The Language, Society and Power Reader

The Language, Society and Power Reader is the definitive reader for students studying introductory modules in sociolinguistics and language in its social contexts.

Highly user-friendly, this wide-ranging collection of key readings introduces students to the thoughts and writings of major writers on language in society. *The Language, Society and Power Reader*:

- is divided into ten thematic sections that explore the nature of language in the following areas: power, thought, politics, media, gender, ethnicity, age, social class, identity and standardisation
- includes classic foundational readings from renowned scholars, but also innovative and contemporary work from new writers in the area
- provides a wealth of editorial support for each section with detailed section introductions and background information, issues to consider, annotated further reading and suggestions for further viewing
- features a glossary with helpful definitions and information on how the readings link to different areas.

While it can be used as a stand-alone text, *The Language, Society and Power Reader* has also been fully cross-referenced with the new companion title: the third edition of *Language, Society and Power* (Routledge, 2011). Together these books provide the complete resource for students of English language and linguistics, media, communication, cultural studies, sociology and psychology.

Readings feature from:
Karin Aijmer • Naima Boussofara-Omar • Deborah Cameron • Diana Eades • Penelope Eckert • Betsy E. Evans • Norman Fairclough • Audrei Gesser • Michael Gos • Karen Grainger • Anthea Irwin • Jennifer Jenkins • Paul Kerswill • Sinfree Makoni • Laura Miller • Geoffrey Nunberg • William Labov • Jacqueline Lam Kam-Mei • John Lucy • John Olsson • Anne Pauwels • Geoffrey Pullum • Anne-Marie Simon-Vandenbergen • Mary Talbot • Joanna Thornborrow • Teun A. van Dijk • Peter R. R. White • Benjamin Lee Whorf

Annabelle Mooney is a Reader in English Language and Linguistics at Roehampton University, UK.

Jean Stilwell Peccei was formerly a Visiting Lecturer in the English Language and Linguistics programme at Roehampton University, UK.

Suzanne LaBelle is a Lecturer in English Language and Communication at Kingston University, UK.

Berit Engøy Henriksen studied Sociolinguistics at Roehampton University, UK.

Eva Eppler is Senior Lecturer and Convenor of the MRes in Sociolinguistics at Roehampton University, UK.

Anthea Irwin is Programme Leader of the Media and Communication degree at Glasgow Caledonian University, UK.

Pia Pichler is a Senior Lecturer in Linguistics at Goldsmiths, University of London, UK.

Satori Soden has taught at both Roehampton Univerisity and Goldsmiths, University of London, UK.

The Language, Society and Power Reader

Edited by

Annabelle Mooney, Jean Stilwell Peccei,
Suzanne LaBelle, Berit Engøy Henriksen,
Eva Eppler, Anthea Irwin, Pia Pichler
and Satori Soden

Routledge
Taylor & Francis Group

LONDON AND NEW YORK

First published 2011
by Routledge
2 Park Square, Milton Park, Abingdon, Oxon OX14 4RN

Simultaneously published in the USA and Canada
by Routledge
711 Third Avenue, New York, NY 10017

Routledge is an imprint of the Taylor & Francis Group, an informa business

British Library Cataloguing in Publication Data
A catalogue record for this book is available from the British Library

Library of Congress Cataloging-in-Publication Data
Mooney, Annabelle, 1974-
    Language, society and power reader : an introduction / Annabelle Mooney...[et al.]. -- 1st ed.
    p. cm.
    1. Sociolinguistics. I. Title.
    P40.M665 2011
    306.44--dc22
    2010036624

ISBN: 978-0-415-43082-1 (hbk)
ISBN: 978-0-415-43083-8 (pbk)

Typeset in Perpetua and Akzidenz-Grotesk by
Saxon Graphics Ltd, Derby

To Jean

Contents

Figures

Tables

Editors

Berit Engøy Henriksen attended The Norwegian University of Science and Technology (NTNU). She then studied at Roehampton University, graduating with an MRes in Sociolinguistics in 2009. Her Master's research examined the communicative norms which develop in video blogging. She continues to pursue research in the field of new media and language.

Eva Eppler is Senior Lecturer and convenor of the MRes in Sociolinguistics at Roehampton University, London. Her research, based on data from the LIDES corpus, focuses on structural and processing aspects of bilingual language use. Recently she has been working on bilingual conversational structures in single and mixed sex groups and processing of bilingual speech, especially in heavily intra-sententially code-mixed utterances. Among her publications are *The LIDES Coding Manual* and the edited volume *Gender and Spoken Interaction* (Palgrave Macmillan 2009, with Pia Pichler), as well as numerous articles on bilingual code-switching. She is presently also working on a monograph entitled *Emigranto*.

Anthea Irwin is Programme Leader of the BA (Hons) Media & Communication degree at Glasgow Caledonian University. She researches discourse reproduction and identity construction in both conversational and media data. Her publications include: 'London adolescents (re)producing power/knowledge: *You know* and *I know*', *Language in Society*, 35(4), 2006; 'Now you see me, now you don't: adolescents exploring deviant positions', in Pichler, P. and Eppler, E. (eds.), *Gender and Spoken Interaction* (Palgrave Macmillan 2009); 'Race and Ethnicity in the Media' in Blain, N. and Hutchison, D. (eds.), *The Media in Scotland* (Edinburgh University Press 2008).

Suzanne LaBelle studied sociolinguistics at the University of Pennsylvania and Essex University. She is a variationist sociolinguist, and a lecturer in English Language and Communication at Kingston University. Her research interests include language change in minority language communities, particularly Welsh, and perception of variation during sound change.

Annabelle Mooney is a Reader at Roehampton University in London. She teaches in fields of gender, narrative, sexist language, and language and the law. She has published on the topics of health and HIV, globalization, religion, gender and law. She is the author of *The Rhetoric of Religious Cults* (Palgrave Macmillan 2005) and co-editor, with Betsy Evans, of *Globalization: The Key Concepts* (Routledge 2007). She is currently working on language and the law.

Jean Stilwell Peccei, formerly a Visiting Lecturer in the English Language and Linguistics programme at Roehampton, has had wide experience in undergraduate teaching. Her publications include: *Child Language* (Routledge Language Workbooks series, second edition, 1999), *Pragmatics* (Routledge Language Workbooks series 1999) and *Child Language: A Resource Book for Students* (Routledge 2006).

Pia Pichler is Senior Lecturer in Linguistics at Goldsmiths, University of London. She has published work in the area of language and gender and on the linguistic construction of identity, with a particular focus on the interplay of local identity practices with gender, ethnicity and social class. She is co-editor of the second edition of *Language and Gender: A Reader* with Jennifer Coates (Wiley-Blackwell 2011) and of *Gender and Spoken Interaction* with Eva Eppler, and author of *Talking Young Femininities* (both Palgrave Macmillan 2009).

Satori Soden completed her PhD at Roehampton University in 2009 and has taught at both Roehampton and Goldsmiths, University of London. Her research interests are media representations, the social construction of ageing, semiotics, advertising and workplace literacies.

Acknowledgements

We'd like to thank Jean Peccei for the formulation of this project. Her clear and detailed map has been our constant orientation point. Without her, the project would never have come about. Her experience, her advice and assistance at all stages of preparation – as well as her writing – have been invaluable. The many students who have taken the course Language, Society and Power at Roehampton University have also provided invaluable help in formulation of this text. We would also like to thank Routledge's anonymous reviewers and readers for their valuable suggestions at the start of the project. Our editors at Routledge, Eloise Cook and Nadia Seemungal, have been unstinting in their enthusiasm, support and patience.

Each of us have benefited from support from our colleagues, family, friends and readers. They have our heartfelt thanks.

Permissions

The authors and publishers would like to thank the following for permission to reproduce copyright material:

Boussofara-Omar, Naima (2006) 'Learning the 'linguistic habitus' of a politician: A presidential authoritative voice in the making' from *Journal of Language and Politics*, 5(3) pp. 325–328. With kind permission by John Benjamins Publishing Company, Amsterdam/Philadelphia, www.benjamins.com.

Cameron, Deborah (1995) 'Verbal Hygiene', Preface, Routledge, London. Reprinted by permission of Routledge.

Eades, D. (2008) 'Telling and Retelling Your Story in Court: Questions, Assumptions and Intercultural Implications', *Current Issues in Criminal Justice*, 20(2) pp. 209–230. Reproduced by permission of Current Issues in Criminal Justice.

Eckert, Penelope (2003) 'The meaning of style' from *Texas Linguistic Forum*, 47. Reproduced by permission of the author.

Eckert, Penelope (2004) 'Adolescent Language' from *Language in the USA: Themes for the Twenty-first Century*. Copyright © Cambridge University Press. Reproduced by permission of Cambridge University Press and the author.

Evans, B. (2010) 'English as official state language in Ohio: market forces trump ideology', from *Language and the Market*, Palgrave Macmillan, London (2010). Reproduced by permission of Palgrave Macmillan.

Fairclough, Norman (1999) 'Global capitalism and critical awareness of language', from *Language Awareness*, 8(2). Copyright © 1999 and reprinted by permission of Taylor & Francis Group, www.informaworld.com.

Fetzer, Anita and Lauerbach, Gerda Eva (2007) 'Political Discourse in the Media: Cross Cultural Perspectives' pp. 31, 32, 33, 37, 38, 48, 49, 50, 52, 53, 54, 55, 56, 57, 58, 66, 67, 68, 69, 70. With kind permission by John Benjamins Publishing Company, Amsterdam/Philadelphia, www.benjamins.com.

Thornborrow, Joanna (2001) 'Authenticating Talk: Building Public Identities in Audience Participation Broadcasting', from *Discourse Studies*, Volume 3(4) p. 21. Copyright © 2001, reprinted by permission of Sage.

van Dijk, T. (2004) 'Racist Discourse', in Cashmere, Ellis (ed.), *Routledge Encyclopaedia of Race and Ethnic Studies*, pp. 351–355, Routledge, London. Reproduced by permission of Routledge.

Whorf, Benjamin Lee (John Carroll, ed.) (1956) *Language, Thought, and Reality: Selected Writings of Benjamin Lee Whorf*, pp. 134–160, ©1956 Massachusetts Institute of Technology, by permission of The MIT Press.

Every effort has been made to trace and contact copyright holders. The publishers would be pleased to hear from any copyright holders not acknowledged here so that this acknowledgements list may be amended at the earliest opportunity.

Bookmaps

These readings... / ... link with these topics	1 Power	2 Thought	3 Politics	4 Media	5 Gender	6 Ethnicity	7 Age	8 Class	9 Identity	10 Standards
PART ONE: Language and power										
1 Cameron	✓	✓								✓
2 Fairclough	✓		✓						✓	
PART TWO: Language and thought										
3 Pullum	✓	✓		✓						
4 Whorf	✓	✓				✓			✓	
5 Lucy			✓							
PART THREE: Language and politics										
6 Nunberg	✓	✓	✓	✓						
7 Boussofara-Omar			✓			✓			✓	✓
8 Simon-Vandenbergen		✓	✓	✓						

These readings… / … link with these topics	1 Power	2 Thought	3 Politics	4 Media	5 Gender	6 Ethnicity	7 Age	8 Class	9 Identity	10 Standards
PART FOUR: Language and the media										
9 Irwin		✓	✓	✓		✓			✓	
10 Miller		✓		✓	✓	✓	✓		✓	✓
11 Thornborrow			✓	✓				✓	✓	
PART FIVE: Language and gender										
12 Pauwels		✓	✓		✓				✓	✓
13 Talbot	✓		✓		✓				✓	
14 Cameron					✓				✓	
PART SIX: Language and ethnicity										
15 Van Dijk	✓	✓	✓	✓		✓			✓	
16 Eades	✓		✓	✓		✓			✓	✓
PART SEVEN: Language and age										
17 Makoni and Grainger	✓					✓	✓		✓	
18 Eckert	✓				✓		✓	✓	✓	
PART EIGHT: Language and social class										
19 Kerswill					✓			✓	✓	✓
20 Labov	✓		✓			✓		✓	✓	✓
21 Gos	✓		✓					✓	✓	✓
PART NINE: Language and identity										
22 Eckert					✓		✓	✓	✓	
23 Olsson	✓								✓	✓
24 Gesser	✓		✓						✓	
PART TEN: Standard Englishes										
25 Kachru/Kam-Mei	✓					✓		✓	✓	✓
26 Evans	✓		✓	✓					✓	✓
27 Jenkins	✓		✓			✓				✓

INTRODUCTION

This selection of readings has been put together as a companion volume for the third edition of the textbook *Language, Society and Power*. The structure of the Reader follows the structure of the textbook, covering the same topics in the same order. The readings provide more depth and some different perspectives from those in the textbook. However, the Reader has been designed to work independently of the textbook. There is a short introduction before each selection of text which offers an overview of the arguments made in the papers. This should not be treated as exhaustive; rather, it should serve as an orientation for your reading, such that you can keep the central issues and arguments in mind. Reading academic journal articles is not always easy. It does take some time to get used to their structure, conventions and language. It is an important skill to develop and we hope the reflective questions will assist in exploring the ideas and implications of the arguments in the articles. Discussion with others, either about sections you're struggling with, or portions that excite you, is an excellent and productive thing to do.

The selections have been chosen with two things in mind. We have tried to keep a balance between including classic sociolinguistic texts and introducing some articles and authors which will be less familiar. We have also sought to include texts from academic as well as more mainstream publications. While some of the papers have been edited, we have tried to keep them as much as possible in their original forms. There is a wealth of work on all of the topics included here. We have made some suggestions for further reading that you may find useful in exploring further. We have also included some suggestions for further viewing.[1] The films we have suggested are largely not academic, thus, any representations and arguments should be considered carefully. At the same time media, like film, can be an excellent way of getting the mind working! No doubt you will think of other examples. We hope you will also notice (and take note of) language examples from your language world that relate to the issues discussed in this book.

A glossary of terms has also been included at the end of this book in order to gloss some terminology which may be unfamiliar.[2] Some terms are used to mean different things by different scholars; we have tried to indicate such polysemy in the glossary entry. Glossary terms appear in bold in the text. We have also indicated through the Bookmaps (p. xx) that the texts often cover more than one area. While papers can only be allocated to one section, do try to keep in mind that the issues are connected and that texts usually cover more than one area.

Notes

1   Thanks to Eva Eppler for this idea.
2   Thanks to Jean Stilwell Peccei for material taken from textbook glossary.

PART ONE

Language and power

Annabelle Mooney

INTRODUCTION

THE PAPERS IN this section answer the questions, what is language and why should we study it? They also raise issues about how linguistics, the study of language, intersects with the views that people have about language and the world in general.

The first text is the preface to Deborah Cameron's seminal work, *Verbal Hygiene*. She defines verbal hygiene as 'Practices … born of an urge to improve or "clean up" language' (1995: 1). Cameron describes encounters with various individuals with particular attitudes about language and, for a linguist, rather odd ideas about what should be done about 'the state of the language'. Most of us have experienced such things, perhaps simply by reading letters to the editor in newspapers. We all have ideas and opinions about our language, but some people invest considerable time and energy by campaigning or by forming associations to protect particular rules relating to syntax or punctuation. Her book examines topics such as political correctness, style guides for newspapers and other publications, as well as critiquing the 'helpful' advice given to women about how to 'improve' their language.

Understanding and engaging with popular ideas about language is as important as it is compelling. While linguists often argue that language change is inevitable, there are still questions to be asked about what kind of change occurs and what motivates it. Obviously, attitudes and behaviour in relation to language can also be subject to the workings of power. This is not to say that a single person makes the 'rules'; language is social.

> Because language-using is paradigmatically a social, public act, talking (and writing and signing) must be carried on with reference to norms, which may themselves become the subject of overt comments and debate. In our everyday interactions we take this for granted; and necessarily so, for without recourse to such ordinary metalinguistic practices as correcting slips of the tongue, asking what someone meant by something and disputing their usage of particular

words, the enterprise of communication would be even more fraught with difficulty than it already is.

(Cameron 1995: 2)

There will always be norms and these will usually be commented on in some way. If we really want to understand language, we need to examine where these norms come from and what consequences they might have. Part of this examination involves paying attention to what we say about language – the **metalinguistic**.

The ideologies that people have about language can uncover a great deal about social interaction. For example, dismissing or stigmatizing a language variety or feature can lead to negative treatment of individuals who use it. As Cameron notes, this can have profound effects in areas like education and, at an individual level, prejudices about language can, and do, translate into prejudice against people. The 'complaint' tradition is hardly new (see Milroy and Milroy 1999). Nevertheless, the details of such complaints vary from time to time and tell us something not only about attitudes to language and people, but can also shed light on what people think linguists do as well as the values that linguists hold.

The arguments of '**language mavens**' and of linguists represent language, and thus the world, in a very particular way. The diversity of views about the 'best' or 'most correct' forms of language demonstrates the existence of different, and opposing, arguments, even in relation to something as small as an apostrophe. Indeed, any argument depends on representing facts and reality in a specific way. The next paper pays attention to this.

Fairclough's arguments can be understood in relation to the representative function of language. Fairclough is seen as the founder of **Critical Discourse Analysis (CDA)**, which examines the detail of language with tools of linguistic analysis in order to explore social and political issues. As well as being grounded in the linguistic theories of Halliday (1985) (which consider both syntax and **semantics**) CDA also draws on sociological theory, especially Foucault's view of power as capillary. This means that, like capillaries in the body, we find the exercise and evidence of power in small places; far from what we might think are the centres of power. Further, power also has an effect on our bodies in that our behaviour is influenced in various ways by powerful **discourses**. This is a theme that runs through this collection; that is, if we really want to understand how power is exercised we need to consider the fine detail of language.

Fairclough's work is concerned with the exercise of power through language, whether this is in politics, the media, economic issues, **globalization** or education. For practitioners of CDA, 'Language is first and foremost a type of social practice', only one of the many '*social practices of representation and signification*' (Kress 1990: 85, emphasis in original). Language is also situated: to really understand what is going on, attention needs to be paid to context. (We see this clearly in the case of **interruptions** in the section on gender.) Fairclough and others working within the CDA paradigm have been instrumental in bringing a political edge to sociolinguistics, creating space to engage with social and political issues by tracing the connections between language, discourse and power.

In the paper included here, Fairclough argues for the importance of critical attention to language and for the inclusion of this in language education. This can be understood as a necessary consequence of the stance he takes about the importance of language in constructing relationships, practices and power. It might also be connected to arguments for empowerment through language education, in the mode of Paulo Freire, who used literacy programmes in Brazil as a way of empowering people. In a frequently cited passage, he writes:

> Education either functions as an instrument which is used to facilitate integration of the younger generation into the logic of the present system and bring about conformity or it becomes the practice of freedom, the means by which men and women deal critically and creatively with reality and discover how to participate in the transformation of their world.
>
> (Freire 1972: 38)

Fairclough can be understood as continuing in this tradition, even though he is advocating a different kind of literacy, one that he argues is essential in the contemporary world. Using the example of how 'flexibility' is deployed in discourse as a positive attribute for workers to have, he argues that this indicates and endorses a particular set of political and economic values. These values may not be positive for individuals. However, to be able to know this, and to be able to argue against these discourses, they first need to be identified. Such identification requires competence in the analysis of language and its effects.

The value of language can be expressed in a number of ways. Understanding and exploiting the functions of language allows us access to '**symbolic capital**'. This concept originated with the French sociologist Bourdieu (1986). We can explore this concept by taking education as an example. Education is a kind of symbolic capital; the qualifications that we have can be 'traded' to, for example, find employment. Thus symbolic capital is valuable in that it allows people opportunities that they might not otherwise have. While it may take effort to acquire this capital, it is not 'spent' when traded, and in this sense is more durable than economic capital. We can understand Fairclough as arguing that critical language awareness is an important form of symbolic capital, especially in the contemporary world, where 'symbol management' is so central to economic and political life.

Issues to consider

1. Do you think that language is significant in making you the person you are? Do you think the way you use language has a particular meaning for other people?
2. Does it matter how we use language to represent things? How can we establish what is true and factual or argue that something is false?
3. If there are always 'rules' and 'norms' with respect to language, how can be decide which are worth protecting?
4. Is language the most important thing to consider when looking at power relations? What other features might need to be considered? Do they link to language at all?
5. How can we think about the relationship between language and power when we have to do this in language?
6. In your own education so far, can you think of any examples that show the connection between language and power?

Further reading

The rest of this Reader deals with these issues in relation to particular variables. The section on Language and Politics (Part 3) may be particularly useful in relating to the issues raised here.

If you're interested in the meaning of words, how they change and how this is documented, you may like:

Butterfield, Jeremy (2008) *Damp Squid: The English Language Laid Bare*, Oxford: Oxford University Press.

For work on language attitudes and folk linguistics, see the following:

Preston, Dennis and Niedzielski, Nancy (2009) 'Folk linguistics' in Coupland, N. and Jaworski, A. (eds.), *The New Sociolinguistics Reader*, Basingstoke: Palgrave Macmillan, pp. 356–373.
Preston, Dennis (2004) 'Language with an attitude' in Chambers, J.C., Schilling-Estes, N. and Trudgill, P. (eds.), *The Handbook of Language Variation and Change*, Oxford: Blackwell, pp. 40–66.

David Crystal covers a wide variety of linguistic topics in a manner which is both astute and accessible:

Crystal, David (2006) *The Fight for English: How Language Pundits Ate, Shot, and Left*, Oxford: Oxford University Press.
— (2007) *How Language Works*, London: Penguin.
— (2007) *Words, Words, Words*, Oxford: Oxford University Press.

Fairclough has written a number of books and articles dealing with different topics. You might be interested in the following:

Fairclough, Norman (2002) 'Language in New Capitalism', *Discourse & Society*, 13(2): 163–166.
— (2003) '"Political Correctness": The Politics of Culture and Language', *Discourse & Society*, 14(1): 17–28.

For work that critically engages with new language in the political arena:

Bourdieu, Pierre and Wacquant, Loïc (2001) 'NewLiberalSpeak: Notes On The New Planetary Vulgate', *Radical Philosophy*, 105: 2–5.

Pinker's work is very readable and often rather entertaining.

Pinker, Stephen (1994) *The Language Instinct: The New Science of Language and Mind*, London: Penguin.
— (2008) *The Stuff of Thought: Language as a Window into Human Nature*, London: Penguin.

Suggestions for further viewing

The Royal Tenenbaums (2001) Wes Anderson.
Manufacturing Consent: Noam Chomsky and the Media (1992) Mark Achbar, Peter
    Wintonick.
Dr Who, 'Planet of the Ood', Series 4, episode 3 (2008), Graeme Harper, Russell T. Davies.
Star Wars Episode V: The Empire Strikes Back (1980) George Lucas; especially the
    character Yoda.

References

Bourdieu, P. (1986). 'The Forms of Capital', in Richardson, J.G. (ed.), *Handbook of Theory
    and Research for the Sociology of Education*, Westport, CT: Greenwood Press, pp.
    241–258.
Cameron, D. (1995) *Verbal Hygiene*, London: Routledge.
Freire, P. (1972) *Pedagogy of the Oppressed*, Harmondsworth: Penguin.
Halliday, M.A.K. (1985) *An Introduction to Functional Grammar*, London: Edward Arnold.
Kress, G. (1990) 'Critical Discourse Analysis', *Annual Review of Applied Linguistics*, 11:
    84–99.
Milroy, J. and Milroy, L. (1999) *Authority in Language: Investigating Standard English*,
    London: Taylor & Francis Ltd.

Chapter 1

Deborah Cameron

PREFACE TO *VERBAL HYGIENE*

'TRADITIONAL BRITISH PASTIMES are under threat', a Sunday newspaper warned recently.[1] It was not talking about the Morris dancing or village cricket so beloved of the heritage industry, nor about such unremarkable suburban pursuits as gardening or home improvement. Rather it was alluding to the strange leisure activities of those who in Britain are disparagingly labelled 'anoraks' (the term refers to an unfashionable style of wind-proof jacket): hobbies such as trainspotting, matchstick model building, collecting old bricks and hoarding memorabilia from long-defunct television programmes.[2] The report did not in fact make much of a case for such pastimes being 'under threat'. On the contrary, it suggested that new and ever more esoteric pursuits are springing up all the time. The Muzzle Loaders Association is dead; long live the Street Lamp Interference Data Exchange!

How is all this relevant to a book entitled *Verbal Hygiene*? One rough definition of the phrase 'verbal hygiene' might be 'the urge to meddle in matters of language'.[3] Expressing that urge in a variety of ways is a traditional and perennially popular pastime—though it is not confined to either Britons or 'anoraks'. Language is, notoriously, something which engenders strong feelings: in Britain and the US we may not have academies to refine and regulate our language, but there is no shortage of enthusiasts who take a proprietary interest in it, dedicating some portion of their leisure time to the collection of unusual linguistic specimens, the tracking down of new or 'misused' expressions and the promotion of various language improvement schemes.

In the US, participants in these activities have a name. They are known as '**language mavens**', as in 'Language mavens will have been keeping a close watch on such-and-such an expression', the formulaic opening of a thousand columns by William Safire in the *New York Times*. Even where the term *maven* is uncommon (as in Britain), the 'language maven' is a recognizable species. Recently I heard it lampooned in a BBC radio skit on 'the British Association of Pedants'. I heard a trailer for this item and made a note to tune in, assuming it would be a report on a real organization.

What do language mavens do? Stereotypically, they write letters to newspapers deploring various solecisms and warning of linguistic decline. The press is an important forum for language mavenry in general: it is striking how many newspapers run regular language columns and how much feature space they devote to linguistic topics. During a single week in May 1992, for example, *The Times* carried a long feature about authority and style, a leader about split infinitives and a sharp exchange of letters debating the use of lower-case type on motorway signs.

Newspapers are not, however, the only reading matter available to people who count language among their recreational interests. Railway station bookstalls and public libraries offer a rich variety of popular literature about language: books with titles like *The Joy of Lex, The Gentle Art of Verbal Self-Defense* and *Parliamo Glasgow* can stay in print for years. There is also a surprisingly large market for more serious (and expensive) works: when the travel writer Bill Bryson published a book on American English in 1994, he remarked that the idea had come from his publishers, who had noticed that while his travel books did poorly in the US, an earlier book on language had 'sold rather well'.[4] A profitable subgenre of publishing caters to the demand for linguistic arcana, ephemera and trivia with dictionaries of this and glossaries of that. As Roy Harris commented in 1983 when reviewing a clutch of these publications in the *London Review of Books*, 'modern **lexicography** is the last refuge of that mania for amassing curiosities and odd tit-bits of information which for so many centuries in Europe passed for "polite" learning' (1983: 13).

The same interest in linguistic 'curiosities' is observable in broadcast media, especially the radio. Over the years, BBC radio has broadcast innumerable features and panel games whose basic premise is that ordinary people are fascinated by new, exotic or otherwise interesting words, and are always ready to hear about such perennial subjects as slang, swearing, **dialects**, **etymology** and linguistic change. I recently listened to a radio request show in which a listener asked for a repeat broadcast of the dramatic tie-breaker from the first British national dictation contest (apparently set to become an annual fixture) in which contestants had to spell *orectic, nescience* and *objicient*. The prize was a facsimile edition of Johnson's *Dictionary*.

Dedicated language mavens also have their own specialist outlets. Just as there are journals and fanzines for people whose interest is guns or comic books or *Star Trek,* so there are publications for readers whose interest is the English language—titles such as *English Today* and *Verbatim,* which (like gun magazines) may include contributions from professional experts, but are not read primarily by experts and cannot be classed as scholarly journals; they are more like the newsletters of hobbyist organizations. Recently, too, a forum has opened up where language mavens can communicate on a global scale. Anyone who has ever wandered through the electronic parallel universe of discussion groups and bulletin boards accessed through the Internet will know that many users regard cyberspace as an ideal arena for swapping linguistic trivia and debating matters of usage.[5]

Some people take their interest in language even further, by joining or forming a society. In Britain, national associations exist to promote plain English, the Queen's English, simplified spelling, the Scots language and Esperanto. Such organizations run the gamut from the ultra respectable mainstream to the esoteric fringe. In the latter category, for instance, there is a California-based group—the International Society for General Semantics—one of whose objectives is to abolish the English verb *to be* on the grounds that it encourages sloppy thinking. This sort of thing is the linguistic equivalent of associations devoted to the mysteries of UFOs and crop circles.

It should not be forgotten that some of the great linguistic projects of the past, whose fruits we now treat as monuments of scholarship, have owed their genesis or their execution to amateurs. *Roget's Thesaurus,* for example, was essentially the product of one man's Utopian desire to bring order to the chaotic realm of meanings; Roget, a physician, turned to it after his retirement. Even that most respected and respectable reference work, *The New* (later *The Oxford*) *English Dictionary,* was much indebted to the labour of volunteers; its present-day editors are still bombarded with correspondence drawing attention to mistakes and omissions.

What these examples show (and they could be multiplied) is that there exists a whole popular culture of language, in which many people participate to some degree. Some are occasional and fairly passive consumers, a few are fanatical crusaders, and there is a continuum of interest and commitment between these two extremes. What is clear, however, is that a great many people care deeply about linguistic matters; they do not merely speak their language, they also speak copiously and passionately *about* it. This book is an attempt both to listen to what such people have to say, and to understand *why* they say the sorts of things they do.

Such a project may puzzle at least two groups of people (both, I hope, among the readers of *Verbal Hygiene*): on one hand those educated language-users who take much of the **discourse** I will be examining as obvious common sense; and on the other hand professional linguists, who find the same discourse obscure, deluded or simply uninteresting.[6] In taking up the subject of verbal hygiene I am, among other things, intervening in an ancient debate between experts and laypeople on the nature of language—what it is, what it should be, why it matters. Furthermore, I am making my intervention from a position that is to some extent critical of both camps.

The story of this book begins with an actual encounter between an 'expert' (me) and a layperson of strong opinions. One day in the mid-1980s, I happened to see a hand-lettered sign tied to a street lamp in London, announcing an exhibition about 'the use and abuse of language' at the Conway Hall. My curiosity aroused, I made my way there and found myself in a room full of newspaper cuttings stuck up on display boards with handwritten commentary. This exhibit, it turned out, had been mounted by a group of concerned citizens who had formed a society to combat the abuse of language. After a few minutes, one of these people approached me and engaged me in conversation. In the course of our talk, I mentioned I was a linguist. At this revelation he became visibly excited. 'A linguist!' he said. 'How marvellous! Do tell me what linguists are doing to combat the abuse of language.' Embarrassed, I made my excuses and left.

Anyone who knows anything about linguistics will understand why I was embarrassed. Linguists typically regard people like the man in the Conway Hall in much the same way that Aristotle regarded the **sophist** Prodicus, whose obsession with the 'correctness of names' he dismissed with the comment: 'this is the sort of thing said by men who love to lay down trivial laws, but have no care to say anything sensible.'[7] Whether or not we go along with Aristotle's opinion, there is clearly a vast gulf between what interests linguists about language and what seems to interest everyone else about it.

The linguistic questions laypeople care most about are questions of right and wrong, good and bad, 'the use and abuse of language'. In fact, it would not be overstating the case to say that most everyday discourse on language is above all evaluative discourse (even the language maven who simply collects unusual words has made a judgement that some words are more interesting than others). This overriding concern with value is the most significant characteristic that separates lay discourse on language from the expert discourse of linguists. As scientists, professional linguists aspire to objectivity and not to moral or aesthetic judgement. So when the man in the Conway Hall asked me what linguists were doing to combat the abuse of language, I did not know what to say. I could hardly give the textbook answer: 'Nothing. That isn't what linguistics is about. Linguistics is descriptive, not prescriptive.' I could not say this, or anything like it, not only because it would have been intolerably rude, but also because my interlocutor would not have understood it.

The incomprehension, it should be said, is mutual. Linguists not only disapprove of the forms that popular interest in language typically take; they find the whole phenomenon somewhat bewildering—much as a chemist might be puzzled by laypeople forming an association devoted to the merits of the inert gases. Reviewing Marina Yaguello's book *Les fous du langage* (translated as *Lunatic Lovers of Language* (1991)) in the Linguistic Society of America's journal *Language,* Robbins Burling can only marvel at the scale of the futile and unnecessary activity Yaguello's study of linguistic obsession reveals: 'it remains' he concludes, 'a striking fact that a wonderful amount of human effort has been invested in attempts to improve on the languages we already have' (Burling 1993: 170). A striking fact, but clearly not one on which Burling feels he can shed much light. On the contrary, he seems to feel it would be better left in decent obscurity—a sentiment in the grand old tradition of experts berating laypeople for their ignorant and silly ideas.

But are the ideas in question uniformly silly, and even if they are, is it enough merely to wonder at them, and then move on to more serious matters? I am certainly not going to argue that popular concerns should dictate the scholar's agenda, or that linguists should jettison their principles for the sake of the man in the Conway Hall. But two things do concern me about the gulf between linguists and lay language-users.

One concern is that when linguists dismiss certain phenomena as unworthy of investigation they are failing to live up to their own descriptive ideals. Silly or not, value judgements on language form part of every competent speaker's linguistic repertoire. One of the things that people know how to do with words is to evaluate them, and I can see no principled justification for neglecting or deriding this **metalinguistic** ability. There is something paradoxical (as opposed to merely patronizing) about labelling ideas irrelevant and meaningless, when the people who hold the ideas patently regard them as relevant and meaningful. The beliefs about language that inform people's use of it arguably fall within the scope of what descriptive linguists ought to be able to give an account of.

The second thing that concerns me is the cultural and political effect of the polarization of the two perspectives, a polarization so extreme they seem unable to engage with one another at any level that is satisfactory to both. On those occasions where something to do with language becomes a matter of widespread public concern (as in the case of the English National School Curriculum, or the debate on 'political correctness'), the result is an exchange carried on very much at cross-purposes, if indeed there is any exchange at all.

On 5 July 1993 I tuned into BBC Radio 4's regular Monday morning cultural discussion programme *Start The Week* to hear my profession being denounced by Michael Dummett, Emeritus Professor of Logic at Oxford University. The topic of the day was the decline of English usage, and Professor Dummett was explaining that he attributed the current parlous state of the language to the widespread influence of ridiculous ideas peddled by professional linguists. Linguistics, he said, had proclaimed to the world that Language Does Not Matter and may therefore be abused with impunity.

The alleged decline of language was a commonplace of educated discourse centuries before the emergence of linguistic science, and holding linguists responsible for it is no longer very original either. What made me sit up and take notice on this occasion was the messenger rather than the message—not just because Professor Dummett is a distinguished academic, but because he is also noted as a liberal supporter of humanitarian causes. And yet on the subject of language, he found himself in agreement with the most philistine and reactionary anti-intellectuals.

The state of the language is among very few concerns capable of producing such improbable alliances between right and left, the inhabitants of the ivory tower and the denizens of the backwoods. It is a subject on which even people of undoubted intelligence, impeccable scholarly credentials and otherwise liberal opinions do not hesitate to talk illiberal and reactionary nonsense. It produces discourse in which opinions—not to say prejudices—do not merely substitute for facts, but are triumphantly paraded as somehow superior to facts; discourse in which it seems that what linguists *know* about language can simply be dismissed, because linguists do not *care* about language.

A linguist might justifiably retort that non-linguists have some funny ways of showing how much they care. Take, for example, a memorandum once issued by William Rees-Mogg when he was editor of *The Times,* which informed editorial staff that '"consensus" is an odious word. It is never to be used, and when it is used it should be spelt correctly'. There is, perhaps, an element of self-mockery about this, but it is nevertheless intended seriously, as an instruction to writers and sub-editors that the word *consensus* is to be avoided in *The Times* in future. And the remarkable thing is that where language is concerned, we see nothing odd in such whimsical injunctions.

Imagine, by contrast, the managing director of a large company issuing a memo informing staff that 'green is an odious colour. It is never to be worn, and when it is worn it should be of the correct shade'. This would surely be considered very odd indeed (just as, when the US presidential candidate Ross Perot pronounced an anathema on men wearing blue shirts, this was cited continually as proof of his eccentricity).

Of course, many organizations do operate dress codes for their staff—I am not claiming there is anything outlandish about prescription *per se*—but the rules are generally expected to be reasonable. Ross Perot is laughed at not for making rules, but for making what most people regard as downright silly rules. People may differ on whether it is right to insist, say, on men wearing ties or women wearing skirts, but normally the issues involved will at least be capable of being discussed. Even those who disagree with a policy will probably be able to imagine a rationale for it (e.g. 'clients expect it'), and will concentrate any resistance on demolishing that rationale. How, by contrast, does one begin to argue with the proposition that such-and-such a word is 'odious'? Why do we routinely allow discussions of language to proceed along these lines, treating pronouncements such as Rees-Mogg's as somehow endearing rather than preposterous?

One might say that at least linguists care enough about language to approach it in a spirit of rational enquiry, eschewing the **cant**, cliché and whimsy that passes for serious discussion among the Dummetts and Rees-Moggs. But one might also wonder whether linguists have thrown the baby out with the bathwater, by criticizing not just silly rules, but the entire evaluative discourse to which those rules belong. The typical response of a linguist faced with somebody like Dummett or Rees-Mogg is not merely to take issue with the specific (and, let us grant, often eccentric) value judgements he is proposing, but to deny that there could be *any* legitimate interest in questions of linguistic value. Rather than insist that discussions about the ethics and aesthetics of language use should be held to the same standard of rational argument that prevails on other subjects, linguists often appear to be suggesting it is a vulgar error to discuss such things at all.

I do not believe that a concern with language and value is by definition irrational and silly. I do believe, however, that the standard of public discourse on linguistic topics is lamentably low. Linguistic debates have a tendency to lapse sooner rather than later into irrationality and mystification, becoming ritual exchanges of received ideas that can only end in stalemate. What is needed to change this unproductive situation is direct critical engagement with the practices and ways of thinking that have produced it. But this requires some understanding of, and perhaps even some sympathy with, the concerns that lie behind it.

As a student, I learned that what lay behind misguided folklinguistic beliefs was simple ignorance and prejudice. Now, although I agree ignorance and prejudice play a part, I take people's continued allegiance to their beliefs (some misguided, some not, and very few of them 'simple') above all as a measure of their commitment to the discourse of value: a discourse with a moral dimension that goes far beyond its overt subject to touch on deep desires and fears. It is important for linguists to acknowledge that there is more to people's beliefs than the ignorance and prejudice that meet the eye; for in order to displace the most powerful **ideology** there is, namely common sense, it is necessary to grasp its hidden principles and to understand the reasons for its enduring popular appeal.

From Aristotle's day to ours, the 'wonderful amount of human effort … invested in attempts to improve on the languages we already have' has persistently been deemed unworthy of serious intellectual consideration. This book, by contrast, is dedicated to the proposition that before we either accept certain ideas about what makes language 'good' as profound and indisputable truths, or dismiss them out of hand as merely trivial and nonsensical, we should make some attempt to elucidate their logic.

Undertaken critically—as it should be, and in these pages, I hope, will be—this enterprise is not incompatible either with a concern about the way language is used or with a linguist's commitment to analyse how it works. If evaluative discourse is an important resource through which people make linguistic phenomena make sense, then there is every reason for linguists to concern ourselves with the beliefs and practices of

Michael Dummett, William Rees-Mogg and the man in the Conway Hall: not in order that we may come to share their outlook on language (though I will argue that at some level we all do share it) but in order to understand it better.

Notes

1   'No hobbies or interests' (*Independent on Sunday*, 13 March, 1994).
2   All of these pastimes are cited in the newspaper report. Most are self-explanatory, if odd; but readers unfamiliar with the traditional British pastime of 'trainspotting' may find a brief explanation helpful. A reference work detailing all the locomotives operating in Britain appears each year: the object of trainspotting is to 'collect' sightings of as many different trains as possible. This usually involved travelling to a major railway terminus, standing there all day and recording the serial numbers of the trains you observe. (The question 'why?' is more difficult to answer satisfactorily.)
3   More precisely, 'verbal hygiene' describes the set of normative metalinguistic *practices* that arise from this urge to meddle. For a full discussion of what I mean by the term, see Chapter 1 [of *Verbal Hygiene*].
4   Quoted in *Time Out*, 29 June–6 July 1994. By August 1994 Bryson's book, *Made in America*, was at the top of the London bestseller lists.
5   I have in fact profited throughout the writing of this book from regular forays into cyberspace; people are very unguarded about expressing their views there, and I take those views as a useful indication of current concerns and the range of opinions they support – always with the proviso that net-users represent a fairly narrow social stratum. Because of the unguarded quality of many posted messages, however, and in the absence of a consensus on questions of privacy/intellectual property, I will not reproduce any material from this source.
6   This is the first in a long series of generalizations about linguists, and the usual, all-generalizations-are-false-including-this-one conditions apply: I accept that not all linguists hold the views I attribute to 'linguists' (though in later chapters [of *Verbal Hygiene*] I will argue that certain views are orthodox within the profession, and it is also significant in my argument that linguists are perceived by non-linguists as collectively holding these views). The various exceptions and qualifications, which need to be made will be discussed in more detail later, particularly in the conclusion [of *Verbal Hygiene*].
7   For an account of Prodicus' life and his beliefs about language, see Guthrie (1969: 275–280).

References

Burling, R (1993) 'Review of *Lunatic Lovers of Language*, by Marina Yaguello', *Language*, 69(1): 168–170.

Guthrie, W.K.C (1969) *A History of Greek Philosophy Vol.III: The Fifth Century Enlightenment*, Cambridge: Cambridge University Press.

Harris, R. (1983) 'All my eye and Betty Martin', *London Review of Books*, 5(22–23): 1–21 December.

Chapter 2

Norman Fairclough

GLOBAL CAPITALISM AND CRITICAL AWARENESS OF LANGUAGE

[…]

I T IS OVER ten years since an initial paper on critical language awareness (CLA) was given at the British Association for Applied Linguistics annual conference (later published in Clark *et al.* 1990, 1991, see also Ivanič 1990; Fairclough 1992). The work on CLA was based upon the conviction that because of contemporary changes affecting the role of language in social life, a critical awareness of language is 'a prerequisite for effective democratic citizenship, and should therefore be seen as an entitlement for citizens, especially children developing towards citizenship in the educational system' (Fairclough 1992: 2–3). We argued that CLA should be a basic concern in language education. Has the case for this weakened or strengthened in the intervening years? I want to argue that as the shape of the new global social order becomes clearer, so too does the need for a critical awareness of language as part of people's resources for living in new ways in new circumstances. Our educational practices have some way to go before they begin to match up to our educational needs. At the same time, although I continue using the expression 'critical language awareness' because it is relatively well known, it has also become clearer that what is at issue is a critical awareness of discourse which includes other forms of **semiosis** as well as language: visual images in particular are an increasingly important feature of contemporary discourse (Kress and van Leeuwen 1996).

An example: the discourse of 'flexibility'

I shall begin with an example which points to a number of features of social life in contemporary ('**late modern**') society which demand a critical awareness of discourse. Most accounts of change in contemporary social life give a more or less central place to change in the economic system: the change from 'Fordism' to 'flexible accumulation', as Harvey (1990) puts it. Fordism is the 'mass production' form of capitalism (named after the car magnate Henry Ford) which dominated the earlier part of [the twentieth] century. Flexible accumulation is a more complex concept but it basically means greater flexibility at various levels – in production (the production process can be quickly shifted to produce small batches of different products), in the workforce (part-time and short-term working, extensive reskilling of workers), in the circulation of finance, and so forth. Harvey points out that some academic analysts see 'flexibility' as no more than a new discourse which is ideologically motivated – if working people can be persuaded that 'flexibility' is an unavoidable feature of contemporary economies, they are more likely to be 'flexible' about their jobs disappearing, the need to retrain, deteriorating pay and conditions of work, and so forth. Harvey disagrees. Flexibility is a real feature of contemporary economies for which there is ample scientific evidence – though that does not mean that 'flexible accumulation' has totally displaced 'Fordism', the reality is rather a mix of old and new regimes. Nor does it mean that the discourse of flexibility is irrelevant to the reality of flexible accumulation. Far from it: *the discourse is an irreducible part of the reality*. The change from Fordism to flexible accumulation is inconceivable without the change in economic discourse. Why? Because the emerging global economy is the site of a struggle between the old and the new, and the discourse of flexibility is a vital symbolic weapon in that struggle. It is as Bourdieu (1998) has put it a 'strong discourse', that is a discourse which is backed by the strength of all the economic and social forces (the banks, the multinational companies, politicians, and so on) who are trying to make flexibility – the new global capitalism – even more of a reality than it already is. Neoliberal discourse contributes its own particular, symbolic, form of strength to the strength of these social forces.

Let me briefly clarify my example. My focus is on the metaphor of 'flexibility' which is at the centre of the economic discourse of 'flexible accumulation' for which Harvey (1990: 47–97) gives an analytical account – including, for example, its construction of the labour market in terms of 'core' and 'periphery' employees. Elements of this discourse, and especially the metaphor of flexibility itself, are widely distributed within many types of non-economic discourse (examples shortly). The discourse of flexible accumulation enters complex and shifting configurations with other discourses within a field I am calling 'neoliberal discourse' – for instance with a management discourse which centres on the 'mission statement' which Swales and Rogers (1995) have described. This is a complex and unstable area which needs detailed research.

One accessible place to find the discourse of flexibility used within this struggle over global economy is in the books written by management 'gurus' which seem to dominate airport and railway station bookshops (for example Peters 1994). But it is a discourse that turns up in many other contexts. One of them is politics – New Labour's 'Third Way', for instance, can be summed up as follows: economic flexibility (on the model of the World Bank and the IMF) is inevitable, but government must strive to include those it socially excludes. Here is Blair in his first major speech after becoming Prime Minister:

> We must never forget that a strong, competitive, flexible economy is the prerequisite for creating jobs and opportunities. But equally we must never

forget that it is not enough. The economy can grow while leaving behind a workless class whose members become so detached that they are no longer full citizens.

(Blair 1997)

But the discourse of flexibility also penetrates into everyday language. Here for instance is an extract from an **ethnographic** interview with 'Stephen' from Cleveland in North-East England who does 'fiddly jobs', i.e. works illegally in the black economy while claiming social benefits. He is talking about the work he does:

It's a matter of us being cheaper. It's definitely easier than having a lot of lads taken on permanently. It would cost them more to put them on the books or pay them off. It's just the flexibility. You're just there for when the jobs come up, and he [the 'hirer and firer'] will come and get you when you're needed. You need to be on the dole to be able to do that. Otherwise you'd be sitting there for half the year with no work and no money at all.

(Quoted in MacDonald 1994: 515)

We might pessimistically think of everyday language as colonised by this discourse of the powerful, and that is no doubt partly true, but here is 'Stephen' appropriating the discourse in constructing his own perfectly coherent rationale for his (illegal) way of living. One aspect of economic flexibility from his perspective is that companies need the flexibility of workers doing fiddly jobs.

Like other prominent discourses, the discourse of flexibility draws some comment and critique – a critical awareness of language is not wholly something which has to be brought to people from outside, it arises within the normal ways people reflect on their lives as part of their lives. But this ordinary form of critique has its limits. People need to know about discourses like this – for instance, what insights it gives us into the way economies work or could work, and what other insights it cuts us off from; whose discourse it is, and what they gain from its use; what other discourses there are around, and how this one has become so dominant. People practically need to know such things, because not knowing them makes it harder for them to manage in various parts of their lives: as trade unionists – whether resisting shifts to part-time and short-time work is fighting the inevitable; as managers – what strengths and limitations the metaphor of flexibility has for their organisations; as citizens – whether there is a 'Third Way'; as parents – what sort of world to prepare their children for. But such knowledge about discourse has to come from outside, from theory and research, via education.

I want to proceed by discussing, with a focus on discourse, several key features of late modern society which this example touches on, and which I think help make the case for critical awareness of discourse. Actually the earlier ones arise more easily from the example of the discourse of flexibility than the later ones. I discuss these features of late modernity under the following headings: the relationship between discourse, knowledge and social change in our 'information' or 'knowledge-based' society; what Smith (1990) has called the 'textually-mediated' nature of contemporary social life; the relationship between discourse and social difference; the **commodification** of discourse; discourse and democracy. [...]

Discourse, knowledge and social change

The example points to a relationship between change in economic discourse, new economic knowledge, and change in economic practices. As I stated earlier, it is a matter of discourse, not just language – knowledges are increasingly constituted in multisemiotic ways in contemporary society (Kress and van Leeuwen 1996; New London Group 1996). Information- or knowledge-based late modern societies are characterised, as Giddens has put it, by enhanced **reflexivity** – we are constantly reshaping our social practices on the basis of knowledge about those practices. This is true in the domain of work but also, for instance, in how people conduct their personal relationships – the media are full of expert advice. On one level, reflexivity is an inherent property of all social practices – any social practice includes the constructions of that practice produced by its practitioners as part of the practice. What is different about late modernity is the ways in which 'expert systems' (such as the sciences and social sciences) are systematically integrated into reflexive processes (Giddens 1991). These expert systems can be thought of as evaluating existing knowledges in the practical domain in focus (for example the economy) and producing new knowledges. Since knowledges are constituted as discourses, particular ways of using language, this means that they are in the business of evaluating and changing discourses. Evaluating discourses means setting them against shifting understandings of what material possibilities there are in the practical domain concerned (for example the economy), which are, in turn, instantiated within new discourses. In such practical contexts, discourses are evaluated not in terms of some impossible 'absolute truth', but in terms of 'epistemic gain' – whether they yield knowledges which allow people to improve the way in which they manage their lives.

The business of evaluating and changing knowledges and discourses is something which an increasing number of people are involved in as part of the work they do. It is a major concern of educational institutions to teach them how to do this, and part of the current preoccupation with 'learning to learn', and other thematisations of 'learning' in contemporary education and business – 'the learning society', businesses as 'learning organisations', 'lifelong learning' – see, for example, the Dearing Report on universities *Higher Education in the Learning Society* (National Committee of Inquiry into Higher Education 1997). What I want to argue is that the resources for learning and for working in a knowledge-based economy include a critical awareness of discourse – an awareness of how discourse figures within social practices, an awareness that any knowledge of a domain of social life is constituted as one discourse from among a number of co-existing or conceivable discourses, that different discourses are associated with different perspectives on the domain concerned and different interests, an awareness of how discourses can work ideologically in social relations of power, and so forth. It is on the basis of such understandings of how discourse works within social practices that people can come to question and look beyond existing discourses, or existing relations of dominance and marginalisation between discourses, and so advance knowledge. If on the other hand language and other **semiotic** modalities are viewed as simply transparent media for reflecting what is, the development of knowledge is likely to be impeded.

Textually-mediated social life

The presence of the discourse of flexibility in Stephen's talk is an illustration of the textual mediation of social life: in contemporary societies, the discourses/knowledges generated by expert systems enter our everyday lives and shape the way we live them. Contemporary societies are knowledge-based not only in their economies but even, for instance, in the ways in which people conduct their personal relationships. Expert knowledges/discourses come to us via texts of various sorts which mediate our social lives – books, magazines, radio and television programmes, and so forth. These processes of textual mediation bind together people who are scattered across societies into social systems – one of Smith's examples is how textually mediated constructions of femininity lock women scattered across social space into the economic system of commodity production and consumption, in that feminity is constructed in terms of the purchase and use of commodities such as clothes (Smith 1990). Moreover, the distances in space and time across which these processes of textual mediation operate are increasing. Modernity can be seen as a process of 'time/space compression', the overcoming of spatial and temporal distance, and late modernity is marked by a twist in that process which is widely referred to as '**globalisation**' (Harvey 1990; Giddens 1991). The vehicles for this spatio-temporally extended textual mediation are the new media – radio, television, and information technology.

As everyday lives become more pervasively textually mediated, people's lives are increasingly shaped by representations which are produced elsewhere. Representations of the world they live in, the activities they are involved in, their relationships with each other, and even who they are and how they (should) see themselves. The politics of representation becomes increasingly important – whose representations are these, who gains what from them, what social relations do they draw people into, what are their ideological effects, and what alternative representations are there? The example of Stephen's talk is a case in point. His representation of his own life in the black economy draws upon the discourse of flexibility. We might question whether his construction of his own life and identity has been ideologically invested, drawn into the social relations between the powerful groups who control economies and back **neoliberalism** and the rest of us. However, the picture is more complex and more hopeful. As I suggested earlier, his talk does not simply reproduce the discourse of flexibility, it works it in a particular – and ironic – way into a rationale for his own way of living based on a perfectly coherent, if non-standard, view of the new capitalism – part of the flexibility that companies need is the flexibility of illegal black labour. The example shows that people are not simply colonised by such discourses, they also appropriate them and work them in particular ways. Textually mediated social life cuts both ways – it opens up unprecedented resources for people to shape their lives in new ways drawing upon knowledges, perspectives and discourses which are generated all over the world. But in so doing it opens up new areas of their lives to the play of power. There is a colonisation-appropriation **dialectic** at work. Whether on balance people gain or lose depends on where they are positioned in social life – the fact that new possibilities are opened up does not mean people are unconditionally free to take them. But my main point is this: if people are to live in this complex world rather than just be carried along by it, they need resources to examine their placing within this dialectic between the global and the local – and those resources include a critical awareness of language and discourse which can only come through language education.

Discourse, social difference and social identity

Discourses are partial and positioned, and social difference is manifest in the diversity of discourses within particular social practices. Neoliberal economic discourse, for instance, is only one of many economic discourses and, as I have indicated earlier, it corresponds to a specific perspective and set of interests. Critical awareness in this case is a matter of seeing the diversity of discourses and their positioned nature.

But there are other aspects of social difference. Late modern societies are increasingly socially diverse societies, not only in that migration has led to greater ethnic and cultural diversity, but also because various lines of difference which were until recently relatively covered over have become more salient – differences of gender and sexual orientation, for example. Differences are partly semiotic in nature – different languages, different social dialects, different communicative styles, different voices, different discourses. The predominant ethos, for instance, in European societies is that differences which have in the past been suppressed should now be recognised. But since people need to work together across difference, differences have to be negotiated. People need to work across differences in work, politics, cultural activities and everyday life. But it is increasingly understood that social difference is not only difference between people but also difference within people. Indeed, recognising the difference within is the basis for being open to a non-suppressive negotiation of differences between people and groups (Barat 1998). Working across differences is a process in our individual lives, within the groups we belong to, as well as between groups. Working across differences entails semiotic **hybridity** – the emergence of new combinations of languages, social dialects, voices, genres and discourses. Hybridity, **heterogeneity**, **intertextuality** are salient features of contemporary discourse also because the boundaries between domains and practices are in many cases fluid and open in a context of rapid and intense social change – the negotiation of social difference includes, for instance, the negotiation of differences between educators, advertisers and business managers, and between students and consumers of commodities, within educational institutions which are increasingly forced into operating in market ways. But negotiating differences is simultaneously negotiating identities – working out how I or we relate to others is simultaneously working out who I am or who we are. The radical disarticulations and rearticulations of contemporary social life radically unsettle social identities, and the search for and construction of identities is a constant process and a major preoccupation, but it should be framed in terms of the problem of learning to live with difference (New London Group 1996). Once again, people need from education a range of resources for living within socially and culturally diverse societies and avoiding their dangers, including chauvinism and racism. A critical awareness of discourse is part of what is needed.

Commodification of discourse

There is still a link, if a more tenuous one, between my next theme and the example of the discourse of flexibility. I referred earlier to the books of management gurus which fill airport bookstalls and are filled with neoliberal economic discourse. These books are about big business, but they are also big business themselves. They are generally rather successful commodities, as one can see from the impressive sales figures which are often emblazoned on their covers. The stuff these commodities are made of is, of course, paper, ink and so forth, but it is also language and other sorts of semiotic stuff. They are worked up into commodities, carefully designed to sell. Semiotic stuff is a feature of a great many commodities these days – the nature of commodities has been changing, with a shift in emphasis broadly from goods that are more physical than cultural (like cars) to goods that are more cultural than physical (like books, or television programmes, or advertisements). Many goods now are services, like what you pay for in a smart restaurant which is not just the food but the ambiance, which includes the appearance, behaviour and talk of the staff – language is part of the service, part of the goods. As commodities become semioticised, discourse becomes commodified (Lyotard 1986/7) – it becomes open to processes of economic calculation, it comes to be designed for success on markets. For instance, service industries are full of forms of ostensibly ordinary talk which are designed to seem ordinary, to mobilise all the selling power of ordinariness in a society which values it even in institutional and organisational contexts.

[…]

Discourse and democracy

The discourse of flexibility is predominant within the political systems of, for instance, Great Britain and the USA – all of the major parties use it and take it for granted. It is part of a widely observed narrowing down of the political spectrum – parties are becoming increasingly similar in their policies, and the differences between them are increasingly differences of style. One aspect of this process is what Marcuse identified 30 years ago as 'the closing down of the universe of discourse' (Marcuse 1964) – the predominance of a single economic-political discourse across the political spectrum.

We might see the narrowing of political discourse as a symptom of the political system becoming cut off from the sources of political diversity and change in social life. This has been widely debated in recent years as a crisis of the 'public sphere' (Habermas 1989; Calhoun 1992), troubles to do with the apparent absence of effective spaces and practices where people as citizens can deliberate over issues of common social and political concern, and their deliberations can shape the policy decisions that are made. The broadcast media are full of dialogue on such issues, but it is a dialogue that is deeply flawed in terms of its public sphere credentials – in terms of who has access to it, in terms of what gets onto its agendas, in terms of who controls its flow, and in terms of it being designed to maximise audience and entertain. The task of reconstructing the public sphere is at the heart of the defence and enhancement of democracy. It is already being undertaken within social movements which are active outside the official political system. But it is also a task for educational institutions including schools and universities, whose standing as public spheres has been undermined by recent institutional changes (Giroux 1997). One way forward here is suggested by Billig (1991): that we conceive of teaching people to think as teaching people to argue, and put our energies into making educational institutions as open as possible as spaces for argument. Negotiating across difference is again a central concern for the contemporary public sphere –

political dialogue in socioculturally diverse societies has to be oriented to alliances around particular sets of issues. In this case, a critical awareness of discourse is essential for the work of experimentation and design which is necessary to find effective forms of dialogue which facilitate open argumentation and forms of action in common which do not suppress difference (Fairclough 1998).

[…]

Critical Discourse Awareness and Education[1]

Recent educational reforms have sharply raised the question of what education is for, and for whom. The dominant view of education – evident, for instance, in the recent Dearing Report *Higher Education in the Learning Society* (National Committee of Inquiry into Higher Education 1997) – sees it as a vocationally-oriented transmission of given knowledge and skills. What is perhaps most distinctive about this view of education is its focus upon the teaching and learning of 'key skills' which are seen as transferable from one sphere of life to another, and as the basis for future success including successful 'lifelong learning'. Given that one of these key skills is 'communication' (the others identified in the Dearing Report are numeracy, information technology and learning to learn), this view of education rests upon a view of discourse – discourse as 'communication skills'.

What is wrong with seeing discourse as communication skills? Let me focus on three problems. First, it is assumed that a communication skill, once learnt, can be freely transferred from one context to another. I think there is an interesting connection between this assumption and the tendencies I have identified as textually-mediated social life and the technologisation of discourse – discursive practices are indeed transferred across contexts in late modern social life. But what this first assumption misses is what I have referred to as the colonisation-appropriation dialectic (which is also a global-local dialectic) – even where such transfers take place, it does not mean that we find the same discursive practice in all contexts, for even the most globally dispersed discursive practice is always locally recontextualised, transformed and appropriated. It is inviting disaster to assume that if you have learnt to interview candidates for admission to university, you know how to interview personalities on a television chat show. Second, it is assumed that there is a simple relationship between what is actually said (or more generally done) in the course of some social practice, and skills, internalised models of how to say/do it – that discourse is a mere instantiation of such models (Fairclough 1988). On the contrary, discourse is a complex matching of models with immediate needs in which what emerges may be radically different from any model, ambivalent between models, or a baffling mixture of models, and where flair and creativity may have more impact than skill. Third, and most seriously, it is assumed that there is a given and accepted way of using language to do certain things, as if discourse was a simple matter of technique, whereas any way of using language which gets to be given and accepted does so through applications of power which violently exclude other ways, and any way of using language within any social practice is socially contestable and likely to be contested. From this point of view, any reduction of discourse to skills is complicit with efforts on the part of those who have power to impose social practices they favour by getting people to see them as mere techniques.

In critiquing the view of discourse as communication skills, I am also critiquing the view of education as a transmission of knowledge and skills. For viewing discourse as skills is just one aspect of viewing knowledge and skills in general as determinate, uncontested, and given externally to the learner; and it is only on such assumptions about what is to be taught and learnt that the process can be viewed as 'transmission'. We can broaden out the argument against discourse as skills into a different view of knowledge and skills in education: they are always provisional and indeterminate, contested and, moreover, at issue in social relationships, within which all teachers and learners are positioned. In a critical view of education, knowledge and 'skills' are indeed taught and learnt, but they are also questioned – a central concern is what counts as knowledge or skill (and therefore what does not), for whom, why, and with what beneficial or problematic consequences. In the Dearing Report, higher education promotes knowledge, skills and understanding; my comments here take understanding to mean a questioning of knowledge and skills, and problematise the foregrounding of 'key skills' in the Report.

Perhaps it has always been the case that education has been relatively critical for some, though usually for a small elite. In the new work order (Gee *et al.* 1996), there is a need for a small elite of symbolic-analytic workers for whom the new system may demand a critical education (including a critical awareness of discourse). The danger is a new form of educational stratification which separates them from those likely to become other categories of workers (routine production workers, and workers in service industries) or to join the 'socially excluded' (including unemployed). That would be in line with the contemporary tendency of the purposes of education to narrow down towards serving the needs of the economy. The alternative is some vision of education for life within which a critical awareness of discourse is necessary for all.

Correspondence

Any correspondence should be directed to Dr Norman Fairclough, Department of Linguistics and Modern English Language, Lancaster University, Lancaster LA1 4SE, UK (n.fairclough@lancs.ac.uk).

Note

1   Although pedagogy is not my major concern here, I envisage the sort of four-part pedagogy set out by the New London Group (1996). Its elements are: development of the ability to engage successfully in a range of practices through immersion in authentic Situated Practice; an awareness and understanding of these practices through Overt Instruction; a capacity to critique those practices as socially particular and partial actualities from within a wider range of possibilities through Critical Framing; and Transformed Practice, experimentation with new practices reflexively informed by Overt Instruction and especially Critical Framing. What is envisaged, then, is a link between awareness and practice, awareness opening up new possibilities for practice.

References

Barat, E. (1998) *Women's identities: A tension between discourses and experience*, paper delivered at conference on Critical Discourse Analysis, Brasilia, May.

Billig, M. (1991) *Ideology and Opinion*, London: Sage.

Blair, Tony (1997) Speech at the Aylesbury Housing Estate, Southwark, 2 June.

Bourdieu, P. (1998) L'essence du neo-liberalisme, *Le Monde Diplomatique*, March.

Calhoun, C. (1992) *Habermas and the Public Sphere*, Cambridge, MA: MIT Press.

Clark, R., Fairclough, N., Ivanič, R. and Martin-Jones, M. (1990) Critical language awareness Part 1: A critical review of three current approaches, *Language and Education*, 4(4): 249–260.

——, ——, —— and —— (1991) Critical language awareness Part 2: Towards critical alternatives, *Language and Education*, 5(1): 41–54.

Fairclough, N. (1988) Register, power and sociosemantic change, in D. Birch and M. O'Toole (eds.), *The Functions of Style*, London: Pinter Publications.

—— (ed.), (1992) *Critical Language Awareness*, London: Longman.

—— (1998) *Democracy and the public sphere in critical research on discourse*, paper given at conference on Discourse, Politics and Identity in Europe, Vienna, April.

Gee, J., Hull, G. and Lankshear, C. (1996) *The New York Order: Behind the Language of the New Capitalism*, London: Allen & Unwin.

Giddens, A. (1991) *Modernity and Self-Identity*, Cambridge: Polity Press.

Giroux, H. (1997) *Pedagogy and the Politics of Hope*, Boulder, CO: Westview Press.

Habermas, J. (1989) *Structural Transformation of the Public Sphere*, Cambridge, MA: MIT Press.

Harvey, D. (1990) *The Condition of Postmodernity*, Oxford: Blackwell.

—— (1996) *Justice, Nature and the Geography of Difference*, Oxford: Blackwell.

Ivanič, R. (1990) Critical language awareness in action, in R. Carter (ed.), *Knowledge about Language – The LINC Reader*, London: Hodder & Stoughton.

Kress, G. and van Leeuwen, T. (1996) *Reading Images: The Grammar of Visual Design*, London: Routledge.

Lyotard, J.-F. (1986/7) Rules and paradoxes and svelte appendix, *Cultural Critique*, 5(winter): 209–219.

MacDonald, R. (1994) Fiddly jobs, undeclared working and the something for nothing society, *Work, Employment and Society*, 8(4): 507–530.

Marcuse, H. (1964) *One-Dimensional Man*, London: Abacus.

National Committee of Inquiry into Higher Education (1997) *Higher Education in the Learning Society (The Dearing Report)*, London: HMSO.

New London Group (1996) A pedagogy of multiliteracies: Designing social futures, *Harvard Educational Review*, 66(1): 60–92.

Peters, T. (1994) *The Tom Peters Seminar*, London: Vintage Books.

Smith, D. (1990) *Texts, Facts and Femininity*, London: Routledge.

Swales, J. and Rogers, P. (1995) Discourse and the projection of corporate culture: The Mission Statement, *Discourse and Society*, 6(2): 223–242.

PART TWO

Language and thought

Annabelle Mooney

INTRODUCTION

THE RELATIONSHIP BETWEEN language and thought is a contentious one, often misunderstood and frequently parodied. It is important to understand the subtleties of the arguments in this area and to be familiar with original works in the field. The readings included here seek to cover these various areas.

The argument that language and thought are closely connected is usually traced back to the work of Whorf and his mentor, Sapir. Whorf's observation of language, both English and other languages, led him to argue for a connection between the words in a language and the way people think and, perhaps most significantly, the way we behave. As he notes early in this paper, he noticed that people's behaviour was affected by the labels attached to things. Thus, a container labelled 'empty' was treated as an appropriate place to throw cigarette butts. This was notwithstanding the residual flammable substances in the container. This insight has implications for human safety, but also for all manner of behaviour. While Whorf's ideas might just seem to be about interaction with things, as outlined in his paper, it also helps understand how we interact with concepts for abstract things, like time. In English, we very often speak of time as something which is valuable; the phrase 'time is money' is commonplace (Lakoff and Johnson 1980). This leads to certain kinds of behaviour being commended (such as efficiency and speed) and other kinds being negatively evaluated.

The so called Sapir-Whorf hypothesis has two components: **linguistic diversity** and **linguistic relativism**/determinism. The first states that languages describe reality in different ways, that is, distinctions made in some languages are not made in others. The second has to be understood as a matter of degree. Very few people would argue that one's language completely determines worldview (**linguistic determinism**). If this was the case, it would be impossible to create and learn new words, or to understand distinctions that other languages make.

Some argue that the Sapir-Whorf hypothesis is outdated. This is usually because it is understood in its extreme form, that is, that language determines our world view pretty much completely. Few would agree that the language we speak constrains us in an inescapable way. Further, to understand language in this way tends to treat languages as static, homogenous and as containing a particular set of cultural norms. However, it is important to understand that contemporary work on **ideology** and **discourse** can be understood as modern versions of linguistic relativism. In particular, Guy Cook argues that relativism finds a contemporary instantiation in **Critical Discourse Analysis** (CDA).

> Though not usually concerned with differences between languages, as the original work on linguistic relativity was, CDA is concerned with how different encodings within one language may affect perceptions of reality. In this, it subscribes to a version of the Whorf hypothesis...
>
> (Cook 2005: 295)

Thus the relationship between language and thought is still important.

As speakers (and thinkers), we may accept dominant ideologies and discourses without question. Certainly we can question these, especially if we pay critical attention to language, but they are influential nonetheless. Lucy's paper has been included to provide a contemporary account of the connection between language and thought. As well as providing an excellent account of the history and issues in this area, he also argues that we have *habits* of thought, thus echoing the title of Whorf's paper included here. These habits can be traced in the way we categorize objects in the world (whether we're dealing with concrete objects like chairs or more abstract entities, like relationships) as well as the way we think about certain issues.

The phrase 'linguistic determinism' may suggest a curtailment of freedom and an inevitably powerless position in relation to the influence of language. Lucy's conception is quite different. If we consider the weaker form, linguistic relativism, it turns out to be a very valuable explanatory account. It can help us understand why people generally think and behave in the way that they do. At the same time, when these habits have been traced and explored, they can also be challenged. Our habits of thought, our ideologies, are often treated as natural, and common sense. When this natural status is challenged, by breaking down the ideologies into their component parts and linguistic symptoms, arguments can be made for change and action can be taken (see Fairclough, Chapter 2 above). This may also be said of our conceptions about theories of language. Lucy traces the history of thinking about the relationship between language and thought. This allows us to see previous models as situated in specific cultural contexts.

Part of the move away from the Sapir-Whorf model may well be linked to the odd things that have written about it. Pullum's paper outlines such an example and details the academic work that went into exposing the myth of Eskimo snow terms. This paper has been included to demonstrate both how attractive people seem to find the Sapir-Whorf hypothesis as well as how apparently easy it is to misunderstand the details of the argument. There is something that can be said here about the stereotypes we apply to 'other' languages and the habits of mind that somehow encourage us to recall and repeat these stereotypes. There are a number of myths about language and language use that are accepted and repeated in the same way that the 'Eskimo snow' story is. The 'strangeness' of other languages (and others use of language) appeals to our ideas about language. At the same time, we tend not to see the 'strangeness' of our own language. This is hardly surprising. We use our own language without thinking too much about what we're doing. Thus, we tend to see popular books about 'correct English' as well as those about 'extraordinary words from around the world' (Jacot de Boinod 2006). The papers in this section can all be understood as arguing for close attention to our own language, and to claims that are made about language. In relation to the latter, it is well to be sceptical and to critically examine the provenance and verifiability of the various claims made about language.

Issues to consider

1. How much of an effect do you think language has on thought? If we don't think in the terms of our language, how do we do it? If we don't think in the terms of our language, how can we communicate this?
2. Do you think you have a particular world view or habits of thought? Is this connected to the language you speak or to something else?
3. Does the way we use language change the way we behave? Try to come up with representations that may change action. For example, you may be happy to eat a 'hamburger' but would you eat a 'ground up cow bun'?
4. How might we try to uncover our own 'common sense'? What kinds of questions do we need to ask and what kind of state of mind might we need to adopt to be able to treat our own behaviour as 'other'?

Further reading

On linguistic relativism:

Gumperz, John and Levinson, Stephen (eds.), (1996) *Rethinking Linguistic Relativity*, Cambridge: Cambridge University Press.
Kay, Paul and Kempton, Willett (1984) 'What is the Sapir-Whorf Hypothesis?' *American Anthropologist*, 86(1): 65–79.
Mertz, Elizabeth (1982) 'Language and Mind: A "Whorfian" Folk Theory in US Language Law', *Duke University Working Papers in Sociolinguistics*, 93: 1–21.

On the connection between language and behavior and culture:

Everett, Daniel L. (2005) 'Cultural Constraints on Grammar and Cognition in Pirahã: Another Look at the Design Features of Human Language', *Current Anthropology*, 46(4): 621–646. (The extended version of this paper includes extended commentary from a number of scholars and as such, gives a good indication of the diversity of approaches still current, as well as the terms of the debate.)
Lakoff, George and Johnson, Mark (2003) *Metaphors We Live By*, Chicago: Chicago University Press.

Wierzbicka, Anna (2006) *English: Meaning and Culture*, Oxford: Oxford University Press.

The following provide wide ranging accounts of issues around language:

Bauer, Laurie and Trudgill, Peter (eds.), (1998) *Language Myths*, London: Penguin.
Pinker, Stephen (1994) *The Language Instinct: The New Science Of Language And Mind*, London: Allen Lane, Chapter 3.

Finally, this text provides analytical tools for the exploration of language:

Simpson, Paul (1993) *Language, Ideology and Point of View*, London: Routledge.

Suggestions for further viewing

The Linguists (2008) Seth Kramer, Daniel A. Miller.
The Manchurian Candidate (2004) Jonathan Demme.
Nemt: A Language Without a People for a People Without a Language (2004) Michel Grosman, Isabelle Rozenbaumas.
Nineteen Eighty-Four (1984) Michael Radford.

References

Cook, Guy (2005) 'Calm seas or troubled waters? Transitions, definitions and disagreements in applied linguistics', *International Journal of Applied Linguistics*, 15(3): 282–301.
Jacot de Boinod, Adam (2006) *The Meaning of Tingo: And Other Extraordinary Words from Around the World*, London: Penguin.
Lakoff, George and Johnson, Mark (1980) *Metaphors We Live By*, Chicago: University of Chicago Press.

Chapter 3

Geoffrey K. Pullum

THE GREAT ESKIMO VOCABULARY HOAX

[…]

MOST LINGUISTICS DEPARTMENTS have an introduction-to-language course in which students other than linguistics majors can be exposed to at least something of the mysteries of language and communication: signing apes and dancing bees; wild children and lateralization; logo-graphic writing and the Rosetta Stone; *pit* and *spit*; Sir William Jones and Professor Henry Higgins; isoglosses and Grimm's Law; *Jabberwocky* and colorless green ideas; and of course, without fail, the Eskimos and their multiple words for snow.

[…]

Linguists have been just as active as schoolteachers or general-knowledge columnists in spreading the entrancing story. What a pity the story is unredeemed piffle.

Anthropologist Laura Martin of Cleveland State University spent some of her research time during the 1980s attempting to slay the constantly changing, self-regenerating myth of Eskimo snow terminology, like a Sigourney Weaver fighting alone against the hideous space creature in the movie *Alien* (a xenomorph, they called it in the sequel *Aliens*; nice word). You may recall that the creature seemed to spring up everywhere once it got loose on the spaceship, and was very difficult to kill.

Martin presented her paper at the annual meeting of the American Anthropological Association in Washington DC in December 1982, and eventually (after a four-year struggle during which bonehead reviewers cut a third of the paper, including several interesting quotes) she published an abbreviated version of it in the 'Research Reports' section of AAA's journal (Martin 1986). This ought to have been enough for the news to get out.

But no, as far as widespread recognition is concerned, Martin labored in vain. Never does a month (or in all probability a week) go by without yet another publication of the familiar claim about the wondrous richness of the Eskimo conceptual scheme:

hundreds of words for different grades and types of snow, a lexicographical winter wonderland, the quintessential demonstration of how primitive minds categorize the world so differently from us.

And the alleged lexical extravagance of the Eskimos comports so well with the many other facets of their polysynthetic perversity: rubbing noses; lending their wives to strangers; eating raw seal blubber; throwing grandma out to be eaten by polar bears; "We are prepared to believe almost anything about such an unfamiliar and peculiar group", says Martin, in a gentle reminder of our buried racist tendencies.

The tale she tells is an embarrassing saga of scholarly sloppiness and popular eagerness to embrace exotic facts about other people's languages without seeing the evidence. The fact is that the myth of the multiple words for snow is based on almost nothing at all. It is a kind of accidentally developed hoax perpetrated by the anthropological linguistics community on itself.

The original source is Franz Boas' introduction to *The Handbook of North American Indians* (1911). And all Boas says there, in the context of a low-key and slightly ill-explained discussion of independent versus derived terms for things in different languages, is that just as English uses separate roots for a variety of forms of water (liquid, lake, river, brook, rain, dew, wave, foam) that might be formed by **derivational morphology** from a single root meaning 'water' in some other language, so Eskimo uses the apparently distinct roots *aput* 'snow on the ground', *gana* 'falling snow', *piqsirpoq* 'drifting snow', and *qimuqsuq* 'a snow drift'. Boas' point is simply that English expresses these notions by phrases involving the root *snow*, but things could have been otherwise, just as the words for lake, river, etc. could have been formed derivationally or periphrastically on the root *water*.

But with the next twist in the story, the unleashing of the xenomorphic fable of Eskimo **lexicography** seems to have become inevitable. What happened was that Benjamin Lee Whorf, Connecticut fire prevention inspector and weekend language-fancier, picked up Boas' example and used it, vaguely, in his 1940 amateur linguistics article 'Science and linguistics', which was published in MIT's promotional magazine *Technology Review* (Whorf was an alumnus; he had done his BS in chemical engineering at MIT).

Our word *snow* would seem too inclusive to an Eskimo, our man from the Hartford Fire Insurance Company confidently asserts. With an uncanny perception into the hearts and minds of the hardy Arctic denizens (the more uncanny since Eskimos were not a prominent feature of Hartford's social scene at the time), he avers:

> We have the same word for falling snow, snow on the ground, snow packed hard like ice, slushy snow, wind-driven flying snow—whatever the situation may be. To an Eskimo, this all-inclusive word would be almost unthinkable; he would say that falling snow, slushy snow, and so on, are sensuously and operationally different, different things to contend with; he uses different words for them and for other kinds of snow.
>
> (Whorf 1940; in Carroll 1956, 216)

Whorf's article was quoted and reprinted in more subsequent books than you could shake a flamethrower at; the creature was already loose and regenerating itself all over the ship.

Notice that Whorf's statement has illicitly inflated Boas' four terms to at least seven (1: "falling", 2: "on the ground", 3: "packed hard", 4: "slushy, 5: "flying", 6, 7, ...: "and other kinds of snow"). Notice also that his claims about English speakers are false; I recall the stuff in question being called *snow* when fluffy and white, *slush* when partly melted, *sleet* when falling in a half-melted state, and a *blizzard* when pelting down hard enough to make driving dangerous. Whorf's remark about his own speech community is no more reliable than his glib generalizations about what things are "sensuously and operationally different" to the generic Eskimo.

But the lack of little things like verisimilitude and substantiation are not enough to stop a myth. Martin tracks the great Eskimo vocabulary hoax through successively more careless repetitions and embroiderings in a number of popular books on language. Roger Brown's *Words and Things* (1958: 234–236), attributing the example to Whorf, provides an early example of careless popularization and perversion of the issue. His numbers disagree with both Boas and Whorf (he says there are "three Eskimo words for snow", apparently getting this from Figure 10 in Whorf's paper; perhaps he only looked at the pictures).[1]

After works like Brown's have picked up Whorf's second-hand misrecollection of Boas to generate third-hand accounts, we begin to get fourth-hand accounts carelessly based on Brown. For example, Martin notes that in Carol Eastman's *Aspects of Language and Culture* (1975), the familiar assertion that "Eskimo languages have many words for snow" is found only six lines away from a direct quote of Brown's reference to "three" words for snow.

But never mind: three, four, seven, who cares? It's a bunch, right? When more popular sources start to get hold of the example, all constraints are removed: arbitrary numbers are just made up as the writer thinks appropriate for the readership. In Lanford Wilson's 1978 play *The Fifth of July* it is "fifty". From 1984 alone (two years *after* her 1982 presentation to the American Anthropological Association meetings on the subject—not that mere announcement at a scholarly meeting could have been expected to change anything), Martin cites the number of Eskimo snow terms given as "nine" (in a trivia encyclopedia, Adams 1984), "one hundred" (in a *New York Times* editorial on February 9), and "two hundred" (in a Cleveland TV weather forecast).

By coincidence, I happened to notice, the *New York Times* returned to the topic four years to the day after committing itself to the figure of one hundred: on February 9, 1988, on page 21, in the 'Science Times' section, a piece by Jane E. Brody on laboratory research into snowflake formation began: "The Eskimos have about four dozen words to describe snow and ice, and Sam Colbeck knows why." The *New York Times*, America's closest approach to a serious newspaper of record, had changed its position on the snow-term count by over 50 percent within four years. And in the *science* section. But hey: nine, forty-eight, a hundred, two hundred, who cares? It's a bunch, right? On this topic, no source can be trusted.

People cannot be persuaded to shut up about it, either. Attempting to slay the creature at least in my locality, I mentioned Martin's work in a public lecture in Santa Cruz in 1985, in the presence of a number of faculty, students, and members of the general public. I drove home the point about scholarly irresponsibility to an attentive crowd, and imagined I had put at least a temporary halt to careless talk about the Eskimo **morpheme** stock within Santa Cruz County. But it was not to be.

Within the following three months, two undergraduate students came to me to say that they had been told in class lectures about the Eskimo's highly ramified snow vocabulary, one in politics, one in psychology; my son told me he had been fed the same factoid in class at his junior high school; and the assertion turned up once again in a "fascinating facts" column in a Santa Cruz weekly paper.

Among the many depressing things about this credulous transmission and elaboration of a false claim is that even if there *were* a large number of roots for different snow types in some Arctic language, this would *not*, objectively, be intellectually interesting; it would be a most mundane and unremarkable fact.

Horsebreeders have various names for breeds, sizes, and ages of horses; botanists have names for leaf shapes; interior decorators have names for shades of mauve; printers have many different names for different fonts (Caslon, Garamond, Helvetica, Times Roman, and so on), naturally enough. If these obvious truths of specialization are supposed to be interesting facts about language, thought, and culture, then I'm sorry, but include me out.

Would anyone think of writing about printers the same kind of slop we find written about Eskimos in bad linguistics textbooks? Take a random textbook like Paul Gaeng's *Introduction to the Principles of Language* (1971), with its earnest assertion: "It is quite obvious that in the culture of the Eskimos … snow is of great enough importance to split up the conceptual sphere that corresponds to one word and one thought in English into several distinct classes …" (p. 137). Imagine reading: "It is quite obvious that in the culture of printers … fonts are of great enough importance to split up the conceptual sphere that corresponds to one word and one thought among non-printers into several distinct classes. …" Utterly boring, even if true. Only the link to those legendary, promiscuous, blubber-gnawing hunters of the ice-packs could permit something this trite to be presented to us for contemplation.

And actually, when you come to think of it, Eskimos aren't really that likely to be interested in snow. Snow in the traditional Eskimo hunter's life must be a kind of constantly assumed background, like sand on the beach. And even beach bums have only one word for sand. But there you are: the more you think about the Eskimo vocabulary hoax, the more stupid it gets.

The final words of Laura Martin's paper are about her hope that we can come to see the Eskimo snow story as a cautionary tale reminding us of "the intellectual protection to be found in the careful use of sources, the clear presentation of evidence, and above all, the constant evaluation of our assumptions." Amen to that. The prevalence of the great Eskimo snow hoax is testimony to falling standards in academia, but also to a wider tendency (particularly in the United States, I'm afraid) toward fundamentally anti-intellectual "gee-whiz" modes of **discourse** and increasing ignorance of scientific thought.

This is one more battle that linguists must take up—like convincing people that there is no need for a law to make English the official language of Kansas (cf. Chapter 14 [of Pullum's original book]), or that elementary schools shouldn't spend time trying to abolish negated auxiliary verbs ("There is no such word as *can't*"). Some time in the future, and it may be soon, you will be told by someone that the Eskimos have many or dozens or scores or hundreds of words for snow. You, gentle reader, must decide here and now whether you are going to let them get away with it, or whether you are going to be true to your position as an Expert On Language by calling them on it.

The last time it happened to me (other than through the medium of print) was in July 1988 at the University of California's Irvine campus, where I was attending the university's annual Management Institute. Not just one lecturer at the Institute but two of them somehow (don't ask me how) worked the Eskimological falsehood into their tedious presentations on management psychology and administrative problem-solving. The first time I attempted to demur and was glared at by lecturer and classmates alike; the second time, discretion for once getting the upper hand over valor, I just held my face in my hands for a minute, then quietly closed my binder and crept out of the room.

Don't be a coward like me. Stand up and tell the speaker this: C.W. Schultz-Lorentzen's *Dictionary of the West Greenlandic Eskimo Language* (1927) gives just two possibly relevant roots: *qanik*, meaning 'snow in the air' or 'snowflake', and *aput*, meaning 'snow on the ground'. Then add that you would be interested to know if the speaker can cite any more.

This will not make you the most popular person in the room. It will have an effect roughly comparable to pouring fifty gallons of thick oatmeal into a harpsichord during a baroque recital. But it will strike a blow for truth, responsibility, and standards of evidence in linguistics.

Appendix: Yes, But How Many Really?

[…]

So how many really? I know you still crave an answer. I will say only this. In 1987, in response to a request from some students at Texas who had read Laura Martin's article, Woodbury put together a list of bases in the Central Alaskan Yupik language that could be regarded as synchronically unanalyzable and had snow-related meanings. All of them are in Steven A. Jacobson's *Yup'ik Eskimo Dictionary* (University of Alaska, Fairbanks, 1984). Some of them are general weather-related words relating to rain, frost, and other conditions; some are count nouns denoting phenomena like blizzards, avalanches, snow cornices, snow crusts, and the like; some are etymologizable in a way that involves only roots unrelated to snow (example: *nutaryug-* is glossed as 'new snow' but originates from *nutar-* 'new' and *-yug-* 'what tends to be', so it means literally 'that which tends to be new' or 'new stuff'), but they have apparently been lexicalized as ways of referring to snow. The list includes both non-snow-referring roots (e.g. *muru-* 'to sink into something') and etymologically complex but apparently lexicalized stems based on them that are usually glossed as referring to snow (e.g. *muruaneq* 'soft deep snow', etymologically something like 'stuff for habitually sinking into'). The list has about a dozen different stems with 'snow' in the gloss, and a variety of other words (slightly more than a dozen) that are transparently derived from these (for example, *natquig-* is a noun stem meaning 'drifting snow' and *natquigte-* is a verb stem meaning 'for snow etc. to drift along ground').

So the list is still short, not remarkably different in size from the list in English (which, remember, boasts not just *snow, slush*, and *sleet* and their derivatives, but also count nouns like *avalanche* and *blizzard*, technical terms like *hardpack* and *powder*, expressive meteorological descriptive phrases like *flurry* and *dusting*, compounds with idiosyncratic meanings like *snow cornice*, and so on; many of the terms on Woodbury's list are much more like these terms than like simple mass nouns for new and unusual varieties of snow).

If it will allow you to rest easier at night, or to be more of an authority at cocktail parties, let it be known that Professor Anthony Woodbury (Department of Linguistics, University of Texas, Austin, Texas 78712) is prepared to endorse the claim that the Central Alaskan Yupik Eskimo language has about a dozen words (even a couple of dozen if you are fairly liberal about what you count) for referring to snow and to related natural phenomena, events, or behavior. Reliable reports based on systematic dictionary searches for other Eskimo languages are not available as far as I know.

For my part, I want to make one last effort to clarify that the chapter above isn't about Eskimo lexicography at all, though I'm sure it will be taken to be. What it's actually about is intellectual sloth. Among all the hundreds of people making published contributions to the great Eskimo vocabulary hoax, no one had acquired any evidence about how long the purported list of snow terms really was, or what words were on it, or what criteria were used in deciding what to put on the list. The tragedy is not that so many people got the facts wildly wrong; it is that in the mentally lazy and anti-intellectual world we live in today, hardly anyone cares enough to think about trying to determine what the facts are.

Note

1   Murray (1987) has argued that Martin is too harsh on some people, particularly Brown, who does correctly see that some English speakers also differentiate their snow terms (skiers talk of *powder*, *crust* and *slush*). But Martin is surely correct in criticizing Brown for citing no data at all, and for making points about lexical structure, perception and **Zipf's Law** that are rendered nonsense by the actual nature of Eskimo word structure (his reference to "length of a verbal expression" providing "an index of its frequency in speech" fails to take account of the fact that even with a single root for snow, the number of actual *word forms* for snow in Eskimo will be effectively infinite, and the frequency of each one approximately zero, because of the polysynthetic morphology).

References

Adams, Cecil (1984) *The Straight Dope: A Compendium of Human Knowledge*, edited and with an introduction by Ed Zotti, Chicago Review Press, Chicago, IL.

Boas, Franz (1911) Introduction to *The Handbook of North American Indians, Vol. I, Bureau of American Ethnology Bulletin* 40, Part 1, Smithsonian Institution, Washington, DC. Reprinted by Georgetown University Press, Washington DC (c. 1963) and by University of Nebraska Press, Lincoln, NE (1966).

Brown, Roger (1958) *Words and Things*, The Free Press, New York.

Carroll, John B. (ed.), (1956) *Language, Thought, and Reality: Selected Writings of Benjamin Lee Whorf*, MIT Press, Cambridge, MA.

Eastman, Carol (1975) *Aspects of Language and Culture*, Chandler, San Francisco, CA; third printing, Chandler & Sharp, Novato, CA, 1980.

Gaeng, Paul A. (1971) *Introduction to the Principles of Language*, Harper & Row, New York.

Jacobson, Steven A. (1984) *Yup'ik Eskimo Dictionary*, University of Alaska, Fairbanks, AK.

Martin, Laura (1986) "'Eskimo words for snow': A case study in the genesis and decay of an anthropological example," *American Anthropologist*, 88(2): 418–423.

Murray, Stephen O. (1987) "Snowing canonical texts," *American Anthropologist*, 89(2): 443–444.

Schultz-Lorentzen, C.W. (1927) *Dictionary of the West Greenlandic Eskimo language, Meddelser om Grønland* 69, Reitzels, Copenhagen.

Whorf, Benjamin Lee (1940) "Science and linguistics," *Technology Review* (MIT) 42(6): 229–231, 247–248. Reprinted in Carroll (1956), pp. 207–219.

Chapter 4

Benjamin Lee Whorf

THE RELATION OF HABITUAL THOUGHT AND BEHAVIOR TO LANGUAGE

[…]

THERE WILL PROBABLY be general assent to the proposition that an accepted pattern of using words is often prior to certain lines of thinking and forms of behavior, but he who assents often sees in such a statement nothing more than a platitudinous recognition of the hypnotic power of philosophical and learned terminology on the one hand or of catchwords, slogans, and rallying-cries on the other. To see only thus far is to miss the point of one of the important interconnections which Sapir saw between language, culture, and psychology, and succinctly expressed in the introductory quotation [see below]. It is not so much in these special uses of language as in its constant ways of arranging data and its most ordinary every-day analysis of phenomena that we need to recognize the influence it has on other activities, cultural and personal.

> Human beings do not live in the objective world alone, nor alone in the world of social activity as ordinarily understood, but are very much at the mercy of the particular language which has become the medium of expression for their society. It is quite an illusion to imagine that one adjusts to reality essentially without the use of language and that language is merely an incidental means of solving specific problems of communication or reflection, The fact of the matter is that the 'real world' is to a large extent unconsciously built up on the language habits of the group. ... We see and bear and otherwise experience very largely as we do because the language habits of our community predispose certain choices of interpretation.
> EDWARD SAPIR, 'The Status of Linguistics as a Science,' *Language*, Vol. V, pp. 209–210 (1929).

The name of the situation as affecting behavior

I came in touch with an aspect of this problem before I had studied under Dr Sapir, and in a field usually considered remote from linguistics. It was in the course of my professional work for a fire insurance company, in which I undertook the task of analyzing many hundreds of reports of circumstances surrounding the start of fires, and in some cases, of explosions. My analysis was directed toward purely physical conditions, such as defective wiring, presence or lack of air spaces between metal flues and woodwork, etc., and the results were presented in these terms. Indeed it was undertaken with no thought that any other significances would or could be revealed. But in due course it became evident that not only a physical situation *qua* physics, but the meaning of that situation to people, was sometimes a factor, through the behavior of the people, in the start of the fire. And this factor of meaning was clearest when it was a *linguistic meaning*, residing in the name or the linguistic description commonly applied to the situation. Thus around a storage of what are called 'gasoline drums' behavior will tend to a certain type, that is, great care will be exercised; while around a storage of what are called 'empty gasoline drums' it will tend to be different—careless, with little repression of smoking or of tossing cigarette stubs about. Yet the 'empty' drums are perhaps the more dangerous, since they contain explosive vapor. Physically the situation is hazardous, but the linguistic analysis according to regular analogy must employ the word 'empty,' which inevitably suggests lack of hazard. The word 'empty' *is* used in two linguistic patterns: (1) as a virtual synonym for 'null and void, negative, inert,' (2) applied in analysis of physical situations without regard to, e.g. vapor, liquid vestiges, or stray rubbish, in the container. The situation is named in one pattern (2) and the name *is* then 'acted out' or 'lived up to' in another (1); this being a general formula for the linguistic conditioning of behavior into hazardous forms. In a wood distillation plant the metal stills were insulated with a composition prepared from limestone and called at the plant 'spun limestone.' No attempt was made to protect this covering from excessive heat or the contact of flame. After a period of use the fire below one of the stills spread to the 'limestone,' which to everyone's great surprise burned vigorously. Exposure to acetic acid fumes from the stills had converted part of the limestone (calcium carbonate) to calcium acetate. This when heated in a fire decomposes, forming inflammable acetone. Behavior that tolerated fire close to the covering was induced by use of the name 'limestone,' which because it ends in '-stone' implies noncombustibility.

A huge iron kettle of boiling varnish was observed to be overheated, nearing the temperature at which it would ignite. The operator moved it off the fire and ran it on its wheels to a distance, but did not cover it. In a minute or so the varnish ignited. Here the linguistic influence is more complex; it is due to the metaphorical objectifying (of which more later) of 'cause' as contact or the spatial juxtaposition of 'things'—to analyzing the situation as 'on' versus 'off' the fire. In reality the stage when the external fire was the main factor had passed; the over-heating was now an internal process of convection in the varnish from the intensely heated kettle, and still continued when 'off' the fire.

An electric glow heater on the wall was little used, and for one workman had the meaning of a convenient coat-hanger. At night a watchman entered and snapped a switch, which action he verbalized as 'turning on the light.' No light appeared, and this result he verbalized as 'light is burned out.' He could not see the glow of the heater because of the old coat hung on it. Soon the heater ignited the coat, which set fire to the building.

A tannery discharged waste water containing animal matter into an outdoor settling basin partly roofed with wood and partly open. This situation is one that ordinarily would be verbalized as 'pool of water.' A workman had occasion to light a blow-torch nearby, and threw his match into the water. But the decomposing waste matter was evolving gas under the wood cover, so that the setup was the reverse of 'watery.' An instant flare of flame ignited the woodwork, and the fire quickly spread into the adjoining building.

A drying room for hides was arranged with a blower at one end to make a current of air along the room and thence outdoors through a vent at the other end. Fire started at a hot bearing on the blower, which blew the flames directly into the hides and fanned them along the room, destroying the entire stock. This hazardous setup followed naturally from the term 'blower' with its linguistic equivalence to 'that which blows,' implying that its function necessarily is to 'blow.' Also its function is verbalized as 'blowing air for drying,' overlooking that it can blow other things, e.g., flames and sparks. In reality a blower simply makes a current of air and can exhaust as well as blow. It should have been installed at the vent end to *draw* the air over the hides, then through the hazard (its own casing and bearings) and thence outdoors.

Beside a coal-fired melting pot for lead reclaiming was dumped a pile of 'scrap lead'—a misleading verbalization, for it consisted of the lead sheets of old radio condensers, which still had paraffin paper between them. Soon the paraffin blazed up and fired the roof, half of which was burned off.

Such examples, which could be greatly multiplied, will suffice to show how the *cue to a certain line of behavior is often* given by the analogies of the linguistic formula in which the situation is spoken of, and by which to some degree it is analyzed, classified, and allotted its place in that world which *is* 'to a large extent unconsciously built up on the language habits of the group.' And we always assume that the linguistic analysis made by our group reflects reality better than it does.

Grammatical patterns as interpretations of experience

The linguistic material in the above examples is limited to single words, phrases and patterns of limited range. One cannot study the behavioral compulsiveness of such material without suspecting a much more far-reaching compulsion from large-scale patterning of grammatical categories, such as plurality, gender and similar classifications (animate, inanimate, etc.), tenses, voices, and other verb forms, classifications of the type of 'parts of speech,' and the matter of whether a given experience is denoted by a unit **morpheme**, an inflected word, or a syntactical combination. A category such as number (singular vs. plural) is an attempted interpretation of a whole large order of experience, virtually of the world or of nature; it attempts to say how experience is to be segmented, what experience is to be called 'one' and what 'several.' But the difficulty of appraising such a far-reaching influence is great because of its background character, because of the difficulty of standing aside from our own language, which is a habit and a cultural *non est disputandum*, and scrutinizing it objectively. And if we take a very dissimilar language, this language becomes a part of nature, and we even do to it what we have already done to nature. We tend to think in our own language in order to examine the exotic language. Or we find the task of unraveling the purely morphological intricacies so gigantic that it seems to absorb all else. Yet the problem, though difficult, is feasible; and the best approach is through an exotic language, for in its study we are at long last pushed willynilly out of our ruts. Then we find that the exotic language is a mirror held up to our own.

In my study of the Hopi language, what I now see as an opportunity to work on this problem was first thrust upon me before I was clearly aware of the problem. The seemingly endless task of describing the **morphology** did finally end. Yet it was evident, especially in the light of Sapir's lectures on Navaho, that the description of the *language* was far from complete. I knew for example the morphological formation of plurals, but not how to use plurals. It was evident that the category of plural in Hopi was not the same thing as in English, French, or German. Certain things that were plural in these languages were singular in Hopi. The phase of investigation which now began consumed nearly two more years.

The work began to assume the character of a comparison between Hopi and western European languages. It also became evident that even the grammar of Hopi bore a relation to Hopi culture, and the grammar of European tongues to our own 'western' or 'European' culture. And it appeared that the interrelation brought in those large subsummations of experience by language, such as our terms 'time,' 'space,' 'substance,' and 'matter.' Since with respect to the traits compared there is little difference between English, French, German, or other European languages with the *possible* (but doubtful) exception of Balto-Slavic and non-Indo-European, I have lumped these languages into one group called SAE, or 'Standard Average European.'

That portion of the whole investigation here to be reported may be summed up in two questions: (1) Are our own concepts of 'time,' 'space,' and 'matter' given in substantially the same form by experience to all men, or are they in part conditioned by the structure of particular languages? (2) Are there traceable affinities between (a) cultural and behavioral norms and (b) large-scale linguistic patterns? I should be the last to pretend that there is anything so definite as 'a correlation' between culture and language, and especially between ethnological rubrics such as 'agricultural,' 'hunting,' etc., and linguistic ones like 'inflected,' 'synthetic,' or 'isolating.'[1] When I began the study the problem was by no means so clearly formulated and I had little notion that the answers would turn out as they did.

[...]

Nouns of physical quantity in SAE and Hopi

We have two kinds of nouns denoting physical things; individual nouns, and mass nouns, e.g., water, milk, wood, granite, sand, flour, meat. Individual nouns denote bodies with definite outlines: a tree, a stick, a man, a hill. Mass nouns denote homogeneous continua without implied boundaries. The distinction is marked by linguistic form; e.g., mass nouns lack plurals,[2] in English drop articles, and in French take the partitive article *du, de la, des*. The distinction is more widespread in language than in the observable appearance of things. Rather few natural occurrences present themselves as unbounded extents; air of course, and often water, rain, snow, sand, rock, dirt, grass. We do not encounter butter, meat, cloth, iron, glass, or most 'materials' in such kind of manifestation, but in bodies small or large with definite outlines. The distinction is somewhat forced upon our description of events by an unavoidable pattern in language. It is so inconvenient in a great many cases that we need some way of individualizing the mass noun by further linguistic devices. This is partly done by names of body-types: stick of wood, piece of cloth, pane of glass, cake of soap; also, and even more, by introducing names of containers though their contents be the real issue: glass of water, cup of coffee, dish of food, bag of flour, bottle of beer. These very common container-formulas, in which 'of' has an obvious, visually perceptible meaning ('contents'), influence our feeling about the less obvious type-body formulas: stick of wood, lump of dough, etc. The formulas are very similar: individual noun plus a similar relator (English 'of'). In the obvious case this relator denotes contents. In the inobvious one it *suggests* contents. Hence the lumps, chunks, blocks, pieces, etc., seem to contain something, a 'stuff,' 'substance,' or 'matter' that answers to the water, coffee, or flour in the container formulas. So with SAE people the philosophic 'substance' and 'matter' are also the naïve idea; they are instantly acceptable, 'common sense.' It is so through linguistic habit. Our language patterns often require us to name a physical thing by a **binomial** that splits the reference into a formless item plus a form.

Hopi is different. It has a formally distinguished class of nouns. But this class contains no formal sub-class of mass nouns. All nouns have an individual sense and both singular and plural forms. Nouns translating most nearly our mass nouns still refer to vague bodies or vaguely bounded extents. They imply indefiniteness, but not lack, of outline and size. In specific statements 'water' means one certain mass or quantity of water, not what we call 'the substance water.' Generality of statement is conveyed through the verb or predicator, not the noun. Since nouns are individual already they are not individualized either by type-bodies or names of containers, if there is no special need to emphasize shape or container. The noun itself implies a suitable type-body or container. One says, not 'a glass of water' but ke.yi 'a water,' not 'a pool of water' but pa.he,[3] not 'a dish of corn-flour' but ngemni 'a (quantity of) corn-flour,' not 'a piece of meat' but sik^{w}i 'a meat.' The language has neither need for nor analogies on which to build the concept of existence as a duality of formless item and form. It deals with formlessness through other symbols than nouns.

Phases of cycles in SAE and Hopi

Such terms as summer, winter, September, morning, noon, sunset, are with us nouns, and have little formal linguistic difference from other nouns. They can be subjects or objects, and we say 'at' sunset or 'in' winter just as we say at a corner or in an orchard.[4] They are pluralized and numerated like nouns of physical objects, as we have seen. Our thought about the referents of such words hence becomes objectified. Without objectification it would be a subjective experience of real time, i.e. of the consciousness of 'becoming later and later'—simply a cyclic phase similar to an earlier phase in that ever-later-becoming duration. Only by imagination can such a cyclic phase be set beside another and another in the manner of a spatial (i.e. visually perceived) configuration. But such is the power of linguistic analogy that we do so objectify cyclic phasing. We do it even by saying 'a phase' and 'phases' instead of, e.g. 'phasing.' And the pattern of individual and mass nouns, with the resulting **binomial** formula of formless item plus form, is so general that it is implicit for all nouns, and hence our very generalized formless items like 'substance,' 'matter,' by which we can fill out the binomial for an enormously wide range of nouns. But even these are not quite generalized enough to take in our phase nouns. So for the phase nouns we have made a formless item, 'time.' We have made it by using 'a time,' i.e. an occasion or a phase, in the pattern of a mass noun, just as from 'a summer' we make 'summer' in the pattern of a mass noun. Thus with our binomial formula we can say and think 'a moment of time,' 'a second of time,' 'a year of time.' Let me again point out that the pattern is simply that of 'a bottle of milk' or 'a piece of cheese.' Thus we are assisted to imagine that 'a summer' actually contains or consists of such-and-such a quantity of 'time.'

In Hopi however all phase terms, like summer, morning, etc., are not nouns but a kind of **adverb**, to use the nearest SAE analogy. They are a formal part of speech by themselves, distinct from nouns, verbs, and even other Hopi 'adverbs.' Such a word is not a case form or a **locative** pattern, like 'des Abends' or 'in the morning.' It contains no morpheme like one of 'in the house' or 'at the tree.'[5] It means 'when it is morning' or 'while morning-phase is occurring.' These 'temporals' are not used as subjects or objects, or at all like nouns. One does not say 'it's a hot summer' or 'summer is hot;' summer is not hot, summer is only *when* conditions are hot, *when* heat occurs. One does not say '*this* summer,' but 'summer now' or 'summer recently.' There is no objectification, as a region, an extent, a quantity, of the subjective duration-feeling. Nothing is suggested about time except the perpetual 'getting later' of it. And so there is no basis here for a formless item answering to our 'time.'

[…]

Habitual thought in SAE and Hopi

The comparison now to be made between the habitual thought worlds of SAE and Hopi speakers is of course incomplete. It is possible only to touch upon certain dominant contrasts that appear to stem from the linguistic differences already noted. By 'habitual thought' and 'thought world' I mean more than simply language, i.e. than the linguistic patterns themselves. I include all the analogical and suggestive value of the patterns (e.g. our 'imaginary space' and its distant implications), and all the give-and-take between language and the culture as a whole, wherein is a vast amount that is not linguistic yet shows the shaping influence of language. In brief, this 'thought world' is the **microcosm** that each man carries about within himself, by which he measures and understands what he can of the macrocosm.

The SAE microcosm has analyzed reality largely in terms of what it calls 'things' (bodies and quasi-bodies) plus modes of extensional but formless existence that it calls 'substance' or 'matter.' It tends to see existence through a binomial formula that expresses any existent as a spatial form plus a spatial formless continuum related to the form as content is related to the outlines of its container. Non-spatial existents are imaginatively spatialized and charged with similar implications of form and continuum.

The Hopi microcosm seems to have analyzed reality largely in terms of *events* (or better 'eventing'), referred to in two ways, objective and subjective. Objectively, and only if perceptible physical experience, events are expressed mainly as outlines, colors, movements, and other perceptive reports. Subjectively, for both the physical and non-physical, events are considered the expression of invisible intensity-factors, on which depend their stability and persistence, or their fugitiveness and proclivities. It implies that existents do not 'become later and later' all in the same way; but some do so by growing, like plants, some by diffusing and vanishing, some by a procession of metamorphoses, some by enduring in one shape till affected by violent forces. In the nature of each existent able to manifest as a definite whole is the power of its own mode of duration; its growth, decline, stability, cyclicity, or creativeness. Everything is thus already 'prepared' for the way it now manifests by earlier phases, and what it will be later, partly has been, and partly is in act of being so 'prepared.' An emphasis and importance rests on this preparing or being prepared aspect of the world that may to the Hopi correspond to that 'quality of reality' that 'matter' or 'stuff' has for us.

Habitual behavior features of Hopi culture

Our behavior, and that of Hopi, can be seen to be coordinated in many ways to the linguistically-conditioned microcosm. As in my fire case-book, people act about situations in ways which are like the ways they talk about them. A characteristic of Hopi behavior is the emphasis on preparation. This includes announcing and getting ready for events well beforehand, elaborate precautions to insure persistence of desired conditions, and stress on good will as the preparer of right results. Consider the analogies of the day-counting pattern alone. Time is mainly reckoned 'by day' (taɹk, -tala) or 'by night' (tok), which words are not nouns but tensors, the first formed on a root 'light, day,' the second on a root 'sleep.' The count is by *ordinals*. This is not the pattern of counting a number of different men or things, even though they appear successively, for even then they *could* gather into an assemblage. It is the pattern of counting successive reappearances of the *same* man or thing, incapable of forming an assemblage. The analogy is not to behave about day-cyclicity as to several men ('several days'), which is what *we* tend to do, but to behave as to the successive visits of the *same man*. One does not alter several men by working upon just one, but one can prepare and so alter the later visits of the same man by working to affect the visit he is making now. This is the way the Hopi deal with the future—by working within a present situation which is expected to carry impresses, both obvious and occult, forward into the future event of interest. One might say that Hopi society understands our proverb 'Well begun is half done,' but not our 'To-morrow is another day.' This may explain much in Hopi character.

This Hopi preparing behavior may be roughly divided into announcing, outer preparing, inner preparing, covert participation, and persistence. Announcing, or preparative publicity, is an important function in the hands of a special official, the Crier Chief. Outer preparing is preparation involving much visible activity, not all necessarily directly useful within our understanding. It includes ordinary practising, rehearsing, getting ready, introductory formalities, preparing of special food, etc. (all of these to a degree that may seem over-elaborate to us), intensive sustained muscular activity like running, racing, dancing, which is thought to increase the intensity of development of events (such as growth of crops), mimetic and other magic, preparations based on esoteric theory involving perhaps occult instruments like prayer sticks, prayer feathers, and prayer meal, and finally the great cyclic ceremonies and dances, which have the significance of preparing rain and crops. From one of the verbs meaning 'prepare' is derived the noun for 'harvest' or 'crop:' na'twani 'the prepared' or the 'in preparation.'[6]

Inner preparing is use of prayer and meditation, and at lesser intensity good wishes and good will, to further desired results. Hopi attitudes stress the power of desire and thought. With their 'microcosm' it is utterly natural that they should. Desire and thought are the earliest, and therefore the most important, most critical and crucial, stage of preparing. Moreover, to the Hopi, one's desires and thoughts influence not only his own actions, but all nature. This too is wholly natural. [...]

Covert participation is mental collaboration from people who do not take part in the actual affair, be it a job of work, hunt, race, or ceremony, but direct their thought and good will toward the affair's success. Announcements often seek to enlist the support of such mental helpers as well as of overt participants, and contain exhortations to the people to aid with their active good will.[7] A similarity to our concepts of a sympathetic audience or the cheering section at a football game should not obscure the fact that is is primarily the power of directed thought, and not merely sympathy or encouragement, that is expected of covert participants. [...]

Some impresses of linguistic habit in Western civilization

It is harder to do justice in a few words to the linguistically-conditioned features of our own culture than in the case of the Hopi, because of both vast scope and and difficulty of objectivity—because of our deeply ingrained familiary with the attitudes to be analyzed. I wish merely to sketch certain characteristics adjusted to our linguistic binomialism of form plus formless item or 'substance,' to our metaphoricalness, our imaginary space, and our objectified time. These, as we have seen, are linguistic.

From the form-plus-substance dichotomy the philosophical views most traditionally characteristic of the 'Western world' have derived huge support. Here belong materialism, psycho-physical parallelism, physics—at least in its traditional Newtonian form—and dualistic views of the universe in general. Indeed here belongs almost everything that is 'hard, practical common sense.' Monistic, holistic, and relativistic views of reality appeal to philosophers and some scientists, but they are badly handicapped for appealing to the 'common sense' of the Western average man. This is not because nature herself refutes them (if she did, philosophers could have discovered this much) but because they must be talked about in what amounts to a new language. 'Common sense,' as its name shows, and 'practicality' as its name does not show, are largely matters of talking so that one is readily understood. It is sometimes stated that Newtonian space, time, and matter are sensed by everyone intuitively, whereupon relativity is cited as showing how mathematical analysis can prove intuition wrong. This, besides being unfair to intuition, is an attempt to answer offhand question (1) put at the outset of this paper, to answer which this research was undertaken. Presentation of the findings now nears its end, and I think the answer is clear. The offhand answer, laying the blame upon intuition for our slowness in discovering mysteries of the cosmos, such as relativity, is the wrong one. The right answer is: Newtonian space, time, and matter are no intuitions. They are recepts from culture and language. That is where Newton got them.

Our objectified view of time is however favorable to historicity and to everything connected with the keeping of records, while the Hopi view is unfavorable thereto. The latter is too subtle, complex, and ever-developing, supplying no readymade answer to the question of when 'one' event ends and 'another' begins. When it is implicit that everything that ever happened still is, but is in a necessarily different form from what memory or record reports, there is less incentive to study the past. As for the present, the incentive would be not to record it but to treat it as 'preparing.' But *our* objectified time puts before imagination something like a ribbon or scroll marked off into equal blank spaces, suggesting that each be filled with an entry. Writing has no doubt helped toward our linguistic treatment of time, even as the linguistic treatment has guided the uses of writing. Through this give-and-take between language and the whole culture we get, for instance:

1.   Records, diaries, book-keeping, accounting, mathematics stimulated by accounting;
2.   Interest in exact sequence, dating, calendars, chronology, clocks, time wages, time graphs, time as used in physics;
3.   Annals, histories, the historical attitude, interest in the past, archaeology, attitudes of introjection towards past periods, e.g., classicism, romanticism.

Just as we conceive our objectified time as extending in the future like the way it extends in the past, so we set down our estimates of the future in the same shape as our records of the past, producing programs, schedules, budgets. The formal equality of the space-like units by which we measure and conceive time leads us to consider the 'formless item' or 'substance' of time to be homogeneous and in ratio to the number of units. Hence our prorata allocation of value to time, lending itself to the building up of a commercial structure based on time-prorata values: time wages (time work constantly supersedes piece work), rent, credit, interest, depreciation charges, and insurance premiums. No doubt this vast system once built would continue to run under any sort of linguistic treatment of time; but that it should have been built at all, reaching the magnitude and particular form it has in the Western world, is a fact decidedly in consonance with the patterns of the SAE languages. [...]

It is clear how the emphasis on 'saving time' which goes with all the above and is very obvious objectification of time, leads to a high valuation of 'speed,' which shows itself a great deal in our behavior.

[...]

Thus our linguistically-determined thought world not only collaborates with our cultural idols and ideals, but engages even our unconscious personal reactions in its patterns and gives them certain typical characters. One such character, as we have seen, is *carelessness*, as in reckless driving or throwing cigarette stubs into waste paper. Another of different sort is *gesturing* when we talk. Very many of the gestures made by English-speaking people at least, and probably by all SAE speakers, serve to illustrate by a movement in space, not a real spatial reference but one of the non-spatial references that our language handles by metaphors of imaginary space. That is, we are more apt to make a grasping gesture when we speak of grasping an elusive idea than when we speak of grasping a doorknob. The gesture seeks to make a metaphorical and hence somewhat unclear reference more clear. But if a language refers to non-spatials without implying a spatial analogy, the reference is not made any clearer by gesture. The Hopi gesture very little, perhaps not at all in the sense we understand as gesture.

[…]

Historical implications

How does such a network of language, culture, and behavior come about historically? Which was first, the language patterns or the cultural norms? In main they have grown up together, constantly influencing each other. But in this partnership the nature of the language is the factor that limits free plasticity and rigidifies channels of development in the more autocratic way. This is because a language is a system, not just an assemblage of norms. Large systemic outlines can change to something really new only very slowly, while many other cultural innovations are made with comparative quickness. Language thus represents the mass mind; it is affected by inventions and innovations, but affected little and slowly, whereas *to* inventors and innovators it legislates with the decree immediate.

The growth of the SAE language-culture complex dates from ancient times. Much of its metaphorical reference to the non-spatial by the spatial was already fixed in the ancient tongues, and more especially in Latin. It is indeed a marked trait of Latin. If we compare, say Hebrew, we find that while Hebrew has some allusion to not-space as space, Latin has more. Latin terms for non-spatials, like *educo, religio, principia, comprehendo*, are usually metaphorized physical references: lead out, tying back, etc. This is not true of all languages—it is quite untrue of Hopi. The fact that in Latin the direction of development happened to be from spatial to non-spatial (partly because of secondary stimulation to abstract thinking when the intellectually crude Romans encountered Greek culture) and that later tongues were strongly stimulated to mimic Latin, seems a likely reason for a belief which still lingers on among linguists that this is the natural direction of semantic change in all languages, and for the persistent notion in Western learned circles (in strong contrast to Eastern ones) that objective experience is prior to subjective. Philosophies make out a weighty case for the reverse, and certainly the direction of development is sometimes the reverse. Thus the Hopi word for 'heart' can be shown to be a late formation within Hopi from a root meaning think or remember. Or consider what has happened to the word 'radio' in such a sentence as 'he bought a new radio,' as compared to its prior meaning 'science of wireless telephony.'

In the middle ages the patterns already formed in Latin began to interweave with the increased mechanical invention, industry, trade, and scholastic and scientific thought. The need for measurement in industry and trade, the stores and bulks of 'stuffs' in various containers, the type-bodies in which various goods were handled, standardizing of measure and weight units, invention of clocks and measurement of 'time,' keeping of records, accounts, chronicles, histories, growth of mathematics and the partnership of mathematics and science, all coöperated to bring our thought and language world into its present form.

In Hopi history, could we read it, we should find a different type of language and a different set of cultural and environmental influences working together. A peaceful agricultural society isolated by geographic features and nomad enemies in a land of scanty rainfall, arid agriculture that could be made successful only by the utmost perseverance (hence the value of persistence and repetition), necessity for collaboration (hence emphasis on the psychology of teamwork and on mental factors in general), corn and rain as primary criteria of value, need of extensive *preparations* and precautions to assure crops in the poor soil and precarious climate, keen realization of dependence upon nature favoring prayer and a religious attitude toward the forces of nature, especially prayer and religion directed toward the ever-needed blessing, rain—these things interacted with Hopi linguistic patterns to mold them, to be molded again by them, and so little by little to shape the Hopi world-outlook.

To sum up the matter, our first question asked in the beginning (p. 43) is answered thus: Concepts of 'time' and 'matter' are not given in substantially the same form by experience to all men but depend upon the nature of the language or languages through the use of which they have been developed. They do not depend so much upon *any one system* (e.g., tense, or nouns) within the grammar as upon the ways of analyzing and reporting experience which have become fixed in the language as integrated 'fashions of speaking' and which cut across the typical grammatical classifications, so that such a 'fashion' may include lexical, morphological, syntactic, and otherwise systematically diverse means coordinated in a certain frame of consistency. Our own 'time' differs markedly from Hopi 'duration.' It is conceived as like a space of strictly limited dimensions, or sometimes as like a motion upon such a space, and employed as an intellectual tool accordingly. Hopi 'duration' seems to be inconceivable in terms of space or motion, being the mode in which life differs from form, and consciousness *in toto* from the spatial elements of consciousness. Certain ideas born of our own time-concept, such as that of absolute simultaneity, would be either very difficult to express or impossible and devoid of meaning under the Hopi conception, and would be replaced by operational concepts. Our 'matter' is the physical sub-type of 'substance' or 'stuff,' which is conceived as the formless extensional item that must be joined with form before there can be real existence. In Hopi there seems to be nothing corresponding to it; there are no formless extensional items; existence may or may not have form, but what it also has, with or without form, is intensity and duration, these being non-extensional and at bottom the same.

But what about our concept of 'space,' which was also included in our first questions? There is no such striking difference between Hopi and SAE about space as about time, and probably the apprehension of space is given in substantially the same form by experience irrespective of language. The experiments of the **Gestalt psychologists** with visual perception appear to establish this as a fact. But the *concept of space* will vary somewhat with language, because as an intellectual tool[8] it is so closely linked with the concomitant employment of other intellectual tools, of the order of 'time' and 'matter,' which are linguistically conditioned. We see things with our eyes in the same space forms as the Hopi, but our idea of space has also the property of acting as a surrogate of non-spatial relationships like time, intensity, tendency, and as a void to be filled with imagined formless items, one of which may even be called 'space,' Space as sensed by the Hopi would not be connected mentally with such surrogates, but would be comparatively 'pure,' unmixed with extraneous notions.

As for our second question (p. 43): There are connections but not correlations or diagnostic correspondences between cultural norms and linguistic patterns. Although it would be impossible to infer the existence of Crier Chiefs from the lack of tenses in Hopi, or vice versa, there is a relation between a language and the rest of the culture of the society which uses it. There are cases where the 'fashions of speaking' are closely integrated with the whole general culture, whether or not this be universally true, and there are connections within this integration, between the kind of linguistic analyses employed and various behavioral reactions and also the shapes taken by various cultural developments. Thus the importance of Crier Chiefs does have a connection, not with tenselessness itself, but with a system of thought in which categories different from our tenses are natural. These connections are to be found not so much by focusing attention on the typical rubrics of linguistic, **ethnographic**, or sociological description as by examining the culture and the language (always and only when the two have been together historically for a considerable time) as a whole in which concatenations that run across these departmental lines may be expected to exist, and if they do exist, eventually to be discoverable by study.

[…]

Notes

1   We have plenty of evidence that this is not the case. Consider only the Hopi and the Ute, with languages that on the overt morphological and lexical level are as similar as, say, English and German. The idea of 'correlation' between language and culture, in the generally accepted sense of correlation, is certainly a mistaken one.

2   It is no exception to this rule of lacking a plural that a mass noun may sometimes coincide in lexeme with an individual noun that of course has a plural; e.g., 'stone' (no pl.) with 'a stone' (pl. 'stones'). The plural form denoting varieties, e.g., 'wines' is of course a different sort of thing from the true plural; it is a curious outgrowth from the SAE mass nouns, leading to still another sort of imaginary aggregates, which will have to be omitted from this paper.

3   Hopi has two words for water-quantities; ke.yi and pa.he. The difference is something like that between 'stone' and 'rock' in English, pa.he implying greater size and 'wildness'; flowing water, whether or not out-doors or in nature, is pa.he, so is 'moisture.' But unlike 'stone' and 'rock,' the difference is essential, not pertaining to a connotative margin, and the two can hardly ever be interchanged.

4   To be sure there are a few minor differences from other nouns, in English for instance in the use of the articles.

5   'Year' and certain combinations of 'year' with name of season, rarely season names alone, can occur with a locative morpheme 'at,' but this is exceptional. It appears like historical detritus of an earlier different patterning, or the effect of English analogy, or both.

6   The Hopi verbs of preparing naturally do not correspond neatly to our 'prepare'; so that na'twani could also be rendered 'the practised-upon,' 'the tried-for,' and otherwise.

7   See e.g. Ernest Beaglehole, *Notes on Hopi Economic Life* (Yale University Publications in Anthropology, No. 15, 1937), especially the reference to the announcement of a rabbit hunt, and on p. 30, description of the activities in connection with the cleaning of Toreva Spring—announcing, various preparing activities, and finally, preparing the continuity of the good results already obtained and the continued flow of the spring.

8   Here belong 'Newtonian' and 'Euclidean' space, etc.

Chapter 5

John A. Lucy

THROUGH THE WINDOW OF LANGUAGE: ASSESSING THE INFLUENCE OF LANGUAGE DIVERSITY ON THOUGHT

[…]

Introduction

The diversity of human languages has long given rise to speculation about its sources and consequences. Why do languages render the same reality so differently and what are the consequences of those differences for human thought? These two questions are in fact intimately related: how we understand *language diversity*, the ways languages differ in their renderings of reality, greatly affects our approach to understanding *linguistic relativity*, the effects of linguistic diversity on thought. The present paper explicates the close interrelationship between these two questions and its significance for current theoretical and empirical approaches.

The shared human capacity for natural language manifests itself in the form of many individual languages differing in important respects. Hence individual speakers do not speak language-in-general but rather one or more specific languages that differ structurally from one another. In this discussion we are concerned specifically then with *structural diversity* among language codes (e.g., Hopi, Chinese, Spanish) and, ultimately, their impact on thought, what we can call, *structural ("linguistic") relativity* (in contrast to generic language effects or those due to specialized institutionalized practices; see Lucy 1996). At issue then are two distinct relationships: each language embodies a particular *interpretation* of reality and these language interpretations can *influence* thought about that reality (Lucy 1997). The interpretation arises from the selection of substantive aspects of experience and their formal arrangement in the verbal code. Such selection and arrangement is, of course, necessary for every language, so the crucial emphasis here is that each language involves a particular interpretation, not a common, universal one. An influence on thought ensues when the particular language interpretation guides or supports cognitive activity more generally and hence the beliefs and behaviors dependent on it. Theory and research about such cognitive effects are shaped in important ways by one's prior orientation to linguistic diversity.

Historical orientations to understanding linguistic diversity

There have been two dominant approaches to understanding the diverse interpretations of reality embodied in language (Aarsleff 1982). First, there are those who view the connection between language and the world as natural (or absolute).

[…]

One can hear echoes of this view in any language **ideology** about the supposed slovenliness of contemporary speech (especially among youth) as contrasted with earlier, more correct or "logical" forms. Alternatively, others discard the historical dimension and simply imagine a pristine linguistic form lying securely within each language and that all we have to do is peel back the superficial encrustation and we will find the natural logic of language revealed. One can hear echoes of this view in all those who speak of underlying competence, deep structures, universal primitives, and the like, all waiting to be excavated from beneath the messy, misleading, and ultimately irrelevant surface diversity.

On the opposing side are those who view the connection between language and experience as artificial (or conventional) and who, therefore, regard diversity as an unavoidable feature of languages. Again, there are two ways to regard this diversity. One classic view celebrates this diversity as of local historical significance. So languages, in this view, contain in their form living traces of history and are to be treasured as repositories of the genius of a people. Thus diversity is embraced, but often with a more or less explicit evaluation of one or another language (or language type) as superior—along with the people who created it. One thinks especially of Humboldt in this regard and his claims that the inflecting languages of Europe were naturally superior as formal instruments for rendering reality (Aarsleff 1988). Alternatively, one can take a more neutral view of this process, but recognize that the lack of a uniform natural relationship presents obstacles to clear communication, especially in philosophy and science, a view classically articulated by Locke. However, in this view, the very conventional nature of language allows us to build up specialized vocabularies and professional jargons as needed to convey our views accurately. So in place of decline and corruption one sees the possibility of progress and perfection in language. Here we find much of the impetus for the rampant multiplication of technical terms that besets contemporary scholarship and for the flight to mathematical formalisms.

Disparate as these two dominant approaches are, they share the common underlying assumptions that there is a *single unitary reality* and *an ideal relation of language to it*, however elusive. Early in the twentieth century these assumptions were challenged by Benjamin Whorf (1956; see Lucy 1992a), a linguist working in the American anthropological tradition founded by Franz Boas. Whorf questioned the existence of a single ideal relation of language to reality and in precisely this sense he also questioned our conceptualization of a unitary reality, since its qualities would vary as a function of the language used to describe it. If there is no ideal relation of language to reality, hence a fundamental scientific uncertainty about the character of that reality, then the whole problem of the relation of language to experience changes. Claims for universality in the relation of language to reality can no longer simply be presumed but require empirical proof. And no language, whether ancient or modern, received or constructed, can be judged inferior or superior, corrupted or perfected in light of its match with reality. In this view, we are lacking a language-neutral standard against which to form such judgments. And, consequently, no single language can provide through its system of categories a reliable guide to reality for the purposes of research. This is the central problem faced by contemporary researchers dealing with the question of linguistic relativity.

Contemporary orientations to linguistic relativity research

Since the appearance of Whorf's formulation of the problem, two main strategies of empirical research have emerged aiming to solve this puzzle of how to provide a neutral ground or frame of reference for comparing languages and cognition (Lucy 1997). Each approach has characteristic advantages and drawbacks.

One approach, which I call *domain-centered*, selects a domain of experience (such as color or time or space) and seeks to describe it on language-independent grounds in order first to ask how individual languages treat the domain and subsequently how speakers regard the domain in cognition. The domain-centered approach seeks to solve the comparison problem by asking how different languages partition the same domain of reality. Although the approach offers a number of advantages for comparative purposes, it tends to suffer from two weaknesses. First, the representation of the domain is typically drawn from one linguistic and cultural tradition. As such it begs the question being asked, namely, whether such representations, or even the domain itself, are universally recognized. Acknowledging this problem, some seek to anchor the description in well-established scientific concepts to help assure neutrality and objectivity. This can be illuminating, but more often one ends up with a description in terms of parameters drawn from that science and not from those semantically or structurally relevant to actual linguistic systems; this in turn can lead to a dramatic misrepresentation of the languages at issue. Further, by adopting one vision of reality, even a scientific one, as the standard for comparison, one still necessarily favors the original language and culture from which it arose. This leads, not surprisingly, to any number of demonstrations of difference in which a hierarchy quietly (re)emerges: in effect such efforts simply show how well languages do or do not represent the semantic values of the system framing the comparison. The method used for creating a neutral system based on reality thus often undermines the very possibility of fair comparison.

[…]

The most successful recent effort at a domain-centered approach has been undertaken in the domain of space (Levinson 2003). Spatial conceptualization has been widely regarded as invariant within philosophical, psychological, and linguistic circles and yet there is variability in its linguistic encoding. For example, speakers of modern European languages tend to favor the use of body coordinates to describe arrangements of objects (e.g., "the man is to the left of the tree"). For similar situations, speakers of other languages such as Guugu Yiimithirr (Australian) and Tzeltal (Mayan) favor systems anchored as cardinal direction terms or topographic features respectively (e.g., "the man is to the east/uphill of the tree"). Careful cross-linguistic comparison using a variety of innovative techniques for referential typology has been undertaken to compare "the meaning patterns that consistently emerge from domain-directed interactive discourse." In a large number of nonlinguistic tasks it appears that speakers of different languages respond in ways congruent with their verbal practices.

This research has attempted to gain the advantages of precise, extensive comparison characteristic of a domain-centered approach while simultaneously avoiding its chief pitfalls by incorporating extensive linguistic description and typology into the project from the outset. And it vigorously avoids entering into an evaluation of which type of semantic system is superior or more natural, seeing each as having characteristic costs and benefits. In these respects this effort escapes the usual weakness of domain-centered approaches. But it does so only by allowing serious slippage with regard to the original concern with linguistic structure: a single "language" may use more than one semantic approach to spatial description and languages considered the "same" in their referential usage may in fact be using radically different structural means. In the end then, the linguistic analysis and typology are not concerned so much with linguistic structure in the traditional sense but rather with patterns of linguistic usage; and a single language structure can be used implement more than one of these usage strategies.

A second approach, which I call *structure-centered*, selects some grammatical structure (such as number or gender or aspect marking), asks how it differs across languages, and how reality might appear differently from the vantage of each relevant system. Structure-centered approaches build squarely on a long tradition of typological work in linguistics (modeled on phonology), seeking to build more neutral and structure-relevant frameworks from the outset, that is, to study languages and the realities they represent through the window of language itself. But the approach is difficult to implement: comparing categories across languages requires extensive linguistic work both in terms of local description and typological framing, and it can be extremely difficult to characterize referential **entailments** suitable for an independent assessment of cognition. Nonetheless, this approach most closely respects the linguistic facts and thus holds the greatest promise for identifying structural differences and directing the search for cognitive influences in appropriate directions.

The classic example of structure-centered work is Whorf's comparison of number marking patterns in English and Hopi (Whorf 1956; Lucy 1992a). Whorf argued that English speakers measure and count cyclic experiences such as the passage of a day or a year in the same way as ordinary objects with a form and a substance. This leads ultimately by analogy to the projection of these cycles as forms for a homogeneous substance 'time.' By contrast, the Hopi language differentiates these cycles as a distinct type of recurrent event and are not therefore led to the same view of time. From these linguistic observations Whorf was led to identify patterns in habitual behavior that he felt bore the impress of this difference in outlook toward time. There are difficulties in Whorf's work to be sure, notably the anecdotal quality of the characterization of effects on thought. But his approach does show how to begin with language structure and to build a characterization of reality through the window provided by the languages themselves. And, crucially, it does not entail any hierarchical evaluation of the languages with respect to a pre-given reality. My own research, discussed in the following section, seeks to develop this approach further, providing a more explicit typological anchor for the linguistic comparison and explicit psychological assessments for the cognitive comparisons.

Structure-centered empirical research: An illustration

I have worked for many years now exploring whether the structural differences between American English and Yucatec Maya, a language indigenous to southeastern Mexico, lead to distinctive effects on habitual cognition. This work represents the most fully developed effort at a structure-centered approach to date and can serve therefore to illustrate an approach to the relation of language, thought, and reality that builds outward from language structure. Only a sample of this work can be presented here. I describe some salient contrasts between the two languages, associated cognitive entailments, and a study assessing these entailments.

Language contrast: Number marking semantics

The focus here will be on how Yucatec Maya and American English differ in their nominal number marking patterns (Lucy 1992b: 56–83). First, the two languages contrast in the way they signal plural for nouns. English speakers obligatorily signal plural for nouns semantically **marked** as referring to discrete objects (e.g. *car*, *chair*) but not for those marked as referring to amorphous materials (e.g. *sugar*, *mud*, etc.). Yucatec speakers are never obliged to signal plural for any referent, although they often do mark plural for animate referents.

Second, the two languages contrast in the way they enumerate nouns. For English nouns marked as having semantically discrete reference, numerals directly modify their associated nouns (e.g., *one candle*, *two candles*); for nouns not so marked, an appropriate unit (or unitizer) must be specified by a form that then takes the number marking (e.g., *one clump of dirt*, *two cubes of sugar*). Yucatec requires that all constructions with numerals be supplemented by a special form, usually referred to as a numeral classifier, which typically provides crucial information about the shape or material properties of the referent of the noun (e.g., *'un tz'íit kib'* 'one long-thin candle', *ká 'a tz'íit kib'* 'two long-thin candle').

In essence all nouns in Yucatec are semantically unspecified as to quantificational unit almost as if they referred to unformed substances. So, for example, the semantic sense of the Yucatec word *kib'* in the example cited above is better translated into English as 'wax' (i.e., 'one long-thin wax')—even though, when occurring alone without a numeral modifier in conditions other than enumeration, the word *kib'* can routinely refer to objects with the form and function that we would call candles (as well as to other wax things). Given the quantificational neutrality of the noun it becomes clear why one must specify a unit when counting, since expressions such as 'one wax' do not make quantificational sense. By contrast, many nouns in English include the notion of quantificational 'unit' (or 'form') as part of their basic meaning—so when we count these nouns, we can simply use the numeral directly without any classifier (e.g., *one candle*). In short, whereas English requires such a unitizing construction only for some nouns, Yucatec requires one for all of its nouns. These complementary patterns of plural marking and numeral modification form part of a unified number-marking pattern evidenced typologically across many languages (Lucy 1992b: 61–71).

Cognitive hypotheses and predictions

To assess whether traces of these contrasting verbal patterns appear in speakers' cognitive activities more generally, we need first to draw out the implications of these grammatical patterns for the general interpretation of experience. If we consider the denotational meaning of nouns referring to discrete concrete referents, that is, *stable objects* that maintain their physical appearance over time, then certain regularities appear from which cognitive implications can be drawn. The quantificational unit presupposed by English nouns referring to objects of this type is frequently the shape of the object. Hence use of these English lexical items routinely draws attention to the shape of a referent as the basis for incorporating it under some lexical label and assigning it a number value. Yucatec nouns referring to objects of this type, lacking such a specification of quantificational unit, do not draw attention to shape and, in fact, fairly routinely draw attention to the material composition of the referent as the basis for incorporating it under some lexical label. If these linguistic patterns translate into a general cognitive sensitivity to these properties of referents of the discrete type, then we can draw the following prediction: Yucatec speakers should attend relatively more to the material composition of stable objects (and less to their shape), whereas English speakers should attend relatively less to the material composition of stable objects (and more to their shape).

Cognitive contrast: Shape versus material preference

The prediction has been tested in a variety of ways with both adult and child speakers from both languages (Lucy 1992b; Lucy and Gaskins 2001, 2003). One example will serve to illustrate the approach. Twelve speakers in each language group were shown fifteen triads of familiar objects. Each triad consisted of an original *pivot* object and two *alternate* objects, one of the same shape as the pivot and one of the same material as the pivot. So, for instance, speakers were shown a plastic comb with a handle as the pivot and asked whether it was more like a wooden comb with a handle or more like a plastic comb without a handle. The expectation was that English speakers would match the pivot to the other comb with a handle whereas the Yucatec speakers would match it with the other comb made of plastic. Speakers were shown a large number of such triads, which, across the stimulus set, controlled for size, color, function, wholeness, malleability, and familiarity.

The predicted classification preference was strongly confirmed with adult English speakers choosing the material alternate only 23 percent of the time and adult Yucatec speakers favoring it 61 percent of the time. Clearly the two adult groups classify these objects differently and in line with the expectations based on the underlying lexico-grammatical structures of the two languages. However, English-speaking and Yucatec-speaking seven-year-olds showed an identical early bias toward

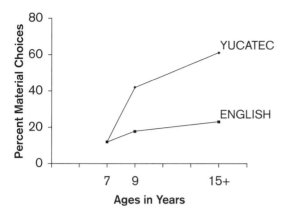

Figure 5.1: Developmental pattern for English and Yucatec classification preferences with stable objects: material versus shape (source: Lucy and Gaskins 2001).

shape—choosing material alternates only 12 percent of the time. But by age nine the adult pattern was visible: English-speaking children continued to favor shape, choosing material alternates only 18 percent of the time whereas Yucatec-speaking children were choosing material alternates 42 percent of the time. Thus, the same kind of language-group difference found among adult speakers is also found in children by age nine—and the result is statistically reliable. The adult and developmental data are jointly displayed in Figure 5.1.

We can summarize these results as follows. Seven-year-olds show clear sensitivity to referent type independently of language group membership. Here we see they prefer shape as a basis of classification with stable objects; in related experiments, with *malleable objects* they prefer material as a basis of classification. Nine-year-olds show differential sensitivity to referent type in line with their language. This suggests that language categories increase in their importance for cognition between ages seven and nine. Adults show a consolidation into a dominant pattern for each group. We can summarize the overall pattern by saying that the two populations begin by grouping different referent types in the same way and end up grouping these same referent types in quite different ways as a function of language type.

Common questions

Three questions are often raised in regard to these findings and therefore deserve some comment. First, are these same verbal and cognitive patterns evident in everyday life? Mayan speakers clearly do exhibit a great sensitivity to the material properties of objects. In the experimental tasks, they constantly evaluate the material composition of the test items before sorting them—feeling how heavy they are, poking their nails into them to test for malleability, scraping the surface to see what material might be under any paint, smelling and tasting the objects, and generally questioning or commenting on their material properties—something English speakers rarely do. In one telling case, a Yucatec woman sorted items into those that would melt if they were burned versus those that would turn to ash, attending to material in a quite striking way. A preference for material over shape also emerges with loan words from Spanish: a kerosene lantern is referred to as a *gas*, a ceramic bowl is referred to as a *porcelina*, etc. On first visits to urban areas villagers pay great attention to materials composing the furniture and floors in homes, hotels, and restaurants. Granted, these sorts of incidents are anecdotal; but cumulatively over time they suggest the everyday vitality of a distinctive orientation to the material world.

Second, are these patterns actually due to language rather than to cultural factors such as lack of education or poverty or rural lifestyle? When one considers the whole array of studies, it seems unlikely that any single cultural 'fact' will account for all the results. Very specific predictions from language have consistently been confirmed, even though they involve different grammatical patterns, different cognitive functions, and different stimulus materials. No informed cultural argument has yet been made to explain these results. Children do not show these cognitive patterns until the language patterns are in place, both educated and uneducated speakers show the patterns, and adults lacking exposure to the language do not develop the usual response patterns.

Finally, similar preferences for material sorting have been reported for urban Japanese speakers who also have a classifier type language but whose culture as well as educational and urban life style contrast with the Maya (see Lucy and Gaskins 2003). The close linkage between language prediction and cognitive result in the absence of any plausible alternative cultural account suggests that the shaping role of language deserves to be taken seriously.

Third, is this a real linguistic relativity? After all, the preference scores are not absolute for either group. Some variability is, of course, expectable in any experiment. But the broader view taken here is not that languages completely or permanently blind speakers to other aspects of reality. Rather they provide speakers with a systematic default bias in their habitual response tendencies. Although some members of each group clearly do not recognize the alternative classification possibility, I believe they could readily be brought to do so fairly quickly, at least for a while. This said, I think the bias would nonetheless return soon after, for it serves a purpose in coordinating social action and guiding individual behavior. That a habitual bias can be recognized and even overcome for a while in special contexts for certain tasks does not render that bias unimportant. In any number of areas such as mastering a foreign language, overcoming racial and gender prejudices, following strict logical inferences, etc., we know that people can modify their behavior for a short while in some contexts, but it is another matter entirely to change habitual behavior wholesale or permanently. In short, we have evidence that language structures bear some relationship to thought, that the direction appears to be from language to thought, and the relationship appears to be robust.

General discussion

Just as language universally mediates culture and mind, helping enable them in all human groups, so too it appears to play a role in producing cultural and mental diversity. The two processes go hand in hand. Only by acceptance of the conventions of one or more particular languages can we speak at all and so gain the advantages of having language support for sophisticated cultural and psychological activities. But this same acceptance of a particular language commits us to the specific conventions of that language and to their consequences for our thinking. Just as with language universals then, linguistic diversity and its influences should be viewed as natural in human life: they are not some unfortunate contextual corruption that needs to be peeled away or some intrinsic defect that needs to be hammered out of each of us. Language influences form part of the foundation of what it is to be human, that is, a species that adapts to its environment by means of diverse yet stable patterns of symbolic representation.

Comparative work on language diversity is essential in all the human sciences. The reasons for this should now be clear. If the natural process is to think in accordance with our own language, then what we take as neutral reality may in fact be a projection of the emphases of our own language. And what we take to be the meaning of a category in another language may be partly a product of our own semantic accent (Lucy 2003). In short, we risk misunderstanding the interpretations of reality implicit in other languages and their influences on thought if we do not control for our own biases. The remedy for these biases lies in taking the observed categories of other languages seriously, exploring empirically their structure and functioning. We will surely fail to progress if we simply ignore the existence of diversity or erase it through the application of interpretive approaches that effectively render other systems in terms of our own.

Expanded developmental research is also essential. Research on very young children cannot provide a full picture of the emerging relation between language and thought, let alone establish that language variation does not matter for thinking. The substantive finding that relativity effects arise in middle childhood is also theoretically illuminating. Other research on middle childhood indicates that this is a crucial period in the development and integration of higher levels of language and thought (Lucy and Gaskins 2001). We also know that this is the age at which children begin to lose their flexibility in acquiring new languages and are increasingly likely to show interference accents in languages subsequently learned (Lucy 2003) and, on the evidence above, show relativity effects. In short, during this age, substantive advances in development come hand in hand with tangible limitations in the capacity to acquire or understand other languages and with measurable effects of language codes on thought.

This suggests an emerging tradeoff whereby higher levels of intellectual and social development are purchased by a deeper commitment to the mediating role of language, that is, to a particular language, one whose system of categories will then quietly shape our thought and culture thereafter. The emerging picture is that each child can achieve the fully developed humanity implicit in the general capacity for language, culture, and mind only by committing to becoming a particular sort of human, that is, one imbued with a historically specific language, culture, and mind. The deeper human universal, then, lies not so much in the substantive commonalities among these historical systems, but rather in the shared functional imperative of the tradeoff, that is, the imperative of engaging particular systems in order to consummate general development.

References

Aarsleff, H. (1982) *From Locke to Saussure: Essays on the Study of Language and Intellectual History*, Minneapolis, MN: University of Minneapolis Press.

—— (1988) "Introduction," in W. Von Humboldt, *On Language: The Diversity of Human Language-Structure and its Influence on the Mental Development of Mankind*, (trans. P. Heath), Cambridge: Cambridge University Press, pp. vii-lxv.

Levinson, S. (2003) *Space in Language and Cognition: Explorations in Cognitive Diversity*, Cambridge: Cambridge University Press.

Lucy, J. (1992a) *Language Diversity and Thought: A Reformulation of the Linguistic Relativity Hypothesis*, Cambridge: Cambridge University.

—— (1992b) *Grammatical Categories and Cognition: A Case Study of the Linguistic Relativity Hypothesis*, Cambridge: Cambridge University.

—— (1996) "The Scope of Linguistic Relativity: An Analysis and Review of Empirical Research," in J. Gumperz and S. Levinson (eds.), *Rethinking Linguistic Relativity*, Cambridge: Cambridge University Press, pp. 37–69.

—— (1997) "Linguistic Relativity," *Annual Review of Anthropology*, 26: 291–312. Palo Alto, CA: Annual Reviews Inc.

—— (2003) *Semantic Accent and Linguistic Relativity*, paper presented at a Conference on Cross-Linguistic Data and Theories of Meaning, Nijmegen, The Netherlands: Catholic University of the Netherlands and the Max Planck Institute for Psycholinguistics.

—— and Gaskins, S. (2001) "Grammatical Categories and the Development of Classification Preferences: A Comparative Approach," in S. Levinson and M. Bowerman (eds.), *Language Acquisition and Conceptual Development*, Cambridge: Cambridge University Press, pp. 257–283.

—— and —— (2003) "Interaction of Language Type and Referent Type in the Development of Nonverbal Classification Preferences," in D. Gentner and S. Goldin-Meadow (eds.), *Language in Mind: Advances in the Study of Language and Thought*, Cambridge, MA: The MIT Press, pp. 465–492.

Whorf, B. (1956) *Language, Thought, and Reality: Selected Writings of Benjamin Lee Whorf*, ed. J.B. Carroll, Cambridge, MA: The MIT Press.

PART THREE

Language and politics

Berit Engøy Henriksen

INTRODUCTION

THE THREE ARTICLES included in this section display different ways of analysing political language with use of data from four languages. They all show that linguistic 'tools' can be used to persuade an audience. While all the areas under consideration here concern politicians, the tools that are used in any persuasive situation are exactly the same.

Nunberg looks at political bias in the media. American conservatives have claimed that US media is biased in labelling conservative politicians as 'conservatives' while liberal politicians are not described as 'liberals'. The argument is that liberals are not labelled because they are considered mainstream and thus do not need to be identified. Nunberg is initially open to believing this claim, though for reasons that differ from those of the conservatives; he believes that the label 'liberal' now has become a somewhat negative term, because of **connotations** and 'tax-and-spend stereotypes', and the media therefore choose not to use this term to label people.

In his analysis he looks at several major US daily newspapers to see how ten well-known liberal and conservative politicians are labelled. The result differs from what was predicted by the conservative argument: there is a 30 per cent greater likelihood that the liberal politician will be given a label than the conservative. This same result is found when Nunberg looks at other public figures in relation to their political affiliation. So does the labelling mean that the media is biased? Nunberg does not believe that the press uses these labels to 'slant its coverage in one direction or the other' (p. 71). He argues that it can be assumed that the labels used are simply meant to be informative, and to give the readers information on where 'a particular politician or group is coming from' (p. 71). Nunberg also claims that by labelling politicians and public figures, both conservatives and liberals, the media is able to place itself 'at a safe distance from extremes on either sides' (p. 71). But the higher number of liberal labels makes Nunberg believe that there might be some conservative bias in the media. He argues that this is because the media have received so much criticism from conservatives. 'If people are disposed to believe that the media have a liberal bias, it's because that's what the media have been telling them all along' (p. 72).

Simon-Vandenberger, White and Aijmer look at **presupposition** as a means for the politicians to 'get their points across and reach their goals as political speaker' (p. 93). Analysing British, Flemish and Swedish TV-debates they examine the strategic use of presupposition. A presupposition can be defined from a semantic and pragmatic perspective. The semantic approach to presupposition involves analyzing the truth of the presupposed utterance: does the utterance hold true under **negation** and questioning. The pragmatic approach to presupposition focuses on common ground and background knowledge: it is assumed that the hearer already knows or is ready to take for granted the given information.

Similar tactics are used in the British, Flemish and Swedish data, as presupposition is used as a strategy to construct solidarity between the politician and the like-minded viewer. And though an opponent often notices this strategy it can be difficult to challenge. There is also the possibility that the viewers who have not been persuaded yet, may not recognize the tactic, and accept the information contained in the presupposition as general knowledge. But most importantly, the use of a presupposition creates a forceful utterance and an image of the politician as 'someone in the know'. There is tremendous manipulative potential in presenting assertions as background and common knowledge instead of as new information. In short, this paper demonstrates the way in which presupposition can be used to great persuasive effect. It is then, no surprise that it is found across these data sets.

Boussofara-Omar is also interested in the persuasive language of politicians, and particularly looks at how a political speech can be used as a tool to 'promote, protect and legitimate their power and voice of authority' (p. 73). In her article she analyzes the changes made to the handwritten draft of the first 'presidential' speech that Ben Ali, the current president of Tunisia, delivered on 7 November 1987. The changes she notes are key in analyzing the construction of both a voice of authority and power for the president and a voice for the collective population. The changes made from the draft to the finished speech show which linguistic choices have been made to establish Ben Ali's presidential voice. We know that there is a link between linguistic choices and political **ideology** and Boussofara-Omar demonstrates the ways in which political ideology is displayed through linguistic practices. Boussofara-Omar states that 'linguistic choices and discursive practices are never 'value-free' or neutral. They are always situated in histories, whether they are personal, local or global' (p. 76).

Establishing a voice of authority and power is important for a new national leader, and this voice must appeal to the public. The previous president, Bourguiba, used a combination of Tunisian Arabic, French and classical Arabic/modern standard Arabic when making public speeches. Ben Ali distinguishes himself from the previous president by choosing to only speak in **fuṣḥaa**. Boussofara-Omar explains that fuṣḥaa subsumes classical Arabic and modern standard Arabic. She states that 'fuṣḥaa is a language that embodies authority and bestows authority on those who know it' (p. 78). In using it, Ben Ali represents himself as someone of honour, prestige, power and authority. The reason for this is that the linguistic code is associated with sacred scriptures and the history of Islamic civilization and culture. Thus, it is important that Ben Ali use fuṣḥaa correctly, and we can see the relevant changes made in his script, removing 'incorrect' and 'inappropriate' words. Had Ben Ali not made changes to his script, and used the code incorrectly he could potentially alienate his audience and he would not be able to establish himself as a voice of authority or a national leader.

These articles make clear that in various ways, and in various settings, the choices made in language are political. Here, the choices relate directly to professional politicians. However, the same tools and strategies are used in other fields, by other people, addressing different groups. By examining presupposition, the construction of authority and labelling practices in the often highly polarized field of politics, we feel keenly the effects of such choices.

Issues to consider

1. Conservatives in America see themselves as unfairly or disproportionately labelled by the media. Can you think of other groups that might feel marked in this way? Which terms are used? Why do you think these terms might be used? Create a hypothesis and discuss how you would go about testing your hypothesis.
2. The British, Flemish and Swedish politicians used presupposition as a tool to persuade their voters. Can you think of other domains where presupposition might be used to persuade? Do you think that presuppositions are more important in some fields than others?
3. Presuppositions can be difficult to challenge. Why is this the case? What norms of communication make these challenges problematic? If a challenge is made, what does the challenger risk?
4. Fushaa is a variety of Arabic used in writing and formal speech. Think of some of the politicians you know – what variety do they use? Do you think the variety they use help give them power as politicians? You might also want to think of varieties you know that, if spoken by a politician, would decrease their authority and power.
5. Is it difficult to untangle the arguments that are made in television broadcasts and political speeches? Why do you think this is the case? Think about whether the mode of communication has any bearing on your answer to this question.

Further reading

Critical discourse analysis is often used in the analysis of political language. The following are excellent examples of this.

Fairclough, N. (2000) *New Labour: New Language?*, London: Routledge.
Wodak, R., de Cillia, R. Reisigl, M. and Liebhart, K. (2009) 'The discursive construction of national identity', in *The Discursive Construction of National Identity*, second edition, Edinburgh: Edinburgh University Press, pp. 7–49.

The intersection of news and the media with politics is significant. The following may be useful in thinking through this connection.

Fowler, R. (1991) *Language in the News. Discourse and Ideology in the Press*, London: Routledge.

Spitulnik, D. (1998) 'Mediating unity and diversity: The production of language ideologies in Zambian broadcasting', in *Language and Ideologies. Practice and Theory*, Oxford: Oxford University Press, pp. 163–189.

Analyzing political language, as with all other language, requires attention to the detail of linguistic choices made. These texts provide some assistance with the kinds of tools that are appropriate to this as well as making the connection with ideology.

Fairclough, N. (2001) 'Critical discourse analysis in practice: description', in *Language and Power*, second edition, London: Longman, pp. 91–117.
Kress, A. and R. Hodge (1993) *Language as Ideology*, second edition, London: Routledge.

Suggestions for further viewing

All the President's Men (1976) Alan J. Pakula.
Jesus Camp (2006) Heidi Ewing, Rachel Grady.
Mr Smith Goes to Washington (1939) Frank Capra.
Primary Colours (1998) Mike Nichols.

Chapter 6

Geoffrey Nunberg

MEDIA: LABEL WHORES

Bernard Goldberg may not be wrong about the presence of bias in the media – he's just wrong that it's "liberal."

L ISTENING TO PEOPLE complain about bias in the media, you're reminded that there is more than one paranoid style in American politics. While the left has busied itself unpacking interlocking directorates and corporate ownership, the right has made a specialty of close reading, with an extraordinary attentiveness to the nuances of usage and address.

There's no better example of this than Bernard Goldberg's claim, in his bestseller *Bias*, that TV broadcasters "pointedly identify conservative politicians as conservatives" but rarely use the word "liberal" to describe liberals. As Goldberg explained the difference: "In the world of the Jennings and Brokaws and Rathers, conservatives are out of the mainstream and have to be identified. Liberals, on the other hand, are the mainstream and don't have to be identified."

To tell the truth, Goldberg's claim about the use of labels didn't sound that implausible to me – not because I assumed the media were biased, but because the word *liberal* itself has become an embarrassment to so many people. Two decades of conservative derision have turned it into "the L-word," to the point where some Democrats won't own up to the label and others are careful to prefix it with "neo-," so as to distance themselves from those "unreconstructed" tax-and-spend stereotypes. And on the left, where suspicion of liberals has always run deep, most people have thrown the word over the side in favor of "progressive." But no one ever talks about "the C-word," and conservatives invariably wear that label proudly. So it wouldn't be surprising to find that the media, too, were more diffident about calling people liberals than about calling them conservatives.

Still, the psychology journals are full of studies that remind us just how deceptive our subjective estimations of statistical tendencies can be. And Goldberg *is* offering an empirical claim, even if he couldn't be troubled to back it up with any research. Granted, it isn't a simple matter to survey the language of TV newscasts, but the language of the press is readily available online. So I went to a Dialog Corporation database that has the contents of more than 20 major US dailies, including *The New York Times*, the *Los Angeles Times*, *The Washington Post*, *The Boston Globe*, *The Miami Herald*, *Newsday*, and the *San Francisco Chronicle*. I took the names of 10 well-known politicians, five liberals, and five conservatives. On the liberal side were Senators Barbara Boxer, Paul Wellstone, Tom Harkin, and Ted Kennedy, and Representative Barney Frank, all with lifetime Americans for Democratic Action (ADA) ratings greater than 90 percent. On the conservative side were Senators Trent Lott and Jesse Helms, Attorney General John Ashcroft, and Representatives Dick Armey and Tom DeLay, all with lifetime ADA averages less than 15 percent. Then I looked to see how often each of those names occurred within seven words of "liberal" or "conservative," whichever was appropriate, a test that picks out ascriptions of political views with better than 85 percent accuracy. (For more complete results click http://people.ischool.berkeley.edu/~nunberg/table.html.)

And indeed, there was a discrepancy in the frequency of labeling, but not in the way Goldberg – or for that matter, I – assumed. On the contrary, the average liberal legislator has a better than 30 percent *greater* likelihood of being given a political label than the average conservative does. The press describes Frank as a liberal two-and-a-half times as frequently as it describes Armey as a conservative. It labels Boxer almost twice as often as it labels Lott, and labels Wellstone more often than Helms. And the proportions of labeling of liberals and conservatives are virtually unchanged when you exclude opinions and letters to the editor. What's more, the discrepancy is almost as high even if you restrict the search to *The New York Times*, *The Washington Post*, and the *Los Angeles Times*, those pillars of the "liberal press."

The tendency isn't limited to legislators. For example, Goldberg writes that "it's not unusual to identify certain actors, like Tom Selleck or Bruce Willis, as conservatives. But Barbra Streisand or Rob Reiner … are just Barbra Streisand and Rob Reiner." But that turns out to be dead wrong, too: The press labels Streisand and Reiner more than four times as frequently as Selleck and Willis. (Nothing if not careful, I screened out examples that might include references to Reiner's portrayal of "Archie Bunker's liberal son-in-law.") Warren Beatty is labeled more often than Arnold Schwarzenegger, and Norman Lear is labeled more often than Charlton Heston.

It goes on. Goldberg claims that former Circuit Judge Robert Bork is always called a conservative whereas Laurence Tribe is identified merely as a Harvard law professor. But it turns out that Bork is labeled only a bit more frequently than Tribe is. And columnist Michael Kinsley gets a partisan label more often than either William Bennett or Jerry Falwell.

It could be, of course, that the figures for people like Lott, DeLay, and Armey were skewed by the fact that they have leadership titles that might take the place of partisan labels in many stories. But the pattern is the same for other legislators. Substitute Richard Shelby or Strom Thurmond in the conservative group and the score for the group goes up a bit; substitute Jeff Sessions or Mitch McConnell and it goes down.

Ditto the liberals – inserting Ron Dellums would raise their score, inserting Nancy Pelosi would lower it.

The fact is, though, that however you cherry-pick the groups, there's no way to make the survey come out as Goldberg claims it should, where conservatives are systematically labeled more than liberals are. True, the proportions of labeling might be different in TV newscasts. But given the way the labels are used in the "liberal press," the burden of proof is on Goldberg and other critics of liberal bias to do the studies that should have been done before making the claim. In the meantime, it's hard to believe the proportions would come out in a radically different way, not unless you're willing to assume that the language used on CBS and CNN is going to turn out to be much more liberal than what you find in *The Washington Post* and *The New York Times*.

Beyond showing that Goldberg is wrong about the use of labels, what does this all prove? If you took his premises at face value, you'd say that the patterns of labeling actually reveal a slight conservative bias in the media. But that misses the point, not just because it takes for granted the right's portrayal of the media as **ideologically** monolithic, but because it assumes that the press is really using these labels to slant its coverage in one direction or the other.

Why does the press use these labels, anyway? At a first pass, we might assume they're purely informative, a way of letting readers know where a particular politician or group is coming from. That does seem to be the way labels are used with interest groups and think tanks, which generally have a much higher rate of labeling than politicians do. This makes sense – groups like these are almost always cited in the course of providing background on the "liberal" or "conservative" point of view on a story, rather than as its subjects. In fact the major finding here wasn't in the relative frequency of labeling of conservative and liberal groups, which was slight, it was in the striking imbalance in the absolute numbers of citations for each side. The numbers confirm what Michael Dolny has shown in a series of annual studies for the group Fairness and Accuracy in Reporting (FAIR): Reporters' Rolodexes stop three times as often at the names of conservative think tanks as at the names of liberal think tanks.

But the informational needs of readers don't explain the labeling of politicians and other public figures. Readers scarcely need to be told where Helms or Kennedy stands on the issues, after all, but a label could helpful in situating McConnell or Pelosi.

It turns out, though, that Helms gets a label anywhere from eight to 10 times as often as Senators Tim Hutchinson or Sessions, and Kennedy gets one much more often than Pelosi or Paul Sarbanes does. Those discrepancies clearly have less to do with views than with viewers – ADA or ACA ratings are less reliable as predictors of how frequently politicians are labeled than the number of times they've appeared on *Hardball* or *Larry King Live*.

In the end, then, the function of political labels isn't to inform or indoctrinate readers about the people and groups they're attached to. Rather, they're a way of reassuring us that the writer and publication are comfortably in the center, at a safe distance from the extremes on either side. And for these purposes, it's more expedient to use the labels with ideological archetypes like Helms or Wellstone than with a McConnell or a Sarbanes.

If there is a media bias in this, it consists, as Jonathan Chait has put it, of "ratifying the stereotypes that already exist." And if the media wind up labeling liberals somewhat more than conservatives, that's chiefly an indication of how phobic they've become about charges of bias from the right. In this sense, the disparities in labeling are chiefly a tribute to the success that critics like Goldberg have had in popularizing their picture of the media – and by the by, to the extraordinary attention that the media have given to views like Goldberg's in the first place.

Shortly after I did a "Fresh Air" commentary about this study, I got an e-mail from a conservative who told me that the best indication of the liberal bias of the media lies in the fact that conservatives complain about bias much more often than liberals do. "If 90 percent of the bias complaints have been coming for years from the right," he wrote, "there must be something to their complaints." That's a misapprehension, of course, but an entirely understandable one. In newspaper articles published since 1992, the word "media" appears within seven words of "liberal bias" 469 times and within seven words of "conservative bias" just 17 times. If people are disposed to believe that the media have a liberal bias, it's because that's what the media have been telling them all along.

Geoffrey Nunberg is a senior researcher at the Center for the Study of Language and Information at Stanford. His most recent book is *The Way We Talk Now*.

Chapter 7

Naïma Boussofara-Omar

LEARNING THE 'LINGUISTIC HABITUS' OF A POLITICIAN: A PRESIDENTIAL AUTHORITATIVE VOICE IN THE MAKING

[...]

Introduction

WE HAVE BECOME increasingly cognizant of "the status of language as a primary site of political process and of discursive mediation of those very activities and events that we recognize as political" (Kroskrity 2000: 1). Politicians use language as the site at which they promote, protect and legitimate their power and voice of authority, and rationalize their visions of political order and their representations of social harmony. Political speeches are a critical locus for translating those visions and representations of reality into words. Presidential political speeches are elaborately composed, scrupulously revised and edited – resulting in numerous drafts – in order to carry the voice of authority and power of the president while they are carefully crafted to be heard as the voice of the collectivity. The final linguistic product of a political speech is the outcome of behind-the-scene efforts to orchestrate the simultaneity of voices (Bakhtin 1984) and to harmonize their multiplicity through a meticulous selection and arrangement of words. But "words", as Thompson (1991: 1) reminds us, "are loaded with unequal weights, depending on *who* utters them and *how* they are said, such that some words uttered in certain circumstances have a force and a conviction that they would not have elsewhere" (emphasis is mine). Implicit in the selection of words and ways of using those words are such major questions as "what to select, what to deflect, how to interpret, and what to make what emblematic *– what to foreground and what to de-emphasize – and what to put under erasure*" (Coe 1993: 372, emphasis is mine). Such questions, which will be closely explored in this essay, are subtly translated into a "dance of words" (Burke 1969: 288) which are primarily a "selection of reality" and are ultimately presumed to "function as a deflection of reality" (Burke 1966: 45).

Rarely, if ever, however, do we have access to drafts of a presidential speech, or any draft of any other text for that matter, with changes (scribbled in red) which visibly map out the processes of orchestration of voices and harmonization of words. Because such drafts are not intended to be shared with the public, the behind-the-scene manipulations, modifications, and changes – brought to a text – are assumed to be invisible. My essay is an analysis of such a document: a handwritten draft of a "presidential" address, officially known as *bayaan s-saabiʕ min nuvambar*, "November 7th Communiqué."[1]

In this paper, I analyze the changes brought to the handwritten draft of the first "presidential" speech that Ben Ali, the current president of Tunisia (then the newly appointed Prime Minister), delivered on November 7, 1987 across the airwaves, to announce the deposition of President Bourguiba and the end of his thirty-year rule since independence (1956–1987), and to proclaim himself the successor of the deposed "old" and "sick" president (Appendix, November 7, 1987 Communiqué). The original handwritten draft charts, in red, the editorial revisions which relate to forms of speaking and styles of speaking. Specifically, the revisions consisted in correcting some grammatical mistakes and spelling errors, altering the structure of some phrases and sentences, changing some words, [and] shuffling the order of some others[...]. In this essay, I will focus on the last [type] of interventions: word order. I demonstrate how the changes capture the processes whereby the new discursive authority and presidential voice are in the making. In other words, through the description and analysis of the changes, I demonstrate how the changes map out the processes whereby the new 'presidential' voice is being crafted in front of our eyes and how the speaker is being initiated, linguistically and pragmatically, into how and when to appropriate 'the colloquy of other voices' (Farmer 1995: 318), their **discourses** and words, and how and when to subtly speak their own voice and words while respecting the pragmatics of appropriateness and appropriation, i.e. norms and principles of what can be said and communicated, what cannot be stated or acknowledged, and what can be appropriated and how and when it can be appropriated in order to find a balance between competing voices (Bakhtin 1986), ideologies, and linguistic habituses (Bourdieu 1991).

By the same token, the analysis explores the intricate interweaving of text and discourse regulation, valuation of forms of speaking and styles of speaking, and political ideology. I am not claiming that there is a transparent or linear correspondence between the visible changes and their significance. I am simply arguing that the analysis of the linguistic changes offers fertile ground to conceptualize ways to "recognize critical linkages between linguistic practices and political-economic activity" (Kroskrity 2000: 3) and interests, I would add, and hence to explore conceptual ways to bridge the gap between the micro-analysis of linguistic patterns and the macro-processes of social and political factors, knowing that "much of the meaning and hence communicative value that linguistic forms have for their speakers lies in the '**indexical**' connections between the linguistic signs and the contextual factors of their use" (Kroskrity 2000: 7). This essay aims to contribute to the on-going discussions of how to find those linkages between political ideology, on one hand, and linguistic practices and ways of using language, and hence voice, within institutions of power, on the other, as it will become clear throughout the essay.

[…] I draw on the studies of scholars who worked on language and its symbolic power, and language ideologies in institutions of power (Bourdieu 1991; Errington 2000; Gal and Irvine 2000; Gal 1999; Hill 2000; Haeri 1997, 2000, 2003; Mertz 1998; Philips 2000; Spitulnik 1998, 1999). But drawing extensively and particularly on some aspects of Bourdieu's (1991, 1998; Bourdieu and Wacquant 1992) *theory of practice*, I demonstrate how his notions of habitus and symbolic power, and his discussions of the nature of political discourse and the social conditions for the efficacy and effectiveness of ritual discourse (e.g. speech making) capture my reading of the manipulations, that were brought to Ben Ali's first political address, as the processes whereby the new speaker is being initiated into learning the presidential linguistic habitus, and finding his own words and voice of authority.

Bourdieu denounced the 'illusion of linguistic communism' according to which the social competence to speak is equally distributed or accessed in a speech community. Any discourse is the result of an encounter between a *linguistic habitus* and a *linguistic market*, Bourdieu argues. He defines the linguistic habitus as:

> [A] set of socially constituted dispositions that imply a propensity to speak in certain ways and to utter determinate things (an expressive interest), as well as a competence to speak defined inseparably as the linguistic ability to engender an infinite array of discourses that are grammatically conforming, and the social ability to adequately utilize this competence in a given situation
> (Bourdieu and Wacquant 1992: 145)

But acquiring the social dispositions, the linguistic competency, and the social ability to use that competence only falls short of making utterances efficacious and effective or turning them into **performative** acts in the political arena. The speaker needs to learn to assess the *linguistic market* in order to make utterances *à propos*, i.e. to know the values and prices of linguistic products on the *linguistic market* because both will, in a way, help the speaker shape his discourse in accordance with the norms of what constitutes legitimate discourse. Bourdieu and Wacquant (1992: 145) define the *linguistic market* as "a system of relations of force which impose themselves as a system of specific censorship, and thereby help fashion linguistic production by determining the 'price' of linguistic products." Utterances derive their efficacy from the *delegated power* of the institution and *symbolic power* is defined by a relation that will create belief in the legitimacy of the words and the person who utters these words but it will not create it unless the hearer wields it. As I will demonstrate throughout the essay, through the analysis of some excerpts from the Communiqué, the power of words and the authority of the speaker's voice derive from far more than just the "right" selection and "appropriate" order of words.

Rites of institution

It is strongly argued and widely acknowledged, within the framework of political economy of language (e.g. Bourdieu 1991; Friedrich 1989; Gal 1988, 1989, 1991; Woolard 1985) and in the literature on the interconnectedness of linguistic ideologies and institutions of power (Errington 1998; Haeri 2003; Spitulnik 1998, 1999; Mertz 1998) that linguistic choices and discursive practices are never 'value-free' or neutral. They are always situated in histories, whether they are personal, local, or global. "[E]ven 'neutrality' is socially constructed", Spitulnik (1998: 164) deftly reminds us. The process of their selection is not merely a matter of finding the right **lexical** words either. Selection of words and choice of their order in institutions of power (e.g. state, courtrooms, school classrooms, medical offices, and media) are strategically tied to the construction and legitimation of their power, among many other things. And as Bakhtin (1981: 293) reminds us:

> [T]here are no "neutral" words and forms – words and forms that can belong to "no one"; language has been completely taken over, shot through with intentions and accents … All words have the "taste" of a profession, a genre, a tendency, a party, a particular person, a generation, and age group, the day and the hour. Each word tastes the context and contexts in which it has lived its socially charged life.

The salience or insignificance of particular words, through their focalization or de-emphasization, and the prevalence or irrelevance of particular voices, through their emphasis or erasure, are themselves forms of power. By speaking in particular ways, speakers activate complex webs of associations that link a wide array of discourses and contexts, and by using language in the specific ways they do, speakers construct linguistic selves and create linguistic images of their selves. Haeri (2003: 18–19):

> Words, particular ways of phrasing matters, certain grammatical constructions, sayings and so on create and are marked by particular times, places and types of persons. In short, different languages and different linguistic usages within them create and evoke "images," or as Bakhtin would say "images of man" (of the actual or imaginary user) in specific times, places, characteristics and so on.

[…]

Bourdieu and Wacquant (1992: 146) argue first that "not all linguistic utterances are acceptable and not all locutors equal". Second, "the habitus of the politician depends on a special training" (Bourdieu 1991: 176):

> This [training] includes in the first instance, of course, the entire apprenticeship necessary to acquire the corpus of specific kinds of knowledge … produced and accumulated by the political work … or to acquire the more general linguistic skills such as the mastery of a certain kind of language and of a certain political rhetoric – that of the *popular orator*, indispensable when it comes to cultivating one's relations with non-professionals … But it is also and above all that sort of *initiation*, with its ordeals and rites of passage, which tends to inculcate the *practical mastery* of the immanent logic of the political field and to impose a *de facto submission* to the values, hierarchies and censorship mechanisms inherent in this field.

What is worth noting from Bourdieu's quote is the dialectical relation between acquiring the skills of the political rhetoric (and speaking the voice of a politician) and learning to obey the constraints of the political game (of the specific socio-political context). Such processes as "training," "apprenticeship," "acquisition," "initiation," "inculcation" need to be accompanied by the "mastery of" or rather "submission to" mechanisms inherent in the political domain. The new speaker has to learn the rhetoric of public speaking and the political rhetoric which, as Bourdieu (1991: 173) forcefully argues, "is subjected to the constraints and limitations inherent in the functioning of the political field" and symbolized by the linguistic code chosen, as I argue in this essay and will demonstrate in the next section.

My analysis of the visible processes of shifting, reframing, and re-articulating Ben Ali's words demonstrates the processes whereby the new speaker is initiated into "the practical mastery of" valuation and evaluation of ways of speaking and "doing things with words" and the "de facto submission" to the constraints that weigh heavily on the choices of "what can be said and thought politically, as opposed to what is rejected as unsayable and unthinkable" (Bourdieu 1991: 176).

Learning "how to do things with words": When word order is shuffled

As I mentioned earlier, in his first address to the Tunisians, Ben Ali chose to speak to the Tunisians across the airwaves. The Communiqué, announcing Bourguiba's deposition and Ben Ali's self-investiture, was broadcast on November 7 at 6:30 AM on the national radio station. Evidently, the presidential paraphernalia (e.g. cameras, microphones, lights, photographers, reporters, dignitaries, ceremonial elite, and distinguished guests), indispensable for the presidential theatrical performance, the legitimization of Ben Ali's first encounter with the Tunisian people and the validation of his authority, was absent. There was no "direct communication" or "close contact" *'ittiṣaal mubaaʃir* with the audience which was Bourguiba's slogan for a thirty-year strategy and stratagem to rally the Tunisians around him and his policies.

Unlike Bourguiba, who used a constellation of linguistic codes (Tunisian Arabic, French, and Classical Arabic/Modern Standard Arabic – which I subsume under the term **fuṣhaa**) in his public political speeches and relished public appearances, Ben Ali chose to deliver his first address, and his skillfully staged subsequent public political speeches later, in fuṣhaa. The presidential habitus of authority, power, detachment, distance, and separation from the "masses" is partially enacted in the choice and use of fuṣhaa; the linguistic locus of eloquence (faṣaaha), ceremonial etiquette, solemnity, formality, and distance. Reclaiming fuṣhaa as the only variety of public political speeches not only makes the other linguistic codes (Tunisian Arabic and French) and practices (e.g. Bourguiba's codeswitching) invisible,[2] but also puts the speaker who advocated their "inappropriate" and "incorrect" use in public speeches under "erasure."[3] Besides, the choice and use of fuṣhaa embodies, in a way, the new "serious" tone of the new regime, and symbolically defines the nature of the to-be-accepted political discourse of the New Era. The physical separation indexes the intended boundaries of participation and involvement of the Tunisians in "running their affairs" *taṣriifi shu'ūnihi* (Appendix, Communiqué 7 November). More importantly, it has accorded primacy to Ben Ali's words and to the "serious" tone and raucous voice uttering those words. Because Ben

Ali's words were going to mark the passage from the Old to the New Era as legitimate, and because they were going to create belief in the legitimacy and authority of an unfamiliar disembodied voice of an unknown speaker, they had to be carefully selected and skillfully ordered. But "words alone cannot create this belief", Bourdieu (1991: 170) argues. In the case of Arabic, I believe words in fuṣḥaa magically, although partially, create this belief. Endowed with its association with the sacred script (i.e. the Qur'an, as the divine word was revealed in Arabic) and regarded as the emblematic carrier of Islamic civilization and culture of the Golden Age (aṣr an-nahḍa, the "Era of [Islamic] Renaissance"), fuṣḥaa "is a language that embodies authority and bestows authority on those who know it" (Haeri 1997: 796). With skillful knowledge and linguistic competency in fuṣḥaa, a constellation of privileges (Bourdieu's **symbolic capital**) accrues to the speaker, namely honor, prestige, power and authority. But as I have demonstrated elsewhere (Boussofara-Omar 2005), the voice of authority of fuṣḥaa does not accrue to its users unless they abide by its linguistic rules and "obey" its pragmatic appropriateness. In other words, fuṣḥaa, as a linguistic capital, is not automatically convertible into symbolic capital unless its users manifestly comply with its authority. Anyone who uses fuṣḥaa, even a soon-to-be president, has to subject their linguistic production to scrutiny and thorough examination to ensure the perfect use of its linguistic rules and pragmatics because as Haeri (2003: 69) rightly argues: "The only authority that is unquestioned belongs to the language." And any "incorrect" or faulty use of fuṣḥaa takes authority away from its users because it remains the variety of Arabic that is canonically associated with the sacred and the prescriptive tradition of correctness, purity, and perfection.

Bourguiba's status (as the president, the charismatic leader, and the Supreme Combatant), his proficiency in fuṣḥaa,[4] the formality of the settings and contexts of some speeches would traditionally have called for the use of fuṣḥaa; the variety of formality and solemnity. But Bourguiba chose deliberately to symbolically "transgress" the normative and prescriptive boundaries between fuṣḥaa and the **dialect** by using Tunisian Arabic – the dialectal variety of the masses – in his public speeches and by drawing on pure Tunisian colloquialisms in those unambiguously formal occasions; thereby distinguishing himself from all those who were not endowed with symbolic capital to make such linguistic violations as his. Bourguiba could take liberties with all the privileges that accured to him over the years by virtue of his position and various titles in the political and social arenas. The conditions under which he spoke concurred closely with the authority to "transgress" the linguistic rules and "violate" pragmatic appropriateness but still reap symbolic capital by speaking in the way he did. His linguistic violations are turned into legitimate speech because they issued from the mouth of si laḥbeeb "Mr. al-Habib"; an expression of endearment that Tunisians use to affectionately refer to Bourguiba. Had such "transgressions" been uttered by another member of the government or were they to be uttered by the current President when addressing the same audience, they would have been heard and perceived mal à propos.

In the case of Ben Ali, the then Prime Minister, self-investiture does not accord the symbolic capital that an elected president may automatically gain. The "Premier Ministère," as a political apparatus with its own constraints and as a political institution that he represents, is not powerful enough politically to license or legitimate the "linguistic violations" that Ben Ali tentatively made in the original draft, as I will demonstrate in my analysis of the changes brought to the draft of the address. The self-proclaimed presidency has to be "sanctioned" and "sanctified" to become public investiture by making it not only known but also, and more importantly, acknowledged or "recognized" (Bourdieu 1991) by the people on whose behalf he will speak and act as their president. So besides acquiring the voice of fushaa, Ben Ali, the then Prime Minister, has to acquire the linguistic habitus of the presidential voice which, ultimately, consists of a complex host of linguistic habituses and "colloquy of voices," e.g. the voice of the people, the voice of the government, the voice of the party, and the voice of the fellow citizen, to name but a few. In other words, the speaker "must acquire a practical sense [sense pratique] or 'feel' for [the political] game, that is a [linguistic] habitus attuned to the specific conditions or constraints of the political field" (Thompson 1991: 27). The main stake in learning the process of presidential linguistic habitus is not a question of learning to produce valid statements but of learning the habitus (i.e. a "set of dispositions," Bourdieu 1991) that is attuned to the gain of symbolic capital. Two examples from the Communiqué are interesting to explore in this section to illustrate a presidential voice and linguistic habitus in the making. They both show how the new speaker is being initiated to have sensitivity to and awareness of the tension between what is to be said versus the constraints that are inherent in particular relations of linguistic production. They also demonstrate how the boundaries between the individual and collective voices are being mapped in front of our eyes and how the tone of the new authoritative voice of the speaker and the contours of the people's voice (as a newly "imagined community" in the post-Bourguiba era) are being redrawn through the corrections scribbled in red in the draft. The proposed alternants are believed to be crucial linguistic mediators that translate better the discursive authority of the New Era which, as I stated earlier, was a disembodied voice on November 7, 1987. They also serve to naturalize the new voice of authority, and rationalize its acceptance.

In the prelude to the announcement of Bourguiba's deposition, which constitutes the introductory passage of the Communiqué, Ben Ali opens his first public address to the Tunisians by emphatically paying tribute to Habib Bourguiba, "the leader and first president of the Republic of Tunisia", and commending him for the "countless and enormous sacrifices" that he courageously ventured to make for the liberation and development of Tunisia (excerpt 1, Communiqué, November 7th).

(Excerpt 1)

ʾinna	at-tadhiyaat	al-jisaam	allati	ʾaqdama	ʿalayhaa	az-zaiim
indeed	the-sacrifices	the-enormous	that	made	on-it	the-leader

al-habib	bourguiba	ʾawwal	raʾiis	li-l-jumhuuriyya	at-tunisiyya
habib	Bourguiba	first	president	to-the-republic	the-tunisian

latuhsaa	wa	la	tuaʿdd
notcount	and	not	counted

"The enormous sacrifices that Bourguiba – the leader and first president of the republic of Tunisia – made are numerous and countless."

Note how with the juxtaposition of the emphatic *'inna* "that" or "indeed" to the noun *tadhiyaat'* "sacrifices," and the choice of the adjective *jisaam* "enormous," suggesting heroic times and great deeds readily recognizable to the audience, Ben Ali appeals to the past as the repository of collective memory filled with sacrifices, glories, victories, and triumphs.

The speaker further adds:

> (Excerpt 2)
> And it is because of these countless and immense sacrifices, we have loved him, we have respected him …

Within an Aristotelian framework such a trope may be read as an instance of pathos: a (nationalistic) discourse that involves arousing an appropriate emotional response in the audience by invoking Bourguiba's contribution to the glorious past. But as Suleiman (2003: 38–39) rightly argues: "Nationalists … use the past as the basis of … embracing change and projecting it as part of the inner fabric of this past in an almost seamless progression of history into the present and beyond." The reference to the past is rooted in a reality of shared experiences, shared memories, and shared history between Bourguiba and his people. It is rather risky for a self-proclaimed successor, even though he presents himself as the legitimate successor and savior, to ignore the strong thirty-year bond between the leader and his people.

> It is not easy to replace a man like me … There is, between the Tunisian people and me, forty years of life passed together, which will not exist with him who comes after me … I have created a nation largely around myself, around my person …
>
> (Bourguiba, 12 January 1972)

In fact, Bourguiba's cult cluttered not only public spaces but also, and more importantly, private spaces (i.e. Tunisians' homes and daily lives) because as Bessis and Belhassen (1989: 302–303) rightly say:

> Bourguiba veut être partout, dans les foyers et les coeurs des citoyens, comme il aime dire, leur tenant compagnie, leur donnant des directives, les couvant de son regard paternel et protecteur.

> Bourguiba wants to be everywhere, in the homes and hearts of the citizens, as he likes saying, keeping them company, giving them instructions, keeping a paternal, protective eye on them.

But the people needed to be reminded that the "leader" was "too old to fulfill his duties as the president of the republic" (Appendix) and that the deposition of the incapacitated leader is *al-waajib al-wataniy* "the national duty" of each Tunisian, as it were. Note the use of the inclusive "we" in "we have loved him, we have respected him" in excerpt 2. Even though ambiguous, it may be perceived as inclusive and heard as a chorus of voices, or a collective "we," i.e. we, the Tunisians. It makes the Tunisians emotionally involved and renders Bourguiba's incapacity to lead a "collective truth" (Bourdieu 1991: 212) and his deposition a collective duty. In a way, the invocation of the past "plays an authenticating and legitimizing role; it signals continuity, cohesion and, therefore, a feeling of intimacy and belonging between members of the nation" (Suleiman 2003: 38).

The phrases acknowledging and reminding the audience of Bourguiba's heroic sacrifices seem to act as "terministic screens," to borrow Burke's (1966) words, serving to deflect our attention from Ben Ali's attempt to engage in challenging Bourguiba's authoritative voice and re-actualizing and appropriating his words.

In the prelude of the original draft and prior to the announcement of Bourguiba's deposition, Ben Ali commends not only Bourguiba but also some other *rijaal barara* 'loyal men' (Appendix) for their sacrifices to liberate Tunisia. The tribute reads:

(Excerpt 3)
The grand sacrifices that courageously ventured – along with loyal men –
the leader Habib Bourguiba – the first President of the Republic of Tunisia –
to make for the liberation and development of Tunisia – are countless.

As we can see, in the original draft, Bourguiba is mentioned as one among many who fought for the liberation and independence of the country. The two phrases that recognize Bourguiba as the "leader" *za'iim* and as "the first president of the Republic of Tunisia" *'awwal ra'iis li-l-jumhuriyya at- tunisiyya* are embedded in a maze of dashes. The dashes, whether their choice was deliberate or spontaneous, are more rhetorical and more persuasive than explicit arguments because they are camouflaged, less likely to be noticed and evaluated critically than propositions presented in the form of an argument. In the draft, not only is Bourguiba acknowledged as one among many other loyal compatriots to whom Tunisians owe independence but, more importantly, he is talked about in the past tense. He is part of the past history of Tunisia already. Furthermore, in recognizing the sacrifices that a group of other fellow citizens made before mentioning Bourguiba's name, the speaker makes an attempt to speak his own voice and give a different reading to the history of the national movement. But the attempt was "censored" and the word order was shuffled because as Bourdieu (1991: 122) rightly argues, "one of the functions of the act of institution [is] to discourage any attempt to cross the line, to transgress."

It is crucial to note here that, in his numerous speeches, Bourguiba never failed to present himself as the "sole savior" and the only "real liberator"; thus undermining the political stature of any potential competitor and eliminating any potential rival. Bourguiba's discursive practices had long served as the key to naturalize the conflation of his person and the history of Tunisia:

Son histoire personnelle résume à ses yeux celle de la Tunisie toute entière.
(Bessis and Belhassen 1989: 137)

In his eyes, his personal story summarizes the history of the whole Tunisia.

Il est un fondateur, un guide, et un père; hors de lui point de salut
(Bessis and Belhassen 1989: 70)

He is a founder [of the nation], a guide, and a father; without him there is no salvation.

He portrayed himself as much of a historical and legendary figure as Jughurta (the Numidian King), and Hannibal (the Carthaginian heroic figure), and his discourse has never allowed any "dialogizing challenge" (Farmer 1995: 307).

[P]our parfaire l'image qu'il veut donner de lui-même, il a besoin d'être le seul acteur de l'histoire. Pas un de ses collaborateurs n'échappe à ses sarcasmes.

(Bessis and Belhassen 1989: 138)

[T]o perfect the image that he wants to project of himself, he needs to be the only actor of history. Not a single collaborator escapes his sarcasm.

Even though his health was failing, and his public speeches and public "acts of theatricalization" (Bourdieu 1991: 185) were becoming less and less frequent, the constellation of Bourguiba's symbolic accountrement (his glasses, a walking stick, a white shawl around his neck in the winter, a bouquet of jasmine in the summer, his cabinet advisers, ministers, and dignitaries flanked by his side), his unique use of Tunisian colloquialisms, and his special way of "doing things with words" were still omnipresent in the 1980s. In his public political speeches, words were swiftly swept away by a swinging arm, a moving voice, a mocking laughter, a gentle smile, a penetrating gaze, an animated face, and a rocking body. Each gesture or facial expression was in total mesh with the linguistic code chosen, the word selected and the intended message delivered (research in progress).

Enfin il convient de ne pas oublier que Bourguiba ne doit pas son prestige et son autorité auprès des masses tunisiennes à ses seuls écrits. Il les doit surtout à sa parole, à son éloquence directe, nerveuse et enflammée qui remue les foules et qui a donné une âme et une raison de vivre à un peuple fier et généreux.

Finally, it is appropriate to keep in mind that Bourguiba does not owe his prestige and authority among the Tunisian masses only to his writings. He owes them especially to *his word, his straightforward, nervous, and firing eloquence* that *emotionally stirs the crowds* and which gave a soul and a reason to live to a proud and generous people (emphasis is mine).

Even though his mental and physical conditions were deteriorating, his regime was weakening, its popular image was fainting and the political and social scene was getting bleaker during the last two decades of his rule, Bourguiba remained the symbol of a constellation of historical accomplishments (e.g. independence, development, and Westernization of Tunisia) and the embodiment of Modern Tunisia.

By virtue of his status as the 'founding father' of modern Tunisia, the "Supreme Combatant" *al-mujaahid al-akbar*, the "king of the kings" *sayyid al-asy-aad*, and the "leader" *az-zaim*, Bourguiba was endowed with the full power and authority to speak and act on behalf of all the Tunisians (the highly educated, the educated, the uneducated, and the illiterate).

With the advent of the New Era, new official imagery and new rhetorical practices had to replace Bourguiba's omnipresent image, voice, and words. But Ben Ali's first attempt to purportedly restore historical facts and may be re-write the history of the national movement for independence was toned down to better resonate with the audience and their attachment to Bourguiba. The editorial touches reflect a shift of emphasis and perception since what was initially de-emphasized or rather put under erasure in the original draft was fore-grounded in the 'cleaned-up version' of the address (excerpt 5). I repeat excerpt 3 under 4 to facilitate the comparison between the two versions of the draft.

> (Excerpt 4: Original draft)
> The grand sacrifices that courageously ventured – along with loyal men – the *leader Habib Bourguiba – the first President of the Republic of Tunisia –* to make for the liberation and development of Tunisia – are countless.

> (Excerpt 5: Revised version)
> The grand sacrifices that ventured to make the *leader Habeeb Bourguiba the first President of Tunisia*, in company with loyal men, for the liberation and development of Tunisia, are numerous and countless, this is why we loved and respected him.

The privileges and personal capital, conferred to Bourguiba, the charismatic leader, were denied to Ben Ali. Note the manipulation of the text through the visible re-arrangement of his words, the selection of their order, and the change of the punctuation. Ben Ali could not play with the linguistic rules of the political game or "transgress in a lawful way" (Bourdieu 1991: 117). Despite his explicit claim, in the Communiqué, to political clout, and hence political capital, in the forms of the jobs that he held not only inside the governmental apparatus but more significantly under Bourguiba's leadership (excerpt 6) – his "personal capital" was lacking.

> (Excerpt 6)
> and we have worked under his leadership in different positions, in our national popular army, and in the government, with *trust*, *loyalty*, and *dedication* (emphasis is mine).

The establishment of an authoritative *ethos* is imperative. There is a need for the speaker to portray himself as legitimate, credible and having a good moral character, as illustrated in his use of such words as "trust," "loyalty," and "dedication" (excerpt 6) and thereby to secure personal capital, professional, and symbolic capital. It is crucial to reiterate the fact that in 1987 Ben Ali was an unknown speaker, a disembodied voice, and an unfamiliar face that not very many Tunisians could relate to or even recognize, had he chosen to appear on their television screens. According to Tuqoi (2002), a French journalist, even a decade or so later, and "despite all the noise [of the propaganda],

Ben Ali remains for the Tunisians, a distant, unknown character that is difficult to frame", "a face, but not a voice."

The symbolic capital of recognition and loyalties, which Bourguiba enjoyed for almost three decades, could not be mobilized or solicited from the masses since the political coup had to be shrouded in total secrecy. Furthermore, Ben Ali did not have the "privileges of the consecration" that Bourguiba had. When he delivered the Communiqué, Ben Ali was not duly empowered to take any liberties to speak his own words or his own voice because the transference of power and the act of delegation had not occurred since he had not taken the oath of office. He would have to undergo the "rites of passage," i.e. the ritual of investiture. His Communiqué was neither a campaign speech, nor an acceptance speech nor an inaugural speech. His desire and will to act, speak, and perform as the new delegate or to appropriate Bourguiba's words are carefully revoked through the significant changes.

[...]

'Learning how to do things with words': Omissions

What renders utterances such as "I name this ship the *Queen Elizabeth*" uttered when smashing a bottle against the stem of a vessel, "I now pronounce you man and wife" or "I do" uttered in the course of a marriage ceremony as plausible performative utterances (or acts) are the conditions under which they are performed (e.g. the place, the time, and the agent). The efficacy of performative utterances is dependent upon an institution – be it political, social, educational or religious – that endows individual speakers with status, power, and legitimacy to carry out the act. Not anyone could stand, on November 7, 1987, in front of the Tunisians to announce the deposition of the president and proclaim the presidency but the Prime Minister who sought the provisions in the Constitution which would allow for the ailing president's removal. There is some irony, however, in the fact that the magical performative utterance that would overtly vest Ben Ali with authority and give him legitimacy to step into Bourguiba's shoes and that would imbue his words with "magical efficacy" (Bourdieu 1991: 72) to change the course of history in Tunisia was missing in the initial draft. The magical words of "the act of authority" or "authorized act" (Bourdieu 1991), "We, Zine Al-Abidine Ben Ali, the Prime Minister of the Republic of Tunisia, have issued the following Communiqué" were clearly squeezed, in red, between the ritualized invocation of Allah *bismi allah ar-rahmaan ar-rahiim* "In the Name of Allah, Most Gracious, Most Merciful," and the address phrase *ayyatuha l-muwatinaat, ayyuha l-muwatinuun* "fellow (female) citizens, fellow (male) citizens," in the draft (Appendix). The invocation of Allah and his *baraka* "grace" is a crucial device in the creation of authoritative discourse. By evoking and creating divine realms, agency is implicitly attributed to those incontestable divine realms. The speaker is acting in accordance with the wishes of Allah. Besides, the invocation of outside authority frames and reconstructs the totality of the social and political space in which the efficacy of the words and the magic of the voice are made possible.

Performatives do not report or describe a state of affairs. Because they indicate the performance of an act or rather the unfolding of an act, they are in the present tense. The present tense indexes the break with the past, the execution of an act, and the passage to a future, i.e. a different if not a new reality. What is unusual about Ben Ali's performative utterance is that it is in the past tense: "We … issued the following Communiqué." The performative verb *ʾaṣdara* "issue" that is going to change the history of Tunisia is used in the past, *ʾaṣdarnaa*, conveying that the action is not concurrent with the time of speaking. The new reality is a *fait accompli*. The passage from the Old to the New Era is accomplished (Ben Ali and his allies were already in control since the coup was staged on the night of November 6, 1987) but the recognition of the act itself (i.e. the acceptance of Bourguiba's deposition and the recognition of the beginning of the post-Bourguiba Era) rests upon the Tunisian people's acceptance and their "active complicity" (Bourdieu 1991). The *taḥawwul mubaarak* "blessed change" needs to be recognized and ratified by the Tunisians, even though they were solicited in absentia: The Tunisians were not physically present when Ben Ali announced the magical words to announce the historical change. Any performative utterance usually requires the physical presence of an audience to "recognize" the act as legitimate. Bourdieu (1991: 125) states:

> Even when the act is accomplished by a sole agent duly empowered to accomplish it and to do so within the recognized forms …, it rests fundamentally on the belief of an entire group (which may be physically present), that is, on the socially fashioned dispositions to know and recognize the institutional conditions of a valid ritual. And this implies that the symbolic efficacy of the ritual will vary – simultaneously or successively – according to the degree to which the people for whom the ritual is performed are more or less prepared, or more or less disposed to receive it.

It is also ironic that the "historical" date and the "historical" title of the address, which will later serve as a leitmotiv in the official presidential and governmental discourse, were also omitted in the original draft (Appendix). It is ironic because shortly after it was delivered, the text was officially adopted as the November 7 Communiqué *bayaan as-saabiʿ min nuvambar*. In a sense, it constituted (and still constitutes) the roadmap of the New Era. The *Bayaan*, Communiqué, as a title and as a text, has become a political ideology. It is profusely cited, quoted in the press, broadcast in the media, and taught in schools when the anniversary of the "blessed change" *at-taḥawwul al-mubaarak* – according to the officials – is festively celebrated a week long. The 'historical' date ended up being placarded onto street, boulevard, square, school, kindergarten, restaurant, and hospital signs. Almost every major city, and even some rural small towns, have their *rawdat sabʿa nuvambar* "November 7 Kindergarten," *madrast sabʿa nuvambar,* "November 7 School," *mustaʃfaa sabʿa nuvambar,* "November 7 Hospital," *ʃaariʿ sabʿa nuvambar,* "November 7 Boulevard," *maṭʿam. sabʿa nuvambar,* "November 7 Restaurant," and their *maqhaa sabʿa nuvambar,* "November 7 Café." The new **semiotic** practice has shifted the history of Tunisia from the cult of a person, through the erection of bronze statues to honor Bourguiba, or the naming of main streets and boulevards after the leader's name (e.g. *saaḥat Bourguiba*, Bourguiba Square, *ʃaariʿ Bourguiba*, Bourguiba Boulevard) to that of a date. It is ironic that the date, which has gradually wiped out Bourguiba's omnipresent name, image and voice, and became the symbol of the 'historical' political change, was inadvertently omitted in the draft. It is also ironic that the title was missing because it has, in a way, determined the nature of the new political rhetoric, defined the to-be-accepted political discourse of the New Era, and reflected the style of the new regime. The Bayaan became the emblem of the change, and more importantly it gave a sound to the disembodied voice of the new speaker. Reframing the analysis of the date and the title of the Communiqué in light of Bakhtin's idea of how language lies at the intersection of multiple voices or speaking positions, the date and the title of the Communiqué of the New Era and the Old Era are not mutually exclusive. It is their tense intersection that gives symbolic meaning to each.

The "corrections" of the omissions and the re-arrangement of Ben Ali's words denote, in a way, a lack of adroitness to skillfully navigate between the private and public spaces and an absence of dexterity to subtly weave in and out of the public and the private voices that could dialogize with the former president's words and voices only implicitly, inferentially, and **indexically**.

Conclusion

Not anyone could have stood in front of the Tunisian people in 1987, solemnly uttered the words "We, X, have issued the following Communiqué," authoritatively announced the deposition of the "old" and "sick" president, swiftly proclaimed the presidency, and promptly been acclaimed as the new president of the New Era and the Commander in Chief of the Tunisian Armed Forces. In order for such words to become a performative utterance (i.e. to be "felicitous," in Austin's terms (1962)) or more specifically to be *heard* and *recognized* (Bourdieu 1991) as an act of power and authority, the speaker must be endowed with authority to speak with authority and recognized as such by those who hear the speech. In fact, the words that Ben Ali, the then Prime Minister, uttered on November 7, 1987 at 6:30 AM on the national radio station could have been uttered by anyone but, most likely, the speaker would have been either committed to a mental institution (because s/he would be regarded as mentally ill) or tried for defamation (because s/he would be regarded as a "thug," or a *jurthuuma*, a "parasite"; Bourguiba's label for anyone who dared challenge his discursive authority). "A performative utterance is destined to fail each time that it is not pronounced by a person who has the power to pronounce it" (Bourdieu 1991: 111). One may wonder: what creates belief in the power of the words and legitimacy of the speaker who utters them?

In my exploration of the question of how a presidential authoritative voice is made, through the linguistic analysis of the changes brought to Ben Ali's "incorrect" and "inappropriate" (*mal à propos*) use of words (or lack thereof), I have demonstrated how intricate the interweaving of the different sources of discursive authority and power is and how the voice of authority that accrues to the speaker comes from inextricably linked sources that are linguistic and extra-linguistic. First, I have argued that authority, in part, comes from the linguistic ideology of the code chosen, i.e. fuṣḥaa, the High variety of Arabic (Ferguson 1959) that is deeply rooted in the divine and symbolic of the Islamic heritage. But I also claimed (and demonstrated elsewhere, Boussofara-Omar 2005) that authority of fuṣḥaa does not accrue automatically or transparently to any user, and that anyone who uses fuṣḥaa, even a soon-to-be president, has to "obey" its authority by subjecting their linguistic production to scrupulous scrutiny to ensure the correct use of its linguistic rules and pragmatic appropriateness. Second, I have demonstrated that words of authority derived from an institution of power (e.g. the Premier Ministère) alone fall short of endowing the speaker with the necessary authority to depose a president and change the course of history of a country (i.e. to make things happen with words only rooted in a state apparatus). Third, I have shown the processes whereby a soon-to-be president's words had to be re-worked in order to orchestrate the tension between the personal, the socio-historical and the political contexts on the one hand, and to harmonize the voices of the personal and the socio-political authorities on the other. In order for a new speaker (in the political field) to acquire symbolic capital, his words and voice have to be heard against the chorus of others' voices and the constellation of others' words with varying degrees of authority. The visible changes of the text, I argued, capture the complex process of "distinguishing between one's own and another's discourse, between one's own and another's thoughts" (Bakhtin 1981: 345) and of creatively re-contextualizing words to establish a balance between "varying degrees of otherness and varying degrees of … own-ness" (Bakhtin 1986: 89, cited in Fairclough 1992: 102). The analysis of those changes has demonstrated the processes whereby the new speaker's words and voice were made dialogically and historically situated to "make the efficacy of the magic of language possible" (Bourdieu and Wacquant 1992: 148).

Naïma Boussofara-Omar is an Assistant Professor of Arabic Studies at the Department of African & African-American Studies at the University of Kansas, USA. She holds a PhD in Applied Linguistics from the University of Texas at Austin where she was also trained in sociolinguistics. Her research interests include language change and variation in the Arab world, language ideology and linguistic choices in political and media discourse.

Appendix

http://www.bibliotheque.nat.tn/VISITE_V/INDEX_A.htm

Declaration of November, 7th 1987
In the name of God, the Clement, the Merciful

We, Zine El Abidine Ben Ali, Prime Minister of the Republic of Tunisia, proclaim the following:

Fellow Citizens,

The great sacrifices made by the Leader Habib Bourguiba, first President of the Republic, together with other men of valor, for the liberation and development of Tunisia, are countless. And that is why we granted him our affection and regard and worked under his leadership for many years confidently, faithfully and in a spirit of self-denial, at all levels, in the ranks of our popular and national army and in the government.

But the onset of his senility and the deterioration of his health and the medical report made on this called us to carry out our national duty and declare him totally incapable of undertaking the tasks of President of the Republic.

Thereby, acting under article 57 of the Constitution, with the help of God, we take up the Presidency of the Republic and the high command of our armed forces.

In the exercise of our responsibilities, we are counting on all the children of our dear country to work together in an atmosphere of confidence, security and serenity, from which all hatred and rancor will be banished.

The independence of our country, our territorial integrity, the invulnerability of our fatherland and our people's progress are a matter of concern for all citizens. Love of one's country, devotion to its safety, commitment to its growth are the sacred duties of all Tunisians.

Fellow Citizens,

Our people has reached a degree of responsibility and maturity where every individual and group is in a position to constructively contribute to the running of its affairs, in conformity with the republican idea which gives institutions their full scope and guarantees the conditions for a responsible democracy, fully respecting the sovereignty of the people as written into the Constitution. This Constitution needs urgent revision. The times in which we live can no longer admit of life presidency or automatic succession, from which the people is excluded. Our people deserves an advanced and institutionalized political life, truly based on the plurality of parties and mass organizations.

We shall be soon putting forward a bill that will concern political parties and another concerning the press, which ensure a wider participation in the building up of Tunisia and the strengthening of its independence in a context of order and discipline.

We shall see that the law is correctly enforced in a way that will proscribe any kind of iniquity or injustice. We shall act to restore the prestige of the State and to put an end to chaos and laxity. There will be no more favoritism or indifference where the squandering of the country's wealth is concerned.

We shall continue to keep up our good relations and positive cooperation with all other countries, particularly friendly and sister countries. We shall respect our international engagements.

We shall give Islamic, Arab, African and Mediterranean solidarity its due importance.

We shall strive ourselves to achieve the unity, based on our common interests, of the Great Maghreb.

Fellow Citizens,

By the Grace of God, we are entering on a new era of efforts and determination.

Love of our country and the call of duty require this of us.

Long live Tunisia!

Long live the Republic!

Notes

1   It is important to note here that the original handwritten draft of the final version of the *bayaan*, Communiqué, was respectively published in 1992 in a book entitled "The Peaceful Revolution" aθ-θawra al-haadiʾa, and in 1995 in ben ali wa aṭ-ṭareeq ʾila at-taʿaddudiyya ("Ben Ali and the Road to Pluralism"). In the first book, the draft was published along with three other official documents: first a copy of a medical report (ironically composed in French) signed by seven medical doctors, at 6:00 AM, proclaiming the president to be incapable of

fulfilling his duties and hence legally entitling Ben Ali to step into Bourguiba's shoes to become the second president of independent Tunisia, second a copy of three annotations ('observations', mulaahadaat according to the official version) that relate to the changes brought to the manuscript, the time of its recording and the typing of the final text, and third a copy of the 'cleaned up' final version. The 'observations' indicate that the Communiqué was 'amended' at 4:30 AM, recorded at 5:45 AM and broadcast on the national radio at 6:30 AM. These documents serve as symbols of the etiquette of the New Era and its new rhetoric of visibility, accessibility, transparency and truth.

2   Spitulnik (1998: 166) argues that "there is an indexical use of a language or a speech variety, which extends beyond the indexing of a social group associated with a code: the code chosen indexes the codes not chosen." Like Spitulnik, I argue that the relational values – that exist between different codes – become particularly salient in a diglossic, bilingual speech-community like Tunisia. Ben Ali's rigorous use of fushaa as the sole variety/language of the public presidential political discourse in the New Era stands as an antithetical discourse to Bourguiba's polyphonic discourse.

3   In their discussion of the tactful semiotic processes of linguistic differentiation, Irvine and Gal (2000: 38) define "erasure" as "the process in which ideology, in simplifying the sociolinguistic field, renders some persons or activities (or sociolinguistic phenomena) invisible".

4   Bourguiba was educated in the prestigious bilingual College Sadiki, founded in 875 by Khereddine Pasha in order to educate a new generation of Tunisian leaders who received good training on both Arabic and French.

References

Austin, J. (1962) *How to Do Things with Words*, Cambridge, MA: Harvard University Press.

Bakhtin, Mikhail (1981) *The Dialogic Imagination: Four Essays by M.M. Bakhtin*, ed. M Holquist, Austin, TX: University of Texas Press.

—— (1984) *Problems of Dostoevsky's Poetics*, Ed. and Trans. Caryl Emerson. Theory and History of Literature 8. Minneapolis, MN: University of Minnesota Press.

—— (1986) *Speech Genres and Other Late Essays*, trans. Vern W. McGee, ed. Caryl Emerson and Michael Holquist, University of Texas Press Slavic Series 8, Austin, TX: University of Texas Press.

Ben Abdallah, Abdelkrim (1992) *7 November: Al-thawra al-haadi'a*, Tunis: Ben Abdallah Press.

Bessis, Sophie and Belhassen, Souhayr (1989) *Bourguiba: Un si Long Régne (1957–1989)*, Paris: Jeune Afrique Press.

Bourdieu, Pierre (1991) *Language and Symbolic Power*, Cambridge, MA: Harvard University Press.

—— (1998) *Outline of a Theory of Practice*, trans. R. Nice, Cambridge: Cambridge University Press.

—— and Wacquant, Loïc J. (1992) *An Invitation to Reflexive Sociology*, Chicago: The University of Chicago Press.

Boussofara-Omar, Naïma (2005) Political transition, linguistic shift: How a political Communiqué (*bayaan*) has come to be what it is, *Perspectives on Arabic Linguistics XVIII*. Philadelphia/Amsterdam: John Benjamins, pp. 195–224.

Burke, Kenneth (1966) *Terministic Screens: Language as Symbolic Action*, Berkeley, CA: University of California, pp. 44–62.

—— (1969) *A Grammar of Motives*, Berkeley, CA: University of California Press.

Coe, Richard (1993) Beyond diction: Using Burke to empower words, and wordlings, *Rhetoric Review*, 11(2): 368–377.

Errington, Joseph J. (1998) *Shifting Languages: Interaction and Identity in Javanese Indonesia*, Cambridge: Cambridge University Press.

—— (2000) Indonesian('s) authority, in: Bambi Shieffelin, Kathryn Woolard and Paul Kroskrity (eds.), *Language Ideologies: Practice and Theory*, Oxford: Oxford University Press, pp. 271–284.

Fairclough, Norman (1992) *Discourse and Social Change*, Cambridge: Polity Press.

Farmer, Frank (1995) Voice reprised: Etudes for a dialogic understanding, *Rhetoric Review*, 13(2): 304–320.

Friedrich, P. (1989) Language, ideology and political economy, *American Anthropologist*, 9l(2): 295–312.

Gal, Susan (1988) The political economy of code choice, in M. Heller (ed.), *Codeswitching*, Berlin: Mouton de Gruyter, pp. 245–265.

—— (1989) Language and political economy, *Annual Review of Anthropology*, 18: 345–367.

—— (1991) Bartok's funeral: representations of Europe in Hungarian political rhetoric, *American Ethnologist*, 18(3): 440–458.

—— (1999) Multiplicity and contention among language ideologies, in Bambi Shieffelin, Kathryn Woolard and Paul Kroskrity (eds.), *Language Ideologies: Practice and Theory*. Oxford: Oxford University Press, pp. 317–331.

—— and Irvine, Judith (2000) Language ideology and linguistic differentiation, in Paul V. Kroskrity (ed.), *Regimes of Language: Ideologies, Polities, and Identities*, Santa Fe, NM: School of American Research Press, pp. 35–83.

Haeri, Niloofar (1997) The reproduction of symbolic capital: Language, state, and class in Egypt, *Current Anthropology*, 38(5): 795–816.

—— (2000) Form and ideology: Arabic sociolinguistics and beyond, *Annual Reviews Anthropology*, 29: 61–87.

—— (2003) *Sacred Language, Ordinary People*, New York: Palgrave Macmillan.

Hill, Jane, H. (2000) Read my article, in: Paul V. Kroskrity (ed.), *Regimes of Language: Ideologies, Polities, and Identities*, Santa Fe, NM: School of American Research Press.

—— and Gal, Susan (2000) Language ideology and linguistic differentiation, in: Paul V. Kroskrity (ed.), *Regimes of Languages: Ideologies, Polities, and Identities*, Santa Fe, NM: School of American Research Press, pp. 35–83.

Kroskrity, Paul (2000) Regimenting languages: Language ideological perspectives, in Paul V. Kroskrity (ed.), *Regimes of Language: Ideologies, Polities, and Identities*. Santa Fe, NM: School of American Research Press, pp. 1–34.

Mertz, Elizabeth (1998) Linguistic ideology and praxis in U.S. law school classrooms, in Bambi Shieffelin, Kathryn Woolard and Paul Kroskrity (eds.), *Language Ideologies: Practice and Theory*, Oxford: Oxford University Press, pp. 149–162.

Murphy, Emma (1999) *Economic and Political Change in Tunisia: From Bourguiba to Ben Ali*, New York: St. Martin's Press.

Philips, Susan (2000) Constructing a Tongon nation-state through language ideology in the courtroom, in: Paul V. Kroskrity (ed.), *Regimes of Language: Ideologies, Polities, and Identities*, Santa Fe, NM: School of American Research Press, pp. 229–257.

Spitulnik, Debra (1998) Mediating unity and diversity: The production of language ideologies in Zambian broadcasting, in Bambi Shieffelin, Kathryn Woolard and Paul Kroskrity (eds.), *Language Ideologies: Practice and Theory*, Oxford: Oxford University Press, pp. 163–188.

—— (1999) The language of the city: Town Bemba as urban hybridity, *Journal of Linguistic Anthropology*, 8(1): 30–59.

Suleiman, Yasir (2003) *The Arabic Language and National Identity: A Study in Ideology*, Washington, D.C.: Georgetown University Press.

Thompson, John B. (1991), Introduction, in Bourdieu, Pierre *Language and Symbolic Power*, Cambridge, MA: Harvard University Press, pp. 1–31.

Tuqoi, Jean-Pierre (2002) Ben Ali L'inconnu, online, available at: www.lemonde.fr/article/0,5987, 3212–277055.

Woolard, K.A. (1985) Language variation and cultural hegemony: Toward an integration of sociolinguistics and social theory, *American Ethnologist,* 12(4): 738–748.

Chapter 8

Anne-Marie Simon-Vandenbergen, Peter R.R. White and Karin Aijmer

PRESUPPOSITIONS AND 'TAKING-FOR-GRANTED' IN MASS COMMUNICATED POLITICAL ARGUMENT: AN ILLUSTRATION FROM BRITISH, FLEMISH AND SWEDISH POLITICAL COLLOQUY

[…]

1. Introduction

RECENT LINGUISTIC RESEARCH on media political language, whether the concern is with the written or the spoken media, can roughly be divided into three groups of studies. In one type of studies the focus is on ways in which language reflects explicit or implicit **ideologies**. Typically these studies have aimed at laying bare the means by which speakers/writers convey political opinions regarding crucial societal issues such as class, gender or race relations. The linguistic framework within which most of these studies are carried out is critical discourse analysis in the broadest sense. The ultimate goal of this type of research is to raise awareness of language as an instrument of power and thereby to attempt to have an impact on power relations, to contribute to lifting inequality. These studies hence have a clear ideological starting-point and purpose. Examples are van Dijk (1998a, 1998b). Fairclough (1995, 2001), Wodak *et al.* (2000), Blommaert and Bulcaen (1997), and many articles in the journal *Discourse and Society*.

The second group of studies on media political language focus on the mechanisms of interaction and ways in which participants engage in talk. These studies are not so much interested in the ideologies of the speakers as in the way media interaction develops in different genres such as radio or television interviews and debates. The linguistic framework within which these studies are to be situated is typically conversation analysis in some variant. Examples of such work are Greatbatch (1992) and Clayman and Heritage (2002).

The third group comprises studies which take a functional approach to **discourse** in a broad sense and concentrate on the linguistic means, **lexical** and grammatical, of persuasion. The focus is on participants' rhetorical strategies by means of which they attempt to get their points across and reach their goals as political speakers. This type of research shares with the first group of studies its interest in the power of linguistic choices and with the second group its interest in the way speakers deal with the demands made by the various genres in which they are involved – for example how is it that speakers answer face-threatening questions, deny accusations or strengthen their own arguments. This type of research tends to go into detailed analyses of linguistic choices as rhetorical devices employed by political speakers to reach certain goals which are crucial in the presentation of themselves in the media. Examples are Harris's study (1991) on answering questions, Simon-Vandenbergen (1996, 1997) on image building, Lauerbach (2004) on political interviews as a **hybrid** genre.

The present article is to be situated within the third group. Its aim is to study strategic uses of lexicogrammatical means in an attempt to persuade. More specifically the focus is on the use of a set of resources which we see as construing 'taken-for-grantedness' – certain formulations by which propositions are treated as generally known or agreed upon, and hence as uncontentious and not at stake argumentatively. Our specific focus will be upon a mode of taken-for-grantedness – that associated with what the literature terms **presupposition** (see e.g. Bertuccelli Papi 1997; Caffi 1998; Lambrecht 1994). The research elaborates on previous work on the use of modality and evidentiality in British political discourse (especially Simon-Vandenbergen 1992) and on cross-linguistic research in this area (especially Simon-Vandenbergen and Aijmer 2005; Lewis 2004). Our goal is threefold.

The first aim is to look at taken-for-grantedness as a persuasive strategy in political TV debates. This paper builds on Sbisà (1999) and takes the argumentation further in the direction of finding an answer to the question why speakers find it useful to treat certain propositions as generally known or agreed upon or otherwise not at issue. […]

The second aim of this paper is of a more general linguistic nature. […] The account in this paper seeks to consider the rhetorical function of taken-for-grantedness in greater depth, and in the context of cross-linguistic comparisons.

Third, the data are taken from political debates in three closely related cultural contexts, the British, Flemish and Swedish ones. We believe that by studying closely linguistic choices in similar data in different languages and cultures the resources which are exploited surface more visibly. Furthermore, if it appears that the choices are similar we can hypothesize that political discourse in these cultures relies on the same tactics. However, in order to reach this third goal of studying strategies from an intercultural point of view much more research is called for, on a larger amount of data from more widely different cultures. We therefore see this third goal as mainly exploratory in nature.

Section 3 discusses the data. […] The use of presupposing constructions across the British, Flemish and Swedish data is dealt with in Section 5. Section 6 gives the discussion of and conclusions from the findings.

[…]

3. The data

The British data used for this study are taken from the programme *Question Time* (BBC1, 8 January 2004) and from a **corpus** comprised of some fifty episodes of the BBC radio programme. *Any Questions* (June 2003–December 2004), the Flemish data[1] are from the programmes *Ter zake Zaterdag* (Canvas, 7 February 2003) and *De Zevende Dag* (Canvas, 8 February 2003). The data cover six debates. The Swedish data are from a debate on nuclear energy broadcast on 21 March 1980.[2] These programmes share a number of features, including that the protagonists are politicians, that the topics are political issues, and hence that these are interactions which all fall under the heading of 'political discourse'. Further, in all cases the interaction is managed by an interviewer or moderator. Third, in all cases these are broadcast programmes, whether on the radio or on television. For the purposes of this study the difference between radio and television programmes is less important. The crucial factor is that the discourse is political, the issues controversial, and the interaction takes place for an audience of viewers or listeners. On the other hand there are some differences between the genres which these data represent that may have an impact on the discursive choices, and thus potentially on the use of presupposition as a tactic. We shall briefly comment on these genres.

The English and the Flemish programmes belong to the genre which Greatbatch (1992) and, following him, Clayman and Heritage (2002) call 'the panel interview'. According to Greatbatch, the advantage of panel interviews over one-to-one interviews is that the former solve the journalist's problem of having to reconcile combative questioning with the preservation of neutrality. By asking questions of two or more interviewees, typically representing different parties and viewpoints, the interviewer can provoke lively debate while maintaining neutrality. The liveliness results from disagreement among the interviewees. The disagreement can be voiced at different places in the **turn-taking** and can be addressed to the interviewer or to another interviewee. Greatbatch (1992) points out that the strength of disagreement in this genre increases with the abandonment of the expected question-answer format and with the identity of the addressee. The extracts given in the discussion will show that both the English and the Flemish data display the features of this genre. Not infrequently do interviewees address each other and in some cases they even deviate from the topic to become personal in an escalation of heated and unmitigated disagreement (see Clayman and Heritage 2002: 313ff. on the escalation from disagreement to confrontation).

The Swedish data are well described in Hirsch (1989). The genre is a formal television debate in which the turn-taking can be characterized as 'mechanistic or almost completely predetermined' (1989: 118). The debate in question took place in the last days before the referendum on nuclear energy in Sweden held on 23 March 1980. In this debate, the representatives of the three lines met. Line 1 is in favour of nuclear energy, while line 3 wants to abolish it. Line 2 is a compromise, neither radically for nor against it. The three lines were represented by four speakers, and a well-known news broadcaster acted as moderator or 'master of ceremonies'. The primary goal of the activity was to influence the voting behaviour of the home audience. From the interaction point-of-view it is important to mention that the turns were very strictly timed, that claims made by one speaker are answered by another speaker only indirectly, and hence that there is no overlapping talk, no **interruptions**, no abandonment of 'institutionalised footing' (Greatbatch 1992: 287), no escalation of disagreement towards confrontation.

The passages given in the following sections as illustrations follow normal orthographic and punctuation conventions for readability's sake. We have opted against a detailed CA transcript for the sake of uniformity: while the Flemish data were recorded and transcribed by us, the Swedish data have been transcribed at the Department of Linguistics, Göteborg University and this transcription has been used here (although some conventions have been changed for the sake of consistency with the other data). The *Question Time* data were transcribed by us, while the data from *Any Questions* were collected from the BBC website at www.bbc.co.uk/radio4/anyquestions.shtml.

[…]

5. The use of presupposition as another tactic

[…]

5.2 The term presupposition

The term *presupposition* covers many different things. One important distinction that has been made is between semantic and pragmatic presupposition. According to Caffi (1998: 752) '[t]he concept of semantic presupposition is quite clear'. This is true to the extent that there are clear criteria which allow us to decide under what conditions we can claim that some material is semantically presupposed. Semantic presupposition is defined in terms of truth-conditions, as a subtype of entailment, in the sense that a proposition which is presupposed remains true under **negation** and questioning. The following example is from Bertuccelli Papi (1997). The sentence 'Sue is dancing a macarena' presupposes that there is a person named Sue and there is a dance which is the macarena. This type of existential presupposition survives even when the sentence is negated or turned into a question: 'Sue is not dancing a macarena' and 'Is Sue dancing a macarena?' Semantic presupposition manifests itself in various lexical expressions and grammatical structures, and Bertuccelli Papi (1997) gives the following list: definite descriptions (including proper names), factive predicates including epistemic verbs (like *know, realize*) and emotive predicates (like *be surprised, regret, forget, deplore, resent*), implicative verbs (like *manage, remember*), change of state, inchoative and iterative verbs (like *stop, start*), verbs of judging (like *accuse, blame, criticize*), clefting and pseudo-clefting, prosodic emphasis, temporal clauses, non-restrictive relative clauses and counterfactuals. Semantic presupposition is conceptually different from pragmatic presupposition, which is defined in terms of common ground or background knowledge. Lambrecht (1994) gives the following definition of pragmatic presupposition:

> The set of propositions lexicogrammatically evoked in a sentence which the speaker assumes the hearer already knows or is ready to take for granted at the time the sentence is uttered.
>
> (1994: 52)

While this definition clearly distinguishes pragmatic from semantic presupposition, in practice it appears that the two concepts are hard to keep apart. The same types of lexicogrammatical structures are given for both types. In fact the distinction has, as Lambrecht points out (1994: 61), 'been all but abandoned in the literature', and Bertuccelli Papi remarks in the same vein that semantic presuppositions 'have to be treated as pragmatic phenomena' (1997:11). The types of lexicogrammatical structures mentioned above are the ones we shall look for in the data at hand, even though what we are interested in are not the truth-conditions but the fact that these structures evoke situations, events which are presented by the speaker as background knowledge, propositions whose truth the speaker takes for granted. Thus when a speaker says *I regret that you told these lies* we have a case of semantic presupposition (the truth of the main proposition depends on the truth of the subordinated proposition, and the presupposition that 'you told these lies' survives under negation in *I don't regret that you told these lies*). However, what is more interesting from the point of view of interaction is that in uttering *I regret that you told these lies* the proposition 'you told these lies' is presented as common ground, while the assertion which is at stake is that 'I regret this'. Why is this the crucial point in interaction?

There are two reasons. One is that by encoding something as background, shared knowledge, the speaker at the same time presents a proposition as one whose truth is accepted by the hearer. In other words, pragmatically it is not the logical entailment which is of interest in the analysis of verbal interaction as much as the speaker's assumption of what can be taken for granted. Second, in terms of information structuring it is important that the presupposed material is backgrounded as old information, while the information in the assertion is foregrounded as new. Presuppositions in this way contribute to the structuring of the discourse, and 'determine the point of view from which the text develops' (Bertuccelli Papi 1997:13). Both these factors play a role in the choices which speakers make with regard to what can be encoded as presupposed material.

The pragmatic view of presuppositions obviously entails that they are not static but are negotiated and interactively construed. But it also entails the possibility of exploitation. Bertuccelli Papi puts it as follows:

> It is therefore legitimate to wonder by whom pragmatic presuppositions should be taken for granted and by whom they are granted. The most plausible answer is that speakers treat presuppositions as noncontroversial, even though they may in fact be controversial and not taken for granted by the addressee.
>
> (1997: 12–13)

Similarly, Lambrecht (1994: 65) mentions the 'conscious or unconscious exploitation of presuppositions for special communicative purposes'. The reason why presuppositions are exploitable is that they are harder to challenge. As Lambrecht points out, the 'lie-test' shows that if the addressee wishes to challenge the 'old' information in the presupposition, he/she has to use other strategies than the straightforward 'That's not true'. For example, if the addressee replies *That's not true* to the utterance *I finally met the woman who moved in downstairs* she is challenging that the speaker met her, not that she moved in downstairs. If the addressee wishes to challenge the taken-for-granted nature of the presupposed proposition she would have to say something like *I didn't know that you had a new neighbour* or *What are you talking about?* (1994: 52). In such cases Lambrecht demonstrates that presuppositions are based on the assumption of shared knowledge which is not put up for discussion. There is, however, also the cognitive principle of 'pragmatic accommodation' (Lambrecht 1994: 66), which means that speakers frequently create a new presuppositional situation which can then be the starting-point for the further development of the conversational exchange. If someone says *My car broke down* this does not necessarily imply that the speaker thinks that the addressee knew that she has a car. Even if the addressee did not have this information she will accommodate to the new situation. Such cases of pragmatic accommodation are, however, to be distinguished from what Lambrecht refers to as 'devious' cases of exploitation (1994: 70). The difference lies in the effects aimed at: devious cases are not aimed at conveying information indirectly but at creating 'a fictitious presuppositional situation' for certain rhetorical purposes. In this paper we shall examine which types of presuppositions are used by political speakers and for what purposes.

It is important to emphasise that, whatever the pragmatic effect in specific contexts, certain lexicogrammatical expressions by themselves trigger presuppositions. It is these expressions that we will examine. We shall, on the other hand, not be concerned with pragmatic presupposition in the very broad sense in which it has been used by some, to include all knowledge that language users have and which is brought into the production and comprehension of utterances. Kempson (1975: 166ff.), for instance, refers to the 'Pragmatic Universe of Discourse', defined as the 'body of facts which both speaker and hearer believe they agree on' in a conversation. Mey (1998: 186) claims that a 'serious theory of pragmatic presuppositions (...) inquires *metapragmatically* into the ways in which an utterance is understood in the context of the language users "common ground"'. And Mey further points out that it is then important not only to inquire how people say things but why they say them at all (1998: 187).

In this paper we are focusing on structures that are traditionally subsumed under semantic presupposition, while recognizing that they need to be studied from a pragmatic point of view; both in their exploitation and their understanding. We are not concerned with pragmatic presupposition in the broadest sense, which includes various forms of implicitness such as conversational **implicatures** (whether particularized or generalized).

[...]

5.4 Presupposition in the data

The following extract from the programme *Question Time* illustrates the type of structures and meanings that we are interested in. The issue of debate is the government's plans to introduce top-up fees for university students, for which they could get a loan. David Willits (W), Shadow Secretary, voices the Conservative party's opposition to this plan. David Dimbleby (D) asks the question:

(13) D: David Willits, you were asked whether Tories will be voting in the lobbies for this because your position purports to be that you're against top-up fees.

W: We are against them, we are against them and we're against them because we don't think we want to see our students any other perhaps on the latest proposals 23,000 [pounds'] of debt when they leave university. I don't think that's the right way to go. And as a Conservative I want to encourage people to save and I hear Ministers in the areas that I debate particularly, pensions, things like that, say they've got to encourage people to save. I don't see how getting saddling young people with 23,000 pounds' worth of debt is gonna help them start off in their lives and we should remember how we got into this. We got into this because the government set a target, an arbitrary target for the expansion of universities, that they should reach this target of 50%. Well, I completely agree with what Phylis James said, I don't think it's in the best interests of the people in this country, you do need a better education to set such a target, they need [interruption by moderator].

The first instance of a construction which exploits presupposition is 'I don't see how ....' This expression is synonymous to other expressions such as 'I don't understand how.' The proposition in the subordinated interrogative clause, in this case a *how*-clause, is in such structures presented as known information, since the only unknown element, the missing bit is the element in the *wh*-word (i.e. *how*). In this concrete example, the speaker presents as presupposed that the government is going to 'saddle young people with 23,000 [pounds'] worth of debt'. The term *saddle* is evaluative, which means that the negative judgement is simultaneously absorbed in the message as presupposed and non-negotiable. We have a similar example in the expression 'we should remember', a factive verb. In the above instance, what needs to be remembered is that the government took the wrong decision ('bad for them'), and again an evaluative term, *arbitrary*, is smuggled into the presupposed material.

The next example is from the Swedish nuclear debate. The speaker is Per Unckel (a member of the Conservative Party and in favour of nuclear energy, line 1). The addressee (Ulla Lindström) is a member of the Social Democratic party and is in favour of line 3 and abolishing nuclear energy.

(14) If Ulia Lindström does not trust lines one and two I suppose Ulla Lindström anyhow trusts the developing countries themselves when they shake their heads and wonder how we in Sweden can think about doing away with nuclear energy/when this implies that the pressure on scanty oil resources/which could be of use to the developing countries becomes still harder.

The tactically relevant presupposed material in this passage is in the two *when*-clauses *when they shake their heads (...)* and *when this implies (...)*. The speaker first presents the disapproving attitude of the developing countries towards Sweden's plans to do away with nuclear energy as self evident by putting the proposition in a *when*-clause. Next, at a deeper level of subordination, the proposition that these plans would harm the developing countries by increasing the pressure on resources, is also presented as presupposed in a *when*-clause.

The following extract is also from the Swedish material. The speaker is Per Unckel (line 1):

> (15) the election is about whether in addition to the global energy crisis we have already to a large extent been affected by, we should place additional burdens which may be too heavy for us.

What is presupposed in the above utterance is that there is 'a global energy crisis'. Further, the comparative **referential** term *additional* is relevant here in terms of presupposition, since it presupposes the current existence of a burden (in the form of the 'global energy crisis').

Here follow some more examples of presuppositional structures from the Flemish and Swedish data.

(i) Factive predicates

The presupposition trigger of factive predicates can be illustrated with the following example from the Flemish data, from an interview with Jean-Luc Dehaene (DH), former Prime Minister of Belgium:

> (16) DH: Well I call that continuing the debate after the elections and so I thought that this hype uh was unnecessary ub totally artificial uh and some people apparently did not see that they were thereby undermining the verve of the innovation . . .
> I: Hmm
> DH: . . . and and and the campaign that should revolve around the innovation.

What is presented as new information is that some people apparently did not see something. That they were undermining the innovation is presented as to be taken for granted. The verb 'see' is indeed frequently used as an evidential and has a factive meaning: you can only see what is there. Another example from the same interview:

> (17) DH: But when I see that this position uh damages my party, that through the way in which they handle this in my party they damage themselves, then I have to stop this.

The following is an example from the Swedish data, with Lennart Dahleus (LD) speaking:

> (18) LD: Yes, Per Unkel knows of course that there are more possibilities for serious accidents than those we have discussed, stcam

explosions, <u>and that</u> nuclear power is a dangerous source of energy <u>and that</u> it contains enormous risks ranging from uranium mining to waste disposal that we probably agree on <u>and that</u> there are risks which have no equivalent in other sources of energy.

(ii) Relative clauses

Consider the following extract from the Flemish data:

(19) RD: This of course doesn't alter the fact that the government has approved an investment plan in the long term, a framework within which the NMBS [National Railways Company] must try to become healthy again, and one thing should certainly not be forgotten and that is a very important thing after all …

I: [overlap] Yes

RD: … in a few months the liberalization of this goods transport starts and therefore …

I: [overlap] Precisely. Uhm.

RD: … we must really urgently take a number of measures which …

I: [overlap] Yes

RD: … <u>in so many years were not taken</u> because otherwise competition is going to bit very hard.

I: [overlap] Well, Mr Van Rompuy, it's the previous government's fault again.

VR: Yes, well, we're getting used to that.

On the face of it the relative clause gives information which is quite innocent: there would be no point in taking measures if they had indeed been taken before. The fact that the information is added at all raises the question of why it is added and why it is added in the form it is. The shared knowledge of the world which we need in order to explain the workings of this utterance is that 'in so many years' is a reference to the previous legislature, when the speaker's party was in the opposition and his opponent in the debate was in the government. This utterance is a way of reversing the tables in holding the opponent responsible for 'what is bad'.

The next extract is an example from the Swedish debate. The speaker is Rune Molin, who represents line 2 in the referendum which was neither clearly for nor against nuclear energy.

(20) RM: It is self-evident that if we use our nuclear plants, the possibilities will increase considerably for cutting a dependence on oil <u>which is wrecking the economy of the whole of Swedish society</u>.

Below is another example from the Swedish debate. The speaker is Per Unckel (line 1):

(21) PU: In this nuclear debate there has been one feature which I myself have appreciated much […] and this is a feature characteristic of

many of those who still support line three [..] <u>which implies a demand for a more tolerant society with room for more human concern and closeness</u> [.] if it was this that this referendum was actually about [.] I think that no one would have any doubts about its outcome.

The relative clause carries the presupposition that people in line three want a more tolerant society with room for human concern and closeness, which is obviously positively evaluated. However, the speaker draws attention to this as already known or old information in order to then foreground that this is not what the referendum is about. His own viewpoint is that this desire for a better society is actually a reason to use nuclear energy not to abolish it. What we have here is a 'put down' of line three's position by presenting its argumentation as an overstatement, something everyone agrees on but which does not solve the problem.

Similarly in the next example from the Swedish data, the addressee is obviously assumed to share the presupposition conveyed in the *which*-clause. The speaker is Per Unckel (line 1) and the addressee Lennar Daleus (line 3):

(22) PU: yes Lennart Daleus was surprised that I spoke about oil in a referendum about nuclear energy/the reason is of course that we have decided to use our nuclear reactors in order to open up the possibility of us being forced to reduce our dependence on oil, <u>which is well on the way to getting out of hand</u>.

(iii) Conditional clauses

(23) VR: Do people feel safer?
RD: [overlap] <u>Well of course if</u> in politics, colleague Van Rompuy, you get important people such as Mr Dehaene is an important man, <u>who want to create the impression</u> among the population that unsafety increases …
VR: Oh, It's Mr Dehaene?
RD: –then I think that's bad. What m …
VR: Oh dear, Mr Dehaene creating unsafety.
RD: … what matters is reality …
VR: [overlap] <u>That is that is</u> …
RD: … and I'll give you another example.
VR: [overlap] very new to us, that is very new.
I: Yes, you must conclude, Mr Daems.
VR: [overlap] that is very new.

By presenting the contestable information in the conditional clause of an *if … then* structure which expresses a general truth that information is backgrounded as given and the focus is on the result, namely the value judgement 'I think that's bad'. It will be noted that the speaker makes use of several closing down strategies at the same time: *of course* (concurrence), subordination in an *if* clause in a general truth statement (presupposition), subordination in a relative clause (presupposition).

The following example is from the Swedish data (the speaker is Per Unckel, line 1):

(24) But it is clear that [.] if one now decides to demolish nuclear reactors [.] which correspond to all the energy that we get from water power [.] then this cannot pass without a trace [.] and line three confirms I suppose also this by claiming that there is no other country which is so dependent on nuclear power as Sweden

In (24) the speaker uses the conditional clause structure, which includes the relative clause with presupposed material, to convey the following message: 'if one decides to do away with nuclear energy, one does away with all the energy we get from water power'.

(iv) Existential structures

By 'existential structures' we refer in this context to structures with definite noun phrases triggering the presupposition of the existence of their referents. A very frequent type in political argumentation is an identifying clause with as subject 'the problem'. It is illustrated by the following example:

(25) RV: The problem of Mr Dewinter is that he only …
      DW: It is linked …
      I: [overlap] Yes
      DW: … to it.
      RV: … looks at the past. And we want to do something …
      I: [overlap] Okay
      RV: … about the future and Mr Dewinter refuses to discuss that.
      I: No, he has a clear thesis. His future is: full is full.
      DW: [overlap] immigration stop.

The topic of discussion is immigration and Robert Voorhamme (RV, Socialist party) is attacking Filip Dewinter (DW, Flemish Bloc) for his thesis that the government policy does not work. He uses the expression 'The problem … is that …'. In this type of structure two propositions are semantically presupposed, namely the identified and identifying elements. In this case these are first that there is a problem which the opponent has (the identified element), and second that he only looks at the past (the identifier element). What is new information is thus that the problem is now identified as such. How do we have to understand the workings of this type of utterance? First, 'problem' is a judgement term: whether something is a problem or not is a subjective assessment of a state-of-affairs. Second, 'he only looks at the past' is pragmatically to be understood as a judgement as well, since our knowledge of the world tells us that politicians need to look at the future. This is indeed explicit in the contrast with the speaker's own party ('And we want to do something about the future'). Through this structure a negative judgement (a criticism of the opponent as a politician) is made into presupposed material.

(v) Pseudo-cleft structures

> (26) DW: [overlap] What you are doing …
> AD: [overlap] That's not possible, according to the law …
> DW: [overlap] … by slowing down …
> VR: [overlap] Mr Dewinter
> DW: [overlap] … by slowing down integration …
> AD: [overlap] human rights …
> DW: [overlap] … is …
> AD: [overlap] … says very clearly …
> DW: [overlap] importing …
> I: [overlap] This is incomprehensible. Let's …
> DW: [overlap] … importing backwardness. And that is the wrong position.

There is a lot here which is presupposed in Filip Dewinter's (DW) statement: that the government is slowing down integration and that there is backwardness associated with the Islam culture. What is presented as new information is that this backwardness is imported. Again, value judgements are thus sneaked in as shared knowledge.

In the following example from Swedish there is a reversed pseudo-cleft summing up what has been presupposed in the preceding context. The speaker is Per Unckel (line 1):

> (27) this is actually so self-evident that even line three ought to be able to agree [..] we can use nuclear power being certain that in spite of its risks [.] it is safer than any other alternative which is at our disposal today [..] and this is what is most important

What is presupposed by the pseudo-cleft construction is that nuclear energy is safer than any other alternative type of energy. However the speaker cannot count on the audience's willingness to go along with the assumption that nuclear power is the safest source of energy and with the positive evaluation conveyed by the pseudo-cleft construction.

[…]

6. Discussion of the results and conclusions

In this article we have shown that 'taken-for-grantedness' is frequently manipulated in media political discourse. In doing this we have adduced further evidence of its importance as a rhetorical strategy. The advantages of the strategy mentioned in the literature are its construal of solidarity with like-minded viewers and the difficulty of challenging by those who hold alternative views. However, it has been shown that this strategy is recognized by the opponent for what it is, i.e. as a rhetorical ploy. The question we can ask is why speakers go on using the tactic anyway. One reason is of course that the first advantage still holds, viz. that the solidarity with the like-minded is confirmed and strengthened. It is the like-minded in the first place who are addressed as the electors. Further, there is always the possibility that the yet-to-be persuaded will not recognize the tactic of taking-for-granted as such and accept the implication of general knowledge. Most importantly however, the tactic has value as a rhetorical device which creates a forceful utterance and as such contributes to the image which politicians wish to project for themselves, i.e. that of someone 'in the know' (cf. Simon-Vandenbergen 1996). As such, the strategy becomes a way of making strong value judgements, likely to be challenged but nevertheless giving the speaker a temporary advantage in the battle for scoring with the audience. We may therefore conclude that such tactics are part of the professional discourse, and hence that interpersonal meanings are as much part of the genre as **ideational** ones.

Second, [...] Our discussion has demonstrated the importance of noting the difference between bare assertions in which some point of contention is presented as new information (the non-presupposing option) and those in which it is presented as background, common knowledge (the presupposing option). As such presupposition has tremendous manipulative potential. [...] The nature of media political debate reshapes presuppositional utterances into strong evaluative statements which cry out for challenging. As such presuppositions are two-faced in this genre. On the one hand, they present as presupposed judgements which the speakers know are not shared by their **interlocutors** and which they know will get challenged. The rhetorical effect is, however, in the saying itself. On the other hand, the presuppositions will work in the 'normal' way with at least part of the television audience, i.e. they will simply be accepted.

Third, we found that similar tactics were used in the British, Flemish and Swedish data. This suggests that the rules of interaction are largely similar in the genre in these cultural contexts. The Swedish data differed from the British and Flemish ones in that the debate was of a more formal and more strictly regulated type, and the rhetorical strategies differed accordingly. The similarities can partly be explained from similar views on linguistic **ideologies** and on how political debate works, what politicians are supposed to do and how the media handle political discussion. However, this aspect is in need of further study on the basis of more and culturally more varied data.

Appendix: Examples in the original languages Flemish and Swedish

(14) PU: om < ulla lindström> inte litar på linjerna ett och två så kan väl < ulla lindström> ändå lita på uländerna själva när dom skakar på huvudet och undrar hur vi i sverige kan överväga att avveckla kärnkraften [.] när detta innebär att trycket på knappa oljeresurser [.] som skulle kunna komma uländerna till del blir ändå hårdare

(15) PU: [.] valet gäller om vi ovanpå den globala energikris vi redan i så hög utsträckning drabbats av [.] ska lägga ytterligare bördor som kan bli oss över-mäktiga [.]

(16) DH: [overlap]: Wel dat noem ik de het het debat verder zetten na de verkiezingen uh dus ik ik vond deze hype uh voor niets nodig uh totaal artificieel uh en sommige mensen zagen blijkbaar niet in

> dat ze daarmee de de de de schwung van de vernieuwing …
>
> I: [overlap]: Hmm.
>
> DH: … en en en de campagne die rood de vernieuwing moet draaien, dat ze dit eigenlijk aan het ondermijnen waren.
>
> (17) DH: Maar als ik dan zie dat die stelling uh kwade. kwaad berokkent aan mijn partij, dat door de manier waarop dat men daarmee omgaat in mijn partij men zichzelf beschadigt bah dan moet ik daar paal en perk aan zetten.

For the sake of readability, all Dutch and Swedish extracts are given in English translation. The original extracts are added in the Appendix. In the transcripts abbreviations stand for the names of political speakers. The letter I stands for 'Interviewer'. In the Dutch transcripts […] in turn final position indicates that the current speaker is interrupted and […] in turn initial position indicates that the speaker continues his/her utterance after interruption or overlap. The symbol [.] indicates a slight pause. The symbol [..] within a turn indicates a longer pause.

Notes

1   The word *Flemish* is used here to indicate that the programmes were broadcast in Flanders (i.e. on Flemish television) and that they were debates between Flemish politicians. When reference is to the linguistic features we prefer to use the term *Dutch*, a variant of which is spoken in Flanders.
2   The Flemish programmes are weekly debates in which a number of politicians take part and in which various topics are discussed. This explains why the examples from the Flemish data are 'heterogeneous' as far as speakers and topics are concerned. In contrast, all Swedish examples are from one debate, on the topic of nuclear energy. The reason why it is used for illustration, even though it is quite old (1980) is that it was a heated as well as much discussed debate at the time. We do not think that the time gap is relevant to the points we want to illustrate.

References

Bertuccelli Papi, M. (1997) 'Implicitness', in J. Verschueren, J.-O. Ostman, J. Blommacrt and C. Bulcaen (eds.), *Handbook of Pragmatics*, Amsterdam: John Benjamins, pp. 1–29.

Blommaert, J. and Bulcaen, C. (eds.), (1997) *Political Linguistics*, Belgian Journal of Linguistics 11, Amsterdam: John Benjamins.

Caffi, C. (1998) 'Presupposition, pragmatic', in J. Mey (ed.), *Concise Encyclopedia of Pragmatics*, Amsterdam: Elsevier, pp. 751–758.

Clayman, S. and Heritage, J. (2002) *The News Interview: Journalists and Public Figures on the Air*, Cambridge: Cambridge University Press.

Fairclough, N. (1995) *Media Discourse*, London: Arnold.

—— (2001) *Language and Power*, second edition, Oxford: Blackwell.

Greatbatch, D. (1992) 'On the management of disagreement between news interviewees', in P. Drew and J. Hertitage (eds.), *Talk at Work: Interaction in Institutional Settings*, Cambridge: Cambridge University Press, pp. 268–301.

Harris, S. (1991) 'Evasive action: How politicians respond to questions in political interviews', in P. Scannell (ed.), *Broadcast Talk*, London: Sage, pp. 76–99.

Hirsch, R. (1989) *Argumentation, Information and Interaction. Studies in Face-to-Face Interactive Argumentation under Different Turn-Taking Conditions*, Department of Linguistics, Göteborg University.

Kempson, R.M. (1975) *Presupposition and the Delimitation of Semantics*, Cambridge: Cambridge University Press.

Lambrecht, K. (1994) *Information Structure and Sentence Form*, Cambridge: Cambridge University press.

Lauerbach, G. (2004) 'Political interviews as hybrid genre', *Text*, 24(3): 353–397.

Lewis, D. (2004) 'Mapping adversative coherence relations in English and French', *Languages in Contrast*, 5(1): 35–48.

Mey, J.L. (1998) *Pragmatics: An Introduction*, second edition, Oxford: Blackwell.

Sbisà, M. (1999) 'Ideology and the persuasive use of presupposition', in J. Verschueren (ed.), *Language and Ideology: Selected Papers from the 6th International Pragmatics Conference*, Antwerp: International Pragmatics Association, pp. 492–509.

Simon-Vandenbergen, A.M. (1992) 'The interactional utility of *of course* in spoken discourse', *Occasional Papers in Systemic Linguistics*, 6: 213–226.

—— (1996) 'Image-building through modality: The case of political interviews', *Discourse and Society*, 7(3): 389–415.

—— (1997) 'Modal (un)certainty in political discourse: A functional account', *Language Sciences*, 19(4): 341–356.

—— and Aijmer, K. (2005) 'The discourse marker *of course* in British political interviews and its Flemish and Swedish counterparts: A comparison of persuasive tactics', in A. Betlen and M. Dannerer (eds.), *Beiträge zur Dialogforschung, Selected Papers from the 9th IADA Conference Salzburg 2003*, Part 2 Media: Tubingen: Nicmeyer, pp. 105–112.

van Dijk, T.A. (1998a) *Ideology. A Multidisciplinary Approach*, London: Sage.

—— (1998b) 'Opinions and ideologics in the press', in A. Bell and P. Garrett (eds.), *Approaches to Media Discourse*, Oxford: Blackwellpp. 21–63.

Wodak, R., de Cillia, R., Reisigl, M., Liebhart, K., Hofstälter, K. and Kargl, M. (eds.), (2000) *The Discursive Construction of National Identity*, Edinburgh: Edinburgh University Press.

PART FOUR

Language and the media

Anthea Irwin

INTRODUCTION

THE MEDIA IS important in informing the public of all manner of events that may have significance for their lives. While part of this is informational, there are also **ideological** processes at work. The public are increasingly involved in the production of news, however they have always had a role as audience members and even as being represented in broadcasts.

The first reading gives you the opportunity to further explore the nuances and complexities of representations of race and ethnicity in news media by providing you with a case study. Irwin talks in her chapter about her research into representations of asylum in the Scottish press. This reading explores representations of minority ethnic people indigenous to or permanently resident in Scotland. The reading is a case study discussing coverage of a young girl named Misbah Rana moving from Scotland to Pakistan. The move is represented variously across time and across news titles as a 'disappearance', an 'abduction' and a 'voluntary flight'. The presuppositions that are made about Misbah and her family, in the early days of the coverage especially, suggest significant stereotyping of the Scottish Pakistani community. It is a good example of how dominant **discourses** about different groups in society are repeatedly reproduced, and causes us to think about what the implications of this might be for both news producers and news consumers. We are reminded that stereotyping or prejudice does not have to be conscious to be problematic. Indeed, during the latter part of the week of reporting that makes up the case study, journalists begin to comment not on the events themselves, but on the earlier coverage of the events, self-critiquing the ways in which their industry has engaged in unconscious stereotyping and prejudicial discourse use.

The second reading explores the Japanese subcultural identity known as 'Kogal' (*kogyaru*), considering what it is visually, linguistically and behaviourally that sets this identity apart from other identities in Japanese society. Specifically, Laura Miller examines how this identity challenges norms of adolescent femininity, and how it is evidence of, unusually in Japanese society, young women setting trends. These challenges appear to be particularly salient and as such are often reported in the media. Thus, 'Kogals are the focus of intense public concern, and media discourses reflect an ongoing obsession with locating and delimiting them' (Miller p. 126).

Kogal style includes 'loose socks', bleached hair, distinctive make-up including light coloured eyeliner and lipstick, short high school uniform skirts, and playful incorporation of anything fake or **kitsch**. The last feature makes the identity somewhat egalitarian because girls do not have to have a lot of money to achieve the look. Kogals are also heavy users of technology, and have developed group specific uses of this technology. They visit *purikura* booths that produce sheets of photo stickers which they then write on in creative ways; both the pictures and the writing are often sexually suggestive or masculine, both of which challenge dominant ideas about what it is to be a young woman in Japan. Such graffiti in a relatively private sphere is a particularly intimate way of expressing identity (see also Carrington 2009). They also have developed their own **emoticons**; something especially common more an increasing number of new technology users (Crystal 2008).

The Japanese language includes gendered forms (where the form of word a speaker should use depends on whether they are make or female), and **honorific** forms, which differentiate people by status. Kogals regularly break both of these norms and could be seen as changing the definition of femininity. Whilst Kogals are not the only group who do this, they are reported to be the group that does it in the most extreme ways. Such changes and challenges to gendering in Japanese continue.

Miller highlights the level of media comment on Kogal behaviour and language, which suggests the Kogal identity is a recognizable cultural phenomenon. Some media coverage likens Kogal language to low status **dialects** of Japanese. Some coverage suggests it comes from a fascination with American popular culture, which is categorized negatively as cultural imperialism, but this is challenged by those (e.g. Suzuki 2002) who say that it refers not to foreign culture, but to 'coolness'. Some coverage constructs somewhat of a '**moral panic**' around Kogals, expressing extreme concern that they are destroying either the Japanese language or Japanese norms of femininity. A minority of coverage recognizes Kogals' identity construction positively, and some anime (Japanese animation) representations of Kogals show them as empowered.

Miller makes clear that Kogal challenges to Japanese norms do not come from any engagement with radical or feminist politics, and she points to some irony in that their 'particular forms of resistance tie them to beauty work that requires increased consumption' (Miller 2000); Kogals are, nonetheless, providing some degree of challenge to Japanese male-centred society.

In the final reading, Joanna Thornborrow explores the specific examples of language use in public participation programmes (this genre includes discussion programmes and radio phone-ins) to see both how participants are positioned by presenters and, more importantly, how participants position themselves. She looks at previous work that differentiates completely between 'expert' talk and the talk of 'ordinary' people, which views the latter as more '**authentic**'; what Thornborrow brings to the discussion is a suggestion that 'ordinary' people actually construct an authentic *public* identity for themselves on public participation programmes.

Whilst presenters tend to introduce experts according to their public status, they tend to introduce ordinary or 'lay' people as simply 'next speaker'. The lay people themselves use strategies to construct or reinforce the relevance of their being a participant on the programme, however. One strategy is to provide information about their status relevant to the topic, for example career, familial role, medical condition, or expertise in a pastime, before going on to make their main point. Participants may also refer to previous participation in the same programme; this is more likely to happen on a radio phone-in show. Thornborrow shows that experts and presenters also validate the relevance of this self-positioning by the participants. Experts allow participants to provide the information before attempting to take the **floor**, and, if the information is *not* provided, presenters will tend to ask for it before allowing the conversation to continue. Finally Thornborrow introduces us to a type of speaker status that cuts through the binary division between experts and lay people. In this case, rather than speakers introducing *themselves* with information that positions them as a relevant participant in relation to the expert's status or knowledge, instead the *host* positions the participant as having something to say that is not only relevant to the interaction in general, but specific to the participant her/himself, thus setting her/him apart from all other speakers and shifting the interaction on to a new topic or sub-topic, where usually it would be an expert speaker who would do this.

A key conclusion of Thornborrow's article is that it is more useful to think of all talk as constructed within situations in ways that are appropriate to those situations, rather than particular kinds of talk having inherent 'authenticity' and others not. In other words, it is more useful to think about 'authenticating' talk than 'authentic' talk.

Issues to consider

1. Is a 'true' of objective account of any event possible? Are there some topics or people who are more likely to be misrepresented by media reports? Why do you think this is the case?
2. People are now participating in the media in new ways. What are some of these new roles? Do they improve the state of the media? Do these ways of participating improve the access that the public has to power?
3. Some events and topics are considered more 'newsworthy' than others. What kinds of issues routinely merit comment? Which do not? Why do you think this is the case?
4. It is more usual to discuss negative representations in the media than positive ones. However, there are arguably many positive images disseminated by the media. Can you think of any? Why are they positive? Why are they chosen to be commented upon? Do you think such positive representation is good for those who are involved?

Further reading

For more on the language of the media, including details on how to analyze the media, see the following:

Bell, A. (1991) *The Language of News Media*, Oxford: Blackwell.

Fowler, R. (1991) *Language in the News: Discourse and Ideology in the Press*, London: Routledge.
Fairclough, N. (1995) *Media Discourse*, London: Edward Arnold.

The representation of race and ethnicity in the media is of ongoing concern. The ideologies and **stereotypes** which are used are well described, even though the focal ethnicity changes from time to time. See also Part 8.

Morris, R. (2000) 'Gypsies, travellers and the media: press regulation and racism in the UK', *Communications Law*, 5(6): 213–219.
Van Dijk, T.A. (1998), 'Opinions and ideologies in the press', in A. Bell and P. Garrett (eds.), *Approaches to Media Discourse*, Oxford: Blackwell, pp. 21–63.
Welsh Media Group (2002) *Welcome or Over-reaction: Refugees and Asylum Seekers in the Media*, Oxford: Oxfam UK Poverty Programme.
Westminster Media Forum (2007) *Ethnicity and the Media*, Bagshot: Westminster Forum Projects, Ltd.

Changes in language in Japanese, especially with respect to gender, have been documented in the following.

Okamoto Shigeko (1995) '"Tasteless" Japanese: less "feminine" speech among young Japanese women', in Hall, K. and Bucholz M. (eds.), *Gender Articulated*, London: Routledge, pp. 297–325.
Reynolds, K.A. (1998) 'Female speakers of Japanese in transition', in Coates, J. (1998) *Language and Gender: A Reader*, Oxford: Blackwell. Also in Coates, J. and Pichler, P. (eds.), (2011) *Language and Gender: A Reader*, second edition, Oxford: Blackwell.
Takano, S. (2005) 'Re-examining linguistic power: strategic uses of directives by professional Japanese women in positions of authority and leadership', *Journal of Pragmatics*, 37(5): 633–666.
Wetzel, P. (1998) 'Are powerless communication strategies the Japanese norm?' in Coates J. (1998) *Language and Gender: A Reader*, Oxford: Blackwell. Also in Coates, J. and Pichler, P. (eds.), (2011) *Language and Gender: A Reader*, second edition, Oxford: Blackwell.

For representations of women, see Part 5.

Suggestions for further viewing

Beautiful Losers (2008) Aaron Rose, Joshua Leonard (co-director).
State of Play (film, 2009) Kevin Macdonald.
State of Play (miniseries, 2003) BBC.
Wag the Dog (1997) Barry Levinson.

References

Carrington, V. (2009) 'I write, therefore I am: texts in the city', *Visual Communication*, 8(4): 409–425.

Crystal, D. (2008) *Txting: the Gr8 Db8*, Oxford: Oxford University Press.

Miller, L. (2000) 'Media typifications and hip *Bijin*', *US-Japan Women's Journal*, 19: 176–205.

Suzuki, Y. (2002) *Nihongo-no-deki-nai-Nihonjin* (Japanese who can't use Japanese correctly), Tokyo: Chuokoron-Shinsha.

Chapter 9

Anthea Irwin

RACE AND ETHNICITY IN THE MEDIA

Introduction

THE BULK OF this chapter will analyse in detail two examples of recent press coverage: one of asylum and in particular unrest in detention, and the other the voluntary flight/abduction of Misbah Rana from Scotland to Pakistan. The two case studies are interesting in and of themselves, but they also throw up more general questions.

　[...]

Discourse analysis

The analysis which follows identifies press coverage as a site of struggle where competing **discourses** vie for dominance and a simplistic distinction between positive and negative portrayals is problematised. It is indebted to the work of Michel Foucault (1980) on **ideology** and power, and to a number of analyses of lexical representation and narrative structure. Fowler (1991) draws our attention to the implications of word choice for how a news actor is viewed, and the implications of transitivity – the verb processes employed – for where responsibility is seen to lie. Fairclough (1995) talks about 'degrees of presence', the fact that different aspects of an event can be foregrounded, backgrounded or presupposed. Van Dijk (1998), whose previous 1989 work is one of the seminal texts on how race and ethnicity are treated in the media, brings in a relational aspect when he observes a common relational pattern in news discourse that he labels the 'ideological square'. This consists of an 'us' group and a 'them' group with the 'good' and 'bad' acts of each being variously highlighted or mitigated. Bell (1991), who has been a working journalist, points out that news narratives, unlike most informal oral narratives, are not chronological, and that it is therefore possible for the order in which events have occurred, and by extension the cause-and-effect relationships between different events, to be 'lost'.

[…]

Case study 2: Misbah Rana

The flight of a young girl from Scotland to Pakistan in the summer of 2006 and the ensuing custody battle threw into question the Scottish media's approach to race and ethnicity. This story ran on and off in the Scottish press for five months, culminating in reports of Misbah (I will refer to her by this name as this is the name by which she has said she wishes to be known) remaining with her father in Pakistan after an out-of-court settlement. The case study will analyse the first week of reporting as it is in some ways a **microcosm** of the coverage as a whole. It illustrates in two ways that imbalance or prejudice do not have to be conscious to be problematic. First, the information that came to light from day three onwards caused journalists and audiences to reassess how they had 'read' the situation and as such provides a good argument for the existence of dominant discourses, and different ones in different societies. Second, within a week of the beginning of the coverage, parts of the press had embarked on a kind of 'metareporting' about *how* the case had been reported and whether/how this was problematic, and as such is an example of that which was backgrounded being forcibly foregrounded (see Fairclough) in order to make sense of it. Again a comprehensive analysis of the full coverage is not possible, so I have chosen to focus on Scotland-based papers due to the relative prominence of the story and the fact that the interplay between Scottish national identity and other aspects of the story is one of the most striking elements of the analysis.

Day one: identities

The first time the story appears in the Scottish press is on 28 August on the front page of the *Evening Times* with the headline 'Girl, 12 "*stolen*" from *Scots home*'; world wide hunt amid fears youngster was kidnapped and flown out to Pakistan'. Although the word 'stolen' is placed in quotation marks, we are never told who the source of this description was, thus allowing it to 'stand alone' and potentially have greater implications for how the reader engages with the story. Although having a Scots home is not synonymous with being Scots, that national identity is certainly implied and is placed front and centre by appearing in the headline. We find out over the course of the coverage that Misbah has dual citizenship of the UK and Pakistan, and does not consider *herself* Scots. Her name, 'Molly Campbell', appears in the fourth sentence and in a highlighted box of text. It is not until the seventh sentence that we are told that she 'is also known as Misbah Iram Ahmed Rana'. This pattern of giving Misbah the name 'Molly Campbell' and including 'Misbah' later as an alternative occurs for several days across papers.

Day two: generalisations

The Scotsman carries the story on 29 August. Different stories appear in the first and third editions of the paper. The first edition story also uses a claim in the headline: 'Girl of 12 taken to Pakistan by father for arranged marriage, says family'. The claim is sourced in this story, but the 'family' is in fact one person, Misbah's maternal grandmother. We do read in the lead sentence that she was '*allegedly* abducted', but this pattern of portraying as a fact in the headline that which is alleged later in the report is repeated in many of the stories. The headline in the third edition is 'Hunt for girl, 12, taken from school and flown to Pakistan by father' and the arranged marriage claim does not appear in this story, suggesting that it may already be in doubt.

On 29 August the *Evening Times* and the *Daily Record* also use the grandmother's claim for headline material. The *Evening Times* headline reads '*Child bride fears* over "kidnap" girl'. Although 'kidnap' appears in quotation marks, 'child bride fears' does not and is arguably given more gravity than it deserves as the fears too are based on the opinion of one person. The *Daily Record's* headline is 'Girl of 12 *kidnapped to wed man*, 25; Exclusive: gran *tells* of Molly's abduction'. Both the abduction and the alleged plan for Molly to enter an arranged marriage appear in this headline, and in the first two sentences of the story, as fact. The use of the word 'tells' is also problematic as Molly's grandmother was not an eyewitness to her granddaughter leaving Lewis. In the sixth sentence we read that Molly's 'given name' is 'Misbah Iram Ahmed Rana', which arguably gives the Islamic name more status than it has had in other coverage.

The Herald runs with the story on the same day with the headline '*Abducted island girl* may now be in Pakistan; Pupil vanishes with sister'. The abduction is presented as fact and national identity is once again front and centre as she is referred to as an 'island girl'. Indeed, focusing on the fact that she lived on Lewis could be seen to reinforce the 'us and them' pattern: there is arguably more symbolic distance between Pakistan and a 'traditional' Scottish location such as Lewis than there is between Pakistan and Scotland in general. This description is surprising, given that the highlight box tells us 'they had moved to Lewis recently'. Having the adjective 'abducted' modify the description of Misbah presents it as fact. Both of these elements of description are somewhat contradictory to the fact that this is the first story to place Misbah's Islamic name in the same sentence as her Scottish one, albeit the Scottish name comes first and the status of the Islamic name is perhaps lower than it has been in other stories as we are told she was '*previously* known as Misbah Rana'.

The only paper not to have the possibility of abduction, emotive or otherwise, in its headline is the *Press and Journal*. The headline on 29 August reads 'Police hunt for missing girl leads to Pakistan'.

Day three: contradictions

The focus of the story shifts on 30 August. *The Scotsman* again runs a slightly different story in its first and third editions, with both headlines focusing on Misbah's mother Louise Campbell's plea for the return of her daughter. This is an interesting choice of focus for the headlines, given that it begins to become apparent on this day that Misbah may have travelled to Pakistan willingly, which is arguably more newsworthy. This suggestion comes both from friends of her father who speak to the media *and* from her mother's statement which includes the words, 'I would like to say to Molly that we miss her so much and we beg her to come home to us. She has to know that she is not in any trouble and we are not angry; we just want her home.' There is a nuanced shift away from the suggestion of abduction from the first-edition headline to the third-edition headline: they read '*Bring* my daughter home to me, begs mother' and 'We miss Molly so much, we just *want* her home'.

The *Evening Times* of 30 August contains two contradictory stories on the subject. The first, on page two, has the headline 'Mum in tearful plea over *abducted Molly*'. Once again we see the abduction presented as fact in the headline, by using the adjective 'abducted' to modify 'Molly', and a shift to saying it is 'alleged' in the lead sentence. The second story, on page six, has the headline 'Girl, 12, "begged" to be taken to Pakistan; Glasgow friend tells of pleas by youngster to dad'. It covers the claims of former Glasgow councillor Bashir Maan, a friend of Misbah's father Sajad Rana. It seems odd for the paper not to have conflated these two stories, or placed them on the same page. The practicalities and time constraints of producing a newspaper notwithstanding, these editorial choices do not shift the focus as far as the content itself would suggest it could have been.

The first time the possibility that this is not an abduction is explicitly stated in a headline is in *The Herald* on 31 August. It reads 'Pakistani father "did not abduct daughter"; New claims by friends over island girl's disappearance'. The story is based on Bashir Maan's claims and introduces for the first time the information that, after her parents' split, Misbah had lived with her father until 2002.

Days four and five: heroes and villains

On 31 August and 1 September a number of stories focus on Glasgow Central MP Mohammad Sarwar having agreed to meet with Misbah in Pakistan, but again the framing is rather different in different papers. The *Daily Record*'s headline is 'I'll *find* Molly; Exclusive: MP Sarwar *pledges to help* mum of girl, 12, *snatched* to Pakistan'. This headline has echoes of traditional narratives (Propp 1968), with Mr Sarwar portrayed as a hero figure being sent out on a quest by Louise Campbell to win Misbah back from the villain who has 'snatched' her. This is rather at odds with *The Scotsman's* coverage which once again includes different headlines in the first and third editions, 'MP hopes to *meet missing* schoolgirl in Pakistan today' and 'MP in Pakistan as an "*honest broker*" to *meet missing* girl'. The second of these shifts the tone to neutral as regards the conflict between Misbah's parents, as does the Aberdeen *Press and Journal*'s 'MP flies to meet Molly as *row rages*'. Contrary to Mr Sarwar going on a quest to 'find' Misbah, we hear of a 'private meeting' having already been arranged. Sarwar also dismisses the arranged marriage claims, which leads to the headline in *The Herald*: 'Sarwar to meet "abducted" girl in Pakistan; Child bride claims rejected'.

Days six and seven: battles

The *Press and Journal*'s use of 'row' foreshadows the next shift: on 2 and 3 September, a large proportion of what is written frames the situation in military discourse, as a 'battle'. Some examples of headlines are: 'Custody *war* as Molly begs to stay with dad; *Tug-of-love* girl, 12, insists she wants to stay in Pakistan' (*Evening Times*, 2 September, p. 6); 'It was my choice. I like it here and want to stay with my father'; 'Parents prepare for *international custody battle* over daughter' (*The Herald*, 2 September, p. 5); 'Molly wins *battle* to stay with dad; judge says girl remains in Pakistan till custody is decided' (*Sunday Mail*, 3 September, p. 2).

'Battle' is of course a common metaphor to use for custody situations, but the front-page coverage in the *Press and Journal* on 2 September extends the discourse in an interesting way. The lead sentence following the headline 'Call me Misbah – and I was not kidnapped' reads 'Schoolgirl Molly Campbell sat *shoulder-to-shoulder* with her father yesterday as she faced the world's media in Pakistan and insisted: I was not kidnapped'. 'Shoulder-to-shoulder' has immediate echoes of its high-profile use during the Iraq war and adds gravity to the situation.

Conclusions: empowering, distancing, metareporting and historicising

It is apparent from the above that many of the news headlines on these two days following Misbah's press conference are presented as direct quotes from Misbah herself. In the headline of its story on page nine on 2 September, the *Daily Record* reinforces this by using upper case and referring to Misbah 'speaking out': 'MY REAL NAME IS MISBAH … I DON'T WANT TO GO HOME; SNATCH PROBE GIRL SPEAKS OUT'. There are two ways to view this trend: does it empower Misbah and give her the voice she has not had thus far? Or does it allow papers to avoid deciding on the wording for headlines that, at least for some of them, are in blatant contradiction to what they had been reporting just a few days earlier?

September 2 and 3, a Saturday and Sunday, see various opinion pieces alongside the latest news reports. The opinion pieces display a range of reporting strategies: distancing strategies similar to the use of Misbah's own words (for example, the *Sunday Mail*'s 'Opinion: Molly must have a say in her future'); discussions about the complexities of the story and Misbah's identity; and a strategy I have labelled 'metareporting', that is reporting which critiques how the press covered the story when it initially broke. It is interesting to view these opinion themes in relation to the previous and current coverage in the papers in which they appear.

On 2 September *The Scotsman's* comment headline contradicts its news headline somewhat. On page four we read the headline 'I was *not kidnapped*, I just want to live with my family', while on page twenty-three we read '*Abduction* leaves a trail of heartache in its wake'. Closer scrutiny demonstrates that the news story is very quote-led, drawing on both Misbah's press conference and an interview with her brother Omar, thus avoiding the need to take a stance on the issue. The paper instead positions itself in a broader sense by using a discourse of traditional family values. The comment piece frames Misbah as a 'victim of marriage breakdown' and paints her as a rather fickle child whose statement must be 'taken with a pinch of salt'. This disempowerment of Misbah continues with the final words of the piece, which play down the gravity of the situation and focus squarely on the centrality of the mother/daughter relationship: 'there will likely come a time, in the not too distant future, when she will want her mum. And what will happen then? Because Lahore is an awfully long way from the Isle of Lewis'. The focus on the personal and the emotional arguably allows the paper to take a position on the issue in a roundabout way: it empathises with Louise Campbell's heartache at the 'abduction; or at least seeming abduction' and likens Louise's situation to that of Lady Catherine Meyer, wife of the former British ambassador to the US, whose sons *were* abducted. The traditional family values discourse is continued in one of the more general comment pieces, 'World of the week', which focuses on 'family' and frames the Misbah story as shattering a family unit.

It is notable that many of the pieces over these two days, both news and opinion, focus on the contestation about Misbah's name. It has become a metaphor for the whole case, and the papers cement its place in public discourse. *The Herald*, which takes a 'metareporting' approach to its coverage over these two days, highlights the name issue in the headline of almost every story it runs on the story. Its front page headline on 2 September is 'Girl wants to stay with her father; MY NAME ISN'T MOLLY, IT IS MISBAH', and the lead sentence of a feature on page fourteen is 'For Molly Campbell of Stornoway, read Misbah Iram Ahmed Rana of Lahore'. The feature is headlined 'A child caught in the middle; Custody decisions do not belong in press conferences', an example of 'metareporting' in that it critiques media involvement in the case, both invited and uninvited. The *Sunday Herald* on 3 September carried an openly critical piece on page six headlined 'Kidnap claim "shows media bias"; RACISM: PRESS UNDER SCRUTINY; Anger at newsrooms' treatment of Misbah Rana case' and an opinion piece on page thirty-nine headlined 'Molly Misbah; A story of our times; When a young girl went missing from her mother's home in Scotland and turned up with her father in Pakistan, the world jumped to conclusions. The wrong ones. Neil Mackay separates fact from fiction'.

This final headline is interesting on several levels and provides an appropriate conclusion to the wider discussion. First, its word choice and structure provide a microcosm of the case as a whole: the two names and the two parents are given presupposed equal status and it is pointed out that 'the world' has thus far not given them this. Second, it positions the *Sunday Herald* in opposition to 'the world' suggesting that it did not engage in jumping to 'the wrong conclusions'. And third, the words 'a story of our times' historicise the Misbah case and present the case as a metaphor for the press treatment of race and ethnicity in this country. This is perhaps unfair, given some of the good practice we have seen in the discussion of asylum coverage, or at least good practice relative to the UK more widely, but undoubtedly the case of Misbah Rana has and will continue to cause journalists to be conscious of the discourses they employ. It also reminds us all of the ideological force of language, and the responsibility which comes along with that.

Although it has not been possible to explore broadcast coverage of both cases here, certainly as far as Misbah Rana is concerned, it would appear to have followed a similar pattern to press coverage, in that it began with a suggestion of abduction, then called that into question and finally moved into 'metareporting' about its own coverage of the story. Further analysis in this area would be welcome.

References

Bell, A. (1991) *The Language of News Media*, Oxford: Blackwell.

Fairclough, N. (1995) *Media Discourse*, London: Edward Arnold.

Foucault, M. (1980) *Power/Knowledge: Selected Interviews and Other Writings, 1972–1977*, New York: Pantheon Books.

Fowler, R. (1991) *Language in the News: Discourse and Ideology in the Press*, London: Routledge.

Propp, V. (1968) *Morphology of the Folktale*, Austin, TX: University of Texas Press.

Van Dijk, T.A. (1998), 'Opinions and ideologies in the press', in A. Bell and P. Garrett (eds.), *Approaches to Media Discourse*, Oxford: Blackwell, pp. 21–63.

Chapter 10

Laura Miller

THOSE NAUGHTY TEENAGE GIRLS: JAPANESE KOGALS, SLANG, AND MEDIA ASSESSMENTS

[...]

Introduction

AMONG THE MANY subcultural identities available to Japanese youth, perhaps none has become the focus of such mainstream anxiety and voyeuristic interest as the young women known as Kogals (*kogyaru*). This article examines critiques and displays of the Kogal, with a particular focus on the way her gender-transgressing identity and language style challenge longstanding norms of adolescent femininity. In addition to providing evidence of Japanese **heterogeneity** and documenting the current struggle for female self-definition, I argue that Kogal subculture is significant as an unusual case of female-centered coolness at the forefront of cultural and linguistic trend setting.

[...]

Girl typologies

The English word *girl*, transliterated as either *gyaru* or *gâru*, is a vintage loanword in Japan. In addition to the prewar Moga, during the 1920s there were Kiss Girls and Boat Girls who exchanged kisses for a modest fee (Nakayama 1995), as well as movie theater ushers called Cinema Girls (*kinema gâru*) and female clerks known as Shop Girls (*shoppu gâru*, Kitazawa 1925). As the 1950s drew to an end, independent and pleasure-seeking postwar young women were called Mambo Girls (*mambo gâru*) (*Time* 1959: 24). By 1956, as Jan Bardsley (2000) notes, there were types called Salary Girls (*sararii gâru*), women who focused on their work lives instead of making plans for marriage. Salary Girls prefigured the postwar Business Girls (*bijinesu gâru*), later renamed Office Ladies or OL (*ôeru*) in the 1980s when women's magazine editors realized there might be an unintended negative meaning for the earlier term. They discovered that *Business Girl* was used in American slang to refer to prostitutes and were concerned that foreigners and Japanese men involved in sex tourism might confuse an office worker with a sex worker. Other Girls of the era were the Body-Conscious Girls (*bodikon gyaru*), young women who worked hard at creating sexy and fit bodies, and the flamboyant Stage Girls (*otachidai gyaru*) who danced in nightclubs. By the 1990s there was the Three Negatives Girl (*san nai gyaru*), who did not work, did not get married, and did not bear children (*hatarakanai, kekkon shinai, kodomo o umaranai*). The Old Guy Girls (*oyaji gyaru*) were young women who affected middle-aged male pastimes such as playing golf and going to pachinko parlors and race tracks. Akihiko Yonekawa (1996: 151–153) also lists the 1986 term Three-*Beru* Girl (*san beru gyaru*), derived from the word for *three* combined with the verbal ending *beru*, for girls who think only about eating, talking, and getting into trouble (*taberu, shaberu, toraberu*), and the 1991 term Old Bag Girl (*ofukuro gyaru*), which refers to a young woman who is totally dependent on her mother. A recent type is the Pajamas Girl (*jinbei gyaru*), a young woman who lazes around the house wearing old-fashioned old-men's-style pajamas.

The unrestrained and creative **hybridity** of Kogal language and fashion, in which diverse global elements are freely incorporated, is viewed as irresistibly cool by some Japanese observers. Catherine Driscoll (2002: 293) suggests that *Kogal* is derived from English *cool girl*, with the "inflection of 'colored girl' as well," but this does not accord with Japanese phonology. If the source were *cool girl*, the form would be *kûru gyaru*; if *colored girl*, it would be *karâdo gyaru*. It has also been suggested that *Kogal* is derived from the **morpheme** *ko* (small) (Jolivet 2001; Watrous 2000). I prefer another candidate **etymology**—that it was coined around 1990 by workers at discos and music clubs, who called the under-18 crowd *kôkôsei gyaru* (High School Girls), a term that was later clipped to *kogyaru*.

The label *Kogal* is most often elicited because of a girl's appearance and consumption patterns, which may overshadow her linguistic construction of a subcultural identity. The Kogal aesthetic (see Figure 10.1) is not straightforward, for it often combines elements of calculated cuteness and studied ugliness. The style began in the early 1990s when high-school girls developed a look made up of "loose socks" (knee-length socks worn hanging around the ankles), bleached hair, distinct makeup, and short school-uniform skirts. Kogal fashion emphasizes fakeness and **kitsch** through playful appropriation of the elegant and the awful. Kogal tackiness is also egalitarian because girls from any economic background or with any natural endowment may acquire the look, which is not true of the conservative, cute style favored by girls who conform to normative femininity.

[…]

Figure 10.1: The Kogal aesthetic (source: photo from *Egg* magazine, August 2000).

Unregulated cultural production

Since the 1990s, teenage girls in Japan have dominated the market for brand-name goods, cell phones, cameras, and a variety of other photographic products. According to the Nomura Research Institute, 95.7 percent of Japanese women under the age of 20 had a cell phone or a pager in 2003 (Asahi Shimbun 2003: 176). Kogals' heavy use of technology has resulted in some interesting script innovations. One is the development of novel **emoticons**, combinations of punctuation marks and accent marks to express affect in telephone text messages and e-mail. The emoticons, called *kao moji* (face characters), are more extensive and complex than the American "smiley-face" emoticons typically created with a colon and a closing parenthesis to resemble a side-ways face, and are processed differently: American emoticons are read horizontally; Japanese ones are read vertically. A few examples are *wai* ('wow') \(808)/, *itai* ('ouch') (>_<), *hakushu* ('applause') (^^) / /, and *kikoenai* ('I can't hear you') <<(-·-)>>.

Kogals are also credited with creating a unique text message code for their cell phones, now referred to as *gyaru moji* (Gal characters). It is a basic substitution system, in which parts or combinations of characters, mathematical symbols, or Cyrillic letters are used in place of the Japanese syllabic characters; there are several alternatives commonly used for each syllable. For example, rather than being written in either the Japanese *katakana* or *hiragana* syllabaries, the syllable *ni*, normally written as k in *hiragana* or = in *katakana*, is written as (=, |=, L=, or I=. The following chart lists three expressions in standard script and in *gyaru moji* versions:

Standard Script	Gal moji
超 かわいい	千ょカゝワヽ
chô-kawaii	
(totally cute)	
チビポラ	千ヒ″ ホ○яа
chibi-pora	
(mini-Polaroid camera)	
なかよし	ナょカゝよ∪
nakayoshi	
(good friends)	

One of the more noteworthy examples of Kogal consumption is the phenomenon of *purikura* booths, from *purinto kurabu* (print club), that manufacture strips of small photo stickers, which are used to decorate objects and are exchanged with friends as a form of social currency. Over time, Kogals began to amend their photos with colored ink captions, taboo words, and unusual script elements. Other girls also create graffiti photos, but Kogals are more risqué in their textual expressions. Their graffiti photos contain a remarkable mix of spoofed cuteness and burlesque freakishness that defies gender normativity. Examples 1 through 3 illustrate their unique characteristics.

1. Hがうまい人
   H *ga umai hito*
   (People good at sex)

2. ♡ my board リペア中! ♡
   my board *ripeachû*
   (While repairing my surfboard)

3. 初めての海外トリツプ in カルフォルニア
   *hajimete no kaigai torippu **in** karuforunia*
   (Our first overseas trip in California)

In Example 1, underneath a photo of two Kogals, the boastful phrase *H ga umai hito* (people good at sex) is written in outlined blue characters and a fat letter *H*. The capital letter *H* stands for the term *eitchi*, which has both adjectival and nominal uses. It has been popular since the late 1970s, when it originally referred to *hentai seiyoku* (abnormal sexual desire) and meant "kinky" or "sleazy". Over time it has come to simply mean "naughty" or "sexy". *Eitchi* is also used as a noun for sexual activity and is often paired with the verb *suru* (to do), as in *eitchi ga suru* (do the wild thing, have sex).

The graffiti photos also contain many instances of script mixing. Because it has four writing systems to exploit—Chinese characters, two syllabic scripts (*hiragana* and *katakana*), and the Roman alphabet—Japanese orthography permits extensive expressiveness. In Example 2, written on a photograph of two Kogals sanding a surfboard, the English phrase *my board* is written in the Roman alphabet rather than in *katakana*, whereas part of the word *ripeachû* (repair) is written in *katakana* (the suffix *-chû* 'while' is written in *kanji*). Working on surfboards is usually a male activity, so this writer is also proclaiming her bold gender transgression. In the third example, found on a photograph of three teenagers, the loanword *torippu* (trip) is transliterated into syllabic *katakana*, yet it is followed by the English preposition *in* written in the Roman alphabet. Perhaps these and similar examples constitute a new genre of writing that is the counterpart of oral **code-switching**. In any case, their polygraphic juxtaposition presents an aesthetically pleasing balance and contrast, something seen in many Japanese writing genres (Miller 2003; Stanlaw 2004). Beginning in the mid-1980s, young women began to audaciously use many unconventional orthographic practices. They continue to substitute Roman letters in novel places and liberally use stars, hearts, emoticons, Roman script, and nonnative punctuation such as exclamation points, ellipses, ampersands, and word spacing in their writings (Horiuchi 1985; Ishino 1985; Kataoka 2003, 1997). Japanese texts originally contained little punctuation, but during the early twentieth century, writers began to experiment with borrowed Western forms and eventually created their own marks (Twine 1984). Kogals use both Western and Japanese punctuation in their writing and graffiti photos.

Kogals highlight the importance of categories of youth in Japan's culture of advanced consumerism, yet Kogals themselves determine how the products of the culture industries are used to articulate their own identities as Girls. Not only in their consumption patterns and writing practices, but also in their use of language, Kogals are creatively contributing to their society.

[…]

In addition to making up their own vocabulary, Kogals and other young women are said to violate language structure itself. Shigeko Okamoto and Shie Sato (Okamoto 1995; Okamoto and Sato 1992) describe the parent culture's distaste for women who use putatively "masculine" language forms and who also fail to use correct **honorific** speech. However, unlike the college-age women they studied, Kogals do not qualify their use of "strongly masculine" forms by giggling or using **hedges** or quotatives in order to indicate a lingering discomfort in breaking gendered language norms. Kogals are not attempting to be masculine; they are changing the definition of femininity, a point Yoshiko Matsumoto (1996) has made about women's changing speech in general.

An example of Kogals' structural changes to Japanese is found in the avoidance of certain infixes. In prestige **dialects**, the potential form of a verb is formed by **infixing** the two morphemes *ra* and *re*. Thus, the verb *miru* (to see) becomes *mirareru* (can be seen), and the verb *taberu* (to eat) becomes *taberareru* (can be eaten). Although the derivation process is different, the potential and the passive forms for the class of verbs that have the dictionary endings *-eru* or *-iru* will both end in *-rareru*. But Kogals often drop the *ra* morpheme, saying *mireru* or *tabereru* instead. This practice is called *ra-nuki* (*ra*-deletion). Although *ra*-deletion is often associated with Kogals, it is not unique to them; it is common in many regional dialects and is found in various age groups. However, the media has singled out *ra*-deletion as one of the worst transgressions of youth speech, and this association with youth is widespread. In 1997 the Ministry of Education Award for Artistic Person of the Year went to playwright Ai Nagai, who wrote an intellectual comedy about generational friction over language use entitled *Ra-Nuki no Satsui* (Intent to Kill Dropped *Ra*) (Nagai 2000). The play revolves around a middle-aged man who detests the speech of young people in his office. They engage in *ra-nuki*, misuse honorifics, insert too many English loanwords, and if women, "talk like Kogals" or use forbidden masculine forms.

[...]

Kogals in mainstream media

Media pundits are fascinated yet disturbed by the way Kogals talk, and exposés of their language have appeared in weekly magazines such as *Josei Seben* and the national newspaper *Mainichi Shimbun*. Some commentators have placed Kogal speech in the same exotic category as other denigrated dialects. For example, although it is not the case at all, some hold the theory that Kogal intonation is very much like that of some northeastern dialects (Kurata 1998: 42). The term *shiriagari*, or '**rising intonation**', is also used to describe their pitch pattern. The media's **metalinguistic** objectification of Kogal speech reached a peak when newspapers, magazines, and television programs latched onto the term *chôberiba* (ultra very bad), formed with the intensifier prefix *chô*, English-derived *beri* (very), and clipped *ba* from *baddo* (bad). Newscaster Tetsuya Chikushi, in puzzlement, once shared the term with his audience as a perfect specimen of *kogyaru-go* (Kogal speech). According to Yonekawa (1996: 217), however, it is debatable if *chôberiba* was ever a real Kogal word. Instead, it seems to have begun among college-age girls and then spread among youth in general. Although the Roppongi Kogals I spent time with never used it, I received numerous e-mails from friends in Japan asking if I knew the "Kogal word *chôberiba*." In an article first published in the *New York Times*, journalist Nicolas Kristoff asserts that Kogals' speech is most characterized by its of English "loanwords" and says that their language is "a secret code by which they can bond and evade surveillance by hostile forces, like parents" (1997: 3). Ignoring at least four decades of domestication and reworking of English (see Stanlaw 2004), he attributes the popularity of Kogal speech to a simple fascination with American popular culture. Japanese linguists and pundits including Yoshisato Suzuki (2002) also bemoan the use of too much borrowing. However, made-in-Japan English has little to do with cultural imperialism because it is more likely to index the cool or the modern rather than the foreign.

Kogals are the focus of intense public concern, and media **discourses** reflect an ongoing obsession with locating and delimiting them.[1] Of course, this sort of surveillance of women is longstanding. Today's tensions about women's roles and aspirations, expressed through satire or heated polemic over Kogals, are not really new at all but have antecedents in prewar and postwar media, in which women have been debated, stereotyped, fictionalized, and caricatured. Common descriptions of Kogal are that they are impertinent, vulgar or indecent, egocentric, lacking manners, absurd or devoid of common sense, garish, and without perseverance. They are said to have brash, self-assured, and loud voices that can slice through tofu. Men complain that they are doing abuse to the "heart" (*kokoro*) or spirit of language. Kogals can be found sitting on the street pavement and on the floors of trains, actions viewed as slovenly and dirty. The increase in this behavior has led to the coinage of a new term to describe groups of squatting or sitting youth, *jibetarian*, a combination of *jibeta* ("squat on the ground") and English *battalion*.

On the other hand, in some media depictions, Kogal are grudgingly applauded. One male commentator makes it clear that he does not find their style attractive but recognizes that Kogals are nevertheless to be admired for creating their own category of identity (Murakami 2001: 169–170). In an episode of the animation series "Super Gals Kotobuki Ran" (*Chô Gyaruzu Kotobuki Ran*), there are amusing scenes in which a pseudoteacher decodes Kogal words by writing them on a chalkboard and "translating" them.[2] Viewers are taught Kogal terms such as *ikemen* (cool dudes) and *chômuka* (really annoying). The anime Kogals get into physical and verbal fights with rival gang Gals, bonk clueless boys on the head, and throw things at them. The main heroine, Ran, also offers up various "Gal rules," such as "Gals never back down from a challenge"; "Gals need eight hours' sleep for good skin, so they may sleep in class if necessary"; "Whatever Gals want, they must get it"; and "Gals never let go of their prey."

Kogals work at appearing brainless and insipid when talking to older men and foreign reporters, producing repetitive inanities and truncated answers to such pithy interview questions as "Until what age will you be a Girl?"; "How many times have you been to a love hotel?"; and "How much money is in your wallet?" (Klippensteen and Brown 2001). They are, however, capable of extended rants concerning older men and the state of their nation. This is what Asuka says:

> I wish they'd [old men] all die at once. Seriously, today's corporations are truly no good. To live in such a world as this, where people are so corrupt. What on earth is the Prime Minister doing?? Instead of worrying about what other nations are doing, he should be thinking about his own political situation. Seriously, if I were the Emperor, I'd fire all those bureaucrats. Fired!! Really, I just don't get it.
>
> (Yoshidô 1998: 48)

[...]

Conclusion

As a response to a stagnated male-centered society, Kogals have been effective in making ripples on the surface representation of Japanese homogeneity and consensus. By saying this I admit to a certain romanticization of resistance (Abu-Lughod 1990). I believe that Kogal language and behavior undermine patriarchal models of propriety used to evaluate and control women. This is not to say that Kogals subscribe to radical or feminist politics, to which they seem rather indifferent. Yet, to borrow from Abu-Lughod (1990: 47), not having any feminist or political agenda nevertheless does not strip Kogal transgressions of value. As members of Japanese society they are enmeshed in the same cultural gender system and its code of sexualized femininity as other women, and regardless of their nature, their rebellions point to a struggle over self-identity and sexual autonomy; resistance "is never in a position of exteriority in relation to power" (Foucault 1978: 95–96). Yet as Kogals use language, fashion, and behavior to set themselves apart from the parent culture, they increasingly entangle themselves in a culture of escalating consumerism and materialism. Their particular forms of resistance tie them to beauty work that requires increased consumption (Miller 2000).

[…]

I have tried to show that mainstream disapproval of Kogals reflects more than customary intergenerational scorn. Understanding media images of Kogals is important because through them we apprehend the public response to the critical role of women in sustaining capitalist consumerism, and to women's struggles for autonomy and independence. Deborah Cameron (1995) observes that controversies over English language use often serve as a cover for other obsessions, particularly moral and sociopolitical concerns. She suggests that panics about grammar may be interpreted as the metaphorical expression of persistent conservative fears that society is losing the values that underpin civilization. Likewise, Japan's mainstream society, forgetting the prewar Moga debates and the other *furyô shôjo* (delinquent maidens) sensationalized in women's magazines, views Kogals as exhibiting an unprecedented depravity. Their casual and exploitative attitudes about sex are considered special evidence of the collapse of Japanese culture. It is clear that Japanese anxiety over women's changing roles is often deflected onto bits of language. Dropped *ras* become a proxy for dropped panties, and published debate about Kogal speech and behavior is aimed not so much at understanding it, but at controlling and curtailing it. The media's angst over the Kogal is really a battle over the redefinition of female body display, sexuality, and selfhood.

What has been argued here is that the Kogal poses a threat to the gender order through her embodiment of criticism of contemporary society. Kogal aesthetics and images have had significant popularity in other parts of Asia, and it will be interesting to see what the consequences will be in the future. Real and media Kogals create a middle ground that could ultimately contribute to a redefinition of girlhood. Even in their marginality, they offer a model for Japanese (and possibly other Asian societies) to imagine the potential for change and for alternative ways of manifesting female identity. Kogals loosen the hold of a mythology of "natural" female restraint, modesty, and delicacy. These misbehaving girls may provide a requisite force for changing Japan's gender ideology.

Notes

1   Kogals are just one of many types of disobedient women who have become the focus of media attention (Miller 1998).

2   "Queen of the Gals" episode aired January 4, 2001, on TV Tokyo. The series is based on the comic by Mihona Fujii (1999).

Acknowledgments

For permission to use images I would like to thank Kazuaki Nakagawa, publisher of *Egg*, and Hiroki Akema, chief editor of *Ribbon*, acting on behalf of Mihona Fujii. I thank panel participants and discussants Mary Bucholtz, Penelope Eckert, and Norma Mendoza-Denton, who provided comments on an early version of this article, presented at the American Anthropological Association annual meeting, San Francisco, 2000. Subsequent versions were presented at the Center for Japanese Studies at the University of California, Berkeley; the Department of Linguistics at Stanford University; and the Reischauer Institute of Japanese Studies at Harvard University. Allison Alexy, Jan Bardsley, Ted Bestor, Rebecca Copeland, Nelson Graburn, Clare Ignatowski, Miyako Inoue, Debra Occhi, Noriko Reider, Shingo Satsutani, and Gavin Whitelaw gave me useful support or comments. Finally, anonymous reviewers offered excellent constructive suggestions for improvement, although perhaps not all of them are reflected here. All translations of Japanese are my own.

References

Abu-Lughod, Lila (1990) The Romance of Resistance: Tracing Transformations of Power through Bedouin Women, *American Ethnologist*, 17(1): 41–55.

Asahi Shimbun (2003) *Japan Almanac 2003*. Tokyo: Asahi Shimbun.

Bardsley, Jan (2000) What Women Want: Fujin Kôron Tells All in 1956, *U.S.-Japan Women's Journal*, 19: 7–48.

Cameron, Deborah (1995) *Verbal Hygiene*, London: Routledge.

Driscoll, Catherine (2002) *Girls: Feminine Adolescence in Popular Culture and Cultural Theory*, New York: Columbia University Press.

Egg Magazine (2000) Fukkatsu tamago nyûzu (Revival Egg News), *Egg*, August, 46: 90.

Foucault, Michel (1978) *The History of Sexuality, Vol. 1: An Introduction*, New York: Random House.

Fujii, Mihona (1999) *Chô gyaruzu kotobuki ran (Super Gals Kotobuki Ran), vol. 1*, Tokyo: Shûeisha Ribbon.

Horiuchi, Katsuaki (1985) Amerikanizumu kara dasseiyoka e (From Americanism to Post-Westernization), *Gengo*, 14(9): 70–77.

Ishino, Hiroshi (1985) Yokomoji ga minna no mono ni natta (The Roman Alphabet Now Belongs to Everyone) *Gengo*, 17(9): 38–44.

Jolivet, Muriel (2001) The Sirens of Tokyo, *Unesco Courier*, vol. 54, July, online, available at: www.unesco.org/courier/2001_07/uk/doss21.htm [accessed June 13, 2002].

Kataoka, Kuniyoshi (1997) Affect and Letter Writing: Unconventional Conventions in Casual Writing by Young Japanese Women, *Language in Society*, 26(1): 103–136.

—— (2003) Form and Function of Emotive Pictorial Signs in Casual Letter Writing, *Written Language and Literacy*, 6(1): 1–29.

Kitazawa, Shûichi (1925) Shoppu gâru (Shop Girls), *Kaizô*, April: 172–173.

Klippensteen, Kate and Brown, Everett Kennedy (2001) Ganguro Girls: The Japanese "Black Face," Budapest: Könemann.

Kristoff, Nicolas (1997) Stateside Lingo Gives Japan Its Own Valley Girls, *New York Times*, October 19: 3.

Kurata, Masumi (1998) Chihô ni kogyaru o sagashi ni iku (In Search of Kogal Localities), in Hiromu Inoue (ed.), *Chô kogyaru tokuhon (The Super Kogal Reader)*, Tokyo: Takarakajimasha, pp. 46–51.

Matsumoto, Yoshiko (1996) Does Less Feminine Speech in Japanese Mean Less Femininity? in Natasha Warner, Jocelyn Ahlers, Leela Bilmes, Monica Oliver, Suzanne Wertheim, and Melinda Chen (eds.), *Gender and Belief Systems: Proceedings of the Fourth Berkeley Women and Language Conference*, Berkeley, CA: Berkeley Women and Language Group, pp. 455–468.

Miller, Laura (1998) "Bad Girls": Representations of Unsuitable, Unfit, and Unsatisfactory Women in Magazines, *U.S.-Japan Women's Journal*, 15: 31–51.

—— (2000) Media Typifications and Hip *Bijin*, *U.S.-Japan Women's Journal*, 19: 176–205.

—— (2003) Male Beauty Work in Japan, in James Roberson and Nobue Suzuki (eds.), *Men and Masculinities in Contemporary Japan: Dislocating the Salaryman Doxa*, New York: Routledge, pp. 37–58.

Murakami, Ryû (2001) *Dame na onna (Women Who Are No Good)*, Tokyo: Kôbunsha.

Nagai, Ai (2000) *Ra-nuki no satsui (Intent to Kill Dropped* Ra*)*, Tokyo: Jiritsu Shobô.

Nakayama, Yoshigoro (1995 [1931]) *Kindai yôgo no jiten shûsei (A Collection of Dictionaries of Modern Terminology), vol. 19: Modango manga jiten (Manga Dictionary of Modern Language)*, Tokyo: Ôzarasha.

Okamoto, Shigeko (1995) "Tasteless" Japanese: Less "Feminine" Speech among Young Japanese Women, in Kira Hall and Mary Bucholtz (eds.), *Gender Articulated: Language and the Socially Constructed Self*, New York: Routledge, pp. 297–325.

Okamoto, Shigeko, and Sato, Shie (1992) Less Feminine Speech among Young Japanese Females, in Kira Hall, Mary Bucholtz, and Birch Moonwomon (eds.), in *Locating Power: Proceedings of the Second Berkeley Women and Language Conference*, Berkeley, CA: Berkeley Women and Language Group, pp. 478–488.

Stanlaw, James (2004) *Japanese English: Language and Culture Contact*, Hong Kong: Hong Kong University Press.

Suzuki, Yoshisato (2002) *Nihongo dekinai nihonjin (Japanese Who Can't Use Japanese Language)*, Tokyo: Chûô Kôronsha.

Time Magazine (1959) Japanese Women: Freedom amid Old Customs, *Time*, March 23.

Twine, Nannette (1984) The Adoption of Punctuation in Japanese Script, *Visible Language*, 18(3): 229–237.

Watrous, Marlena (2000) *Hello Kitties*, online, available at: http://cobrand.salon.com/people/feature/2000/03/08/kogaru/ [accessed June 12, 2002].

Yonekawa, Akihiko (1996) *Gendai wakamono kotoba ko (Analysis of Contemporary Youth Language)*, Tokyo: Maruzen.

Yoshidô, Hiroe (1998) Te yû ka, maji chô raburabu na "kogyaru nikki" (The, How Do You Say, Seriously Super Love Diary of a Kogal), in Hiromu Inoue (ed.), *Chô kogyaru tokuhon (The Super Kogal Reader)*, Tokyo: Takarakajimasha, pp. 46–51.

Chapter 11

Joanna Thornborrow

AUTHENTICATING TALK: BUILDING PUBLIC IDENTITIES IN AUDIENCE PARTICIPATION BROADCASTING

[...]

THIS ARTICLE FOCUSES on the talk of lay participants in public participation broadcasting on radio and television, and the nature, or perhaps more precisely, the *production* of '**authentic** talk' within this mediated context. Typically, public participation programmes offer the space for a range of discourse activities: discussion, argument, advice seeking, opinion giving and opinion seeking on matters such as health, finance, legal issues and issues of public concern, including political agendas. As such, they provide an occasion for 'fresh' talk, in Goffman's terms. I want to consider the kind of talk produced in these contexts as a form of authentic talk; however, contrary to previous research, where 'authenticity' is one attribute in a set of **dichotomous** criteria which distinguish 'expert' from 'lay' talk (Livingstone and Lunt 1994),[1] I examine how ordinary people produce talk on such occasions which authenticates their public role as ratified participants in relatively spontaneous, unscripted, unrehearsed, mediated events.

[...]

2. Establishing participant status: expert and lay identities

In public participation broadcasting, expert or professional participants[2] are identified according to that status before they start to talk. This occurs usually by a host's introduction (on radio) and by on-screen naming as well as host introduction on TV. Here are three typical examples from both TV and radio sources of hosts' identification of expert participants:

(1)   BBCR4/MBL
      Host: [—] with me in the studio and I have two chartered accountants
                (.) (.hh) John Whiting . of Price Waterhouse Coopers (.) and
                David Rothenburg from (Blick Rothenburg)

(2)   BBCRI/ECI
      Host: [—] tonight I'm joined by the prime minister Mrs Thatcher (.)
                good evening
      MT: good evening
      Host: thank you for coming and let's get straight to the calls

(3)   BBCTV1/FP
      Host: John Bird who's the- you're the editor of the Big Issue (.)
                you've been hearing these two points of view (.) which stri-
                what strikes you (.) so far

In these examples, the host attributes a public identity to the experts by naming
them and by giving their profession (here editor, prime minister, chartered accountant).
In contrast, lay participants in these programmes do not usually have such an identity
attributed to them. Although callers to radio phone-ins are routinely named and
geographically located by hosts before they start to speak, this naming functions to
identify and nominate them as 'next speaker' in order to bring them into the
participatory frame, rather than to identify them according to any other criteria: [...]
      [...]
      [...] In these sequences, a recurring feature of lay speakers' uptake of the **floor** is
the production of further information explicitly relating to identity and status, which is
given before they get round to the main business, or topic, of their call. The following
set of extracts contain instances of lay speaker self-identification from both radio and
TV data:

(5)   BBCR1/EC1
      Host: Keith M (.) from Barnstaple in North Devon good evening
      Caller: hello yes uh my question uh to the prime minister is on
                → health .hh I'm a nurse in (.) a London teaching hospital

(6)   BBCR1/EC6
      MT: =that was Roger was it=
      Host: =Roger [yes it was]
      Caller: [it is yeah] (xx)
                → er I work for a local building society (.) and in order to get
                  promotion (.) er I need to move down south [—]

(7)   IRP/MT
      PM: [—]'n we now take our first call (.) it's Jim in Finchampstead
                who wants to talk about the teachers good morning Jim
      Caller: good morning

MT: .hh good morning (.) [sir
Caller: [good morning prime minister=
MT: =good
            morning
Caller: uh my question is- follows on from (.) the uh subject
          → you've been talking about [—] I'm the parent of two boys (.)
            my question how are you going to get the teachers back to
            work and get politics out of the classroom.

(8) BBCTV1/E9
      Host: Sir you wanted to speak
      Man: → I've just (.) I-I'm divorced I- I have uh (.) a- a child fr- from the
               divorce and I- I would like to think that (.) that he has a much
               wider family now [—]

(9) BBCTV1/E5
      Host: Sir yes
      Man: → yeah Esther I'm nineteen and (.) I'm quite lucky my parents
               have been married for twenty five years [—]

(10) ITV/TTTP2
      Host: the lady back here (.) what do you say
      Woman: → um I'm a (tai) boxer I've been (tai) boxing and kick boxing
               for ten years (.) believe me I'm a hundred per cent woman

In these examples, we can see that participants are doing something more than just giving an opinion. In each case, in their first turns these speakers produce a self-identification which goes beyond that of selected next speaker provided by the hosts' prior turn. This selection is accomplished by naming and locating the next speaker in radio phone-ins, or in talk shows simply by the host saying: 'Sir yes' or 'the lady back here' (extracts (9) and (10)). So in extract (6) the caller has been identified by the host as 'Roger', but in his first turn after the clarification of his name, Roger's first action is to provide more information about himself: 'I work for a local building society'. The caller identified in (5) as 'Keith from Barnstaple' does similar further self-identification: 'I'm a nurse in a London teaching hospital'; Jim in (7) is 'the parent of two boys'. In extract (10), where the speaker is an unnamed member of the studio audience picked out by the host as 'the lady back here', the first part of her turn is also taken up with self-identification: 'I'm a (tai) boxer'; this also happens in extract (9): 'I'm nineteen and I'm quite lucky'. The form of identification given by the participant in (9) is slightly different, and I return to its relevance in Section 3.

For the moment, it seems clear that all these participants are making a salient comment on some aspect of their own personal status and identity, before going on to state their opinion, ask their question, or say whatever it is they have to say as a contribution to the talk. However, I suggest that lay speakers invoke particular identities in this way, not through a concern to establish their individual personal social status, but more through a concern to warrant the relevance of their public participation at that moment. Consequently, the construction of lay speaker identity in these programmes is closely tied to whatever it is they have to say next, and as such, has to be accomplished through local, situated means. This is a very different matter from the attribution of status to the expert participants, whose identities are institutionally already given matters; lay participants have to establish their own 'expertize' in relation to their contributions.

3. Building local identity through discursive grounding

As can be seen from the above examples, lay speakers' production of some further identifying detail is a fairly common feature of the opening talk in calls to radio phone-in programmes, as well as of many opening turns in TV talk shows. This detail is also routinely offered *before* speakers get to the main point of their call, or before they move on to what they have to say about whatever issue is up for discussion. So for instance, the caller in extract (11) structures his opening turn first with a greeting response token, then a transitional 'yes uh',[3] followed by some pre-question framing 'my question to the prime minister is on health', and then some identifying information:

(11)
>
> Host: Keith M (.) from Barnstaple in North Devon good evening
> Caller: hello yes uh my question uh to the prime minister is on
> → health .hh I'm a nurse in (.) a London teaching hospital and (.)
>   my question is this [——]

All this precedes the question itself, which gets produced later on in the turn, after his re-orientation to the discursive role of questioner through: 'my question is this'.

A similar pattern can be observed in extracts (6), (7) and (8) quoted earlier, where the speakers all provide further self-identification in the form of membership of a professional or social category: 'I work for a local building society', 'I'm the parent of two boys', 'I'm divorced'. However, self-categorization according to professional or social status is only one resource that lay speakers have available for establishing a locally relevant participant identity. The categories that participants make salient in these opening turns vary according to the particular theme of the programme, and various discursive strategies can be used to produce them. In the following extracts, selected from a range of programmes, I show how speakers design their local participant identities in other contextually relevant ways. For example, in calls to a family medical advice line on talk radio, callers routinely give information about the nature of their condition, before getting to their question. The callers in the following two extracts both establish their contextual identity as sufferers from a particular problem, whether it is a known medical condition 'I'm a diabetic', or something rather less specific 'I have a problem with my hand':

(12) LBC/FMM1
>
> Host: [——] Mary in West Hampstead with a question for you (.) uh
>   good afternoon Mary go ahead
> Caller: ((hi)) good afternoon Robbie good afternoon doctor

> Doctor: Mary
>   (.)
> Caller: → I have a problem with my hand (.) er the fingers of my hand
>   [—]

(13) LBC/FMM3
>   Host: but let's go to Sheila in Neasden see if we can help afternoon
>   Sheila
>   Caller: oh good afternoon Robbie and doctor
>   Doctor: hi Sheila
>   Caller: → oh hello doctor um I'm a diabetic=
>   Doctor: =mhhmm

As we have already seen in one of the earlier extracts, callers to a pre-election phone-in about party policy gave information about their professional or social status:

(14) BBCR1/EC8
>   Caller: → yeah I come from a one parent family (.) a difficult(y) my
>   mother has found in finding work (.) is the poverty tr- trap (.)
>   where the initial tax paid is (.) too high (.)

while participants in a talk show discussing gay and lesbian adoption rights offered personal information about their families and their reproductive experiences, as in the following extract:

(15) BBCTV1/KDU8
>   Host: [—] don't well what are you saying up at the top
>   Woman: → well I'm infertile I'm infertile and my husband we have an
>   adopted child (.)

Callers to a phone-in dealing with personal and relationship problems similarly gave information about their personal circumstances:

(16) TR/LAD4
>   Host: [—] and my next caller is Rachel Rachel what can I do for you
>   Caller: oh hi Anna I have spoken to you before my I um I have four
>   children of the marriage I am (.) divorced=
>   Host: =yeah

In this particular case, the caller mentions that she has previously made a call to the programme, thereby implicitly reinforcing a relevant identity in this context as someone with ongoing problems, and warranting her participatory status as just such a person, as well as giving information about her personal circumstances.

To return to the participant in extract (9) above, who begins his turn with 'I'm nineteen and I'm quite lucky', the rather different category types he makes salient here, those of age and condition, rather than status, nevertheless function in a similar way to categories such as 'nurse' or '(tai)boxer'. They establish the grounds for that speaker's participation by building a locally specific identity that warrants what he has to say next. Invoking such specific personal or social identities early in their first turns is, then, one way in which lay speakers display that what they are going to say is contextually relevant at that juncture.

[...]

[...] I want to turn briefly to hosts' and experts' treatment of lay speakers' initial grounding talk by looking at two examples where callers breach what appear to be the normative aspects of this activity. We can see that some preliminary contextual grounding is treated by recipients as procedurally relevant in the following call to a medical advice line where the doctor withholds giving his opinion until the caller has formulated her question (line 9):

(24) LBCR/FMM3
1. Caller: [—] and I called the doctor and my doctor is on holiday=
2. Doctor: =hmm,
3. Caller: and um (.) they very (.) I have a lot of pain suddenly
4.   on my joint (.) and I was told there's a young doctor
5.   and they told me that the doctor is on holiday .hh but
6.   I don't know w- maybe it's nothing but uh (they) told me
7.   maybe you can have an xray if you want=
8. Doctor: =hmm,
9. Caller: → and I just wonder what could ↑I↓ do
10.   (.)
11. Doctor: okay. [.hh
12. Caller: [if there's anything else [because I feel very=
13. Doctor: [okay.
14. Caller: =[uncomfort]able=
15. Doctor: [.hh b-   ]
16. Caller: =and I feel I have a lot of pain on the joint [(xxx)   ]
17. Doctor: [mhmm I]
18.   was gonna ask is it the actual joints [—]

Here, the doctor at first treats the caller's grounding information as relevant by minimally responding with a continuer: 'mhmm' (lines 2 and 8). But once the caller gets to her question in line 9: 'and I just wonder what could I do', he begins his next turn with 'okay' (line 11), getting ready to respond. The short pause in line 10, after the question and before the doctor's next turn, seems to indicate that this caller has now completed her turn, and that speaker transition is appropriate here. However, in this case the caller continues to talk after she has produced her question. After that pause, rather than holding off his own turn until she has finished, the doctor tries to take the floor and respond to her question. Despite these clear signals that he is getting ready to speak ('okay' in lines 11 and 13, and the marked intake of breath in line 15), the caller continues to talk in overlap with him. It is only at line 17 after three previous attempts that the doctor gets the floor with an **interruption** (he talks in overlap with her until she stops), and asks a further question of his own: 'I was gonna ask is it the actual joints'. His use of the frame *I was gonna ask* also nicely marks that this is a legitimate overlap, tying his question to her mention of 'pain on the joint'. So while the expert (the doctor in this case) listens through the caller's preliminary discursive grounding, and waits for a question to be produced, once this has happened a relevant transition point has been reached, and a response to that question is now in order.

By way of contrast, in the next extract the caller does not provide any preliminary grounding in his first turn, and asks his question directly he is given the floor. Rather than proceeding to the next stage of the call by getting the expert to provide an answer to this caller's question, in his next turn the host explicitly requests more personal, detailed information from the caller:

> (25) BBCR4/MBL1
> Host: right we'll get to our calls now .hh and uh our first one is uh ↑Brian in Rochdale
> Caller: er (is) indic- indexation of capital gains likely to be continued and how far can you go back at present if you haven't e::r calculated it for previous years
> Host: → have you got some shares to sell Brian?
> Caller: uh always hhh.
> Host: → right and these were acquired some years ago.
> Caller: yes uh (.) an now I've been told six years by somebody [—]

Here then, it is the host who does the work of eliciting the grounds for this caller's question when he asks 'have you got some shares to sell Brian?', thereby providing the space for a possible relevant identity to be produced by the caller (in this case, someone who has shares to sell, and who might have had them for some time). In contrast to other callers, Brian seems quite resistant to giving any specific information, as can be seen in the slightly jokey tone of his first response 'always', and in the brevity of his next response 'yes' in answer to how long ago he acquired his shares. Although it might be possible to provide an answer to Brian's question without such information, the fact that the host pursues the matter seems to indicate that such warrants are expectable on these occasions. In each of the above examples, either when the discursive work of grounding a caller's question was not produced prior to the question, or conversely in extract (24), when it went on for too long, then the recipients (host or expert) work either to establish those grounds, or to curtail them.

[…]

6. Host-attributed identities

Finally, I turn to some situated speaker identities which are constructed by the host, rather than by participants. There is a category of participants in TV talk shows who have already been identified prior to going on air as people with a particular contribution to make, and who the host calls upon to talk at relevant moments during the programme. It is here that the binary division between participants in terms of expert and lay begins to collapse from an interactional point of view, and a more discursively differentiated speaker status comes into play based on the way in which participants are brought into the frame of talk. In each of the following extracts, the host brings a new speaker into the frame in a way that is different from the examples I have given so far:

(40)
> Host: now tell us your story
> Woman: well we split up (.) a few times an' got back together [—]

(41)
> Host: your divorce was very different (.) wasn't it
> Woman: yes it was very acrimonious

(42)
> Host: oh you disagree don't you ma'am don't you dis[-
> Woman: [I definitely do I'm
> just waiting on my turn as a lady
> Host: and what do you think

(43)
> Host: there's a gentleman here you don't agree with this I understand
> Man: in most cases I don't [—]

In these four extracts, it is the host who constructs a locally relevant identity for participants to speak from, based on prior knowledge of their potential contribution. In each case, these participants' first turns are designed very differently from those seen in previous examples. The host's next speaker-selecting turn clearly constructs a discursive identity for that next speaker as someone with a story to tell, or a disagreement to voice, whereas in the extracts discussed earlier, that work is accomplished by the lay participant after the host has either explicitly nominated them, or indicated by some other means that they are ratified next speaker. In the above examples, a position to speak from is set up by the host prior to the new speaker's entry into the talk, and the form of this host eliciting turn determines the form of the response from the addressed next speaker. So a story prompt elicits a story in (40), a declarative tag question gives rise to a confirmation in (41) and (42), as does the host's negative declarative 'you don't agree with this I understand' in (43).

[…]

In the public sphere of TV and radio public participation broadcasting, where there is no explicit status of 'expertize' attributed to lay participants, a key move in their participation as currently selected next speaker is to establish these local identities before moving on to their question, opinion or point. In terms of what we might construe as hearably authentic discourse in mediated contexts such as those I have examined here, then the way in which lay speakers handle the situated, public production of a locally relevant identity constitutes a particular form of authenticating talk. Lay participants not only have to take up the role that, in Goffman's terms, is made situationally available to them, i.e. their structural role in the participatory framework as next speaker, but they also have to display the relevance, or validity, of their occupancy of that role in relation to whatever it may be that they are going to say next. Finally, to return to Sacks' (1995) point that speakers design interactionally sensitive descriptions of themselves through contextually relevant and available categories, in this article I have attempted to identify some of the discursive resources that lay speakers use to build these descriptions, in particular their public identities, through the initial work of grounding or framing utterances in their opening turns.

Acknowledgements

I would like to thank Adam Jaworski and Theo van Leeuwen for their helpful comments on an earlier draft of this paper.

Joanna Thornborrow is Senior Lecturer in Language and Communication at Cardiff University. Her research falls broadly within the field of discourse and conversation analysis, with a focus on institutional interaction and media discourse. Other research interests include children's talk in institutional settings, and stylistics. Her most recent book on institutional interaction, *Power Talk*, is in press with Longman (now Pearson Education). She has published numerous book chapters and journal articles on both stylistics and media discourse, including papers in *Text, Language & Literature, Discourse & Society, Discourse Studies* and *Language in Society*, guest editing a special issue of *Text* 17(2), 1997, on broadcast talk. ADDRESS: Centre for Language and Communication Research, Cardiff University, PO Box 94, Cardiff CF10 3XB, Wales, UK [email: thornborrowj1@cardiff.ac.uk].

Notes

1   This is not to say that the talk of 'experts' cannot be considered as 'authentic' in its own right. The dichotomy suggested by Livingstone and Lunt (1994) is based on a set of broadly oppositional criteria which in practice often break down when the discursive roles and interactions of participants in these shows is examined more closely (see Thornborrow 1997).

2   This binary categorization of expert and lay refers simply to the public, institutional status of participants in the programme, although the label is not necessarily as clearcut as it may first appear (see Note 1). An interesting example of so-called non-professionals being accorded a form of 'expert' status was a programme involving a discussion of begging on the streets of London, where a group of beggars were seated front of stage in the studio and in many respects treated as 'experts in begging' by the host. However, they were neither named individually, nor labelled on screen, despite their high level of participation in the programme.

3   Hutchby (1999) discusses the function of these as 'buffer' devices through which callers orient to their institutional role as speakers.

Appendix: key to transcription symbols

[—]	previous or subsequent omitted talk in a turn
(.)	short pause of less than .5 of a second
(1.3)	timed pause in seconds
hello=	
= hello	latching (no hearable gap) between the end of one turn to the beginning of the next
[good evening]	
[hello]	overlapping talk
(bar)	best hearing of indistinct talk
((laughs))	para-linguistic features
so in <u>our</u> way	marked stress
.hh	marked intake of breath
.	falling tone
?	rising tone
ar-	cut off syllable or word

References

Hutchby, I. (1999) 'Frame Attunement and Footing in the Organisation of Talk Radio Openings', *Journal of Sociolinguistics*, 3(1): 41–63.

Livingstone, S. and Lunt, P. (1994) *Talking on Television*, London: Routledge.

Sacks, H. (1995) *Lectures on Conversation, Vol. II*, Oxford: Blackwell.

Thornborrow, J. (1997) 'Having Their Say: The Function of Stories in Talk Show Discourse', *Text*, 17(2): 241–262.

PART FIVE

Language and gender

Pia Pichler

INTRODUCTION

THIS PART PRESENTS papers from a range of areas in the field of language and gender. The first focuses on **sexist language**, that is, discriminatory language and **ideology** *about* women, and feminist campaigns against it. The second and third paper focus on language use *by* women and men, the former on mixed-sex interaction, the latter on same-sex talk. All three papers show how language, gender and power are intertwined in numerous, but very different, ways.

Anne Pauwels's paper demonstrates how labels used to represent women reveal sexist ideologies, and how feminist campaigners have been challenging these representations and ideologies since the 1970s. The chapter offers a wide variety of examples of sexist language practices from different languages, including English, German and Dutch. Pauwels also discusses different stages of feminist campaigns, from the initial two stages where problematic issues are highlighted and proposals for change are made to the last two stages where changes are implemented and, finally, the success of feminist language reforms is assessed. There are many issues that feminist language campaigners have documented regarding the asymmetry of gendered representations in language (Spender 1980; Cameron 1992; Hellinger and Bussman 2001; Mills 2008). Whereas the male form is presented as the norm, the female is either subsumed in **generic** expressions using masculine forms, or linguistically **marked**, that is, the word used to represent women is a grammatical derivative of the male equivalent. Examples of the former in English are the use of generic 'he' (the person – he), examples of the latter are act*ress* in English and Schauspiel*erin* in German. Pauwels introduces different feminist strategies that have been adopted to achieve linguistic equality of the sexes in different languages.

She refers to the two main strategies as 'gender-neutralization' and 'gender-specification'. The former will be more familiar to English language users, where feminists have campaigned to discontinue the use of marked female forms such as 'actress', 'police woman', 'lady doctor' in favour of the **unmarked**, generic 'actor', 'police constable' and 'doctor' in order to 'do away with, "neutralize", or minimize the linguistic expression of gender and/or gender marking in relation to human referents' (p. 153). The opposite strategy is gender-specification or 'feminization', whose supporters argue for the 'explicit and symmetrical marking of gender in human referents' (p. 153). This strategy is particularly prominent in German, where forms such as 'der Lehrer und die Lehrerin' or even 'der/die LehrerIn' seek to make women more visible and signal that, for example, occupations are equally accessible to both sexes. The success of feminist language change is difficult to measure although certain conclusions can be drawn. In English, there have been many reports of decreased use of masculine generic nouns and pronouns, for example writers frequently use forms such as 'her or she' or even 'they' instead of generic 'he'. What appears to have been less successful is the introduction of the title 'Ms' instead of 'Mrs' and 'Miss' in British English, whereas the form 'Ms' has been adopted more widely in US, Canadian and Australian English. It is perhaps significant to add, that other languages such as German or Italian have opted to phase out the equivalent form of 'Miss', so that 'Fräulein' or 'Signorina' have now been replaced by 'Frau' and 'Signora' in many contexts. It is of course easier to comment on non-sexist alternatives, and much more difficult to assess the social effectiveness of these feminist campaigns. However, feminist language campaigns have certainly contributed to raising awareness of gender bias in language, casting women in the new role as linguistic norm-makers. The question remains whether this new awareness contributes towards a change of gender ideologies and power relations beyond the linguistic realm.

The second and third papers in this part focus on the talk of women and men, the former on mixed-sex conversation, the latter on same-sex talk. Power remains an issue in both papers, as **conversational dominance** in mixed-sex talk in the next paper by Mary Talbot, and in the form of **hegemonic** discourses of masculinity in the final paper by Deborah Cameron.

Talbot's paper invites the reader to reflect on approaches to the analysis of (gendered) **turn-taking** and (unequal) speaking rights, arguing that it is not sufficient to simply count linguistic features if one is to understand the roles and relationships of speakers and the significance of issues such as power and gender in spoken interaction. The paper shows that **interruptions**, a feature many students examine in their analyses of mixed-sex talk, are not easy to identify.

Talbot discusses a range of different methods for identifying interruptions, critically examining previous research on gendered turn-taking/turn violations before offering her own data and conclusions on the topic. The chapter starts with a summary of research which has become known as a typical example of the 'dominance approach' in language and gender research. Zimmerman and West's (1975) and West and Zimmerman's (1983 [1978]) data suggest that men interrupt women systematically, thereby both reflecting and re-enacting the power asymmetry that exists between women and men in society at large. However, Talbot is critical of the methods used in this research, particularly of the 'crude word or syllable counting' which forms the basis of the studies' differentiation between various types of interruptions and overlaps. She then examines two further studies, which use different approaches to identify interruptions (Beattie 1983; Murray 1985). Their findings challenge Zimmerman and West's conclusions about women, men and interruptions, but more importantly, their methods show that interruptions should not only be identified on the basis of syntactic criteria, that is, by their position in relation to the utterance of the current/interrupted speaker. Gestures, eye contact and functional criteria should be considered. Murray's functional criteria consist of the 'microhistorical context' - what has gone on in a conversation before – which speakers draw on to judge the severity of an instance of **simultaneous speech**. For example, if somebody has already been talking for a long time, according to Murray's notion of 'distributive justice', the interruption is felt to be less severe.

Talbot argues that the analysis of interruptions needs to be approached from a qualitative rather than a quantitative perspective, in order to 'see interruptions in action' (p. 177). Although she is in favour of using functional criteria for the identification of interruptions, her own data show that the notion of 'distributive justice' is problematic. Adopting Beattie's classification of simultaneous speech and interruptions in combination with Murray's functional criteria she presents an extract of conversation between a husband and a wife (and their friends). The husband has been taking many more turns in telling a story with himself and his wife as protagonists, but still feels that his speaking rights have been violated by his wife's collaboration (at times in the form of simultaneous speech). This indicates that some speakers feel they are entitled to more speaking time than others. There are many possible reasons for speakers to feel that way, for example due to their higher social status or more powerful situational role. In the case of the married couple whose talk Talbot investigates neither of these reasons apply. Instead, just as various other feminist scholars have found (Spender 1980; Herring *et al.* 2011), gender is likely to be responsible for the asymmetrical speaking rights.

The second paper on talk and gender was published five years later and does not need to make a case for qualitative analysis of language (and gender). Cameron's data consist of the talk of five, 21-year-old US white middle-class college students. Cameron discusses turn-taking features (including simultaneous speech, **latching** and joint utterance production), as well as **hedges** such as 'you know', 'like' and **minimal responses**. All of these formal features have been explored by scholars interested in the talk of women and men. Like Talbot, however, Cameron warns that it is very difficult to determine the function of these linguistic forms. She argues that the young men's linguistic style contains features which could be interpreted as achieving both 'competition', traditionally associated with men's talk, and 'collaboration', traditionally associated with women's talk. Moreover, despite talking about very stereotypically 'male topics', such as wine, women and sports, Cameron notes that the young men also engage in a speech activity, which is mostly associated with women: gossip.

Should we therefore assume that the young men are using a 'feminine' conversational style? Far from it. Even though the young men gossip and provide some features of conversational support, they still 'perform … the same old gendered script' (p. 190). The way they do this is by drawing on dominant/powerful heterosexist discourses about other men whom they describe as 'gay'. But, being 'gay' in this group does not actually mean being homosexual, instead the label is used to mark deviant masculinity: to ridicule young men whose body, clothing and language is deemed to be not masculine enough. By distancing themselves from these insufficiently masculine young men the five college students are doing important gender work – they are reasserting their own masculinity – positioning themselves as 'red-blooded heterosexual males' (p. 190).

What this paper shows us is, firstly, that gender identities are continually being 'performed' (Butler 1990). We all continue to construct ourselves as either feminine or masculine. We may do this by using linguistic features which have traditionally been associated with femininity or masculinity, for example a 'collaborative' or a 'competitive' linguistic style. However, as this paper shows, gender performances do not necessarily rely on these formal language features. Instead, scholars like Cameron have turned their attention to 'discourses', that is, to 'gender scripts', ways of talking and thinking which reflect particular worldviews or ideologies (on gender). The young college students here are voicing discourses which reaffirm normative views about the appearance and behaviour of 'real'/heterosexual men. So, secondly, this paper shows us that we may restrict our analysis if we focus solely on formal conversational features without considering the discourses that speakers voice. As Cameron argues, we must not focus on the 'style, rather than the substance, of what is said' (p. 190), if we seek to understand gender performances more fully.

Issues to consider

1. List a number of linguistic changes which you attribute to feminist language reforms and discuss to what extent these have been 'effective'.
2. What are the issues you need to consider when identifying, classifying and analyzing interruptions? Why is it problematic to simply count all instances of simultaneous speech?
3. What other linguistic features could you focus on if you were interested in the analysis of asymmetrical speaking rights in an extract of talk?
4. How do speakers 'perform' gender identities in their talk? Is there only one way of performing gender?

Further reading

For more on the issues involved in research on language and gender:

Bucholtz, M., Liang, A.C. and Sutton, L.A. (eds.), (1999) *Reinventing Identities: The Gendered Self in Discourse*, Oxford: Oxford University Press.
Coates, J. (2004) *Women, Men and Language*, third edition, London: Longman.
—— and Pichler, P. (eds.), (2011) *Language and Gender: A Reader*, second edition, Oxford: Blackwell.
Eckert, P. and McConnell-Ginet, S. (2003) *Language and Gender*, Cambridge: Cambridge University Press.
Holmes, J. and Meyerhoff, M. (eds.), (2003) *The Handbook of Language and Gender*, Oxford: Blackwell.
Talbot, M. (1998) *Language and Gender: An Introduction*, Cambridge: Polity.

For work that focuses on spoken interaction:

Bucholtz, M. and Hall, K. (2005) Identity and interaction: a sociocultural linguistic approach. *Discourse Studies*, 7(3): 585–614.

Coates, J. (1996) *Women Talk: Conversation between Women Friends*, Oxford: Blackwell.
Pichler, P. (2009) *Talking Young Femininities*, Houndmills: Palgrave MacMillan.
— and Eppler, E. (eds.), (2009) *Gender and Spoken Interaction*, Houndmills: Palgrave MacMillan.

The following are some texts you might find useful if you want to explore issues of representation and ideology.

Cameron, D. (1995) *Verbal Hygiene*, London: Routledge.
Mills, S. (2008) *Language and Sexism*, Cambridge: Cambridge University Press.
Sunderland, J. (2004) *Gendered Discourses*, Houndmills: Palgrave MacMillan.

Suggestions for further viewing

Bombay Eunuch (2001) Alexandra Shiva.
The Handmaid's Tale (1990) Volker Schlöndorff.
Orlando (1992) Sally Potter.
She's The Man (2006) Andy Fickman.

References

Beattie, Geoffrey (1983) *Talk*, Milton Keynes: Open University Press.
Butler, Judith (1990) *Gender Trouble: Feminism and the Subversion of Identity*, London: Routledge.
Cameron, Deborah (1992) *Feminism and Linguistic Theory*, second edition, Houndmills: Palgrave.
Hellinger, Marlis and Bussman, Hadumod (eds.), (2003) *Gender Across Languages: The Linguistic Representation of Women and Men, 3 volumes*, Amsterdam: John Benjamins.
Herring, Susan, Johnson, Deborah and DiBenedeto, Tamara (2011 [1992]) Participation in electronic discourse in a 'feminist' field, in J. Coates and P. Pichler (eds.), *Language and Gender: A Reader*, second edition, Oxford: Blackwell.
Mills, Sara (2008) *Language and Sexism*, Cambridge: Cambridge University Press.
Murray, Stephen (1985) Toward a model of members' methods for recognizing interruptions, *Language and Society*, 14: 31–40.
Spender, Dale (1980) *Man Made Language*, London: Routledge.
West, Candace and Zimmermann Don H. (1983) Small Insults: A Study of Interruptions in Cross-Sex Conversations between Unacquainted Persons, in Barrie Thorne, Cheris Kramarae and Nancy Henley (eds.), *Language, Gender and Society*, Roweley: Newbury House, pp. 103–118.
Zimmerman, Don H. and West, Candace (1975) Sex roles, Interruptions and Silences in Conversations, in Barrie Thorne and Nancy Henley (eds.), *Language and Sex: Difference and Dominance*, Roweley: Newbury House, pp. 105-129. Also in J. Coates and P. Pichler (eds.), (2011) *Language and Gender: a Reader*, second edition, Oxford: Blackwell.

Chapter 12

Anne Pauwels

LINGUISTIC SEXISM AND FEMINIST LINGUISTIC ACTIVISM

1. Women and men as language users and regulators

THE POPULAR PORTRAYAL of women and men as language users has stressed their fundamental differences. A quick perusal of some writings about male and female speakers across languages (e.g. Baron 1986) leaves no doubt that men are perceived not only as powerful speakers but especially as authoritative language users. Women, on the other hand, are often seen as garrulous, frivolous, and illiterate language users. These popular **stereotypes** gained in stature when they were endorsed by or validated in the "academic" and "scientific" literature of the day (for an overview see e.g. Baron 1986; Kramarae 1981). This "scientific" validation in turn led to the desire for the codification and regulation of women's speech, and of women as speakers. Cameron (1995; this volume) as well as other scholars of language and gender have documented the many rules, codes, and guides that were developed to codify and control women's language behavior over the past centuries. Essentially this action cemented men's status as norm-makers, language regulators, and language planners. Men signaled their authority in language through their roles in the dictionary-making process, in the writing of normative grammars, in the establishment of language academies and other normative language institutions, and through their involvement in language planning activities. The history of women as language regulators is very different. As stated above, women were subjected to linguistic regulation much more than men. However, women were given some authority in language regulation as norm enforcers: both as mothers and as school teachers (especially in elementary education) women were to ensure that children learned to use language according to the prescribed norms.

It was the linguistic activism associated with the women's movement starting in the 1970s that posed the first major female challenge to male dominance in language regulation and planning. Women of all walks of life started to expose the biased portrayal of the sexes in language use and demonstrated that this portrayal was particularly discriminatory and damaging to women. Furthermore, their activities targeted the uncovering of the gendered nature of many linguistic rules and norms. For example, Bodine's (1975) paper on "Androcentrism in prescriptive grammar" showed that sex-indefinite *he* gained its dominant status as **generic** pronoun as a result of male regulation. Baron's (1986) comprehensive analysis of grammar in relation to gender similarly exposes **androcentric** practices. Another powerful expression of language regulation is the dictionary. Scholars such as Kramarae (1992), Pusch (1984), and Yaguello (1978) revealed sexism in lexicographic practices, especially in older versions of dictionaries of English, German, and French: the works of the "best" male authors were a major source for dictionary definitions of words. Female authors or women-oriented publications (especially women's magazines) were seldom included in the source material. These exposures of bias cast women in the role of critical commentators on "men's rules." Some women reacted to the bias by becoming *norm-breakers* who subverted established norms and rules: examples include the use of *she* as sex-indefinite pronoun, and in German, the introduction of the word *Herrlein* (literally, little man) for a single man to match the existing *Fräulein* (literally, little woman – Miss).

Perhaps most threatening to men's role as norm-makers were the attempts women made at becoming norm-makers themselves through the formulation of proposals and guidelines for non-sexist language use. Developing women's own norms and implementing them across a speech community is clearly the strongest challenge, if not threat, to male authority in language regulation. This assumption is borne out by the often vehement reactions expressed by (male-dominated) language academies and other linguistic authorities against analyses of linguistic sexism and against proposals for non-sexist language use (for details see e.g. Blaubergs 1980; Hellinger 1990; Pauwels 1998). In many negative reactions to the guidelines the author tries to discard a proposed change by questioning the linguistic expertize of the feminist language planner or linguistic activist. In other words, he or she expresses the belief that the female language planner does not have the knowledge or the expertize to propose new language norms.

In the following sections I will examine the language (planning) activities which were triggered by the newly gained female consciousness associated with women's movements across the Western world during the 1970s and 1980s. I will also examine the extent to which their attempts at becoming *norm-makers* have been successful.

2. Feminist linguistic activism – non-sexist language reform

2.1 Feminist non-sexist language campaigns as an instance of language planning

It is important to acknowledge that the debates, actions, and initiatives around the (non-) sexist language issue are a form of language planning. The marginalization of feminist perspectives on gender and communication in the 1970s and early 1980s had a particularly strong effect on the recognition of feminist linguistic activism as a genuine case of language planning, in this instance a form of *corpus planning* (see Kloss 1969). In fact, "mainstream" literature on language planning either ignored or denied the existence of feminist language planning until Cooper's (1989) work on language planning and social change which includes the American non-sexist language campaign as one of its case-studies.

It will become clear from the description and discussion below that feminist campaigns to eliminate sexist bias from language have all the trademarks of language reform. In my previous work (e.g. Pauwels 1993, 1998) I have analyzed feminist language reform using a sociolinguistic approach to language planning (e.g. Fasold 1984). The sociolinguistic approach emphasizes the fact that reforms are directed at achieving social change, especially of the kind that enables greater equality, equity, and access. Within this framework the language planning process is divided into four main stages. The *fact-finding* stage is concerned with documenting the problematic issues and concerns. The *planning* stage focuses on the viability of change as well as on developing proposals for change. In the *implementation* stage the methods and avenues for promoting and implementing the changes are assessed and the preferred proposals are implemented. In the *evaluation/feedback* stage language planners seek to assess to what extent the planning and implementation processes have been successful in terms of achieving the goal of the language planning exercise. This involves examining whether the changes are being adopted by the speech community and how they are being used.

2.2 Documenting sexist language practices

Exposing and documenting sexist practices in language use and communication has been, and continues to be, a grassroots-based activity by feminists with an interest in language and the linguistic representation of the sexes. There is no denying that feminist activists in the USA were the trailblazers in both exposing sexist bias and proposing changes. Amongst a (linguistic) academic readership the works of Lakoff (1975) and Spender (1980) and the collection of essays in Nilsen *et al.* (1977) became the main reference points for elaborate descriptions of linguistic sexism as it affected the English language. Other speech communities in which feminists took an early and active interest in exposing sexist linguistic practices included Norway (Blakar 1977), France (Yaguello 1978), Germany (e.g. Troemel-Ploetz 1978; Guentherodt 1979; Guentherodt *et al.* 1980; Hellinger and Schräpel 1983) as well as Spain (e.g. Garcia 1977). More recently the documentation of gender bias has spread to languages such as Chinese, Icelandic, Lithuanian, Italian, Japanese, Polish, and Thai (see Hellinger and Bussman 2001; Pauwels 1998).

Feminist explorations into the representation of women and men revealed commonalities across speech communities as well as across languages. A striking feature across many languages and speech communities is the *asymmetrical treatment* of women and men, of male/masculine and female/feminine concepts and principles. The practice of considering the man/the male as the prototype for human representation reduces the woman/female to the status of the "subsumed," the "invisible," or the "marked" one: women are invisible in language when they are subsumed in generic expressions using masculine forms. Generic reference in many languages occurs via the use of forms which are identical with the representation of maleness (e.g. *he* as generic and masculine pronoun, generic nouns coinciding with nouns referring to males). When women are made visible in language, they are "marked": their linguistic construction is often as a derivative of man/male through various grammatical (morphological) processes.

This asymmetry also affects the lexical make-up of many languages. The structure of the lexicon often reflects the "male as norm" principle through the phenomenon of lexical gaps, that is, the absence of words to denote women in a variety of roles, professions, and occupations (e.g. Baron 1986; Hellinger 1990; Sabatini 1985; Yaguello 1978). The bias against women in the matter of lexical gaps is particularly poignant when we consider the reverse, namely, the absence of male-specific nouns to denote men adopting roles or entering professions seen to be female-dominant. The male lexical gaps tend to be filled rather quickly, even to the extent that the new male form becomes the dominant one from which a new female form is derived. An example of this practice is found in German where the word *Hebamme* (midwife) is making way for the new word *Entbindungspfleger* (literally "birthing assistant") as a result of men taking up the role of midwife. Meanwhile a female midwife has been coined *Entbindungspflegerin*, a form derived from *Entbindungspfleger*.

The semantic asymmetry that characterizes the portrayal of women and men in language is of particular concern to feminist activists, as it is an expression of women's and men's perceived values and status in society. The core of this semantic asymmetry is that woman is a sexual being dependent on man, whereas man is simply defined as a human being whose existence does not need reference to woman. Schulz (1975) highlights the practice of semantic derogation which constantly reinforces the "generic man" and "sexual woman" portrayal. Schulz (1975: 64) finds that "a perfectly innocent term designating a girl or a woman may begin with neutral or positive **connotations**, but that gradually it acquires negative implications, at first only slightly disparaging, but after a period of time becoming abusive and ending as a sexual slur." This practice has also been observed and examined for French (e.g. Sautermeister 1985), German (e.g. Kochskämper 1991), and Japanese (e.g. Cherry 1987).

Linguistic *stereotyping* of the sexes was also seen as problematic, especially for women as it reinforced women's subordinate status. Stereotyped language was particularly damaging to women in the context of the mass media and educational materials. It is therefore not surprising that both these spheres of language use were subjected to thorough examinations of sexism (see e.g. Nilsen *et al.* 1977).

Community reaction to these feminist analyses was predominantly negative: the existence of linguistic sexism was vigorously denied. Reasons for its denial varied according to the status and linguistic expertize of the commentator. Whereas non-experts rejected the claim on (folk) etymological assumptions, or because of an unquestioned acceptance of the wisdom of existing language authorities, linguistic experts refuted the claims by arguing that feminist analyses of the language system are fundamentally flawed as they rest on erroneous understandings of language and gender, particularly of grammatical gender. For example, the reaction of the Department of Linguistics at Harvard University to suggestions from students at the Divinity School to ban *Man, man*, and generic *he* as they are sexist, and the reaction by the German linguist Hartwig Kalverkämper (1979) to a similar observation for the German language by fellow linguist Senta Troemel-Ploetz (1978), stated that feminist analysts held a mistaken view about the relationship between grammatical gender and sex. These denials were in turn scrutinized and refuted by feminist linguistic commentators who exposed historical practices of grammatical gender reassignment (e.g. Baron 1986; Cameron 1985) or who presented evidence from experimental work on people's perceptions of gender and sex in language (e.g. Mackay 1980, Pauwels 1998).

2.3 Changing language: How?

Most feminist language activists were and are proponents of language change as a measure for achieving a more balanced representation of women and men in language. Taking linguistic action to improve the plight of women was seen as an integral part of women's liberation. Furthermore, many language activists subscribe to an interactionist view of language and reality which has its origins in a weaker version of the Sapir-Whorf hypothesis: language shapes and reflects social reality.

Despite this consensus on the need for linguistic action there is considerable diversity in the activists' and planners' views on how to change sexist practices in language. Their views on strategies for achieving change are shaped by many factors, including their own motivation for change, their understanding and view of language, and the nature and type of the language to be changed. Planners whose motivation to change is driven by a belief that language change lags behind social change will adopt different strategies from those activists whose main concern is to expose patriarchal bias in language. Whereas the former may consider linguistic amendments as a satisfactory strategy to achieve the linguistic reflection of social change, the latter activists would not be satisfied with mere amendments. Proposals for change are also shaped by one's understanding of the language system, of how meaning is created, and of how linguistic change occurs. For example, a linguist's suggestions for change may be heavily influenced by his or her training – training in recognizing the distinctive structural elements and properties of language such as phonemes, morphemes, and grammatical categories, and in recognizing how these elements contribute to creating meaning. Reformers without such training may focus their efforts for change mainly at the lexical level as this level is often considered the only one susceptible to change. The nature and type of language also influences proposals for change: languages that have grammatical gender pose different challenges from those that do not.

Among this multitude of opinions and views on the question of change, three main motivations for change can be discerned: (1) a desire to expose the sexist nature of the current language system; (2) a desire to create a language which can express reality from a woman's perspective; or (3) a desire to amend the present language system to achieve a symmetrical and equitable representation of women and men.

Causing *linguistic disruption* is a strategy favored by those wishing to expose the sexist nature of the present language system. Its advocates claim that this strategy helps people to become aware of the many subtle and not so subtle ways in which the woman and the female are discriminated against in language. This disruption is achieved through various forms of linguistic creativity including breaking morphological rules, as in *herstory* (based on *history*), or grammatical conventions, such as the generic use of the pronoun *she*; using alternative spellings, as in *wimmin*, *LeserInnen* (female readers); or inverting gender stereotypes, as in "Mr X, whose thick auburn hair was immaculately coiffed, cut a stunning figure when he took his seat in Parliament for the first time since his election." The revaluation and the reclaiming of words for women whose meaning had become trivialized or derogatory over time (e.g. *woman, girl, spinster*) is another form of linguistic disruption, as is the creation of new words (e.g. *male chauvinism, pornoglossia*) to highlight women's subordination and men's domination.

More radical proposals have come from those activists who do not believe that the present language system is capable of expressing a woman's point of view. They call for the creation of a new woman-centered language. Examples range from the experimental language used by Gert Brantenberg (1977) in her (Norwegian) novel *The Daughters of Egalia*, the creation of the Láadan language by the science fiction writer and linguist Suzette Haden Elgin "for the specific purpose of expressing the perceptions of women" (Elgin 1988: 1), to the experiments in "writing the body" – écriture féminine – emerging from the postmodern feminist theories and approaches associated with Hélène Cixous and Luce Irigaray. To date these experiments in women-centered languages and discourses have remained largely the domain of creative writers.

More familiar to the general speech community are feminist attempts at achieving linguistic equality of the sexes by proposing amendments to existing forms, rules, and uses of language (sometimes labeled *form replacement* strategy). *Gender-neutralization* and *gender-specification* are the main mechanisms to achieve this. Whereas gender-neutralization aims to do away with, "neutralize," or minimize the linguistic expression of gender and/or gender-marking in relation to human referents, the gender-specification (also called *feminization*) strategy promotes the opposite: the *explicit* and *symmetrical* marking of gender in human referents. An illustration of gender-neutralization is the elimination in English of female occupational nouns with suffixes such as *-ess, -ette, -trix* (e.g. *actress, usherette, aviatrix*). An example of gender-specification in English is the use of *he or she* to replace the generic use of *he*. The application of both mechanisms has been confined mainly to word level as there was a belief that changes at word level could have a positive effect on eliminating sexism at discourse level.

Given the prominence of the linguistic equality approach and the form replacement strategy it is worthwhile examining which factors influence the feminist language planners in opting for gender-neutralization or gender-specification.

2.4 Choosing non-sexist alternatives

Social and linguistic factors play a role in the selection of the strategies. Social factors revolve around questions of social effectiveness: the chosen strategy should achieve linguistic equality of the sexes by both *effecting* and *reflecting* social change relating to women and men in society. This is particularly relevant with regard to occupational nomenclature. Linguistic factors focus on the issue of *linguistic viability* as well as on matters of *language typology*. Proposed changes need to take account of the typological features and the structural properties of a language; for example, languages which mark gender through morphological processes may have different options from those that don't. Linguistic viability is also linked to linguistic prescriptivism: proposed alternatives which are seen to violate deeply ingrained prescriptive rules or norms could obstruct or slow down the process of adoption in the community.

Most non-sexist language proposals generated for a range of languages contain explicit or implicit evidence that these social and linguistic factors have played a role in the choice of the principal strategy (gender-neutralization or gender-specification).

However, feminist activists and language planners proposing changes for the same language may differ in the priority they assign to arguments of social effectiveness and of linguistic viability, or how they interpret these concepts. This has led to debates about the preferred principal strategy. [...] Languages with a grammatical gender system classify nouns into gender categories on the basis of morphological or phonological features (see Corbett 1991). Whilst many have claimed that a grammatical gender system which classifies nouns in the masculine, feminine, or neuter categories is a purely linguistic invention, and is not linked to the extralinguistic category of biological sex, Corbett (1991: 34) acknowledges that "there is no purely morphological system" and that such systems "always have a semantic core." This is particularly obvious in the gender assignment of human (agent) nouns, with most nouns referring to women being feminine, and those referring to male persons being masculine.

[...]

[...] In the case of English there has been little if any debate about gender-neutralization being the principal strategy in promoting linguistic equality. Discussions have been more about selecting alternative forms within the gender-neutralization strategy: for example, should the word *chairman* be replaced by an existing, semantically related noun, such as *president, chair*, or should a new form be created, for example, *chairperson*? Replacing generic *he* by pronouns such as singular *they*, by a new pronoun, or by generic *she, it*, or *one* is another example of this (e.g. Bodine 1975; Mackay 1980; Baron 1986; Henley 1987).

2.5 Implementing changes – guidelines for non-sexist language use

A crucial component in language planning is the implementation of the proposed changes. Language planners need to identify pathways and mechanisms to implement their proposals so that these can reach and spread through the speech community. In many forms of corpus planning (e.g. orthographic reform) implementation is top-down with language academies and other authoritative language bodies leading, and educational authorities facilitating the implementation process. However, in the case of feminist language planning these language authorities were and are often strongly opposed and resistant to the proposed changes. Being principally a grassroots-driven phenomenon, feminist language planning had limited (if any) access to, and cooperation from, the main channels for the implementation of language change. These include the education system, the media, legislative measures, and linguistic authorities. Instead their main mechanisms for spreading change were, and remain, promotion through personal use, the use of role models, and pressure on key agencies to adopt guidelines for non-sexist language use.

The promotion of linguistic disruption and a newly created woman-centered language was primarily achieved through personal language patterns, often in speech but mainly in writing. Prominent feminist activists who practiced forms of linguistic disruption became role models for and of feminist linguistic change. Mary Daly's (1978) linguistic practices in *Gyn/ecology: The Metaethics of Radical Feminism* are a typical illustration of this. Feminist publications – both academic and general – became vehicles for spreading feminist linguistic practices throughout the feminist community. For example, in its early publication days the German feminist magazine *Emma* played an important role in familiarizing German feminists with, and promoting, feminist language change. The magazine practiced gender splitting, used the new indefinite pronoun *frau* (instead of *man*, meaning "one"), and created many new compounds with -*frau* (-woman) to make women more visible in language. The creative work of feminist novelists and poets such as Monique Wittig, Audre Lorde, Adrienne Rich, Gert Brantenberg, Verena Stefan, and others who experiment with new forms of language use is a further illustration of this.

Exerting pressure on key agencies in language spread became a prominent mechanism for the promotion of change emanating from the linguistic equality approach. Feminist individuals and women's action groups not only developed guidelines and policies on non-sexist language use but also acted to convince professional organizations and key agencies to adopt the policies. These language-oriented actions were often part of general initiatives by women's groups to eliminate gender-biased practices from society. Early targets for feminist linguistic activism were publishers of educational material, the print media, education, and legislative writing. These agencies were targeted because of their key role in shaping the representation of women and men and because of their potential to facilitate and spread change through a community. Feminist language activists also used the introduction of Sex Discrimination, Equal (Employment) Opportunity and Human Rights Acts, and other legislative measures to demand linguistic changes. A case in point is the need to amend professional and occupational nomenclature to comply with Equal Employment Opportunity (EEO) Acts. Terminology commissions, education ministries, employment councils, language academies, and other public agencies charged with making amendments to official (occupational) nomenclature and terminology called upon feminist language planners to assist them in this task. This in turn triggered requests for non-sexist language guidelines and policies to be developed for other public and private agencies covered under EEO and antidiscrimination legislation. To date non-sexist language policies are in place in most public sector and in many large private sector organizations in English-language countries. They are also increasingly found in European countries and in supranational organizations such as UNESCO (see Pauwels 1998; Hellinger and Bussman 2001).

2.6 Assessing feminist language planning

The success of feminist language activism needs to be judged ultimately against the goals it set out to achieve. These include raising awareness of the gender bias in language and getting the speech community to adopt the proposed changes in a manner that promotes gender equality. The relatively recent nature of feminist language planning activities (from the mid-1970s at the earliest) and the scant number of investigations (Fasold 1987; Fasold *et al.* 1990) to date which have charted non-sexist language changes make a comprehensive assessment of success or failure as yet impossible. Nevertheless some comments can be made with regard to evidence of a greater community awareness of gender bias in language. Furthermore, the findings of recent and current research projects (admittedly small-scale) can shed some light on the adoption patterns of some non-sexist proposed changes in the community.

2.7 Increased awareness of gender bias

There is no doubt that in English-language communities and in some other speech communities (mainly European) the awareness of gender bias in language has been raised markedly as a result of feminist linguistic activism. Although many people still disagree with the claim that there is a gender bias in language, or refuse to adopt non-sexist language changes, they have nevertheless been made aware of the problematic nature of language in this respect. A growing number of people display **metalinguistic** behavior which points toward a greater awareness of sexist language. This includes apologizing for the use of generic *he* – some authors now feel compelled to justify the use of generic *he* in textbooks, or for using -*man* compounds in a generic context. Others self-correct generic *he* constructions or comment about title use and gender stereotypes. Whilst many such comments continue to be made in a deprecatory manner they nevertheless show awareness of the problem. The community's awareness is also evident in surveys on issues such as gender stereotyping, masculine generic *he* use, linguistic asymmetries in occupational nouns, and terms of address and naming practices (for an overview, see Pauwels 1998). For example, in 1986, 13 percent of 250 female respondents were not familiar with *Ms* as an alternative title for women; by 1996 this had decreased to 4 percent of 300 women (Pauwels 2001a). It is not possible at this stage to discern whether this awareness has been raised more through contact with linguistic disruption strategies or through language guidelines striving for linguistic equality.

2.8 Adopting feminist language change

Investigating the adoption of feminist language change is a much more complex issue. It involves exploring which types of feminist language change are being adopted: change resulting from linguistic disruption strategies, women-centered language developments, or form replacement proposals. It also requires investigating the process by which these changes spread through a speech community. Does change spread from public forms of written discourse to public speech? Which sector of the community leads the change and how does it spread from this group to other groups in the community? Furthermore, there is the fundamental question of whether the adoption and spread of non-sexist language through a community occurs in such a way that it promotes gender equality and eliminates the bias against women in language.

   To date many of these questions have not yet been addressed and present an opportunity for further research, especially in communities which have witnessed feminist linguistic activism for a number of years. To my knowledge there have not yet been any systematic investigations into community adoption of changes linked to the strategies of linguistic disruption or women-centered language developments. In fact the linguistic disruption strategy was not intended to be adopted by the community at large; rather, it was used by linguistic activists to raise the community's awareness, sometimes in a more provocative manner. There is certainly evidence that some feminist publications in English, German, Dutch, French, and Spanish continue to use linguistic disruption as a way of keeping readers aware of gender bias in language.

Developing women-centered languages has remained a preoccupation of poets and creative writers.

The adoption of proposals emerging from the linguistic equality approach and involving form replacements has received more attention. To date most such explorations have focused on the adoption and spread of non-sexist alternatives for generically used nouns and pronouns and on symmetrical naming practices or title use. The reduction or avoidance of gender-stereotyped language has also been examined. Although these investigations are relatively small-scale and mainly involve English, they nevertheless allow an insight into the issue of the adoption and spread of feminist language planning.

2.9 Non-sexist generic nouns and pronouns in writing

The studies by Cooper (1984), Markovitz (1984), Ehrlich and King (1994), and Pauwels (1997, 2000), among others, concern the adoption of non-sexist generic nouns and pronouns in English. All report a decrease in use of masculine generic nouns and pronouns in favor of non-sexist alternatives both in forms of written discourse and in public speech. Cooper's (1984) **corpus** of 500,000 words taken from American newspapers and magazines covering the period 1971 to 1979 noted a dramatic decline in the use of masculine generic nouns (including -*man* compounds) and some decline in the use of generic *he*. Markovitz (1984) and Ehrlich and King's (1994) work focuses on university documents and reveals that the use of non-sexist alternatives for masculine generic nouns and generic *he* had increased markedly. Pauwels' (1997) survey of non-sexist generic nouns and pronouns in 2,000 job advertisements in Australian newspapers found a very high degree of use of such forms. Only 5.4 percent of all generic nouns (i.e. 128 different occupational and human agent nouns) used in the advertisements could be considered sex-exclusive terms: there were a few instances of -*man* compounds and of -*ess* words. With the exception of *chairman* and *handyman*, all -*man* compounds occurred less than their gender-inclusive counterparts. There were many instances of -*man* compounds having been replaced by -*person* compounds such as *chairperson, draftsperson, foreperson, groundsperson, handyperson*, even *waitperson*. The investigation also showed that the (already) few female-exclusive terms had been abandoned in favor of gender-neutral ones. For example, there were no *air hostesses*, only *flight attendants*; no *salesgirls, saleswomen*, or *salesladies*, only *salesperson(s)* or *salespeople*. The study also revealed zero use of generic *he*. In job advertisements generic *he* was replaced mainly by the practice of repeating the generic noun, although there were some instances of *He/She*.

In more recent work I have started to investigate the use of non-sexist alternatives to masculine generic nouns and pronouns in public, non-scripted speech (Pauwels 2000, 2001b). A comparison of (non-scripted) speech derived from radio programs and parliamentary debates recorded in Australia between the 1960s and 1970s and in the 1990s showed a steep decline in the use of generic *he* from the pre-feminist reform period (i.e. between the 1960s and 1970s) to the post-feminist reform period (in the 1990s). In the pre-reform period approximately 95 percent of all generic pronouns were generic *he*. Singular *they* recorded less than 1 (0.4) percent, and *he or she* only 2.25 per cent. The post-reform period revealed a significant turnaround for singular *they*, which had become the most frequently used generic pronoun recording a 75 percent usage rate. Generic *he* had dropped from 95 to 18 percent, whereas *he or she* had increased only slightly to 4.5 percent. The users of these pronouns were mainly educated speakers including health professionals, journalists, lawyers, judges, members of the clergy, academics, teachers, and athletes. Changes in the patterns of generic noun use could not be investigated as there were very few examples of morphologically marked masculine generic nouns in the pre-and post-reform database.

Another recent study (Pauwels 2000) explored generic pronoun use by Australian academics and educators when they were lecturing or giving papers at conferences, or in workshops or symposia. This study revealed that generic *he* has become the exception rather than the norm in generic pronoun use, as can be gleaned from Table 12.1.

These investigations also reveal some difference in the choice of pronoun which is most likely linked either to type of speaker, or to type of speech genre, or both. Educators and academics display a greater use of *he or she* than other educated speakers, whose preference is for the gender-neutral alternative singular *they*. The observed difference may also reflect the type of speech genre: the first study (Pauwels 2001b) consisted mainly of parliamentary debates and one-on-one interviews on radio programs, whereas the second study (Pauwels 2000) focused on lectures in university or other educational settings.

[...]

2.10 Naming practices and titles

Another prominent aspect of feminist linguistic reform concerned naming practices and terms of address for women (e.g. Kramer 1975; Stannard 1977; Spender 1980; Cherry 1987). Symmetrical use of titles and terms of address for women and the elimination of derogatory and discriminatory naming practices were the goals of feminist linguistic activism. There is some evidence of change in this arena of language use as well: an increasing number of women adopt naming practices which assert their linguistic independence from men. Women are more likely to keep their pre-marital name after marriage; there is a growing tendency for the mother's surname to be chosen as the family surname upon the birth of children; naming practices which render women invisible (e.g. Mrs John Man) are starting to disappear.

Table 12.1: Generic pronoun use by academics and teachers

Pronouns	Number (2,189)	%
Singular *they*	763	34.85
He or she	1,105	50.47
Generic *he*	258	11.78
Generic *she*	60	2.74
It	3	0.13

Investigations to date have focused on the introduction and spread of the new title *Ms* as a term of address for women, replacing *Miss* and *Mrs* (for a discussion of the viability of *Ms* as a new title for women, see Pauwels 1998). Evidence from English-language countries (especially the USA, Canada, and Australia) shows that women are increasingly adopting the new title, with estimates for the USA ranging between 30 and 45 percent (Atkinson 1987; Pauwels 1987). For Australia I examined the use of *Ms* among women in 1986 and again in 1996 (Pauwels 1987, 2001a). In 1986 approximately 20 percent of 250 women used *Ms*. This percentage had almost doubled by 1996: 37 percent. The 1996 study also collected socio-demographic information on the *Ms* users, revealing that women with a tertiary education and between the ages of 25 and 65 (i.e. the working population) lead the adoption of *Ms*. Education was the most significant factor in determining title use. Age was also significant but because of the large age groupings it was not possible to pinpoint the most significant age group for *Ms* use. Correlations between marital status and title use showed that *Ms* is being adopted first by those who fall "outside" the traditional categories of "married" and "single/unmarried," but *Ms* use is increasingly found among the latter groups. Although these studies reveal an increase in the use of *Ms* there is not yet strong evidence that *Ms* is in fact replacing the titles *Mrs* or *Miss*. At this stage *Ms* has been added as a new option besides *Mrs* and *Miss* with the latter titles unlikely to become obsolescent in the near future. As to men's use of *Ms* to address women, preliminary evidence from Australia suggests that few attempts are made by men to use *Ms*, even where a woman's preference for this form is known.

3. Are the changes effective?

Investigating the effectiveness of the changes is the most important form of evaluation of the success or failure of (social) linguistic reform. Non-sexist language reform can be considered truly successful if there is not only evidence of the adoption of non-sexist alternatives but also evidence that these alternatives are being used in a manner promoting linguistic equality of the sexes. The investigation of the social effectiveness of non-sexist language reform is still in its infancy. The basis for most comments on the effectiveness of this reform is anecdotal evidence. For example, there is some evidence that the newly created *-person* compounds are not used generically but simply replace *-woman* compounds (Ehrlich and King 1994; Pauwels 2001a). Another observation is that some feminist linguistic creations are not used in their intended manner, leading to a depoliticization of these innovations: Ehrlich and King (1994: 65) comment that "while feminist linguistic innovations (such as *feminism, sexism, sexual harassment*, and *date rape*) pervade our culture, it is not clear that their use is consistent with their intended, feminist-influenced, meanings." To what extent the current usage patterns of *Ms* are an indication of potential failure is less clear cut: it is certainly true that the feminist intention of *Ms* being a replacement for *Miss* and *Mrs* has not yet been achieved and may not be achieved for a long time. In fact at the moment it is being used as an additional option to the existing titles of *Mrs* and *Miss*, leading to even greater asymmetry than before. However, my research into the use of *Ms* does show that women who use *Ms* do so with its intended meaning. The effectiveness of non-sexist alternatives to generic *he*, especially *he or she* and singular *they*, has also received mixed feedback: studies into the mental imagery associated with masculine generic nouns and pronouns had shown that the use of more gender-inclusive or gender-neutral forms reduced the maleness of the mental imagery (e.g. Moulton *et al.* 1978; Hamilton 1988; Wilson and Ng 1988). Khosroshahi's (1989) study, however, revealed no real difference in the mental imagery associated with masculine generic and gender-inclusive or gender neutral generic forms, except in the case of women who had reformed their language. She concludes that the adoption of gender-inclusive/gender-neutral forms will only be effective if there is a personal awareness of the discriminatory nature of the other forms and there is a personal commitment to change. This view concurs with Cameron's (1985: 90) comment that "in the mouths of sexists, language can always be sexist." However, I do not believe that this observation is cause for a pessimistic assessment of the effectiveness of non-sexist language reform: there is evidence that feminist linguistic activism has raised the community's awareness of gender bias in language. There is also proof that those who adopt the changes do so because they are aware of the bias and have a personal commitment to change. Of course, ultimately meanings are not fixed and will change over time and according to context. This applies as much to feminist meanings as to any other meanings.

4. Concluding remarks

In this chapter I have discussed feminist linguistic activism as a genuine form of language reform, showing women in the new roles of critical linguistic commentators, norm-breakers, and norm-makers. Even if the ultimate goals of feminist language reform may not be achieved these linguistic initiatives and actions, many of which have been undertaken at the grassroots level, have made a major contribution to exposing the ideologization of linguistic meanings to the speech community at large and to challenging the **hegemony** of the meanings promoted and authorized by the dominant group or culture, in this case men.

References

Atkinson, Donna L. (1987) Names and titles: Maiden name retention and the use of Ms, *Women and Language*, 10: 37.

Baron, Dennis (1986) *Grammar and Gender*, New Haven, CT/London: Yale University Press.

Blakar, Rolv M. (1977) *Språk er makt [Language and Power]*, Oslo: Pax.

Blaubergs, Maija (1980) An analysis of classic arguments against changing sexist language, *Women's Studies International Quarterly*, 2(3): 135–147.

Bodine, Ann (1975) Androcentrism in prescriptive grammar: Singular "they", sex-indefinite "he", and "he or she," *Language in Society*, 4(2): 129–146.

Brantenberg, Gert (1977) *Egalias døttre [Daughters of Egalia]*, Oslo: Novus.

Cameron, Deborah (1985) *Feminism and Linguistic Theory*, London: Macmillan.

—— (1995) *Verbal Hygiene*, London: Routledge.

Cherry, K. (1987) *Womansword: What Japanese Words Say about Women*, Tokyo: Kodansha International.

Cooper, Robert L. (1984) The avoidance of androcentric generics, *International Journal of the Sociology of Language*, 50: 5–20.

—— (1989) *Language Planning and Social Change*, Cambridge: Cambridge University Press.

Corbett, Greville (1991) *Gender*, Cambridge: Cambridge University Press.

Daly, Mary (1978) *Gyn/ecology: The Metaethics of Radical Feminism*, Boston, MA: Beacon Press.

Ehrlich, Susan and King, Ruth (1994) Feminist meanings and the (de)politicization of the lexicon, *Language in Society*, 23(1): 59–76.

Elgin, Suzette Haden (1988) *A First Dictionary and Grammar of Láaden*, Madison, WI: Society for the Furtherance and Study of Fantasy and Science Fiction.

Fasold, Ralph (1984) *The Sociolinguistics of Society*, Oxford: Blackwell.

—— (1987) Language policy and change: Sexist language in the periodical news media, in Peter Lowenberg (ed.), *Language Spread and Language Policy*, Washington, DC: Georgetown University Press, pp. 187–206.

——, Yamada, Haru, Robinson, David, and Barish, Steven (1990) The language planning effect of newspaper editorial policy: Gender differences in *The Washington Post*, *Language in Society*, 19(4): 521–539.

Garcia, Meseguer A. (1977) *Lenguaje y discriminación sexual* [*Language and Sex Discrimination*], Madrid: Editorial Cuadernos para el Diálogo, S.A. Edicusa.

Guentherodt, Ingrid (1979) Berufsbezeichnungen für Frauen. Problematik der deutschen Sprache im Vergleich mit Beispielen aus dem Englischen und Französischen [Occupational nouns for women. Problems for German in comparison with examples from English and French], *Osnabrücker Beiträge zur Sprachtheorie*, Beiheft 3: 120–132.

Guentherodt, Ingrid, Hellinger, Marlis, Pusch, Luise, and Troemel-Ploetz, Senta (1980) Richtlinien zur Vermeidung sexistischen Sprachgebrauchs [Guidelines for the elimination of sexist language use], *Linguistische Berichte*, 69: 15–21.

Hamilton, Mykol C. (1988) Using masculine generics: Does generic "he" increase male bias in the user's imagery? *Sex Roles*, 19(11–12): 785–799.

Hellinger, Marlis (1990) *Kontrastive Feministische Linguistik* [*Contrastive Feminist Linguistics*], Ismaning: Hueber.

—— and Bussmann, Hadumod (eds.), (2001) *Gender Across Languages: The Linguistic Representation of Women and Men*, Amsterdam: John Benjamins.

—— and Schräpel, Beate (1983) Über die sprachliche Gleichbehandlung von Frauen und Männern [About linguistic equality of women and men], *Jahrbuch für Internationale Germanistik*, 15(1): 40–69.

Henley, Nancy (1987) The new species that seeks a new language: On sexism in language and language change, in Joyce Penfield (ed.), *Women and Language in Transition*, Albany, NY: State University of New York Press, pp. 3–27.

Kalverkämper, Hartwig (1979) Die Frauen und die Sprache [Women and Language], *Linguistische Berichte* 62: 55–71.

Khosroshahi, Fatemeh (1989) Penguins don't care, but women do: A social identity analysis of a Whorfian problem, *Language in Society*, 18(4): 505–525.

Kloss, Heinz (1969) *Research Possibilities on Group Bilingualism: A Report*, Quebec: International Center for Research on Bilingualism.

Kochskämper, Birgit (1991) Language history as a history of male language policy: The history of German *Mensch, Frau, Mann, Mädchen, Junge, Dirne* … and their Indo-European cognates, *Working Papers on Language, Gender and Sexism*, 1(2): 5–17.

Kramarae, Cheris (1981) *Women and Men Speaking*, Rowley, MA: Newbury House.

—— (1992) Punctuating the dictionary, *International Journal of the Sociology of Language*, 94(1): 135–154.

Kramer, Cheris (1975) Sex-related differences in address systems, *Anthropological Linguistics*, 17(5): 198–210.

Lakoff, Robin (1975) *Language and Woman's Place*, New York: Harper and Row.

Mackay, Donald G. (1980) Psychology, prescriptive grammar and the pronoun problem, *American Psychologist*, 35(5): 444–449.

Markovitz, Judith (1984) The impact of the sexist language controversy and regulation on language in university documents, *Psychology of Women Quarterly*, 8(4): 337–347.

Moulton, Janice, Robinson, George M., and Elias, Cherin (1978) Sex bias in language use: neutral pronouns that aren't, *American Psychologist*, 33(11): 1032–1036.

Nilsen, Aileen P., Bosmajian, Haig, Gershuny, H. Lee, and Stanley, Julia P. (eds.), (1977) *Sexism and Language*, Urbana, IL: National Council of Teachers of English.

Pauwels, Anne (1987) Language in transition: A study of the title "Ms" in contemporary Australian society, in Anne Pauwels (ed.), *Women and Language in Australian and New Zealand Society*, Sydney: Australian Professional Publications, pp. 129–154.

—— (1993) Language planning, language reform and the sexes in Australia, *Australian Review of Applied Linguistics* (Series S), 10: 13–34.

—— (1997) Of handymen and waitpersons: A linguistic evaluation of job classifieds, *Australian Journal of Communication*, 24(1): 58–69.

—— (1998) *Women Changing Language*, London: Longman.

—— (2000) *Women Changing Language. Feminist Language Change in Progress*, paper presented at the First International Gender and Language Association Conference, Stanford University, CA, May 2000.

—— (2001a) Spreading the feminist word? A sociolinguistic study of feminist language change in Australian English: The case of the new courtesy title "Ms," in Marlis Hellinger and Hadumod Bussmann (eds.), *Gender Across Languages: The Linguistic Representation of Women and Men*, Amsterdam: John Benjamins, pp. 137–152.

—— (2001b) Non-sexist language reform and generic pronouns in Australian English, *English World Wide*, 22(1): 105–119.

Pusch, Luise (1984) *Das Deutsche als Männersprache* [*German as a Men's Language*], Frankfurt/Main: Suhrkamp.

Sabatini, Alma (1985) Occupational nouns in Italian: Changing the sexist usage, in Marlis Hellinger (ed.), *Sprachwandel und feministische Sprachpolitik: Internationale Perspektiven* [*Language Change and Feminist Language Policy: International Perspectives*]. Opladen: Westdeutscher, pp. 64–75.

Sautermeister, Christine (1985) La femme devant la langue [The woman before language], in *Frauenthemen im Fremdsprachenunterricht* [*Women's Topics in Foreign Language Teaching, Working Papers*], *Arbeitsberichte 3*, Hamburg: University of Hamburg, Zentrales Fremdspracheninstitut, pp. 63–97.

Schulz, Muriel (1975) The semantic derogation of women, in Barrie Thorne and Nancy Henley (eds.), *Language and Sex: Dominance and Difference*, Rowley, MA: Newbury House, pp. 64–73.

Spender, Dale (1980) *Man Made Language*, London: Routledge and Kegan Paul.

Stannard, Una (1977) *Mrs Man*, San Francisco, CA: Germainbooks.

Troemel-Ploetz, Senta (1978) Linguistik und Frauensprache [Linguistics and women's language], *Linguistische Berichte*, 57: 49–68.

Wilson, Elizabeth and Ng, Sik H. (1988) Sex bias in visuals evoked by generics: A New Zealand study, *Sex Roles*, 18(3–4): 159–168.

Yaguello, Marina (1978) *Les Mots et les femmes* [*Words and Women*], Paris: Payot.

Chapter 13

Mary Talbot

'I WISH YOU'D STOP INTERRUPTING ME!': INTERRUPTIONS AND ASYMMETRIES IN SPEAKER-RIGHTS IN EQUAL ENCOUNTERS

THE PRESENT STUDY draws upon approaches to the identification of **interruptions** used by Geoffrey Beattie (1983) and Stephen Murray (1985). Beattie's classification of kinds of speaker-switch provides a subtle framework for identifying candidate interruptions. Murray's approach provides the notions of level of severity, distributive justice and infringement of speaker rights. I will first refer to Don Zimmerman and Candace West (1975) and West and Zimmerman (1983 [1978]), since these studies have been highly influential in correlating use of interruptions and male dominance, since they propose that interruptions are violations of speakers' rights, and since they are explicitly refuted by both Beattie and Murray.

According to West and Zimmerman, interruptions are constant 'reminders' of women's social position as subordinates. In the field of language and gender, their two studies of interruptions are often put forward as evidence of male dominance. They are referred to categorically and without criticism, in a way that is, quite honestly, disturbing.[1] In both statistical studies they had the same findings: put bluntly, that men interrupted women and that women didn't interrupt men. But what are interruptions anyway? What did they count? In their 1975 study they examined 31 dyads of acquainted persons, all white middle class Americans living in southern California, whom they had tape-recorded in coffee shops and drug stores. An *interruption* in this first study was taken to be where a speaker cuts across more than one 'lexical constitutent' (word) of a prior speaker's utterance. A second category, *overlap*, allows for a margin of error, referring to all smaller stretches of **simultaneous speech**. These two categories allowed them to distinguish between 'violations' of speakers' rights and 'transition errors'. Briefly, their findings were as follows (see Table 13.1, Table 13.2; the second table gives the number of interruptions and overlaps (in parentheses) and their distribution as a percentage for each dyad).

Table 13.1: Interruptions and overlaps, same sex (20 dyads)

Interruptions	7 ('violations')
Overlaps	22 ('transition errors')

Table 13.2: Interruptions and overlaps, cross-sex (11 dyads)

	M	F	Total
Interruptions	96% (46)	4% (2)	100% (48)
Overlaps	100% (9)	–	100% (9)

There was apparently no discernible pattern to the incidence of interruptions in same sex dyads, i.e. no clear distinction between female–female and male–male dyads. What the results do show is that there was more interrupting going on in mixed-sex dyads, virtually all of it by men. The women scarcely initiated simultaneous speech at all. Zimmerman and West interpret their findings as follows:

> This contrast in the distribution of interruptions vis-à-vis overlaps ... suggests, if anything, that interruptions are idiosyncratic in same-sex conversations and systematic in cross-sex conversations. For example, one possibility is that males conversing with females orient themselves to the role of listener differently than they do with one another. For, if interruptions are viewed as violations of a speaker's rights, continual or frequent interruption might be viewed as disregard for a speaker, or for what a speaker has to say. Here, we are dealing with a class of speakers, females, whose rights to speak appear to be casually infringed upon by males.
> (Zimmerman and West 1975: 116–117)

Anxious as they are to identify the male oppressor, Zimmerman and West neglect to observe women's conversational practices. According to their findings women interrupt and overlap one another but not men. I suggest that, just as men consistently violated women's turns as speakers, women consistently avoided such violation of men's turns, deferring to them.

In their 1978 study (reprinted 1983), West and Zimmerman examined a smaller sample: videotapes of five mixed sex dyads (the quotations below are from the 1983 reprint). The informants were strangers; only the first 15 minutes of talk were used. West and Zimmerman argue that the informants were therefore maximally polite and in the kind of encounter where they were least likely to talk over their **interlocutor**. They claim that:

> reproduction of a similar pattern of predominantly male-initiated interruption under these conditions offers evidence for the robustness of the phenomenon.
> (West and Zimmerman 1983: 106)

An interruption in this second study is taken to be an incursion of more than two syllables into a prior speaker's turn:

> We intend the term *interruption* to refer only to those deep incursions that have the potential to disrupt a speaker's turn.
>
> (West and Zimmerman 1983: 104)

Excluded from the analysis in this second statistical study were *overlaps* (defined as simultaneous speech lasting less than one syllable, and including **backchannel feedback**, i.e. marginally longer stretches of simultaneous speech with 'some facilitative warrant') and *shallow interruptions* (within two syllables). The results of this second study are presented in Table 13.3, which again gives the number of interruptions (in parentheses) and their distribution as a percentage for each dyad.

In this statistical study, as in the one appearing in 1975, West and Zimmerman establish a correlation between sex of speaker and occurrence of interruption and make the claim that men use interruptions in order to position women as subordinates in conversation, just as they are positioned as subordinates in other social institutions:

> The gestures of power – minor in import viewed one by one – are an integral part of women's *placement* in the social scheme of things.
>
> (West and Zimmerman 1983: 110)

West and Zimmerman make the interesting observation that interruptions are "a way of 'doing' power in face-to-face interaction" (1983: 111). In other words, interruptions are not just a reflection of unequal relations of power between women and men, but enactments of these unequal relations.

It has to be said that West and Zimmerman's methods were rather crude. This, coupled with the fact that the data they collected are no longer available (apparently they destroyed the tapes to protect their informants), lays them wide open to being discredited. Two researchers, Stephen Murray and Lucille Covelli, have done just this, accusing West and Zimmerman of "fixing" their results ("we feel confident that they

Table 13.3: Interruptions in five cross-sex conversations between unacquainted persons

Conversation	Amount of interruption		
	M	*F*	*Total*
DYAD 1	75%	25%	100% (4)
DYAD 2	100%	0%	100% (4)
DYAD 3	67%	33%	100% (6)
DYAD 4	83%	17%	100% (6)
DYAD 5	63%	37%	100% (8)
Total	75% (21)	25% (7)	100% (28)

overinterpreted what they selected" (Murray and Covelli 1988: 108)) and of soiling the good name of Conversation Analysis. In a replication of the first study, Murray and Covelli achieved precisely the opposite results, using data from interviews, staff meetings and parties. They claim that "women *are* capable of interrupting" (1988: 103; original emphasis) in a wide range of situational contexts and reject all connection between interruptions and male dominance.[2]

Geoffrey Beattie's linguistic investigation of interruptions is certainly far more sophisticated than the crude word or syllable counting in the studies above. Using considerable improvements in classification taken from Nicola Ferguson (1977) and some refinements of his own, Beattie (1983) presents a far more complex picture, in which every attempt at a change in speaker can be labelled. Rather than finding interruptions mechanically, he identifies them on the basis of three criteria: success, presence of simultaneous speech and utterance completion. Supportive feedback is not excluded mechanically (by syllable counting) but on functional grounds. It is assumed to be brief. Rather than focusing only on occurrences of simultaneous speech, he looks more broadly at flaws in speaker-switch. Figure 13.1 presents his classification of attempted speaker-switches.

Beattie's data were videotapes of ten tutorial groups, with three to six students in each group, and two televised political interviews. His approach is more complex than West and Zimmerman's in three respects:

(i) he uses Ferguson's classification of types of speaker-switch (as reproduced in Figure 13.1);
(ii) he attends to gestures and eye-contact accompanying speaker-switch;
(iii) he presents his findings in terms of the relative frequency of each category, expressed as a percentage of the total number of interruptions. In the tutorials study, the effects of sex and status as variables are presented in separate sets of complex statistics.

The results indicate a correlation between the social position of speaker and the occurrence of *overlap*. It tended to be tutors who produced *overlaps*; the other kinds of speaker-switch were distributed across participants. Beattie interprets this as evidence of a psycholinguistic skill acquired by "experts":

> In the first study of non-dyadic tutorials the frequency of different types of interruptions was shown to be related to a number of social variables. The status of interactants but not their sex was shown to have a significant effect on the number and types of interruption that arose. Tutors tended to overlap with students more than vice versa. This is a type of interruption which … requires considerable psycholinguistic skill demanding as it does the ability to predict a possible completion point. Students, on the other hand, used simple interruptions more frequently than tutors.
>
> (Beattie 1983: 149)

The results showed women interrupting men, as well as vice versa. Beattie interprets this as evidence that women can and do interrupt when they want "to make an

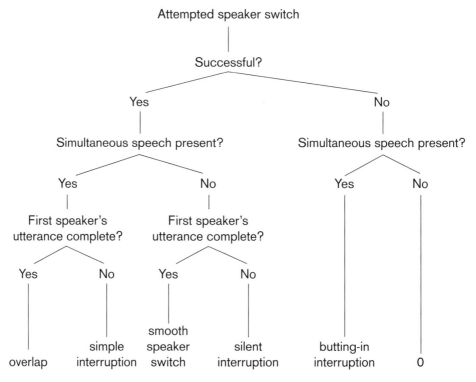

Figure 13.1: Attempted speaker-switches (from Beattie 1983).

impression". He has a psychologist's view of conversational phenomena as the skills of individuals, rather than sharing West and Zimmerman's (albeit undertheorised) view that they place interlocutors in social positions.

The contrast between the two approaches, in terms of the way interruptions are evaluated as features of interaction, is quite striking. West and Zimmerman see them as violations, cutting short speakers' contributions. Beattie sees them as a part of speakers' "interactional competence" (with an unexamined assumption that this involves knowing how to *compete*). Indeed, Beattie takes West and Zimmerman's claims that women do not interrupt as much as men to be a slur on women, an insinuation that women are incompetent in interaction. In his speculations about the contrast between his and West and Zimmerman's findings, he reveals some rather telling assumptions about the nature of 'personal' male–female interactions:

> One may speculate that sex differences in conversational behaviour of the type observed by Zimmerman and West (1975) may be limited to those types of conversation in which women are not deliberately trying to make an impression – this presumably would be especially true in many dyadic male–female conversations where there is not a third party observing the proceedings.
>
> (Beattie 1983: 125)

Why *especially* true in **dyadic** male–female conversations? What kind of cultural assumptions about relationships between women and men are creeping in here? Beattie suggests that the women did not initiate interruptions because they were not "trying to make an impression". So why did the men initiate so many? The implication is that the men interrupted so often in order to make an impression, presumably on their female interlocutors.

The approach to the analysis of interruptions proposed by Stephen Murray (1985) is very different from either Beattie's or West and Zimmerman's. He claims that syntactic or acoustic criteria alone are insufficient to identify potential points for speaker-switch or the presence of interruption, and proposes that what counts as an interruption for interactants depends on their sense of "distributive justice". According to Murray, participants' judgements are wholly functional:

> members judge the intention both of the person already speaking and of the one who begins to speak while the other continues, along with the content of what both say and a folk weighing of distributive justice, which included how long someone has been talking and whether anyone else has some particular claim to reply or comment.
>
> (Murray 1985: 32)

This "members' model of interruption", as he calls it, has four levels of severity, according to opportunities given to a speaker to make "points". Participants decide whether a speaker is interrupting to make a first point, in which case the intrusion is not serious, or whether the speaker is taking more turns than she is entitled to. For these judgements (which presumably do not involve conscious deliberation), participants draw on the "microhistorical context" (1985: 36), i.e. on what has gone before. Put simply, the more turns you have already had in which to make "points", the more serious an interruption is as an infringement on the other interactants' rights to contribute. Out of candidate violations of speaker rights, Murray pinpoints those that participants take to be violations by attention to their production of palliatives: apologies, etc. Presence of these phenomena is taken as proof that interlocutors think that an infringement of speaker rights has taken place. To illustrate the differences in severity of interruptions he contrasts his examples (6) and (7):

(6)
F1:   Can I ask you specifically / about what was going on at eighty-four
      and five?
M1:   yeah   yeah

(F1): when you're trying to fade out/ and you kind of take—
F2:   Yeah/I was / I was just
      going to remark about that because it seemed to me ...
M1:   yeah

According to Murray's severity criterion, the interruption in the example above is a more serious infringement of speaker rights than the interruption in:

(7)
F2: … I think if I were the student / under those circumstances / which are somewhat *threat*-ening to begin with um   then
M1:   uh-huh
(F2): I would find it very difficult to discuss/ the answer to the question the professor might want/ so there's that /OK/ the-e-e-n I noticed that once I listened—
M2:   Can I pop up/before you run on/this reminded me of/something hit me …

(Murray 1985: 36–37)

The reasons Murray gives for his claim that (6) is a more serious infringement than (7) are as follows:

> By the criterion of severity of interruption, F2's interruption of F1 is more severe than M2's of F2, because in (7), F2 had made a point (affirmed lexically: 'so there's that'), and eventually made others, whereas in (6), F1 had not made any point yet in the interaction and never regained the **floor**. Although in (7) F2 signaled an intent to continue (recognized by what M2 says), M2 enters, albeit late, after a completion point ('so there's that'). In contrast, in (6) F2 takes over nowhere near a possible completion point.
>
> (Murray 1985: 36)

As Murray goes to great pains to point out, there is no evidence of anyone being aware of the way F2 has barged in over F1. F2 shows no sign of awareness of any infringement; that is to say, she offers no palliatives. A clear case of distributive injustice. Something rather odd happens to Murray's argument here. Instead of observing, as by his own groundrules he should, that F1's rights are of no import, or, more to the point, that she *has* no rights, he considers F2's failure to notice or compensate for her treatment of F1 as a factor adding to its seriousness:

> Moreover, M2 later (again lexically) recognized that F2 had been interrupted and should be allowed to resume speaking, which neither F2 nor anyone else did for F1.
>
> (Murray 1985: 36–37)

He then asserts that F2's sense of 'violation' by the interruption in (7) had:

> less to do with possible completion points than with the insult to her (or possibly women as a class) in 'before you run on'.
>
> (Murray 1985: 37)

His approach, since it depends on the participants' own sense of distributive justice, will automatically reproduce any distributive *in*justices, as he points out. But he seems to lose track of this insight when confronted by F2's disregard for F1.

At this point I begin to get the impression that Murray's main concern is in fact to demonstrate that women interrupt other women, and that feminists who attribute a feeling of being insulted by men to interruptions are really responding to something else altogether. On the one hand, he is saying that interactants' sense of what is an interruption is based on a notion of distributive justice, which can be focused on by turning attention to apologies, etc. On the other hand, he is saying that when interactants do *not* appear to be using the model that he has given them, then they are reneging on their own sense of justice. There is an assumption, a quite unwarranted assumption, underlying his notions of speaker rights and distributive justice – namely, that interactants have equal rights. I think one of the difficulties is that Murray does not clearly distinguish between his own and his informants' judgements: between what *he* thinks, on the basis of his framework of supposed "members' own" judgements, and what his informants demonstrate by their production of palliatives.

Interruptions are appropriations of a right to speak. In interrupting, a speaker is laying claim to a turn. What are going to differ are participants' notions of what their rights are, and what distribution of turns they think is just or appropriate. The example below, taken from Schegloff (1972), shows a repair mechanism in action (Schegloff uses it as evidence that people orient towards Transition Relevance Points (TRPs):

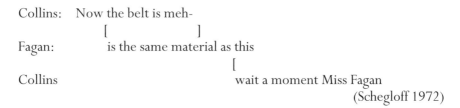

Collins: Now the belt is meh-
                     [   ]
Fagan: is the same material as this
                                                [
Collins   wait a moment Miss Fagan
                                                          (Schegloff 1972)

We can see that Collins corrects Fagan, so it must be an interruption; she seized a turn out of order. Since Schegloff gives no hint as to the situational or cultural context in which it was produced, I will have to guess. For the sake of argument, let's assume that Fagan is a shop assistant and Collins is her male boss. (I make this highly informed guess on the basis of (i) Collins' apparent interruption of Fagan, (ii) his choice of address-term, (iii) his lack of **mitigation** in correcting her.) Collins responds to Fagan's contribution – we know from the presence of a repair mechanism that he feels interrupted. Could Fagan do the same? Is she entitled to judge his utterances as interruptions? Can she challenge him with a "just a moment Mr Collins"? Not, I suggest, if she values her job!

Clearly, deciding what counts as an interruption is no simple matter. Murray's tentative solution proposal goes part of the way to resolving the problem of how to identify them. As he rightly observes, we need to take into account what participants themselves think. Interactants define interruptions not by counting syllables but functionally. Whatever else interruptions may be, they are appropriations of a right to speak. In interrupting, a speaker claims a turn. What are going to differ are participants' notions of what their rights are and what distribution of turns they think is just or appropriate. We need to look at discoursal activity, which means more than counting syllables.

I will now go on to examine a more substantial sample of conversation. This conversation took place in my own home in 1985. I am W2 in the transcript – the silent one, who is taping the whole proceedings.[3] I have taken the somewhat unusual transcription layout from some unpublished data analysis by Norman Fairclough. This layout is particularly useful for presenting data with frequent speaker shifts and simultaneous speech. The conversation contains an example of a speaker complaining about being interrupted, by his wife. This complaint is on "stave" 16; the husband is evidently aware of being repeatedly interrupted, and is irritated by it. Using Beattie's classification of speaker switches I have identified all candidate interruptions.[4] The onset of these are entered on the chart below. A great deal of the simultaneous speech is supportive feedback. Like other analysts, I do not consider supportive feedback as interruption since it does not constitute an attempted speaker-switch. I include quite lengthy stretches of talk in this category. When a speaker begins a turn over supportive feedback, I do not judge that to be interrupting either (see Figure 13.2).

The transcript in Figure 13.2 contains part of a couple's account of their vacation. H1 and W1 are giving an account of their passage through customs. They made a great deal of eye contact with each other and were clearly collaboratively remembering the details. H1's contribution is a single narrative strand. The other interactants support him, especially W1, who assists in remembering details, provides supportive feedback and deals with queries. For the most part, H1 ignores divergences from his own narrative; it is left to W1 to respond to H2's "interested questions". (There are just three exceptions: in stave 7, following a questioning repeat, where he expands briefly on W1's confirmation; in stave 11, in response to a direct request for explanation; and in stave 14, where he interrupts his wife's response to one of H2's "interested questions" to answer it himself.) As we can see from Figure 13.2, speaker-shifts identifiable as interruptions are quite evenly distributed:

	Simple interruption	Silent interruption	Butting-in
H1	(4) over H2 "whe whe when …" (14) over W1 "no that was …" (15) over W1 "over"		
H2	(3) over W1 "oh did you …"	(4) across H1 "use it as …" (8) across H1 "rabies?"	
W1	?(3) over H2 "yeh" (3) over H1 "no it was …"	(4) across H1 "somebody gave him …"	(14) across H1 "no that-" (10) over H1 "no er-"

Oddly, W1's turn immediately preceding H1's complaint is not one of the candidate interruptions entered on the transcript – it did not qualify by the criteria given by any of the approaches to the identification of interruptions. Her four interruptions of H1 on the chart are a simple interruption and two butting-in interruptions to correct specific details of their story ("no it was …" "no er-" and "no that-") and a silent interruption, after H1's lengthy hesitation, continuing a side topic with H2 ("somebody gave him …").

Figure 13.2: Transcript of family conversation (own data).

Key: - incompletion indicated with hyphen e.g. the er customs-
      . untimed pauses of about a second indicated with fullstop

1
h1 i'd forgotten that they distinguish between . still table wines and er sparkling wines yknow fizzy wines . so we brought back
h2
w1   oh gosh yeh
w2

2
h1 i think was it eight bottles of . of table wine . and er we were only allowed something like . six four yknow anyway . so i'm
h2   mm
w1
w2

3
h1 shittin myself   because-
h2   oh did you bring some of y y   mum's schnaps
w1 no it was the schnaps that made it because if you bring some spirits   in it halves it   yeh
w2

4
h1   whe whe when we got to the er-   the er customs-
h2 from home?   huhm   use it as paint
w1   mm   somebody gave him some industrial schnaps as well

Figure 13.2: continued

5
```
h1                       er normally they just wave you straight through yknow      but er well this guy just
h2  stripper for the door                                                      yeh
w1                                        ah heh heh
w2                               heh heh
```

6
```
h1  leans over an says . bay number six sir . oh shit yknow we'd gone through the green zone yknow nothing to declare and silvie'd
h2                                            heh
w1
w2                                                   ah
```

7
```
h1  got some plants under the seat which were illegal to bring in anyway        colorado beetle        grief
h2                                      plants?                                  oh good
w1                        oh gosh            yeh                                 mm
w2                              really illegal . plants oh yes                                    and rabies
```

8
```
h1  an er an er-
h2  rabies?
w1  yeh cos if an animal that has rabies spits on the leaves lying on the floor some other animal could catch it
w2
```

9
```
h1                           and er ..silvie's mother'd bought me this telescope for a . birthday present yeh
h2  good grief                                                                              oh yeh
w1        so heh heh plants are really out heh
w2                            heh heh
```

Figure 13.2: continued

10
h1   well was combined birthday and christmas present   . and that also ought to have been declared
h2
w1   no er-   combined birthday and christmas present
w2

11
h1   = well they're cheaper over there than it's like when you buy watches or optical instruments   you've got to declare
h2   why =   good   grief
w1
w2

12
h1   it because you pay import duty on it . erm so w we got got quite a lot've gear   it's all small stuff   but cu cumulative
h2   mm   mm   yeheh
w1
w2

13
h1   and my air of innocence would have been stretching its cred credulity somewhat . i'd got er . a bought er . a pack of 250 grams
h2   mm
w1
w2

14
h1   of tobacco yknow . for you and martin . and mary of course yknow heh   and er-   yeh well-   no that was within the
h2   heh was that over as well?
w1   no   that-
w2

Figure 13.2: continued

15

h1   limit . but I forgot . that i'd also got a couple of packets of gitane which i'd been smoking myself =   over

h2

w1   = yeh but they were open

w2

16

h1   but one pack I wish you'd stop interruptin me   there's one packet which er was unopened and one packet which i was smoking

h2   heheh

w1   heh

w2   heh

17

h1   but i'd forgotten about that was floatin about the car yknow . and it all sort've came   wow . bay number six sir . urrk

h2   mm   mm

w1

w2   heh heh

18

h1   heh heh s'was pulled in . and there was a woman there as well when you get the er w usually find the women er customs officer

h2

w1

w2

19

h1   are really officious . because once last time i spoke to one she was really bloody bitchy yknow

h2   yeheh

w1

w2

According to Murray, interactants work with a sense of distributive justice, so that interruptions are more serious coming from someone who has been hogging the floor than from someone who cannot get a word in. But H1, judging by his complaint, thinks W1's contributions are violations of his speaking rights, even though he talks *more* than she does. (I have not counted the number of turns taken by each participant, but a glance at the transcript is enough to give a rough idea of the distribution of talk, since the participants have a line each.) I think we are entitled to ask what conception of "distributive justice" Murray is working with. As with the case of Collins and Fagan above, it may be that differential rights are at issue. How many turns at talk does H1 think he is entitled to if W1's collaboration in the telling of their story is seen as a violation of his rights? The lion's share, presumably. If this is the case, H1 gets his way. After his complaint to her, the transcript "flatlines", as it were; that is, the other participants no longer contribute. It continues like this for several minutes, until he has finished "his" narrative, with a noticeable reduction in **minimal responses**.

By looking at interactants' management of interruptions, then, we can pinpoint asymmetries in speaking rights in informal situations among groups of people whom we would probably think of as equals. I think a similar approach to the one I have adopted above could be used to account for the discrepancy in the treatment of F2 and F1 in Murray's data. It is difficult to comment on such small isolated fragments, of course – I tentatively suggest that palliatives are offered for F2 because she is a force to be reckoned with, a troublesome feminist who complains when she is interrupted. Unlike Murray's F1 perhaps, for whom no palliatives were offered.

In conclusion, I suggest that a statistical approach to interruptions is of limited value. It is far more interesting to see interruptions in action – as in the struggle between husband and wife over who gets to tell their story. Zimmerman and West's studies of interruptions clearly had a political function. The correlation they made between interruptions and male dominance was of course far too straightforward. The strong negative reactions the studies have elicited should serve as warnings to feminists of the pitfalls of using quantification as a rhetorical device. Anything put forward as evidence of men dominating women was bound to be contested – we are after all living in patriarchy.

Correspondence to: M. Talbot, 5 Bairstow St., Preston PR1 3TN, UK.

Notes

1   A recent example of such uncritical citation is found in Cate Poynton (1990). She provides a useful checklist of differences between the speech of women and men under three headings: the discourse stratum, the lexico-grammatical stratum and the phonological stratum. Under the first of these headings, the discourse-stratum, her first example is:
     "*Interruption:* men interrupt women and not vice versa in mixed-sex conversations." (1990: 70)

2   See also the debate that followed Murray and Covelli's article in the same issue of *Journal of Pragmatics* (Talbot 1988; Murray 1988).

3   The participants were not aware of being taped, but I played it back to them immediately afterwards and gained their permission to use it as data.

4   In applying Beattie's approach to the classification of speaker switches I will not attempt to distinguish between simple interruption and overlap. I find the distinction difficult to work with. From Beattie's examples, the difference between these two categories seems to lie in

the actions of the interruptee. If the person interrupted stops speaking before finishing, the interrupter has produced a simple interruption. If the interruptee doggedly finishes her contribution, then the interrupter is overlapping.

References

Beattie, Geoffrey (1983) *Talk*, Milton Keynes: Open University Press.

Ferguson, Nicola (1977) Simultaneous speech, interruptions and dominance, *British Journal of Social and Clinical Psychology*, 16(4): 295–302.

Murray, Stephen (1985) Toward a model of members' methods for recognizing interruptions, *Language and Society*, 14(1): 31–40.

—— (1988) The sound of simultaneous speech: the meaning of interruption, *Journal of Pragmatics*, 12(1): 115–116.

—— and Covelli, Lucille (1988) Women and men speaking at the same time, *Journal of Pragmatics*, 12(1): 99–111.

Poynton, Cate (1990) *Language and Gender: Making the Difference*, Oxford: Oxford University Press.

Schegloff, Emanuel (1972) Sequencing in conversational openings, in John Gumperz and Dell Hymes (eds.), *Directions in Sociolinguistics*, New York: Holt, Rinehart and Winston, pp. 346–380.

Talbot, Mary (1988) The operation was a success, unfortunately the patient died: Comment on Murray and Covelli's "Women and men speaking at the same time", *Journal of Pragmatics*, 12(1): 113–114.

West, Candace and Zimmerman, Don (1983 [1978]) Small insults: A study of interruptions in cross-sex conversations between unacquainted persons, in Barrie Thorne, Cheris Kramarae and Nancy Henley (eds.), *Language, Gender and Society*, Rowley, MA: Newbury House, pp. 103–117.

Zimmerman, Don and West, Candace (1975) Sex roles, interruptions and silences in conversation, in Barrie Thorne and Nancy Henley (eds.), *Language and Sex: Difference and Dominance*, Rowley, MA: Newbury House, pp. 105–129.

Chapter 14

Deborah Cameron

PERFORMING GENDER IDENTITY: YOUNG MEN'S TALK AND THE CONSTRUCTION OF HETEROSEXUAL MASCULINITY

Introduction

IN 1990, A 21-year-old student in a language and gender class I was teaching at a college in the southern USA tape-recorded a sequence of casual conversation among five men; himself and four friends. This young man, whom I will call 'Danny',[1] had decided to investigate whether the informal talk of male friends would bear out generalizations about 'men's talk' that are often encountered in discussions of gender differences in conversational style – for example that it is competitive, hierarchically organized, centres on 'impersonal' topics and the exchange of information, and foregrounds speech genres such as joking, trading insults and sports statistics.

Danny reported that the stereotype of all-male interaction was borne out by the data he recorded. He gave his paper the title 'Wine, women, and sports'. Yet although I could agree that the data did contain the stereotypical features he reported, the more I looked at it, the more I saw other things in it too. Danny's analysis was not inaccurate, his conclusions were not unwarranted, but his description of the data was (in both senses) *partial*: it was shaped by expectations that caused some things to leap out of the record as 'significant', while other things went unremarked.

I am interested in the possibility that Danny's selective reading of his data was not just the understandable error of an inexperienced analyst. Analysis is never done without preconceptions, we can never be absolutely non-selective in our observations, and where the object of observation and analysis has to do with gender it is extraordinarily difficult to subdue certain expectations.

[…]

[What this suggests is that] the behaviour of men and women, whatever its substance may happen to be in any specific instance, is invariably read through a more general discourse on gender difference itself. That discourse is subsequently invoked to *explain* the pattern of gender differentiation in people's behaviour; whereas it might be more enlightening to say the discourse *constructs* the differentiation, makes it visible *as* differentiation.[2]

I want to propose that conversationalists themselves often do the same thing I have just suggested analysts do. Analysts construct stories about other people's behaviour, with a view to making it exemplify certain patterns of gender differences; conversationalists construct stories about themselves and others, with a view to performing certain kinds of gender identity.

Identity and performativity

In 1990, the philosopher Judith Butler published an influential book called *Gender Trouble: Feminism and the Subversion of Identity*. Butler's essay is a postmodernist reconceptualization of gender, and it makes use of a concept familiar to linguists and discourse analysts from speech-act theory: *performativity*. For Butler, gender is *performative* – in her suggestive phrase, 'constituting the identity it is purported to be'. Just as J.L. Austin (1961) maintained that illocutions like 'I promise' do not describe a pre-existing state of affairs but actually bring one into being, so Butler claims that 'feminine' and 'masculine' are not what we are, nor traits we *have*, but effects we produce by way of particular things we *do*: 'Gender is the repeated stylization of the body, a set of repeated acts within a rigid regulatory frame which congeal over time to produce the appearance of substance, of a "natural" kind of being' (p. 33).

This extends the traditional feminist account whereby gender is socially constructed rather than 'natural', famously expressed in Simone de Beauvoir's dictum that 'one is not born, but rather becomes a woman'. Butler is saying that 'becoming a woman' (or a man) is not something you accomplish once and for all at an early stage of life. Gender has constantly to be reaffirmed and publicly displayed by repeatedly performing particular acts in accordance with the cultural norms (themselves historically and socially constructed, and consequently variable) which define 'masculinity' and 'femininity'.

This 'performative' model sheds an interesting light on the phenomenon of gendered *speech*. Speech too is a 'repeated stylization of the body'; the 'masculine' and 'feminine' styles of talking identified by researchers might be thought of as the 'congealed' result of repeated acts by social actors who are striving to constitute themselves as 'proper' men and women. Whereas sociolinguistics traditionally assumes that people talk the way they do because of who they (already) are, the postmodernist approach suggests that people are who they are because of (among other things) the way they talk. This shifts the focus away from a simple cataloguing of differences between men and women to a subtler and more complex inquiry into how people use linguistic resources to produce gender differentiation. It also obliges us to attend to the 'rigid regulatory frame' within which people must make their choices – the norms that define what kinds of language are possible, intelligible and appropriate resources for performing masculinity or femininity.

A further advantage of this approach is that it acknowledges the instability and variability of gender identities, and therefore of the behaviour in which those identities are performed. While Judith Butler rightly insists that gender is regulated and policed by rather rigid social norms, she does not reduce men and women to automata, programmed by their early socialization to repeat forever the appropriate gendered behaviour, but treats them as conscious agents who may – albeit often at some social cost – engage in acts of transgression, subversion and resistance. As active producers rather than passive reproducers of gendered behaviour, men and women may use their awareness of the gendered meanings that attach to particular ways of speaking and acting to produce a variety of effects. This is important, because few, if any, analysts of data on men's and women's speech would maintain that the differences are as clear-cut and invariant as one might gather from such oft-cited dichotomies as 'competitive/cooperative' and 'report talk/rapport talk'. People *do* perform gender differently in different contexts, and do sometimes behave in ways we would normally associate with the 'other' gender. The conversation to which we now turn is a notable case in point.

The conversation: Wine, women, sports … and other men

The five men who took part in the conversation, and to whom I will give the pseudonyms Al, Bryan, Carl, Danny and Ed, were demographically a homogeneous group: white, middle-class American suburbanites aged 21, who attended the same university and belonged to the same **social network** on campus. This particular conversation occurred in the context of one of their commonest shared leisure activities: watching sports at home on television.[3]

Throughout the period covered by the tape-recording there is a basketball game on screen, and participants regularly make reference to what is going on in the game. Sometimes these references are just brief interpolated comments, which do not disrupt the flow of ongoing talk on some other topic; sometimes they lead to extended discussion. At all times, however, it is a legitimate conversational move to comment on the basketball game. The student who collected the data drew attention to the status of sport as a resource for talk available to North American men of all classes and racial/ethnic groups, to strangers as well as friends, suggesting that 'sports talk' is a typically 'masculine' conversational genre in the US, something all culturally competent males know how to do.

But 'sports talk' is by no means the only kind of talk being done. The men also recount the events of their day – what classes they had and how these went; they discuss mundane details of their domestic arrangements, such as who is going to pick up groceries; there is a debate about the merits of a certain kind of wine; there are a couple of longer narratives, notably one about an incident when two men sharing a room each invited a girlfriend back without their roommate's knowledge – and discovered this at the most embarrassing moment possible. Danny's title 'Wine, women, and sports' is accurate insofar as all these subjects are discussed at some length.

When one examines the data, however, it becomes clear there is one very significant omission in Danny's title. Apart from basketball, the single most prominent theme in the recorded conversation, as measured by the amount of time devoted to it, is 'gossip': discussion of several persons not present but known to the participants, with a strong focus on critically examining these individuals' appearance, dress, social behaviour and sexual moves. Like the conversationalists themselves, the individuals under discussion are all men. Unlike the conversationalists, however, the individuals under discussion are identified as 'gay'.

The topic of 'gays' is raised by Ed, only a few seconds into the tape-recorded conversation (6):[4]

> ED: Mugsy Bogues (.) my name is Lloyd Gompers I am a homosexual (.) you know what the (.) I saw the new Remnant I should have grabbed you know the title? Like the head thing?

'Mugsy Bogues' (the name of a basketball player) is an acknowledgement of the previous turn, which concerned the on-screen game. Ed's next comment appears off-topic, but he immediately supplies a rationale for it, explaining that he 'saw the new Remnant' – *The Remnant* being a deliberately provocative right-wing campus newspaper whose main story that week had been an attack on the 'Gay Ball', a dance sponsored by the college's Gay Society.

The next few turns are devoted to establishing a shared view of the Gay Ball and of homosexuality generally. Three of the men, Al, Bryan and Ed, are actively involved in this exchange. A typical sequence is the following (14–16):

> AL: gays=
> ED: =gays w[hy? that's what it should read [gays why?
> BRYAN: [gays]   [I know]

What is being established as 'shared' here is a view of gays as alien (that is, the group defines itself as heterosexual and puzzled by homosexuality: 'gays, why?'), and also to some extent comical. Danny comments at one point, 'it's hilarious', and Ed caps the sequence discussing the Gay Ball (23–25) with the witticism:

> ED: the question is who wears the boutonnière and who wears the corsage, flip for it? or do they both just wear flowers coz they're fruits

It is at this point that Danny introduces the theme that will dominate the conversation for some time: gossip about individual men who are said to be gay. Referring to the only other man in his language and gender class, Danny begins (27):

> DANNY: My boy Ronnie was uh speaking up on the male perspective today (.) way too much

The section following this contribution is structured around a series of references to other 'gay' individuals known to the participants as classmates. Bryan mentions 'the most effeminate guy I've ever met' (29) and 'that really gay guy in our Age of Revolution class' (34). Ed remarks that 'you have never seen more homos than we have in our class. Homos, dykes, homos, dykes, everybody is a homo or a dyke' (64). He then focuses on a 'fat, queer, goofy guy … [who's] as gay as night' [sic] (78–80), and on a 'blond hair, snide little queer weird shit' (98), who is further described as a 'butt pirate'. Some of these references, but not all, initiate an extended discussion of the individual concerned. The content of these discussions will bear closer examination.

'The Antithesis of Man'

One of the things I initially found most puzzling about the whole 'gays' sequence was that the group's criteria for categorizing people as gay appeared to have little to do with those people's known or suspected sexual preferences or practices. The terms 'butt pirate' and 'butt cutter' were used, but surprisingly seldom; it was unclear to me that the individuals referred to really were homosexual, and in the one case where I actually knew the subject of discussion, I seriously doubted it.

Most puzzling is an exchange between Bryan and Ed about the class where 'everybody is a homo or a dyke', in which they complain that 'four homos' are continually 'hitting on' [making sexual overtures to] one of the women, described as 'the ugliest-ass bitch in the history of the world' (82–89). One might have thought that a defining feature of a 'homo' would be his lack of interest in 'hitting on' women. Yet no one seems aware of any problem or contradiction in this exchange.

I think this is because the deviance indicated for this group by the term 'gay' is not so much *sexual* deviance as *gender* deviance. Being 'gay' means failing to measure up to the group's standards of masculinity or femininity. This is why it makes sense to call someone '*really* gay': unlike same- versus other-sex preference, conformity to gender norms can be a matter of degree. It is also why hitting on an 'ugly-ass bitch' can be classed as 'homosexual' behaviour – proper masculinity requires that the object of public sexual interest be not just female, but minimally attractive.

Applied by the group to men, 'gay' refers in particular to insufficiently masculine appearance, clothing and speech. To illustrate this I will reproduce a longer sequence of conversation about the 'really gay guy in our Age of Revolution class', which ends with Ed declaring: 'he's the antithesis of man'.

> BRYAN: uh you know that really gay guy in our Age of Revolution class who sits in front of us? he wore shorts again, by the way, it's like 42 degrees out he wore shorts again [laughter] [Ed: That guy] it's like a speedo, he wears a speedo to class (.) he's got incredibly skinny legs [Ed: it's worse] you know=
>
> ED: =you know like those shorts women volleyball players wear? it's like those (.) it's l[ike
>
> BRYAN: [you know what's even more ridicu[lous? when
> ED: [French cut spandex]
>
> BRYAN: you wear those shorts and like a parka on ... (5 lines omitted)

BRYAN: he's either got some condition that he's got to like
     have his legs exposed at all times or else he's got really
     good legs=
ED: =he's probably he'[s like
CARL: [he really likes

BRYAN: =he
ED: =he's like at home combing his leg hairs=
CARL: his legs=

BRYAN: he doesn't have any leg hair though= [*yes* and oh
ED: =he *real*[*ly* likes

ED: his legs=
AL: =very long very white and very skinny

BRYAN: those ridiculous Reeboks that are always (indeciph) and goofy
     white socks always striped= [tube socks
ED: =that's [right

ED: he's the antithesis of man

In order to demonstrate that certain individuals are 'the antithesis of man', the group engages in a kind of conversation that might well strike us as the antithesis of 'men's talk'. It is unlike the 'wine, women, and sports' stereotype of men's talk – indeed, rather closer to the stereotype of 'women's talk' – in various ways, some obvious, and some less so.

The obvious ways in which this sequence resembles conventional notions of 'women's talk' concern its purpose and subject-matter. This is talk about people, not things, and 'rapport talk' rather than 'report talk' – the main point is clearly not to exchange information. It is 'gossip', and serves one of the most common purposes of gossip, namely affirming the solidarity of an in-group by constructing absent others as an out-group, whose behaviour is minutely examined and found wanting.

The specific subjects on which the talk dwells are conventionally 'feminine' ones: clothing and bodily appearance. The men are caught up in a contradiction: their criticism of the 'gays' centres on their unmanly interest in displaying their bodies, and the inappropriate garments they choose for this purpose (bathing costumes worn to class, shorts worn in cold weather with parkas which render the effect ludicrous, clothing which resembles the outfits of 'women volleyball players'). The implication is that real men just pull on their jeans and leave it at that. But in order to pursue this line of criticism, the conversationalists themselves must show an acute awareness of such 'unmanly' concerns as styles and materials ('French cut spandex', 'tube socks'), what kind of clothes go together, and which men have 'good legs'. They are impelled, paradoxically, to talk about men's bodies as a way of demonstrating their own total lack of sexual interest in those bodies.

The less obvious ways in which this conversation departs from stereotypical notions of 'men's talk' concern its *formal* features. Analyses of men's and women's speech style are commonly organized around a series of global oppositions, e.g. men's talk is 'competitive', whereas women's is 'cooperative'; men talk to gain 'status', whereas women talk to forge 'intimacy' and 'connection'; men do 'report talk' and women 'rapport talk'. Analysts working with these oppositions typically identify certain formal or organizational features of talk as markers of 'competition' and 'cooperation' etc. The analyst then examines which kinds of features predominate in a set of conversational data, and how they are being used.

In the following discussion, I too will make use of the conventional oppositions as tools for describing data, but I will be trying to build up an argument that their use is problematic. The problem is not merely that the men in my data fail to fit their gender stereotype perfectly. More importantly, I think it is often the stereotype itself that underpins analytic judgements that a certain form is cooperative rather than competitive, or that people are seeking status rather than connection in their talk. As I observed about Deborah Tannen's vignettes, many instances of behaviour will support either interpretation, or both; we use the speaker's gender, and our beliefs about what sort of behaviour makes sense for members of that gender, to rule some interpretations in and others out.

Cooperation

Various scholars, notably Jennifer Coates (1989), have remarked on the 'cooperative' nature of informal talk among female friends, drawing attention to a number of linguistic features which are prominent in data on all-female groups. Some of these, like **hedging** and the use of epistemic **modals**, are signs of attention to others' face, aimed at minimizing conflict and securing agreement. Others, such as **latching** of turns, **simultaneous speech** where this is not interpreted by participants as a violation of **turn-taking** rights (cf. Edelsky 1981), and the repetition or recycling of lexical items and phrases across turns, are signals that a conversation is a 'joint production': that participants are building on one another's contributions so that ideas are felt to be group property rather than the property of a single speaker.

On these criteria, the conversation here must be judged as highly cooperative. For example, in the extract reproduced above, a strikingly large number of turns (around half) begin with 'you know' and/or contain the marker 'like' ('you know like those shorts women volleyball players wear?'). The functions of these items (especially 'like') in younger Americans' English are complex and multiple,[5] and may include the cooperative, **mitigating**/face-protecting functions that Coates, and Janet Holmes (1984), associate with hedging. Even where they are not clearly hedges, however, in this interaction they function in ways that relate to the building of group involvement and consensus. They often seem to mark information as 'given' within the group's discourse (that is, 'you know', 'like', 'X' presupposes that the addressee is indeed familiar with X); 'you know' has the kind of hearer-oriented affective function (taking others into account or inviting their agreement) which Holmes attributes to certain tag-questions; while 'like' in addition seems to function for these speakers as a marker of high involvement. It appears most frequently at moments when the interactants are, by other criteria such as intonation, pitch, loudness, speech rate, incidence of simultaneous speech, and of 'strong' or taboo language, noticeably excited, such as the following (82–89):

> ED: he's I mean he's **like** a real artsy fartsy fag he's *like* (indeciph) he's so gay he's got this **like** really high voice and wire rim glasses and he sits next to the ugliest-ass bitch in the history of the world

> ED: [and
> BRYAN: [and they're all hitting on her too, like four

> ED: [I know it's like four homos hitting on her
> BRYAN: guys [hitting on her

It is also noticeable throughout the long extract reproduced earlier how much latching and simultaneous speech there is, as compared to other forms of turn transition involving either short or long pauses and gaps, or **interruptions** which silence the interruptee. Latching – turn transition without pause or overlap – is often taken as a mark of cooperation because in order to latch a turn so precisely on to the preceding turn, the speaker has to attend closely to others' contributions.

The last part of the reproduced extract, discussing the 'really gay' guy's legs, is an excellent example of jointly produced discourse, as the speakers cooperate to build a detailed picture of the legs and what is worn on them, a picture which overall could not be attributed to any single speaker. This sequence contains many instances of latching, repetition of one speaker's words by another speaker (Ed recycles Carl's whole turn, 'he really likes his legs', with added emphasis), and it also contains something that is relatively rare in the conversation as a whole, repeated tokens of hearer support like 'yes' and 'that's right'.[6]

There are, then, points of resemblance worth remarking on between these men's talk and similar talk among women as reported by previous studies. The question does arise, however, whether this male conversation has the other important hallmark of women's gossip, namely an egalitarian or non-hierarchical organization of the **floor**.

Competition

In purely quantitative terms, this conversation cannot be said to be egalitarian. The extracts reproduced so far are representative of the whole insofar as they show Ed and Bryan as the dominant speakers, while Al and Carl contribute fewer and shorter turns (Danny is variable; there are sequences where he contributes very little, but when he talks he often contributes turns as long as Ed's and Bryan's, and he also initiates topics). Evidence thus exists to support an argument that there is a hierarchy in this conversation, and there is competition, particularly between the two dominant speakers, Bryan and Ed (and to a lesser extent Ed and Danny). Let us pursue this by looking more closely at Ed's behaviour.

[...]

So far I have been arguing that even if the speakers, or some of them, compete, they are basically engaged in a collaborative and solidary enterprise (reinforcing the bonds within the group by denigrating people outside it), an activity in which all speakers participate, even if some are more active than others. Therefore I have drawn attention to the presence of 'cooperative' features, and have argued that more extreme forms of hierarchical and competitive behaviour are not rewarded by the group. I could, indeed, have argued that by the end, Ed and Bryan are not so much 'competing' – after all, their contributions are not antagonistic to one another but tend to reinforce one another – as engaging in a version of the 'joint production of discourse'.

Yet the data might also support a different analysis in which Ed and Bryan are simply *using* the collaborative enterprise of putting down gay men as an occasion to engage in verbal duelling where points are scored – against fellow group members rather than against the absent gay men – by dominating the floor and coming up with more and more extravagant put-downs. In this alternative analysis, Ed does not so much modify his behaviour as 'lose' his duel with Bryan. 'Joint production' or 'verbal duelling' – how do we decide?

Deconstructing oppositions

One response to the problem of competing interpretations raised above might be that the opposition I have been working with – 'competitive' versus 'cooperative' behaviour – is inherently problematic, particularly if one is taken to exclude the other. Conversation can and usually does contain both cooperative and competitive elements: one could argue (along with Grice 1975) that talk must be definition involve a certain minimum of cooperation, and also that there will usually be some degree of competition among speakers, if not for the floor itself then for the attention or the approval of others (see also Hewitt 1997).

The global competitive/cooperative opposition also encourages the lumping together under one heading or the other of things that could in principle be distinguished. 'Cooperation' might refer to agreement on the aims of talk, respect for other speakers' rights or support for their contributions; but there is not always perfect co-occurrence among these aspects, and the presence of any one of them need not rule out a 'competitive' element. Participants in a conversation or other speech event may compete with each other and at the same time be pursuing a shared project or common agenda (as in ritual insult sessions); they may be in severe disagreement but punctiliously observant of one another's speaking rights (as in a formal debate, say); they may be overtly supportive, and at the same time covertly hoping to score points for their supportiveness.

This last point is strangely overlooked in some discussions of women's talk. Women who pay solicitous attention to one another's face are often said to be seeking connection or good social relations *rather than* status; yet one could surely argue that attending to others' face and attending to one's own are not mutually exclusive here. The 'egalitarian' norms of female friendship groups are, like all norms, to some degree coercive: the rewards and punishments precisely concern one's status within the group (among women, however, this status is called 'popularity' rather than 'dominance'). A woman may gain status by displaying the correct degree of concern for others, and lose status by displaying too little concern for others and too much for herself. Arguably, it is gender-stereotyping that causes us to miss or minimize the status-seeking element in women friends' talk, and the connection-making dimension of men's.

How to do gender with language

I hope it will be clear by now that my intention in analyzing male gossip is not to suggest that the young men involved have adopted a 'feminine' conversational style. On the contrary, the main theoretical point I want to make concerns the folly of making any such claim. To characterize the conversation I have been considering as 'feminine' on the basis that it bears a significant resemblance to conversations among women friends would be to miss the most important point about it, that it is not only *about* masculinity, it is a sustained performance *of* masculinity. What is important in gendering talk is the 'performative gender work' the talk is doing; its role in constituting people as gendered subjects.

To put matters in these terms is not to deny that there may be an empirically observable association between a certain genre or style of speech and speakers of a particular gender. In practice this is undeniable. But we do need to ask: in virtue of what does the association hold? Can we give an account that will not be vitiated by cases where it does *not* hold? For it seems to me that conversations like the one I have analyzed leave, say, Deborah Tannen's contention (1990) that men do not do 'women's talk', because they simply *do not know how*, looking lame and unconvincing. If men rarely engage in a certain kind of talk, an explanation is called for; but if they do engage in it even very occasionally, an explanation in terms of pure ignorance will not do.

I suggest the following explanation. Men and women do not live on different planets, but are members of cultures in which a large amount of discourse about gender is constantly circulating. They do not only learn, and then mechanically reproduce, ways of speaking 'appropriate' to their own sex; they learn a much broader set of gendered meanings that attach in rather complex ways to different ways of speaking, and they produce their own behaviour in the light of those meanings.

This behaviour will vary. Even the individual who is most unambiguously committed to traditional notions of gender has a range of possible gender identities to draw on. Performing masculinity or femininity 'appropriately' cannot mean giving exactly the same performance regardless of the circumstances. It may involve different strategies in mixed and single-sex company, in private and in public settings, in the various social positions (parent, lover, professional, friend) that someone might regularly occupy in the course of everyday life.

Since gender is a relational term, and the minimal requirement for 'being a man' is 'not being a woman', we may find that in many circumstances, men are under pressure to constitute themselves as masculine linguistically by avoiding forms of talk whose primary association is with women/femininity. But this is not invariant, which begs the question: under what circumstances does the contrast with women lose its salience as a constraint on men's behaviour? When can men do so-called 'feminine' talk without threatening their constitution as men? Are there cases when it might actually be to their advantage to do this?

When and why do men gossip?

Many researchers have reported that both sexes engage in gossip, since its social functions (like affirming group solidarity and serving as an unofficial conduit for information) are of universal relevance, but its cultural meaning (for us) is undeniably 'feminine'. Therefore we might expect to find most men avoiding it, or disguising it as something else, especially in mixed settings where they are concerned to mark their difference from women (see Johnson and Finlay 1997). In the conversation discussed above, however, there are no women for the men to differentiate themselves from; whereas *there is* the perceived danger that so often accompanies Western male homosociality: homosexuality. Under these circumstances perhaps it becomes acceptable to transgress one gender norm ('men don't gossip, gossip is for girls') in order to affirm what in this context is a more important norm ('men in all-male groups must unambiguously display their heterosexual orientation').

In these speakers' understanding of gender, gay men, like women, provide a contrast group against whom masculinity can be defined. This principle of contrast seems to set limits on the permissibility of gossip for these young men. Although they discuss other men besides the 'gays' – professional basketball players – they could not be said to gossip about them. They talk about the players' skills and their records, not their appearance, personal lives or sexual activities. Since the men admire the basketball players, identifying *with* them rather than *against* them, such talk would border dangerously on what for them is obviously taboo: desire for other men.

Ironically, it seems likely that the despised gay men are the *only* men about whom these male friends can legitimately talk among themselves in such intimate terms without compromising the heterosexual masculinity they are so anxious to display – though in a different context, say with their girlfriends, they might be able to discuss the basketball players differently. The presence of a woman, especially a heterosexual partner, displaces the dread spectre of homosexuality, and makes other kinds of talk possible; though by the same token her presence might make certain kinds of talk that take place among men *impossible*. What counts as acceptable talk for men is a complex matter in which all kinds of contextual variables play a part.

In this context – a private conversation among male friends – it could be argued that to gossip, either about your sexual exploits with women or about the repulsiveness of gay men (these speakers do both), is not just one way, but the most appropriate way to display heterosexual masculinity. In another context (in public, or with a larger and less close-knit group of men), the same objective might well be pursued through explicitly agonistic strategies, such as yelling abuse at women or gays in the street, or exchanging sexist and homophobic jokes. *Both* strategies could be said to do performative gender work: in terms of what they do for the speakers involved, one is not more 'masculine' than the other, they simply belong to different settings in which heterosexual masculinity may (or must) be put on display.

Conclusion

I hope that my discussion of the conversation I have analyzed makes the point that it is unhelpful for linguists to continue to use models of gendered speech which imply that masculinity and femininity are monolithic constructs, automatically giving rise to predictable (and utterly different) patterns of verbal interaction. At the same time, I hope it might make us think twice about the sort of analysis that implicitly seeks the meaning (and sometimes the *value*) of an interaction among men or women primarily in the style, rather than the substance, of what is said. For although, as I noted earlier in relation to Judith Butler's work, it is possible for men and women to performatively subvert or resist the prevailing codes of gender, there can surely be no convincing argument that this is what Danny and his friends are doing. Their conversation is animated by entirely traditional anxieties about being seen at all times as red-blooded heterosexual males: not women and not queers. Their skill as performers does not alter the fact that what they perform is the same old gendered script.

Transcription conventions

Horizontal sequencing of utterances represents (impressionistically) their relative arrangement in time.

Other symbols used:
=	latching
[	turn onset overlaps previous turn
[]	turn is completely contained within another speaker's turn
?	rising intonation on utterance
(.)	short pause
(indeciph)	indecipherable speech
italics	emphatic stress on italicized item

Notes

1   Because the student concerned is one of the speakers in the conversation I analyze, and the nature of the conversation makes it desirable to conceal participants' identities (indeed, this was one of the conditions on which the data were collected and subsequently passed on to me), I will not give his real name here, but I want to acknowledge his generosity in making his recording and transcript available to me, and to thank him for a number of insights I gained by discussing the data with him as well as by reading his paper. I am also grateful to the other young men who participated. All their names, and the names of other people they mention, have been changed, and all pseudonyms used are (I hope) entirely fictitious.

2   The German linguist Karsta Frank (1992) has provocatively argued that so-called gender differences in speech-style arise *exclusively* in reception: women and men are heard differently, as opposed to speaking differently. I do not entirely accept Frank's very strong position on this point, but I do think she has drawn attention to a phenomenon of some importance.

3   I mention that this was 'at home' because in the United States it is also common for men, individually or in groups, to watch televised sports in public places such as bars and even laundromats; but this particular conversation would probably not have happened in a public setting with others present. It appears to be a recurrent feature of male friends' talk that the men are engaged in some other activity as well as talking. The Swedish researcher Kerstin Nordenstam, who has an impressive corpus comprising data from twelve different single-sex friendship groups, has found that the men are far less likely than the women to treat conversation as the exclusive or primary purpose of a social gathering. Many of the women's

groups recorded for Nordenstam were 'sewing circles' – a traditional kind of informal social organization for women in Sweden – but they frequently did not sew, and defined their aim simply as 'having fun'; whereas the men's groups might meet under no particular rubric, but they still tended to organize their talk around an activity such as playing cards or games. (Thanks to Kerstin Nordenstam for this information.)

4   Numbers in parenthesis refer to the lines in the original transcript.

5   For example, *like* has a 'quotative' function among younger US speakers, as in 'and she's like [= she said], stop bugging me, and I'm like, what do you mean stop bugging you?' This and other uses of the item have become popularly stereotyped as markers of membership in the so-called 'slacker' generation.

6   It is a rather consistent research finding that men use such minimal responses significantly less often than women, and in this respect the present data conform to expectations – there are very few minimal responses of any kind. I would argue, however, that active listenership, involvement and support are not *absent* in the talk of this group; they are marked by other means such as high levels of latching/simultaneous speech, lexical recycling and the use of *like*.

References

Austin, J. L (1961) *How to Do Things with Words*, Oxford: Clarendon Press.

Butler, Judith (1990) *Gender Trouble: Feminism and the Subversion of Identity*. New York: Routledge.

Coates, Jennifer (1989) 'Gossip revisited', in J. Coates and D. Cameron (eds.), *Women in Their Speech Communities*, London: Longman, pp. 94–121.

Edelsky, Carole (1981) 'Who's got the floor?' *Language in Society*, 10(3): 383–422.

Grice, H. P. (1975) 'Logic and conversation', in P. Cole and J. Morgan (eds.), *Syntax and Semantics, Vol 3: Speech Acts*, New York: Academic Press, pp. 41–58.

Hewitt, Roger (1997) '"Box-out" and "taxing"' in Sally Johnson and Ulrike Meinhof (eds.), *Language and Masculinity*, Oxford: Blackwell, pp. 27–46.

Holmes, Janet (1984) 'Hedging your bets and sitting on the fence: some evidence for hedges as support structures', *Te Reo*, 27: 47–62.

Johnson, Sally and Finlay, Frank (1997) 'Do men gossip? An analysis of football talk on television', in Sally Johnson and Ulrike Hanna Meinhof (eds.), *Language and Masculinity*, Oxford: Blackwell, pp. 130–43.

Frank, Kartsa (1992) *Sprachgewalt*, Tübingen: Niemeyer Verlag.

Tannen, Deborah (1990) *You Just Don't Understand: Women and Men in Conversation*, New York: Ballantine Books.

PART SIX

Language and ethnicity

Satori Soden

INTRODUCTION

ETHNICITY, **LIKE OTHER** ways of expressing identity, is not straightforward. The difference between the two papers in this section can be seen in that the first deals with 'race' and the second with 'ethnicity'. We deal with racist discourse first, however, it is important to remember that such discourse treats membership of an ethnic group as straightforward. The difference is signalled in some ways in the difference between 'race' and 'ethnicity'. Just as sex is something considered fixed, talk about race takes this as fixed. Thus, individuals will be seen by others as belonging to a certain racial group on the basis of physical characteristics and, at times, by less obvious biological attributes (such as examination of blood or DNA). On the other hand, ethnicity is more like gender in that it is socially constructed. Because of this, it can be variously claimed and attributed to people.

Teun van Dijk has written extensively on racist discourse. At the start of this paper, he points out that it 'is a form of discriminatory social practice that manifests' in various ways (p. 199). It is important to note the 'social practice', that is, racist discourse is an action; it is done by a person to another person or people. There is also an important power dimension, which is clear when he refers to the 'dominant ethnic group'. Racist discourses differ depending on who is dominant. This may not be dominance because of numerical majority; one only needs to think of the patterns of dominance in **apartheid**-era South Africa to see that dominance is about power. This power may be as much **ideological** as anything else.

Van Dijk identifies two kinds of racist discourse. The first is directed *at* the minority; the second is discourse *about* the minority. Note with the first that racist practices are not confined to insults and direct forms of verbal abuse. A full range of impoliteness strategies, dominating tactics and straightforward silencing can be used as forms of racist practice. The key difference is that such behaviour is routine. This means that it is treated as normal and that it is unrelenting. Being interrupted from time to time is certainly annoying; if this happens all the time, it is a form of violence. When it is done because of ethnicity, it is racist.

Racism about the other is also embedded in everyday life. van Dijk provides a number of different areas where such discourse may be found, from newspaper reports, to laws and jokes. It is here that the distinction between 'us' and 'them' is significant. That is, it is possible to see all kind of apparently normal uses of language as nevertheless being informed by the idea that there is a fundamental difference between the dominant group (us) and the oppressed (them).

We can also see a kind of racism in the situation that Eades describes in the second paper in this section. Diana Eades has worked for many years on the way the criminal justice system treats indigenous Australians. In this paper, she reports on one particular case, for which she was an expert witness. This makes clear that while Aboriginal English (AE) may seem to be the same as Standard Australian English (SE), there are important differences which – as in this case – result in injustice to the point of incarceration. The story that Eades tells is one in which an Aboriginal woman, Robyn Kina, was prevented from telling her story to legal professionals and the court. Kina was effectively silenced by the legal process. That is, something was 'done' to her as a result of the conflict between AE language and SE language.

Eades explores what it means to say that 'Kina was communicating in an Aboriginal way' (p. 207). As with other language varieties (Labov 1972), Aboriginal English is a logical linguistic system. The legal system, however, is not designed to accommodate the **communicative competence** that AE speakers have. Aboriginal modes of seeking information, for example, differ fundamentally from SE. When an AE speaker is telling a story, they are allowed to keep the **floor**; they will not be interrupted or stopped, even if to SE ears they seem to have strayed from 'the point'. For AE speakers, information is valuable; it is not something that should be given to just anyone. The status of information may result in the speaker being silent. AE speakers are comfortable with silence; it may indicate that the silent party is thinking or that they are taking seriously the question. This is problematic in a legal situation as in SE silence generally indicates that a speaker lacks knowledge, is being uncooperative, or is simply guilty (see Eades 2000).

Another significant difference is the use of AE gratuitous concurrence; that is, answering 'yes' to a **closed question** whether the speaker agrees or not. This is a linguistic norm of politeness, one that would be clear for speakers of AE. It would be far from clear, however, to anyone not aware of the convention. The reason for choosing this particular reading from Eades is that it so clearly shows how some communicative contexts work for AE speakers. Thus, Robyn's counsellor had the communicative repertoire available to deal with silence, the valuing of information, and the importance of extended narrative. Obviously it is more than just the skills the **interlocutor** has, the constraints of the professional engagement are also relevant. Lawyers want to get the information they need quickly and efficiently; counsellors have more time at their disposal simply because of the way the professional interactions are structured. Eades' careful documentation of the various interlocutors Robyn Kina encountered, helps to explain how the miscarriage of justice occurred and also how to prevent such events in future.

With ongoing migration and increasingly stringent immigration laws around the world, these kinds of issues are of increasing importance (see Eades 2003, 2005). The intersection of language and the law, especially the criminal law, makes clear how much power can be lost if the 'right' variety is not the one possessed.

Issues to consider

1. We are often told that 'words can't hurt' us. Can this be reconciled with van Dijk's arguments about racist discourse directed at people?
2. Racist discourse often uses the same topics over and over again. van Dijk identifies crime and immigration as two key areas for racist discourse. In what other topic areas are we likely to find racist discourse? You might want to collect some data in order to answer this question.
3. If identity (and especially ethnic identity) is such a slippery concept, why does it get talked about so much?
4. Do you think the communicative conventions of the legal arena can be considered racist? What kind of evidence can be found for this?
5. Do you think it's possible to be fully bicultural, that is, to master two very different sets of rules for communicative competence?

Further Reading

For more on ethnicity and representation; see also Part 3.

Hall, S. (1997) 'The spectacle of the "Other"', in S. Hall (ed.), *Representation: Cultural Representations and Signifying Practices*, London: Sage, pp. 223–290.
Labov, W. (1972) 'Academic ignorance and black intelligence', *The Atlantic*, June (72.06) (see Chapter 20).

For work that deals with language variation and ethnicity:

Boberg, C. (2004) 'Ethnic patterns in the phonetics of Montreal English', *Journal of Sociolinguistics*, 8(4): 538–568.
Goebel, Z. (2009) 'Semiosis, interaction and ethnicity in urban Java', *Journal of Sociolinguistics*, 13(4): 499–523.
Gumperz, J.J. (2003) 'Cross cultural communication', in R. Harris and B. Rampton (eds.), *The Language, Ethnicity and Race Reader*, London: Routledge, pp. 267–275.
Schilling-Estes, N. (2004) 'Constructing ethnicity in interaction', *Journal of Sociolinguistics*, 8(2): 163–195.

For work that explicitly addresses issues of authenticity:

Coupland, N. (2003) 'Sociolinguistic authenticities', *Journal of Sociolinguistics*, 7(3): 417–431.
Cutler, C. (2003) '"Keepin' it real": white hip-hoppers' discourses of language, race, and authenticity', *Journal of Linguistic Anthropology*, 13(2): 211–233.
Shenk, P.S. (2007) '"I'm Mexican, remember?" Constructing ethnic identities via authentication discourse', *Journal of Sociolinguistics*, 11(2): 194–220.

For an excellent collection covering many issues around language and the law:

Cotterill, J. (ed.), (2002) *Language in the Legal Process*, Basingstoke: Palgrave.

Suggestions for Further Viewing

In the Name of the Father (1993) Jim Sheridan.
Rabbit Proof Fence (2002) Phillip Noyce.
The Ballad of Gregorio Cortez (1982) Robert M. Young.
The N Word (2004) Todd Williams.
The Wire (2002-8) David Simon, HBO.
Trainspotting (1996) Danny Boyle.

References

Eades, Diana (2000) "I don't think it's an answer to the question: Silencing Aboriginal witnesses in court" *Language in Society* 29: 161–195.
— (2003) "Participation of Second Language and Second Dialect Speakers in the Legal System", *Annual Review of Applied Linguistics*, 23: 113–133.
— (2005) "Applied Linguistics and Language Analysis in Asylum Seeker Cases" *Applied Linguistics*, 26(4): 503–526.
Labov, William (1972) 'Academic Ignorance and Black Intelligence'. *The Atlantic* 72.06.

Chapter 15

Teun A. van Dijk

RACIST DISCOURSE

R ACIST DISCOURSE IS a form of discriminatory social practice that manifests itself in text, talk and communication. Together with other (nonverbal) discriminatory practices, racist discourse contributes to the reproduction of racism as a form of ethnic or "racial" domination. It does so typically by expressing, confirming or legitimating racist opinions, attitudes and **ideologies** of the dominant ethnic group. Although there are other racisms elsewhere in the world, the most prevalent and devastating form of racism has historically been European racism against non-European peoples, which will be the focus of this essay.

Two forms of racist discourse

There are two major forms of racist discourse:

1. racist discourse *directed at* ethnically different Others;
2. racist discourse *about* ethnically different Others.

The first form of racist discourse is one of the many discriminatory ways that dominant group members verbally interact with members of dominated groups: ethic minorities, immigrants, refugees, etc. They may do so blatantly by using derogatory slurs, insults, impolite forms of address, and other forms of discourse that explicitly express and enact superiority and lack of respect.

Since today such blatant forms of verbal discrimination are generally found to be "politically incorrect," much racist discourse directed at dominated ethnic group members tends to become more subtle and indirect. Thus, white speakers may refuse to yield the **floor** to minority speakers, interrupt them inappropriately, ignore the topics suggested by their **interlocutors**, focus on topics that imply negative properties of the ethnic minority group to which the recipient belongs, speak too loudly, show a bored face, avoid eye contact, use a haughty intonation, and many other manifestations of lack of respect. Some of these verbal inequities are more generally a problem of multicultural communication; others are genuine expressions of racial or ethnic dominance of white speakers.

In other words, these are the kinds of discourse and verbal interaction that are normally considered deviant or unacceptable during conversation with in-group members, and therefore are forms of domination that have been called "everyday racism." Of course, they also occur in conversations with people of the "own" group, but are then sanctioned as being rude or impolite. The fundamental difference is that minority group members *daily* are confronted with such racist talk, and not because of what they do or say, but only because of what they are: different. They are thus subjected to an accumulating and aggravating form of racist harassment that is a direct threat to their well-being and quality of life.

The second form of racist discourse is usually addressed to other dominant group members and is *about* ethnic or "racial" Others. Such discourse may range from informal everyday conversations or organizational dialogues (such as parliamentary debates), to many written or multimedia types of text or communicative events, such as TV shows, movies, news reports, editorials, textbooks, scholarly publications, laws, contracts, and so on.

The overall characteristic of such racist discourse is the negative portrayal of *Them*, often combined with a positive representation of *Ourselves*. The corollary of this strategy is to avoid or mitigate a positive representation of Others, and a negative representation of our own group. Typical for the latter case is the denial or mitigation of racism.

These overall strategies may appear at all levels of text and talk, that is, at the level of visuals, sounds (volume, intonation), syntax (word order), semantics (meaning and reference), style (variable uses of words and word order), rhetoric (persuasive uses of grammar or of "figures" of style), pragmatics (speech acts such as assertions or threats), interaction, and so on.

Topics

Thus, *topics* of conversation, news reports, political debates or scholarly articles about minorities or immigrants may be biased in the sense that they focus on or imply negative **stereotypes**. Thus, immigration may be dealt with in terms of an invasion, a deluge, a threat, or at least as a major problem, instead of as an important and necessary contribution to the economy, the demography or the cultural diversity of the country.

Research into conversation, media, textbooks and other discourse genres has shown that of a potentially infinite number of topics or themes, text and talk about minorities or immigrants, typically clusters around three main topic classes.

The first class features topics of discourse that emphasize the *difference* of the Others, and hence their distance from Us. Such emphasis may have a seemingly positive slant if the Others are described in exotic terms. More often than not, however, the difference is evaluated negatively: the Others are portrayed as less smart, beautiful, fast, hardworking, democratic, modern, etc. than We are. These topics are typical in everyday conversations, textbooks and especially the mass media. This first step of in-group–outgroup polarization in discourse, which also characterizes the underlying attitudes and ideologies expressed in these discourses, usually also implies that They are all the same (and We are all individually different).

The second group of topics takes polarization between Us and Them one step further and emphasizes that the behavior of the Other is *deviant*, and hence breaks Our norms and rules: They do not (want to) speak our language, they walk around in funny dress, they have strange habits, they eat strange food, they mistreat their women, and so on. The **presupposition** or conclusion of such topics is generally that They do not, but should, adapt to Us. On the other hand, even when they totally adapt, the Others will still be seen as different.

Third, the Other may be portrayed as a *threat* to Us. This happens from the moment they arrive, for instance when immigration is represented as an invasion, until the new citizens have settled in "our" country, in which case they may be seen as occupying our space, running down our neighborhood, taking our jobs or houses, harassing "our" women, and so on.

The most prominent threat theme however is crime. All statistics on the coverage of immigrants – or otherwise marginal or marginalized people – show that in everyday conversations, the media and political discourse, various kinds of crime invariably show up as a permanent association with minorities and immigrants: passport fraud, assault, robbery, and especially drugs. Indeed, the quite common expression "ethnic crime" suggests that such crime is seen as a special and different category: crime thus becomes racialized. Doing drugs in the USA and other countries is seen as a typically "black" crime. On the other hand, "normal" topics, such as those of politics, the economy, work, or ("high") culture are seldom associated with minorities. If they are reported positively in the news, blacks do so mostly as champions in sports or as musicians.

According to the overall strategy of positive Self-presentation and negative Other-presentation, neutral or positive topics about Us are preferred, whereas the negative ones are ignored or suppressed. Thus, a story may be about discrimination against minorities, but since such a story is inconsistent with positive Self-presentation, it tends to be relegated to a less prominent part of the page or newspaper.

The discursive logic of racist positive Self-presentation and negative Other-presentation not only controls the fundamental level of global content or topics, but extends to all other levels and dimensions of discourse. Thus, lexicalization, or the choice of words, tends to be biased in many ways, not only in explicit racial or ethnic slurs, but also in more subtle forms of discourse, beginning with the very problem of naming the Others. There has been opposition to changes in naming practices: for example, the movement from (among other terms) "colored," "Negro," "Afro American," "African American" to "people of color" was opposed at different stages in history and by different groups, including, we might add, some African Americans.

Another well-known way to emphasize *Their* bad things is to use sentence forms that make bad agency more salient, such as active sentences. On the other hand, if *Our* racism or police harassment needs to be spoken or written about, the grammar allows us to **mitigate** such acts that are inconsistent with a positive Self-image, for instance by using passive phrases ("They were harassed by the police," or "They were harassed") or nominalizations ("harassment") instead of the direct active phrase ("Police harassed black youths").

Similar forms of emphasis and mitigation are typically managed by rhetorical figures, such as hyperbole and euphemisms. Thus, few Western countries or institutions explicitly deal with (own!) racism, and both in political discourse and well as in the media, many forms of mitigation are currently being used, such as "discrimination," "bias," or even "popular discontent." On the other hand, the opposite takes place whenever the Others do something we do not like. Thus, for starters, and as we have seen, immigration is often described using the military metaphor of an invasion. Similarly, large groups of immigrants or asylum seekers are described not only and simply in large numbers, but typically in terms of threatening amounts of water or snow in which We may drown: waves, floods, avalanches, etc. The same is true for the so-called "number game," used broadly in politics and the media, a strategy that emphasizes the number of immigrants in society by constantly emphasizing how many new people have arrived.

Strategies of presentation

Discourse is more than just words or sentences. It is typically characterized also at more global levels of analysis, as we have seen for the study of topics. In the same way, discourse has more global forms, formats or schemas that may become conventionalized, such as the typical format of a story, a news report in the press, a scientific article or a mundane everyday conversation. Although these formats are quite general and hence do not normally change in different contexts, and hence are the same in (say) racist or antiracist discourse – indeed, a racist story or joke is just as much a story or joke as an antiracist one – there are some interesting ways in which such structures may be related to different intentions or opinions of language users.

Thus, we found that in negative everyday stories about foreign neighbors, people tended to emphasize the *Complication* category, contrasting it with the peaceful *Orientation* category ("I was just walking on the street, and then suddenly..."), but often leave out the *Resolution* category, as if to stress that the presence of foreigners is a problem which cannot be resolved. Typically, the less-biased speakers in such a case *do* mention some form of (positive) resolution, even if they were initially confronted with some "trouble."

Similarly, in parliamentary debates, editorials, scientific articles and any other discourse in which arguments are very important, we also may expect ways in which the argumentation tends to be biased against the Other. Authoritative sources, such as the police or (white) experts, are being mentioned in order to "prove" that the immigrants are illegal, cannot be trusted, or need to be problematized, marginalized, removed or expelled. This move is typical for the well-known fallacy of "authority." Immigration debates are replete with such fallacies, for example, the fallacy of exaggeration, in which the arrival of a small group of refugees may be extrapolated to a national catastrophe by a comment such as, "if we have lax immigration laws, all refugees will come to our country."

Finally, discourse is also more than words and global structures in the sense that it is semiotically associated with visual information, such as page layout, placement, pictures, tables, and so on, as is the case in the press, or for film on TV, or on the internet. These nonverbal messages are also powerful ways of implementing the general strategy of positive Self-presentation and negative Other-presentation. Thus, articles in the press that are about *Their* crime or violence (such as urban disturbances defined as "race riots") tend to appear on the front page, on top, in large articles, with big headlines, with prominent pictures in which *They* are represented as aggressive or *We* (or Our Police) as victims. On the other hand, our racism, or the harassment of blacks by "Our" police will seldom occupy such a prominent place, and will tend to be relegated to the inner pages, to less substantial articles, and not emphasized in headlines.

In sum, we see that in many genres, and at all levels and dimensions of text and talk, racism and prejudice may daily be expressed, enacted and reproduced by discourse as one of the practices of a racist society.

Such discourse, however, does not come alone, and takes its conditions, consequences and functions in communicative, interactional and societal contexts. Biased or stereotypical news is produced in media organizations, by journalists and other professionals. Parliamentary debates are conducted by politicians. Textbooks, lessons, and scholarly publications are produced by teachers and scholars. They do so in different roles and as members of many different professional and other social groups, and as part of daily routines and procedures. News is gathered under the control of editors, and typically under majority institutions and organizations, such as government agencies, the police, the universities or the courts. Minority groups and sources are systematically ignored or attributed less relevance or expertize. The newsrooms in North America, Europe and Australia are largely white. Minority journalists are underemployed and discriminated against, with the usual fake arguments. No wonder that the dominant discourse of society, especially also about ethnic affairs and minority communities, is badly informed and hence informs badly. In other words, racist societies and institutions produce racist discourses, and racist discourses reproduce the stereotypes, prejudices and ideologies that are used to defend and legitimize white dominance. It is in this way that the symbolic, discursive circle is closed and dominant elite talk and text contributes to the reproduction of racism.

Fortunately, the same is true for antiracist discourse. And once such discourse is engaged in by responsible leaders in the media, politics, education, research, the courts, corporate business and the state bureaucracies, we may hope that society will become diverse and hence truly democratic.

[...]

Reading

Discourses of Domination: Racial Bias in the Canadian English-Language Press by Frances Henry and Carol Tator (University of Toronto Press 2002) presents a critical discourse analysis of a number of case studies of the ways the Canadian media portray minorities and immigrants and of the difficulties minority journalists have to get a job within the white media; this may productively be read in conjunction with *Debating Diversity: Analysing the Discourse of Tolerance* by Jan Blommaert and Jef Verschueren (Routledge 1999), which focuses on debates on immigration in Belgium; and *Die vierte Gewalt: Rassismus in den Medien* (*The Fourth Power: Racism in the Media*), edited by Siegfried Jäger and Jürgen Link (Duisburg, Germany, DISS 1993), which presents studies of the way in which the German media, and especially also the tabloids, deal with immigration. This is one of many studies on racism published by the Duisburg Institute for Language and Social Research.

Mapping the Language of Racism: Discourse and the Legitimation of Exploitation by Margaret Wetherell and Jonathan Potter (Harvester-Wheatsheaf 1992) is a discursive sociopsychological study of racism and discourse in New Zealand; this may be read alongside Philomena Essed's *Understanding Everyday Racism* (Sage 1991), a study of the daily experiences of African American women in California and Surinamese women in the Netherlands, which provides a detailed theoretical account of the notion of "everyday racism." Prejudice in discourse by Teun van Dijk (Benjamins 1984) is the first monograph in English of the author's long-term research program on racist discourse. This study focuses especially on racism in everyday conversation and storytelling, and presents his first theoretical framework for a multidisciplinary study of racist discourse. Other work by the same author includes: *Communicating Racism* (Sage 1987), a social psychological study on how ethnic and racial prejudices are expressed and reproduced by discourse, based on data collected in the Netherlands and California; *Racism and the Press* (Routledge 1991), a quantitative and discourse-analytical study of the portrayal of immigrants and minorities in the Dutch and English press; *Elite Discourse and Racism* (Sage 1993), which summarizes the author's earlier research on racist discourse, emphasizing the prominent role of the elites in the reproduction of racism, and offers new data and analyses of parliamentary debates, textbooks, scholarly discourse, and discourse in business enterprises; and *Racism at the Top: Parliamentary Discourses on Ethnic Issues in Six European Countries*, edited with Ruth Wodak (Drava Verlag 2000), which features studies by the team of the international project "Racism at the Top," in which parliamentary debates on immigration and ethnic affairs in seven western European countries (Austria, Italy, Spain, France, the Netherlands, the UK and Germany) are being studied.

The Semiotics of Racism: Approaches in Critical Discourse Analysis, edited by Martin Reisigl and Ruth Wodak (Vienna: Passagen 2000), is one of a series of books on the critical discourse analysis of racism and anti-Semitism edited and written by the team directed by Ruth Wodak at the University of Vienna; the papers contributed to this volume deal with such topics as explaining right-wing violence, diversity, the discourse of social exclusion, parliamentary debates on immigration, linguistic discrimination, and visual racism; it may be read alongside *Discourse and Discrimination: Rhetorics of Racism and Antisemitism* by Reisigl and Wodak (Routledge 2000), which is a discourse-historical study of racism and anti-Semitism in Austria, dealing with everyday anti-Semitic discourse, political and media about a petition by right-wing leader Jorg Haider, as well as bureaucratic discourse refusing residence permits.

Diana Eades

LEGAL RECOGNITION OF CULTURAL DIFFERENCES IN COMMUNICATION: THE CASE OF ROBYN KINA

Introduction

A BORIGINAL PEOPLE ARE grossly over-represented in the Australian prison population. The Royal Commission into Aboriginal Deaths in Custody found that an Aboriginal person is more than 20 times more likely than a non-Aboriginal person to be taken into custody, and 15 times more likely to be imprisoned (Royal Commission into Aboriginal Deaths in Custody 1991).[1]

The Royal Commission found many 'underlying causes' of the 'overimprisonment' of Aboriginal people including racism, social, economic and educational factors, as well as the history of dispossession. The Commission saw the fundamental question as relating to empowerment and self-determination.

Elsewhere (Eades 1994) I have argued that language and communication issues are also relevant to this question. It is becoming increasingly obvious that access to justice is partly a linguistic issue. This point is made very clearly in the case of Robyn Kina.

Most Aboriginal people speak a variety of Aboriginal English in their dealings with the law. Aboriginal English (AE) is the **dialect** of English spoken by Aboriginal people throughout Australia, which differs from Standard Australian English (SE) in systematic ways. There is considerable variation in the varieties of AE spoken, with the heaviest (or most basilectal varieties) being spoken in more remote areas, and the lightest (or most acrolectal) being spoken in urban and metropolitan areas. My work over the last 12 years has shown that even where the grammatical differences between SE and AE are not great, there are significant pragmatic differences, which have implications for cross-cultural communication (e.g. Eades 1984, 1988, 1991, 1993). The case of Robyn Kina shows that Aboriginal ways of communicating must be taken into account if Aboriginal people are to be treated fairly by the justice system.

Summary of Robyn Kina's case

Robyn Kina is an Aboriginal woman who was born in 1959 and grew up in an Aboriginal environment in south-east Queensland. Kina was one of 14 children living in difficult family circumstances, which included an alcoholic father. She left school at the age of 12 to look after three younger brothers and sisters. Her teenage years were characterised by sexual abuse, prostitution, alcoholism and trouble with the police. By the time she was 20, Kina had been charged with a number of the offences which are characteristic of the criminal record of many Aboriginal people: obscene language, assaulting the police, resisting arrest, and wilful and unlawful destruction of police property (such as police documents). This litany of offences shows how the criminal justice system filters Aboriginal people into the population of 'criminals', with the initial trivial charge of using obscene language, and the resulting conflict between the charged Aboriginal person and the police.[2]

At the age of 19 Kina served 20 months in prison for her role in an attack on another drinker in a pub brawl. In her mid-20s Kina stopped prostitution and stopped drinking alcohol and started a relationship with Tony Black (a non-Aboriginal man). Black had bouts of extreme violence towards Kina, particularly when he was drunk, almost from the beginning of their relationship. During the three years of their relationship Kina was subjected to much punching, pulling of her hair, kicking with steel capped boots and anal rape. During an argument one morning early in 1988, in which Black threatened to rape her 14-year-old niece who was living in the house at the time, Kina stabbed Black once in the chest as he came towards her with a chair raised above his head. Kina was shocked to see Black stagger and fall to the ground and he died in hospital shortly after.

On this day the drama of violence ended for Kina, but the drama of the legal process was about to begin.

Most Aboriginal people in the criminal justice system are unable to afford private legal representation, and their cases are handled by either the Legal Aid Commission (LAC) or the Aboriginal Legal Services (ALS). Both of these legal services are seriously underresourced, and lawyers have responsibility for an extremely high case load.[3] Kina was represented by ALS at the initial committal hearing in March 1988, and by LAC at her trial in September of that year. In fact, her case was passed on to a number of consecutive lawyers, due to several factors, including the difficulty experienced by lawyers in taking instructions from her. Table 16.1 shows the total number and duration of all visits to Kina by her lawyers from the time of her imprisonment in January until the trial on 5 September.

Kina pleaded not guilty to murder on the grounds that she had not intended to kill Black. She did not give evidence, and no witnesses were called to give evidence to support her case. The trial was one of the shortest in Queensland's history, with less than three hours of evidence, and only 50 minutes required for the jury to return its verdict of 'guilty'. Kina was sentenced to life imprisonment with hard labour.

Some years later, public interest was aroused in Kina's case by two Australian Broadcasting Commission television documentaries, screened in September 1992 (*Without Consent*) and May 1993 (*Excuse to Murder*). These documentaries raised legal and moral issues concerning victims of domestic violence who kill their violent spouse in situations of self-defence and provocation. As a result of interviews with Kina on these documentaries, the Queensland Attorney-General contacted her and a new appeal was

Table 16.1: Legal visitors to Robyn Kina before her trial

Solicitor A	24 February	1 hr 10 mins
Solicitor B	26 April	1 hr 45 mins
Solicitor B (with C)	27 July	l hr 37 mins 1 hr 56 mins
Barrister D (with E)	11 August	27 mins
Barrister D (with A)	31 August	'brief'
Solicitor A	1 September	30 mins

initiated. The grounds of the appeal were that she should not have been found guilty of murder because she had acted in self-defence and under provocation. Evidence to support this appeal was clear from her TV interviews although it had never been presented to the jury at her trial.

Sociolinguistic evidence in the appeal[4]

The most important question which her lawyers needed to answer at the appeal was this: why did Kina talk about this self-defence and provocation to TV journalists in 1991 and 1992, but not to her lawyers in 1988?

This question was answered by experts in three different fields: psychiatry, social work, and sociolinguistics.[5]

It is the sociolinguistic perspective on this question which I was asked to provide, and which forms the focus of this paper. On the basis of my work on cross-cultural miscommunication between Aboriginal and non-Aboriginal people in the legal system (e.g. Eades 1992), I had some general ideas about how this question might be answered. In order to give a specific answer I read many documents relating to the case, including affidavits from Kina, her lawyers and TV journalists as well as her counsellor. I also spent a couple of hours talking to Kina in prison to find out about her background, and to assess her linguistic and sociolinguistic situation, and interviewed her counsellor, a key person in the story.

The sociolinguistic answer which I provided to the question central to the appeal can be summarised as follows:

In 1988 Kina was communicating in an Aboriginal way. The lawyers who interviewed her were not able to communicate in this way, and they were not aware that their difficulties in communicating with her involved serious cultural differences. Also at this time she did not have the ability to communicate in a non-Aboriginal way. Thus the communication difficulties were not about personalities but about cultural differences in language usage (which I will illustrate below). The way that lawyers are trained and the way that they generally interview clients is not conducive to Aboriginal ways of communicating.

On the other hand, the way that the TV journalists and the counsellor communicated with Kina was quite similar, as it happens, to Aboriginal ways of communicating (also illustrated below).

I concluded therefore that it was no surprise that Kina told TV journalists in 1992 and 1993 about important things which she did not tell her lawyers about in 1988: the manner in which information emerged in Kina's story is totally consistent with her Aboriginality and with this information being accurate and honest, even though this may seem extraordinary to a non-Aboriginal person.

Aboriginal and non-Aboriginal ways of seeking information

What does it mean to say that 'Kina was communicating in an Aboriginal way'? The most relevant aspect of Aboriginal communication relates to the cultural assumptions and linguistic strategies used in finding out information, and the way in which these contrast with the assumptions and strategies used in interviews.

The interview is a speech event specific to Western societies. Many assumptions in Western societies about the sociolinguistics of interviewing become culturally inappropriate, bad manners and ineffective when applied in Aboriginal societies.

The most detailed evidence on Aboriginal ways of seeking information comes from my research carried out over the last 15 years in south-east Queensland (the region in which Kina grew up and spent most of her life).[6]

The following summary of the way that Aboriginal people seek information in Aboriginal interactions is quoted from the handbook I wrote to assist lawyers in Queensland to communicate more effectively with their Aboriginal clients (Eades 1992, pp. 27–28):

> Aboriginal societies in Australia function on the basis of small-scale interaction between people who know each other and are often related to each other. Information or knowledge is often not freely accessible. Certain people have rights to certain knowledge. Direct questions are used in some settings, particularly to find out background details, e.g. *'Where's he from?'* However, in situations where Aboriginal people want to find out what they consider to be significant or certain personal information, they do not use direct questions. It is important for Aboriginal people to respect the privacy of others, and not to embarrass someone by putting them 'on the spot'. People volunteer some of their own information, hinting about what they are trying to find out about. *Information is sought as part of a two-way exchange. Silence, and waiting till people are ready to give information, are also central to Aboriginal ways of seeking any substantial information.*
>
> *Although we can recognise these ways of seeking information in Standard English, we use them in mainstream society only in sensitive situations. In Aboriginal interactions these are the everyday strategies used to seek substantial information.* This is a very significant difference in the way English is used between Aboriginal societies and mainstream societies in Australia. And an awareness of this difference is crucial to understanding why lawyers commonly have so much difficulty in interviewing Aboriginal clients.

In contrast, everyday ways of seeking information in Western societies are often based on the assumption that direct questioning is the most effective strategy. Silences are avoided, as they are frequently interpreted as some kind of breakdown in the communication. Many people who need to find out information from Aboriginal people are unaware of these subtle but important cultural differences, and use non-Aboriginal ways of communicating with them. This is particularly true of professionals, such as lawyers, teachers, and government workers who need to conduct interviews with Aboriginal people. The fundamental assumptions and strategies of the one-sided interview, which are central to many Australian institutions, such as the law, are quite contrary to the assumptions and strategies involved in Aboriginal ways of seeking information, as discussed above.

These differences between Aboriginal and non-Aboriginal ways of seeking information were exemplified and highlighted in Kina's case. From my interview with her and a careful reading of many documents in her file, as well as years of study of Aboriginal communicative style, I concluded that her communication patterns in 1988, specifically in relation to interviews, would have been characterised by the following features.

- A one-sided interview which was basically structured by a large number of questions would have been difficult for her to participate in successfully.
- In particular, she would have found it extremely difficult to provide information about embarrassing personal details in the context of a one-sided interview.
- She would have responded to many questions with silence. My research (which has involved interviewing legal professionals who encounter such silences) indicates that such silence is often wrongly interpreted by an interviewer as unwillingness to answer, or lack of relevant knowledge, or agreement with a proposition.
- As information is seen as part of a relationship, every time that Kina's legal counsel changed (i.e. three times after the committal hearing and before the trial) she would have felt the need to develop a new relationship with the new solicitor before much significant information could be 'given away'. It appears that little ground was made in developing such a relationship with any of the solicitors who worked with her leading up to her trial.

Aboriginal people often find it difficult to express their confusion and to ask for clarification about 'white business' if they are being rushed and have not had the chance to build up some kind of personal rapport with the appropriate person. People commonly wait to talk such important matters over with a white person with whom they have a relationship of trust. But they may not signal that this is their intention. The Aboriginal silence, which means 'I have to think about this some more', and may include time to talk it over with someone else, may be wrongly misinterpreted as acquiescence. This is one of the reasons why it is important not to rush Aboriginal people into decisions over complex legal matters. In Kina's case, she told me that she thought she would be giving evidence right up until the morning of the trial, when Solicitor A advised her not to do so.

Attempts by non-Aboriginal people to seek information from Kina

After the attack on Tony Black, Kina was interviewed by a number of lawyers and a counsellor (in 1988) and two TV journalists (in 1991–1992).

In order to understand the similarities and differences between these interviews, I will briefly highlight the function or purpose of each of these interviews and their characteristic patterns of interaction.[7] Although the central question in the appeal compared the lawyer interviews with the journalist interviews, it is also relevant to examine the counsellor interviews, because they were conducted in the same time period as the lawyer interviews. That is, it cannot be argued that the main factor which differed between the lawyer interviews and the journalist interviews was the passing of time. This is because, during the weeks in 1988 that Kina's lawyers were unable to find out any useful information related to her case, her counsellor was able to find out a great deal of this information.

Interviews with lawyers

The primary purposes of the interview which a criminal lawyer carries out with the client are:

- to ascertain factual circumstances;
- to take instructions about what the client wishes to be done with this information; and
- to ascertain the client's criminal record ('personal antecedents').

A very high functional load is borne by the fact-finding function of the interview. It is also a function of such interviews that the lawyer explains relevant legal matters to the client, and advises the client on possible courses of action and probable outcomes.

It is important to note that many interviews between lawyer and client take place under pressures of time, and in circumstances dominated by the need to organise factual information in legally relevant categories (e.g. related to pleas, types of offence, taxonomies of defence etc.). In this case, it appears that there were significant time constraints on the contact between Kina and the solicitor who obtained her written instructions that she would not give evidence at her trial (Solicitor A).

In affidavits to the 1993 appeal, lawyers A, B and D all gave evidence about their interviews with Kina which highlighted that they found her 'extremely difficult to communicate with'. (They also each pointed out that, at the time of interviewing Kina in 1988, they had received no training or advice on communicating with Aboriginal people.)

The following quote from the affidavit of Solicitor A provides some evidence of the way in which these lawyer interviews proceeded.

> During my years with the ALS, I found that Aboriginal clients were often extremely difficult to interview. They usually presented as reticent and uncommunicative, and would not volunteer information unless questioned in detail. In my experience, an important matter could be overlooked in

that situation because it was not volunteered by the client, and not asked about by the solicitor. I expected to experience some of these problems with the appellant, but even so found her to be one of the most difficult clients for whom I acted at the ALS

(quoted in President and Davies 1993: 18)

Interviews with the counsellor

In contrast, the primary purpose of the interview which a counsellor carries out with his or her client is to help the client to develop ways of dealing with particular situations. One of the major concerns of the counsellor is to develop a situation of trust in which the client feels comfortable to talk about personal matters. While there are aspects of a counsellor's work which involve the gathering of information, this is not the primary function of the counsellor interview. Further, unlike the lawyer, the counsellor is not constrained by a rigid and complex system which requires the assemblance of facts for the client into complex institutional categories. In many ways, the counsellor is able to treat each situation as unique, to negotiate outcomes with the client, and to follow the pace set by the client. In this way then the counsellor is not under the same institutional and time pressure as the lawyer.

In Kina's case specifically, a major factor is that she initiated contact with the counsellor, asking for his assistance and saying she wanted to talk something out with him. In my interview with the counsellor he recalled that Kina had made it clear from the outset that she had something to tell him. In appropriate counselling style he just waited until she was ready to tell him.

From the beginning of his work with Kina, she made the following clear.

she was having problems communicating with the people from the Public Defender's Office who were preparing her case. She said she had not been able to talk about her personal details with her solicitor, Solicitor B

(counsellor's affidavit, quoted in President and Davies 1993: 26)

As well as trusting her counsellor with some of the embarrassing details relevant to her case[8] she sought his assistance in presenting this material to her solicitor.

Here Kina was using a typical Aboriginal strategy of giving important information as part of a trusting relationship, rather than to a person with a designated role (such as lawyer). She was also using another typical Aboriginal strategy of using a spokesperson to help her speak about important issues (see Eades 1992: 93). Both she and her counsellor believed that he would be able to assist her in communicating this information to the lawyers, with whom she was having trouble communicating. But in fact the counsellor experienced a number of difficulties in carrying out this task, and 'he eventually received an intimation [from LAC] that he should not interfere in the proceedings' (McPherson 1993: 9).

Linguistic characteristics of the counselling interview and its relationship to Aboriginal communication

Much of the skill of counselling lies in the ability of the counsellor to help to draw out of the client what the client wants to say, which can be embarrassing and very personal, as it was in Kina's case. A key strategy in effective counselling, which Kina's counsellor told me is crucial to his approach, is that of listening to the client.

There are several features of the counselling technique which coincide with normal Aboriginal ways of communicating and particularly with Aboriginal ways of finding out information.

1. Both Kina and her counsellor reported in their interviews with me that in the early counselling sessions there were often quite lengthy silences. While this is effective counselling technique, it is also appropriate Aboriginal conversational strategy, but would undoubtedly be frustrating for a lawyer and capable of being misunderstood.
2. Many of the strategies of counselling are in fact quite similar to the sharing of information which is so central to Aboriginal information seeking. The relevant counselling strategies involve the counsellor picking up something said by the client and either repeating it, echoing it or paraphrasing it before inviting further comment from the client or commenting on it himself. Further, after the counselling session, it was the practice of Kina's counsellor to send her a letter which outlined the things they had talked about during the session. This written contribution from the counsellor was a part of the on-going exchange between them that was a part of the successful relationship which developed.
3. In both the counsellor interview, and Aboriginal conversational interactions, *uninterrupted* narratives are a valued contribution, no matter how rambling or seemingly off-the-point.
4. In both the counsellor interview, and Aboriginal conversational interactions, important personal details are shared as part of the relationship which develops. Such details are communicated in trust and at the time at which the person is ready to talk about such matters.

In his letter to Solicitor B in June 1988, the counsellor has this to say about the information he was conveying concerning the horrifying personal details of abuse suffered by Kina which led to her attack on Tony Black (p. 5).

> Obtaining this information from Kina has been an extremely slow, circuitous process, due to her shyness and extreme embarrassment. The information had been obtained by a counselling rather than information-seeking approach, which leads me to believe that she has been genuine.

This statement provides evidence of the Aboriginal way that Kina was using to communicate this personal and embarrassing detail to her counsellor.

Contrast with the lawyer interview

In contrast, it appeared that the interviews carried out by lawyers with Kina were quite unsuccessful. General comments from both Kina (in her interview with me) and the lawyers (in their written affidavits) reveal the common tendency for people to interpret different approaches to communication in terms of personality and intention rather than in terms of cultural difference (see, for example, Gumperz 1982).

Kina's analysis of the different styles of interviewing is totally consistent with an Aboriginal approach to effective ways of finding out information. It is not surprising that she found the lawyers to be 'not interested', 'not listening' and 'not communicating', 'in a hurry' and 'using big words'.

The lawyers, on the other hand, described her as 'extremely reticent in her communication with [them]', 'appear[ing] passive and uninterested in the entire process of the preparation of her defence', and generally 'a difficult client'.

My on-going research with Aboriginal people and the lawyers who interview them, combined with an interpretation of such reactions, suggests the following general analysis, comparing the lawyer interview with the characteristics of the counselling interview, described above.

1.   The lawyer interview usually proceeds without productive silences. This is primarily because it is a norm of non-Aboriginal Australians that silence is an indication that communication has broken down. Unlike counsellors, lawyers are not trained to use silences as a positive and productive part of interviews. Further, it is common for lawyers to interrupt the silence of Aboriginal people, not recognising that it is a part of their answer. Unless they are trained either in counselling techniques, or in effective communication with Aboriginal people,[9] lawyers tend wrongly to interpret Aboriginal silence in answer to a question as either unwillingness to answer, or as lack of relevant knowledge. Similarly, they interpret silence in response to suggestions as acquiescence. In both instances the Aboriginal person is most likely to be thinking through the issue at hand before formulating a response.

2.   There is frequently little of the sharing strategy in these interviews. While this may be provided by discussion of allegations against a client (e.g. 'the police have said …'), much of the lawyer interview is a one-sided interview typical of many mainstream white institutions including education and employment.

3.   Narratives are frequently interrupted so that the lawyer can understand the information being provided in terms of the legal constraints and constructs within which the particular case is operating. In addition, the need to collect specific details on a large number of points can necessitate the interruption of the client's telling 'in her own words'.

4.   Frequently, in these interviews there is simply no opportunity to wait until a relationship develops before important personal details are sought from the client. Table 16.1 has shown how impossible it would have been for Kina to build up such a relationship with any of the lawyers who represented her in 1988.

Interviews with TV journalists

There is considerable variation in the way that TV journalists conduct their interviews, for example depending on whether the interview is pre-recorded or live, and on the particular style of journalism.

Fortunately we have some of the necessary information for this report from the affidavit of one of the two documentary producers. She explains that the director of the initial documentary (David Goldie) flew to Brisbane to speak to Kina before any formal or recorded interviews took place.

> Our standard procedure in situations like this is to ensure that the person to be interviewed has our confidence, and feels secure in speaking to us ... One of David's purposes in seeing Robyn before the interview was to make her feel comfortable with us and what we were doing.

Further, when the film crew went to interview Kina, they did the interview in her own space (her room), and Goldie and his team talked to her for some time before turning on the camera.

Relationship between the TV interview and Aboriginal communication

The following three features of the way in which the David Goldie (TV) interview was conducted are culturally appropriate to Aboriginal ways of finding out information.

1. The interviewers took the time to establish some sort of relationship with Kina before conducting the TV interview.
2. The interviewers provided the opportunity for Kina to give several uninterrupted narrative accounts in telling different parts of her story.
3. Unlike the lawyer interviews, the TV interviews were primarily concerned with hearing Kina's story. Having no need to structure the information, the journalists used prompts to encourage her to say what she wanted to say. In contrast, in the lawyer interview, the lawyer needs to find out about certain aspects which are determined to be legally relevant.

The central question

The sociolinguistic analysis found that the way in which the counsellor and the TV journalists communicated with Kina involved features that were culturally appropriate to the task of finding out sensitive and embarrassing personal details from an Aboriginal person. These features have been discussed above.

On the other hand, the way in which the lawyer interviews were carried out were much less culturally appropriate to the task of finding out sensitive and embarrassing personal details from an Aboriginal person. These features have also been discussed above.

The major differences between the counsellor and TV interviews on the one hand, and the lawyer interviews on the other, would be attributable not primarily to personality differences in the interviewers involved, but to the functions and natures of the different interviews, as also discussed above. The lack of continuity of lawyers representing Kina leading up to the trial was also a major problem in terms of trusting important personal information to a person with whom one has developed a relationship.

Another relevant factor in answer to this question relates to the timing of the interviews. The first of the TV interviews was done in October 1991, by which time Kina was developing considerable bicultural competence, as discussed above. Had she been interviewed at this time by a lawyer who had taken some time to establish rapport, it is quite likely that she would also have spoken to that person about these embarrassing personal details. (But note that many of these embarrassing personal details had been revealed to the counsellor in 1988.) It seems quite likely that psychological factors are also relevant to this question, particularly regarding the comparison between the interviews with lawyers in 1988, and with the TV journalists in 1991. The development of Kina's self-confidence and sense of self-worth are issues that were raised by the psychiatrist.

The issue of time was undoubtedly also relevant to the reason why the threat made by Black to rape Kina's 14-year-old niece was not revealed to the lawyers or the counsellor, but was revealed on the TV interviews some years later. Also relevant here is Kina's responsibility to look after her sister's daughter, and what would have been a strong cultural constraint not to 'shame' her sister by talking about such a threat. Kina did not talk about this threat until after her sister's death (in 1990), and the counsellor's reassurance that this niece had settled down, re-enrolled at school and was secure in her family environment.

The role of Kina's diary notes

It is important to point out that Kina did in fact attempt to communicate to her lawyers some detail about the abuse she suffered in the days preceding her attack on Tony Black. This was in the form of nine pages of handwritten diary notes, made by her in prison some months before her trial, as she recollected the days leading up to her fatal attack on Black. These notes gave graphic detail of much of the physical abuse inflicted on her by Black in these few days. In the Statement of Fact produced by her lawyer on 8 July 1988 she refers to these notes saying that she adopts this diary 'as my instructions to the Public Defender'.

The cultural significance of this form of communication (written diary notes) is that it enabled Kina to tell her story in her own words, and in her own time without interruption. In this way she avoided the worst problems encountered in the lawyer interview. She was effectively employing the uninterrupted narrative method of providing information.

These diary notes could have formed the basis of an exchange between Kina and her lawyer, as they could have been taken back to her for clarification, expansion and other further discussion. However, the diary notes were not used, and it seems that the lawyers were focused on eliciting information from their client by means of interview.

The decision not to give evidence at the trial

Kina's 'decision' that she would not give evidence at her trial obviously had drastic consequences, as the jury had no evidence about any circumstances that could have contributed to Kina's acting out of provocation or in self-defence when she stabbed Black. A number of cultural and linguistic factors are relevant to understanding this 'decision' that she would not give evidence.

1. Kina's understanding as conveyed to me (when I interviewed her in October 1993) was that the lawyers were not encouraging her to give evidence and that they actually encouraged her not to give evidence. Her feeling was that '...you're supposed to go with whatever your solicitor tells you'. She could have only gone against her lawyers' advice, if she had spent sufficient time with them to build a relationship of trust. (However, the President of the Appeal Court pointed out during the appeal hearing that Kina could not have been any worse off if she had given evidence at her trial.)

2. The communication style of courtroom evidence is also relevant. Kina would have had to answer many questions asked by people, some of whom she had never seen before, and none of whom she felt she had established a rapport with. Further, these questions would be about very personal and embarrassing details, exactly the worst kind of information to provide in this format.

    It is relevant to point out that Kina's trial took place prior to the enactment of the 1989 amendment of Section 21A of the *Evidence Act* 1977 (Qld), which makes provision for witnesses who are disadvantaged as a result of cultural difference to give evidence either wholly or in part by videotape. (However, this provision appears to be rarely used for Aboriginal witnesses.)

3. Not being encouraged to give evidence, Kina's Aboriginal way of dealing with 'white business' such as the Court, would guide her not to oppose her lawyers. Further, as her counsellor was on holiday immediately preceding the trial, Kina's inability to discuss this issue with someone with whom she had rapport and trust was also an important issue.

4. The manner in which Kina was questioned at the trial did not directly seek her own views, as illustrated with this quote from the trial transcript.

HIS HONOUR:	Robyn Bella Kina, do you intend to adduce evidence in your defence before your Counsel addresses the jury?
MR SHANAHAN:	It is not intended to give evidence or to call evidence.
HIS HONOUR:	Robyn Bella Kina, you have heard your Counsel answer and what he said?
ACCUSED:	Yes.

Even if Kina had interpreted the Judge's second question above to mean, 'Do you agree with your lawyer?', an answer of 'Yes' may not have indicated 'I don't want to give or call evidence'.

Such a question beginning with 'Do you agree …?' invites a 'yes' of gratuitous concurrence from an Aboriginal person, rather than seeking their genuine opinion (see Eades 1992). A more appropriate question would have been something like, 'We need to know what you want to do about this …'.

Sociolinguistic evidence accepted

In accepting the sociolinguistic evidence, the Queensland Court of Criminal Appeal established a new precedent in Australia.[10] In fact, the same court had, some seven years earlier, ruled linguistic evidence (presented by the same expert) as inadmissible in the case of Kelvin Condren (see Eades 1988, 1993, 1995b). Somewhat to my surprise, no objection to the evidence was entered by the Crown. I was not called to give oral evidence, as my report, tendered in the form of a 17-page statement, was accepted in total.

It is difficult to assess the weight that was attached to the sociolinguistic evidence, in comparison with the psychiatric evidence and the evidence of what appeared to point to elements of mishandling by various legal representatives.

The finding of the three appeal court judges is summarised in this extract from 'Reasons for Judgment' by the President and Davies (1993: 35, 36):

> In this matter [i.e. Kina's case], there were, insufficiently recognised, a number of complex factors interacting which presented exceptional difficulties of communication between her legal representatives and the appellant because of:
>
> (i)   her aboriginality
> (ii) the battered woman syndrome; and
> (iii) the shameful (to her) nature of the events which characterised her relationship with the deceased.
>
> These cultural, psychological and personal factors bore upon the adequacy of the advice and legal representation which the appellant received and effectively denied her satisfactory representation or the capacity to make informed decisions on the basis of proper advice.
>
> In the exceptional events which occurred, the appellant's trial involved a miscarriage of justice.

As a result, Kina's murder conviction was quashed and she was released from prison. Although the appeal court judgments recommended a new trial, in which she would undoubtedly have been found guilty of manslaughter, the Attorney-General exercised the prerogative not to proceed with the trial (presumably because she had already served nearly five years in prison, the likely maximum sentence, given the self-defence and provocation involved in the fatal attack.)

Consequences of the case

The Court's recognition of cultural differences in communication and the need for these differences to be accommodated by the law has far-reaching consequences as the following points indicate.

- On a practical level, the Legal Aid Office of Brisbane organised workshops for its staff on cross-cultural communication in law, as a direct response to the judgments in Kina's case (this was the office that had represented Kina so unsuccessfully at her trial).
- In the public debate and discussion that followed the quashing of Kina's conviction, the Attorney-General made a strong statement about the cultural disadvantage experienced by many Aboriginal people in the legal system. Speaking on a television current affairs show on the day following the decision in Kina's appeal, he said:

> ... I think the law is going to have to find ways, and the legal system is going to have to find ways to make special provisions frequently for Aboriginal witnesses ...

and that

> ... the problem of crosscultural communication is one which the legal system needs to have knowledge of and needs to be sensitive to ...
>
> (*7.30 Report,* 30 November 1993)

- While the cultural disadvantage which was so crucial to Kina's appeal had been argued through expert sociolinguistic testimony, the need for legislative reform, rather than individual expert witnesses in specific cases, was argued by the President of the Queensland Court of Appeal in a 1995 judgment (Pringle 1995: 18):

> There is increasing acceptance of the need for greater cultural awareness in the legal system, but problems such as cultural disability would be better addressed legislatively, after proper consultation and debate directed by a body such as the Law Reform Commission.

The issue of the legal systems' knowledge of and sensitivity to the problem of cross-cultural communication was raised in 1995 in the Magistrate's Court in Brisbane, in the way in which three Aboriginal boys were cross-examined in a trial in which they were prosecution witnesses. In their cross-examination these boys became victims of serious miscommunication, exactly of the sort that was raised in Kina's case, and spoken about so clearly by the Attorney General (see Eades 1995b). As a result of the public outcry over this case, the Queensland Criminal Justice Commission has instituted a research project into 'Aboriginal Witnesses', addressing the issue of 'problems in the way Queensland's criminal courts deal with the evidence of Aboriginal witnesses ... in particular ... any cultural or linguistic factors which affect Aboriginal English speakers as witnesses.[11]

It is possible that this inquiry will recommend legislative reform which will make some changes to the rules of evidence, making it more difficult for cultural and linguistic differences to hinder the presentation of Aboriginal evidence. Kina's case shows that legislative reform is not enough: a cross-cultural understanding of the assumptions and practices inherent in the interview process are essential prerequisites for any lawyer who represents an Aboriginal client.

Acknowledgements

I am grateful to Andrew Boe for his advice on a number of legal matters, and to Mee Wun Lee and Jeff Siegel for their helpful comments on this paper. All remaining errors are my responsibility.

Notes

1   Although the major report of this Commission was published in 1991 (RCIADC 1991) with 339 recommendations, it appears that little has changed. In 1994 Behrendt and Cunneen (1994: 4) found that the national rate of Aboriginal deaths in custody had not declined.
2   To understand this situation more fully it is necessary to examine the issue of the culturally biased determination of obscene (or offensive) language, the 'offence' which often triggers off the 'litany of offences' mentioned (see Langton 1988; Walsh 1995; Taylor 1995).
3   For example, it was reported to me by a lawyer working for Aboriginal Legal Services that his case load is ten times that of his load when he previously worked in a private criminal practice.
4   In fact, Kina had written to her lawyers shortly after her trial (in 1988) and asked for an appeal. This appeal was carried out without any consultation between Kina and any lawyer, and was heard on 23 November 1988. It was unsuccessful. The appeal in 1993 was therefore actually the second appeal, but it was the first chance Kina had to present the evidence of self-defence and provocation to the court, which she did mainly in affidavit (written) form.
5   While the psychiatric and sociolinguistic evidence was accepted, without objection, evidence from the social worker was objected to by the prosecution on the basis that the necessary expertise was in psychology, not social work. The court decided that it was unnecessary and undesirable to rule on the admissibility of this social work evidence 'because there was no real investigation of [the social worker's] qualifications and much of her evidence need not be relied upon for the appellant's present purposes' (President and Davies 1993: 32).
6   On-going investigations over the last ten years and communications from Aboriginal and non-Aboriginal people in every state indicate that the patterns which were revealed in Southeast Queensland are widely found all over Australia.
7   I do not intend to express any views as to the relevant value of the professions involved. Nor do I intend to make an evaluation of the competence of any individuals involved.
8   One of the details, namely Black's threat to rape Kina's 14-year-old niece, was not revealed to the counsellor, but was first revealed in the TV interviews several years after the counsellor and lawyer interviews (see p. 215).
9   Kina's trial took place in 1988, at which time there was no training or literature available for lawyers on this topic.
10   Note, however, that sociolinguistic evidence presented by Michael Cooke had been accepted in a 1990 Coronial Inquest into the death of an Aboriginal man on Elcho Island (Cooke, 1995, personal communication). Cooke's evidence related to cultural differences in the acceptable response to a request. For a discussion of interpreting issues in this inquest see Cooke (1995).
11   The boys had been allegedly abducted by six police officers in three separate vehicles late one night and dumped in an industrial wasteland some 14 km away. The boys were witnesses for the prosecution in the trial of the six police officers. As a result of serious linguistic and cultural manipulation of their evidence, questions were raised as to the boys' credibility and

the charges against the police officers were dropped. Following an unsuccessful Supreme Court Review of the magistrate's decision, the case is now closed.

References

Behrendt, J. and Cunneen, C. (1994) Report to the National Committee to Defend Black Rights: Aboriginal and Torres Strait Islander custodial deaths between May 1989 and January 1994, *Aboriginal Law Bulletin*, 3(68): 4–6.

Cooke, M. (1995) Aboriginal evidence in the cross-cultural courtroom, in D. Eades (ed.), *Language in Evidence: Issues confronting Aboriginal and Multicultural Australia*, Sydney: University of New South Wales Press, pp. 55–96.

Eades, D. (1984) Misunderstanding Aboriginal English: the role of socio-cultural context, in G. McKay and B. Sommer (eds.), *Applications of Linguistics to Australian Aboriginal Contexts*, Melbourne: Applied Linguistics Association of Australia, pp. 24–33.

—— (1988) They don't speak an Aboriginal language, or do they? in I. Keen (ed.), *Being Black: Aboriginal Cultures in 'Settled' Australia*, Canberra: Aboriginal Studies Press, pp. 97–115.

—— (1991) Communicative strategies in Aboriginal English, in S. Romaine (ed.), *Language in Australia,* Cambridge: Cambridge University Press, pp. 84–93.

—— (1992) *Aboriginal English and the Law: Communicating with Aboriginal English Speaking Clients: A Handbook for Legal Practitioners*, Brisbane: Queensland Law Society.

—— (1993) The case for Condren: Aboriginal English, pragmatics and the law, *Journal of Pragmatics*, 20(2): 141–162.

—— (1994) A case of communicative clash: Aboriginal English and the legal system, in J. Gibbons (ed.), *Language and the Law*, London: Longman, pp. 234–264.

—— (1995a) Aboriginal English on Trial: the case for Stuart and Condren, in D. Eades (ed.), *Language in Evidence: Issues Confronting Aboriginal and Multicultural Australia*, Sydney: University of New South Wales Press, pp. 147–174.

—— (1995b) Cross-examination of Aboriginal children: the Pinkenba case, *Aboriginal Law Bulletin*, 3(75): 10–11.

Gumperz, J. (1982) *Discourse Strategies*, Cambridge: Cambridge University Press.

Langton, M. (1988) Medicine Square, in I. Keen (ed.) 1988 *Being Black: Aboriginal Cultures in 'Settled' Australia*, Canberra: Aboriginal Studies Press, pp. 201–225.

McPherson, J.A. (1993) The Queen v Robyn Bella Kina: Reasons for Judgment, unpublished MS (C.A. No. 221 of 1993).

President (P. Fitzgerald) and Davies, J.A. (1993) The Queen v Robyn Bella Kina: Reasons for Judgment, unpublished MS (C.A. No. 221 of 1993).

Pringle, K. (1995) Questioning 'Evidence' in R v An Aboriginal, *Youth Aboriginal Law Bulletin*, 3(74): 16–18.

Royal Commission into Aboriginal Deaths in Custody (RCIADC) 1991 *National Report*, Canberra: Australian Government Printing Service.

Taylor, B. (1995) Offensive language: linguistic and sociolinguistic perspective, in D. Eades (ed.), *Language in Evidence: Issues confronting Aboriginal and Multicultural Australia*, Sydney: University of New South Wales Press, pp. 219–258.

Walsh, B. (1995) Offensive language: A legal perspective, in D. Eades (ed.) *Language in Evidence: Issues confronting Aboriginal and Multicultural Australia*, Sydney: University of New South Wales Press, pp. 203–218.

PART SEVEN

Language and age

Jean Stilwell Peccei

INTRODUCTION

THESE TWO READINGS have been chosen in order to look in detail at two age identities: the elderly and adolescents. While we think of age as being an absolute marker, something determined simply by date of birth, we see in these readings that age is a socially constructed identity category. While we ascribe age identities to the individuals we meet, part of this also depends on how these people construct, or style, their own identities.

In the first reading, Makoni and Grainger examine how elderly people in care homes are spoken to. While age is a reason for being in these institutions, there are other identities and tasks that need to be considered. The authors argue that these interactions need to be understood in relation to their particular context. For example, in the South African data, ethnicity is salient because of the former apartheid regime with which all participants will be familiar. This political and legal history is thus available for use in conversation, with some residents making an issue of ethnicity and invoking racist discourses from this period. In terms of a more local context, Makoni and Grainger argue that in analysing the talk of nurses, we need to remember the various professional tasks they are required to undertake. While conversation is certainly part of caring and nursing, the nurses have particular tasks that need to be completed; making sure residents are fed, given their medication and so on. The need to accomplish these tasks has a bearing on the way that interaction takes place. However, it should be remembered that showing care for residents, emotional labour, is an important part of this profession (Hochschild 1983).

These tasks result in the use of particular discourses. That is, we can understand the nurses as drawing on the following discourses: managerial, affective and nursing. The authors note that while most discourse is task oriented, the tasks, and thus discourses, involved, may be in conflict. When trying to accomplish a task, to administer medication, for example, a nurse may use affective discourse strategies in order to fulfil this managerial task. While this is easily understood as strategic, any real concern for the resident will be secondary to the completing of the task.

These conflicts in role and discourse mean that threats to face may occur. 'Face' is a concept generally associated with politeness theory scholars that helps to analyze and understand the way we interact with others (Brown and Levinson 1987). In short, there are two 'kinds' of face: **positive and negative face**. Negative face is the desire to do what one wants to do. It is thus concerned with the way individuals value their autonomy. Thus, when we ask someone to do something for us, we **mitigate** the request either by suggesting that it is small imposition ('Could you do me a small favour?') or by being especially deferential ('if it's not too much trouble, and you wouldn't mind, could you possibly pass the salt'). Positive face, on the other hand, is wanting to be approved of. Thus, when expressing disapproval of someone, it is 'polite' to **hedge** this in some way ('I'm not sure that's such a great idea'). Asking someone to do something or disapproving of them in some way are both potentially face threatening acts (FTA). To reduce the face threat, the strategies just suggested may be used. However, there is also the issue of power to be considered. Whether we care about threatening someone's face depends very much on our relationship to them. Makoni and Grainger draw attention to the hierarchy of staff in these nursing homes which may influence the choices available. Further, some of the nurses are not happy with their own English skills. Given the subtle cues needed to mitigate FTAs, and given that these are not the same across all languages and cultures, what was intended as a polite request can easily be construed as an impolite demand (Thomas 1983). What an utterance means is not straightforward. This is clear in the discussion of 'infantilization discourse'. While the use of endearments (such as 'dear') may appear to treat the resident much the same as a child, it can also be understood as offering reassurance and care. How it is construed will depend on the individuals involved. While one person may interpret 'dear' as friendly, someone else may hear it as patronizing. As always, forms have multiple functions and we need to look closely at the details of interaction to discover what these functions are.

Makoni and Grainger collected their data by participant observation. They focused on sampling specific routines rather than specific timeframes and recorded the interactions on audio. They also video recorded all the interactions to provide non-verbal contextual information (apart from those routines when residents did not wish to be filmed, such as toileting). Residents on short-stay or respite care were excluded from the study, as were those who were 'non-alert'. Classifying a person as 'non-alert' was based on nurses' judgements, a mental status questionnaire or medical records indicating Alzheimer's or Parkinson's disease or other conditions which seriously impaired their ability to both use and understand language.

Penelope Eckert's paper looks closely at a much younger group of language users who are also institutionalized: teenagers. Historically, the category 'teenager' is a relatively recent one. In many ways they are marginalized; they don't belong to the privileged group of children, nor are they considered full adults. Thus, their language use, and other habits, are stigmatized. Eckert notes that teenagers are often blamed for ruining the language, even though their innovations are no different in kind from those that adult speakers engage in. The **stereotypes** that are associated with teenagers' behaviour are transferred to their language use. Gal and Irvine (1995) call this process '**iconization**'. It is important to distinguish iconization from Labov's use of stereotype (1964) because of the association of iconization with stereotype in a different sense. Labov's 'stereotype' is a feature that is so associated with a variety and so stigmatized that speakers avoid it. The process of iconization is an **ideological** one; 'stereotype' here is used in the usual sense of a set of cultural ideas about a group. Teenagers' language use is viewed through the same ideological lens that they are.

Eckert argues that teenagers, like the elderly, are institutionalized and cared for by professionals. The primary institution for teenagers is that of the school. Adolescents orient to this institutional context in making choices about linguistic style. This research makes clear that like other groups, adolescents do not constitute a homogenous whole. There is a great deal of diversity in the way they construct their identities, not only with respect to their language, but with respect to other identity markers too (such as clothes and activities). The stylistic choices made confer particular kinds of **social capital**. While aligning with the values of school provides a particular kind of capital, going against these values provides another. Thus while 'jocks' seek to accumulate the kind of social capital valued by their educational establishment, 'burnouts' do exactly the opposite. The social capital that jocks accrue is analogous to Labov's **overt prestige**; while the burnouts' is more like **covert prestige** (1972). It is important to remember that this is capital related to language and other activity. Further, the way individuals seek this prestige is influenced by other identity categories, such as gender. Thus, burnout women are more extreme than their male counterparts in their use of relevant variables. The same is true for jock women. If we look at the extremes of variation, we find women at both ends.

Questions to consider

1. Grainger and Makoni are looking at elderly people in institutions. Is the way they are spoken to outside such institutions different? How? Why?
2. Usually more than one factor will be relevant to identity and interaction. Thinking of yourself, what are the most salient factors for your interactions? Does this differ according to context? Is there a hierarchical ranking of these?
3. Teenagers are viewed through certain stereotypes/ideologies. Can you think of other groups that are treated according to similar ideas? What are the ideologies? How might this play out in terms of iconization?
4. Groups are represented and spoken about in particular ways. Are there real links between the way members of these groups actually use language and what is said about these groups?

Further reading

On language and the elderly:

Hamilton, H.E. (ed.), (1999) *Language and Communication in Old Age: Multidisciplinary Perspectives*, New York: Garland.
International Journal of the Sociology of Language (2009), 200, Special issue on ageing.

Journal of Aging Studies (1993) 7(3), Special Issue: Discourse, Institutions and the Elderly.

Taylor, B.C. (1992) 'Elderly Identity in Conversation: Producing Frailty', *Communication Research*, 19(4): 493–515.

On the elderly in particular settings:

Backhaus, P. (2009) 'Politeness in institutional elderly care in Japan: A cross-cultural comparison', *Journal of Politeness Research*, 5(1): 53–57.

Coupland, J., Robinson, J.D. and Coupland, N. (1994) 'Frame Negotiation in Doctor-Elderly Patient Consultations', *Discourse and Society*, 5(1): 89–124.

Grainger, K. (1993) '"That's a Lovely Bath Dear": Reality Construction in the Discourse of Elderly Care', *Journal of Aging Studies*, 7(3): 247–262.

The journal *Communication and Medicine* will also be a useful source here.

On the relationship between the language used with children and that used with adults deemed to be 'childish':

Sealy, Alison (2000) *Childly Language*, London: Longman.

On language and adolescents:

Androutsopoulos, J.K. and Georgakopoulou, A. (2003) *Discourse Constructions of Youth Identity*, Amsterdam: John Benjamin.

Bucholtz, M. (1999) '"Why Be Normal?": Language and Identity Practices in a Community of Nerd Girls', *Language in Society*, 28(2): 203–223.

Cheshire, J. and Fox, S. (2009) 'Was/Were Variation: A Perspective from London', *Language Variation and Change*, 21(1): 1–38.

Cutler, C.A. (1999) 'Yorkville Crossing: White Teens, Hip Hop and African American English', *Journal of Sociolinguistics*, 3(4): 428–444.

Huffaker, D. and Calvert, S. (2005) 'Gender, Identity, and Language Use in Teenage Blogs', *Journal of Computer-Mediated Communication*, 2005, 10(2), online, available at: http://jcmc.indiana.edu/vol10/issue2/huffaker.html.

Tagliamonte, S.A. (2008) 'So different and pretty cool! Recycling intensifiers in Toronto', *English Language and Linguistics*, 12(2): 361–394.

Tagliamonte, S. and Hudson, R. (1999) 'Be Like et al. beyond America: The Quotative System in British and Canadian Youth', *Journal of Sociolinguistics*, 3(2): 147–172.

Studies using corpora:

Barbieri, F. (2007) 'Older men and younger women: A corpus-based study of quotative use in American English', *English World-Wide*, 28(1): 23–45.

Mautner, G. (2007) 'Mining large corpora for social information: the case of elderly', *Language in Society*, 36(1): 51–72.

Stenstrom, A.-B., Andersen, G. and Hasund, I.K. (2002) *Trends in Teenage Talk: Corpus Compilation, Analysis and Findings*, Amsterdam: John Benjamins.

Suggestions for further viewing

Mean Girls (2002) Mark Waters.
On Golden Pond (1981) Mark Rydell.
Outnumbered (2007–10) Hat Trick Productions, UK (series).
Outnumbered (2009) Bryan Gordon (film, USA).
Venus (2006) Roger Mitchell.

References

Brown, P. and Levinson, S. (1987) *Politeness: Some Universals in Language Usage*, Cambridge: Cambridge University Press.
Gal, S. and Irvine, J.T. (1995) 'The boundaries of languages and disciplines: how ideologies construct difference', *Social Research*, 62(4): 967–1001.
Hochschild, A.R. (1983) *The Managed Heart: Commercialization of Human Feeling*, Berkeley, CA: University of California Press.
Labov, W. (1964) 'Stages in the acquisition of Standard English', in R.W. Shuy (ed.), *Social Dialects and Language Learning*, Champaign: National Council of Teachers of English.
— (1972) *Sociolinguistic Patterns*, Philadelphia, PA: University of Pennsylvania Press.
Thomas, J. (1983) 'Cross-cultural pragmatic failure', *Applied Linguistics*, 4(2): 91–112.

Chapter 17

Sinfree Makoni and Karen Grainger

COMPARATIVE GERONTOLINGUISTICS: CHARACTERIZING DISCOURSES IN CARING INSTITUTIONS IN SOUTH AFRICA AND THE UNITED KINGDOM

Results

A LTHOUGH THE FOCUS of this study is the actual dialogue between staff and residents, it is perhaps noteworthy that our observations indicate that in many ways the living conditions and daily routines for residents in both cultural contexts are essentially similar. Residents spend most of the day seated in a day room, their chairs arranged around the sides of the room with the chair backs to the wall. This arrangement makes it difficult for residents to interact with one another but is easier for the staff to have access to the residents and to move around the ward. Most residents sit "parked" in their chairs most of the day, usually not talking and otherwise inactive. The television is almost always on in the background.

The daily routine is fairly invariant and consists of taking care of the basic physical needs of the residents: washing, dressing, eating, toileting, and administering medication and treatments. The nurses' job is task-oriented and the completion of routine physical tasks is given priority over individual resident desires. Indeed, our conversations with the nurses revealed that they feel so much pressure to complete these tasks that any demands for attention from residents that do not fit in with these tasks are regarded as interfering with the accomplishment of their routine tasks (Berdes and Eckert 2001).

Descriptions of the Staff

There are clearly hierarchical differences in all institutions. The following quote addresses these differences in institutions for the elderly (Williams and Nussbaum 2001: 207):

Those who do the caring within nursing homes range from highly paid educated physicians to volunteers. At risk of over generalization, it has been our experience that physicians rarely enter the nursing home, that nurses are typically administrators, and that nurse aides interact most frequently with the older residents. Nurse aides are the least educated, most poorly paid, and youngest therefore, most inexperienced of the professional staff. The majority of intergenerational communication that transpires within the nursing home is between the older residents and these nurse aides.

Personnel records at each of the institutions provide details about the background of the nurses observed in this study. In Britain there were 41 nurses in total. Their background and training were as follows: auxiliaries (nurse aides): 24 (with no previous training), student nurses: 2 (currently in training), state enrolled nurses: 12 (two years of training), state registered nurse: 1 (three years of training), ward sister: 1, physiotherapist: 1. Parallel data for the 15 South African nurses are as follows: auxiliaries: 7 (no previous training), state enrolled nurses: 5 (two years of training), state registered nurses: 3 (three years of training).

Controlling discourse

The controlling dimension of nurse-resident interaction is presented in Tables 17.1 and 17.2. As the data suggest below, the controlling dimension of discourse achieves the three established elements of institutional caregiving, specifically: service-provision, showing concern, and doing practical tasks. We find the nurse issues instructions/ **directives** (e.g. "stand up," "move up"), accompanied by endearments ("sweetheart," "darling"), in the same speech act. Table 17.1 is a feeding exchange taking place in a general ward during lunchtime. The nurse is a Black state registered nurse in her early twenties. This is her first professional nursing job after completion of training. She has been working in the nursing home for less than a year. Her mother tongue is **Xhosa** and English is her second language. The resident is in her mid-70s. She has been in the nursing home for five years.

In Table 17.1 the nurse issues an instruction to the resident. The overt commands are toned down with the use of an endearment ("sweetheart") tagged at the end, after a pause. The data include a number of other endearment forms that other nurses use when interacting with residents such as "darling," "lovey," "my man." The endearment terms co-occur with instructions to residents. The co-occurrence of instructions and endearments could be construed as an attempt by the nurses not to impose unnecessarily on the residents. Instructions violate **negative face** because they might be read as impositions by the resident(s), although conversations with the same nurse in Table 17.1 reveal that her intention was not to instruct the residents. She explains that her English is not as good as she would like. Due to the nurse's limited English proficiency, her interactional style is likely to be construed by the resident as instructive, contravening the resident set of norms, which is an unfortunate situation. The nature of the nurse's bilingualism and the differences arising from the fact that the caregiver is a second language speaker caring for a native English speaker creates a tension between the physical and linguistic expression of caring by the nurse. In Table 17.1, the resident

Table 17.1: Directives, pleas and endearments in the United Kingdom data

Nurse:	stand up ((then)) sweetheart (.) up she comes (.) right up
Resident:	ooh mind now don't be rough girl
Nurse:	try not to be
Resident:	yes you are (4.0) ((3 syllables)) (2.0) ((you're)) too rough see
Nurse:	oh I'm trying not to be Ellen (.) but you're awful heavy (3.0) there we are (.) alright now?
Resident:	yes thank you
Nurse:	good girl

Table 17.2: Directives, pleas and endearments in the South Africa data

Nurse 1:	move up (pause) please darling
Resident:	I don't want
Nurse 2:	carry on
Nurse 1:	you must mo!
Nurse 2:	move move up move up (pause) your pillows
Nurse 1:	move up Mrs. Smith you must eat now
Nurse 2:	move up be a darling

positions herself as a service-recipient or manager in that she also issues orders to the nurse and asserts her authority, partly by virtue of age and racial status by addressing her as "girl." Despite this, the nurse re-invokes her "motherly" role (partly controlling, partly nurturing) when she praises the resident ("good girl").

In Table 17.2 there is also some ambiguity of role being negotiated as the nurse pleads with the resident to cooperate. At this point the nurse's controlling role is reduced and becomes more like that of service provider. Notice, the last utterance in Table 17.2 incorporates a directive ("move up"), a plea ("be a darling") and an endearment, capturing in one turn of speech several dimensions of institutional caring: control, nurture, and service provision. The overt instructions are toned down with the use of endearments tagged at the end after a considerably long pause. The endearment expressions co-occur with instructions and pleas.

Service-provider discourse is also present but is less prevalent. The nurse in Table 17.3 is a state registered nurse in her early forties, who, according to institutional records, has been working at the same nursing home since "**apartheid** days," i.e. before 1994. She is more senior in age and professional rank than the other nurses she is working with on her ward. In Table 17.3 the nurse refuses to take the role of service provider, despite having been told by the wife of the resident that he wishes to go to

Table 17.3: Managerial and controlling discourse in South Africa data

Nurse:	you want to go to bed. I know that
Resident:	uhm
Nurse:	later later

bed. Instead she invokes a managerial and controlling role in which it is she who decides when he should go to bed.

The similarities in these data from two widely different cultural contexts would suggest that, in this respect at least (and in both data **corpora** this type of interaction is extremely common), the practice of caring in terms of interaction is manifested in very similar linguistic forms which, despite the cultural function of these forms (for example, the social meaning of first-naming in the United Kingdom and in South Africa may not be identical) may be determined by a *universal* need to balance the conflicting aspects of institutional caring. We can couch this in terms of politeness theory (which claims to be a universal theory; Brown and Levinson 1987). That is, the physical act of caring for someone involves threats to both negative and **positive face** (i.e. intrusion and inflicting discomfort or pain) which have to be redressed with positive politeness strategies such as the expression of love and intimacy (Grainger (1993) argues that the institution has to sustain conflicting definitions of reality, and that this is achieved in part through nurses' and residents' use of various "modes" of discourse).

We do not want to argue, however, that controlling styles of communication such as the above are inevitable given the demands inherent in institutional caring. While institutional caregivers may need to incorporate these elements to some degree in their professional role, the precise balance that is constructed and achieved depends on macro contextual factors. We maintain that because of the similarities in the institutional regime in both the United Kingdom and South Africa settings (that is to say, because in both cases the caring process is very much defined as task-oriented, the nurses feel under pressure to complete a set number of practical caring tasks at the expense of personal integrity of the residents), the majority of nurses' talk is in the service of the task-management goal.

Infantilization discourse

The discourse of task-management is achieved by nurses in interesting ways. In general, nursing staff positions the residents in a powerless role through constructing an appearance of intimacy. This simultaneously maintains a benevolent and concerned role for the nurses. So, for example, endearments and "loving," sympathetic talk often have the effect of infantilizing the residents such that they are in a relatively powerless position, as in Table 17.1. But infantalization is not necessarily negative. It is a strategy by caregivers to protect themselves against a violation of the independence and private spaces of the care receivers (van Dongen 1999).

Although the loving and playful discourse modes are prevalent in our data, at other times nurses and residents are clearly antagonistic towards one another. These instances demonstrate, in Brown and Levinson's (1987) terms, "bald-on-record" face threatening acts. In the United Kingdom data, residents are frequently rude to nurses, usually when protesting at having some procedure carried out for them. This is the case with the auxiliary nurse and elderly woman resident in her seventies described in Table 17.4. In this interaction, the resident first pleads with the nurse not to give her the bath. She then repeatedly calls her "cruel," a threat to the nurse's positive face wants. However, while the nurse responds to the resident ("we're only washing your hair"), she is not deterred from her task. The resident's utterances may be damaging to some extent to the nurse's nurturing identity (since she is asserting "on record" that she is not a caring person). This is perhaps treated lightly because this resident is considered to be "confused" and, therefore, not able to make judgments about what is good for her. Furthermore, the bathing task is seen as a prime nursing task and, therefore, essential to the professional identity of the nurse (Nolan and Grant 1993).

In the South Africa data, face-threatening behavior between staff and residents takes the form more of "malignant racism" than "anachronistic racism" (Berdes and Eckert 2001). Table 17.5 is an exchange between a state registered nurse and a White elderly man. The nurse is in her early twenties and has just joined the staff of the nursing home from a psychiatric hospital. She is trying to get the resident to bathe, but the resident is refusing. Both the resident and the nurse feel the water and it looks as if the resident is complying, but the resident then gets into the water with his clothes and shoes on. In Table 17.5, it is the resident who is exhibiting face-threatening behavior, both in his words and in his actions. In his first utterance he issues the negative face-threat, "you can't bath me," accompanied by a racial slur ("pikinini"). He then indirectly insults (threatens positive face) the nurse by implying that she is uncivilized ("you bath in rivers") and that she should not be where she is ("where do you come from? … what are you doing here?") and thereby may have broken a law of the former apartheid regime. Subsequently, the resident gets into the bath fully clothed. Since this resident cannot be described as "confused," according to the scores from the Mini-Mental Status Questionnaire (MMSE) and the nurse's evidence, this seems to be an act of defiance. The first nurse appears not to tolerate the insults and walks away (although presumably she is used to "difficult" residents if she previously worked in a psychiatric hospital). This is something that is unlikely to happen in the United Kingdom, where resident non-compliance and aggression is usually not taken seriously by the nurses. This is surely because racial insults strike a politically rebellious chord in the Black nurses. They have a particular salience for Black nurses in a South Africa, recently emerging from a period of institutionalized racism.

Interestingly, the South African nurses do not use skin color and ethnic background to insult the residents. Rather, they refer to their supposed or known right wing political affiliations, as in Table 17.6. (The AWB is an extreme racist political gang, and Terreblanche is a well-known racist bigot.)

In Table 17.6, the nurses' insults are not directed at the resident directly. The nurses are commenting about the resident within the resident's hearing. This strategy achieves the effect of an insult without being directly confrontational. While this may save the face of the nurse, it is arguably doubly face-threatening for the resident since it implies that her presence is insignificant accelerating a process of de-individuation of the resident (Makoni *et al.* 2000). In **accommodation theory** terms, we see this as

Table 17.4: Affectionate and playful discourse in the United Kingdom data

The resident is being given a bath	
Resident:	please no (.) no please (.) no
Nurse:	((colour)) look at the colour of your hands
Resident:	no no (.) oh you're cruel (.) you girls are cruel ((4 or 5 syllables)) ((You're cruel things)) (.) You're cruel (2.0) (moans)
Nurse:	let me cut your nails
Resident:	you're cruel
Nurse:	we're only washing your hair
Resident:	you're cruel you're cruel

Table 17.5: Face threatening behavior between nurses and residents in the South African data

Resident:	you can't bath me you pikinini nurse
Nurse:	(smiles)
Resident:	you bath in rivers ((inaudible)) where do you come from?
Nurse:	Johannesburg
Resident:	what are you doing here?
(The nurse walks out and after some time another nurse enters)	
Nurse 2:	would you like me to bath you?
Resident:	any time any time
Nurse 2:	how would you like your water—warm, hot?
Resident:	uhm uhm
Nurse 2:	just feel the water

the nurses promoting their own sense of group belonging and constructing the resident as a member of an oppositional out-group. Thus, it is contra-accommodative (Coupland *et al.* 1991).

It is interesting to note, too, that while the nurses clearly hold this resident in contempt, labeling her as a racist and fat, they address her in terms of endearment. Clearly, then, the endearments are meaningless in the sense of reflecting any true feelings of affection. This underlines our claim that the nurturing and playful modes of discourse are merely a form of "posturing," a veneer, which makes the practice of intimate care giving tasks acceptable.

Table 17.6: Non-face threatening insults which are non-confrontational in the South Africa data

Nurse 1:	(addressing a resident who is wandering off) where are you going to?
Nurse 2:	she doesn't like blacks this one
Nurse 1:	yes yes
Nurse 2:	Terreblanche
Nurse 1:	leave her (pointing to resident) AWB
Nurse 2:	sit down my darling, sit down, and sit down
Resident:	bugger off
Nurse 1:	do you want a cup of tea?
Nurse 1:	why are you shouting?
Resident:	I'm trying to be funny
Nurse 2:	(referring to resident) do you hear the noise she makes, this fat one she is getting fat every day

Playful discourse

Indication of an intimate relationship is through the use of playful modes of discourse. The South African data show considerable use of flirting tactics between female nurses and male residents, a sub-category of playfulness. In Table 17.7, the fact that Nurse 1, an auxiliary nurse, enters the lounge and kisses "Mr. G" on the forehead is indicative of how she usually relates to this resident. Nurse 2, whose salary is supplemented by the family of the resident to look after him, suggests that this behavior is inappropriate when the resident's wife is about to visit. The response of Nurse 1, however, is perhaps a tactless reminder of the potential long-term association between herself and the resident: "she comes and goes (.) We stay here forever." In the final turn in Table 17.7, Nurse 1 "speaks for" the resident (Schiffrin 1994), claiming he wants a cigarette without consulting him. The action of "speaking for" another can be reflective of solidarity in the relationship in that it shows that the speaker is familiar with the likely thoughts and feelings of the other. However, speaking for another also deprives the one who is spoken for of his or her turn at talk and, as such, is a threat to negative face (Schiffrin 1994). In this sense, flirtatious behavior and "speaking for another" have in common that they both assume a level of intimacy. Whether or not such intimacy exists or is desired is crucial in determining whether such behavior is welcomed by the recipient. The nurse's last comment, "she is going to buy cigarettes when you are better," although uttered in a light-hearted manner, has a bitter edge to it when the resident will not improve. While this interaction gives the appearance of a light-hearted and affectionate relationship between the nurses and residents, it is akin to sexual harassment in that this level of familiarity and sexual innuendo may not be welcomed by the resident when there is no real intimacy between the nurse and resident (see Grainger 1993) and the

Table 17.7: Playful discourse in South Africa data

Nurse 1 is entering a lounge in which there are other residents and nurses.	
Nurse 1:	(jocular tone) good morning ladies I love you all (.) hello (.) I still love you (kisses one of the residents, Mr. G., on the forehead)
Nurse 2:	I wonder what the wife is going to say?
Nurse 1:	(still joking) she comes and goes (.) we stay here forever (Laughter)
Nurse 2:	OK
Nurse 1:	he is looking for a cigarette (.) shame (.) your wife hasn't brought you a cigarette (.) she is going to buy cigarettes when you are better

resident is not in a position to reciprocate the behavior. The joking and laughter is at the expense of the resident, not in collaboration with him.

In Table 17.8, the nurse is a state enrolled nurse. The resident is an Afrikaans speaking man in his seventies. The Afrikaans speaking resident was recently admitted to the nursing home. This resident explicitly refers to the sexual nature of the nurse's behavior towards him and at the same time rejects the implied relationship. While the United Kingdom data do not exhibit instances of flirting, there are playful encounters involving sexual innuendo, as in Table 17.9 with a young auxiliary nurse.

Humor in Table 17.9 suggests that there is a friendly relationship between the participants since in some institutional situations humor promotes solidarity between **interlocutors** (see Ragan 1990). However, in this case, unlike in Ragan's data, the joviality is not based on the common experiences of the caregiver and care-recipient. Rather, it is based on an assumption of asexuality and debility in the resident. After all, the humor in the nurse's comments about "sexy" knickers and "going out on the town" arises largely from the supposition that the resident is, in reality, unlikely to possess or make use of sexually alluring underwear, and is unable to sample the city's night life. "Near the bone" humor such as this may be permissible in truly intimate relationships (as a reflection of that intimacy) but despite the resident's apparent acceptance of the joke in this case, it is unlikely to contribute to the forging of a close personal relationship. In fact what we would like to argue here is that in these encounters, because of the physical intimacy of the caring task and the need to carry it out regardless of residents' wishes, the nurses are assuming a level of intimacy in discourse that would be more appropriate in domestic caring relationships. To assume familiarity where it does not exist and where attempts to create it are not reciprocated, however, is likely to lead to frustrating communicative encounters, for both the residents and nurses.

Table 17.8: Playful discourse with sexual overtones in the South Africa data

The nurse has just finished kissing a resident, 'Mr. S'. He responds in Afrikaans:	
Resident:	het jy nie n'man sie? (don't you have a man?)

Table 17.9: Playful discourse with sexual overtones in the United Kingdom data

Nurse (female):	shall we dress you (.) mm? You like that idea do you? (10.0) (She holds up a pair of the resident's knickers) rather sexy these aren't they?
Resident (female):	(laughs)
Nurse:	do you see the ones Beatrice had the long black ones?
Resident:	Nurse Sally put them on
Nurse:	did she? (.) Oh!
Resident:	(laughs)
Nurse:	going out on the town tonight are you Shee (short for Sheila)?
Resident:	well her her (.) hers inclined to be frivolous
Nurse:	(laughs) frivolous is she?
Resident:	mm (.) yes (.) mm

Discussion and conclusions

We conclude from examining data from these two contexts that the discourse of caring is similar in important respects. In both cases, the discourse reflects the two elements of "caring" within instructional and endearing modes. Because this is public and institutional caring there is also an element of service provision. These modes place the caregivers simultaneously in the roles of manager (controller), service-provider, and nurturer. However, it is the controlling dimension which takes precedence, and even when endearing and playful modes of discourse are in use these merely serve to secure the controlling position of the nurses, while at the same time satisfying the professional requirement of apparent benevolence and concern. The aggressive interactions identified in these data suggest that the occurrence of verbal markers of solidarity (playfulness, endearments, speaking for another) do not necessarily reflect any personal familiarity between the nurses and the residents. The similarities in types of interactions across the two settings suggest the importance of the role of the (total) institutional environment. In both contexts, the routine is invariant and is paramount as far as the caring staff is concerned—it (not the patients) is the most important consideration in the working day. This puts pressure on the nurses both physically and interactionally: They have to find ways to balance the twin requirements of efficiency (involving depersonalization of the residents) and showing concern. This is achieved in large part through discourse. Thus, many of the strategies we have discussed above can be seen as coping strategies. Similarly the care recipients are coping with the depersonalizing effects of the institution and they do this sometimes through aggression, sometimes through passivity.

The differences between the two settings become most apparent in situations where the residents are resistant to the nurses' exertion of control. In each context both nurses and residents are closer to the bottom of the institutional hierarchy. In the South African situation, however, one might argue that it is not clear who is positioned at the absolute bottom and interaction becomes a contest to determine who is *not* at the bottom (Makoni 1997). Because of their race and skin color it is possible that the Black nurses have more of a struggle to maintain their relative authority and this leads them to produce the face-threatening utterances we see in the data. Another factor may be that they have, also, a cultural history of reacting to oppression and conflict in an overt and aggressive manner. Similarly, the White residents may be less willing to accept a lowly position relative to the nurses because of their perceived racial superiority, and, hence, we find the racial slurs in the data. In the United Kingdom data, a "power struggle" is present but is not as sharply defined. Here, there is arguably more acceptance of the nurses' controlling position, therefore, there are not as many instances of aggression on either side. In any case, these verbal struggles could not, of course, take place along racial lines as they do in South Africa. However, it should be noted that Berdes and Eckert (2001) documented evidence of discrimination and mistreatment across racial lines in caregiving relationships in institutional settings in the United States. These differences demonstrate that the institutional environment is certainly not the only factor influencing the caring discourse: The broader social and cultural contact is also reflected in these encounters.

References

Berdes, C. and Eckert, J.M. (2001) Race relations and caregiving relationships, *Research on Aging,* 23(1): 109–126.

Brown, P. and Levinson, S. (1987) *Politeness: Some Universals in Language Use*, Cambridge, UK: Cambridge University Press.

Coupland, J., Nussbaum, J. and Coupland, N. (1991) The reproduction of aging and ageism in intergenerational talk, in N. Coupland, H. Giles, and J. Wiemann (eds.), *"Miscommunication" and Problematic Talk*, London: Sage, pp. 85–102.

Grainger, K. (1993) "That's a lovely bath dear": Reality construction in the discourse of elderly care, *Journal of Aging Studies,* 7(3): 247–262.

Makoni, S. (1997) Gerontolinguistics in South Africa, *International Journal of Applied Linguistics*, 7(1): 57–66.

——, Ridge, E. and Ridge, S. (2000) Through different lenses: An analysis of the writing history of a dementia person over fifty years, *Southern African Journal of Applied Language Studies*, 19: 35–50.

Nolan, M. and Grant, G. (1993) Rust out and therapeutic reciprocity: Concepts to advance the nursing care of older people, *Journal of Advanced Nursing*, 18(8): 1305–1314.

Ragan, S. (1990) Verbal play and multiple goals in the gynaecological exam interaction, in K. Tracy and N. Coupland (eds.), *Multiple Goals in Discourse*, Clevedon, UK: Multilingual Matters, pp. 67–84.

Schiffrin, D. (1994) *Approaches to Discourse*, Oxford, UK: Blackwell Publishing.

van Dongen, E. (1999) Space and time in the lives of people with longstanding illness: An ethnographic account, *Anthropology and Medicine*, 4(1): 89–103.

Williams, A. and Nussbaum, J. (2001) *Intergenerational Communication Across the Life Span*, Mahwah, NJ: Lawrence Erlbaum Associates.

Chapter 18

Penelope Eckert

ADOLESCENT LANGUAGE

The power of age

WE TEND TO notice styles that are unlike our own – we come to see some ways of talking, acting, and looking as "normal," unremarkable, and others as "different." The world is full of people who think they don't have an **accent** – that everyone else, or certainly every other region, has an accent, but that their own way of speaking is normal or neutral. But the fact is that everyone has an accent – after all, we all have to pronounce the phonemes of our language some way or another. Some people, however, are in a position to define their own way of pronouncing those phonemes as "normal." Indeed, part of what constitutes power in society is the ability to define normality – to get others to view one's own style as unremarkable, as not a style at all. This domination of others by making them complicit in their oppression (rather than by imposing brute force) has been called **hegemony** (Gramsci 1971). In any community, most middle-aged adults speak somewhat differently from most adolescents. And these differences are not viewed neutrally, but are evaluated in favor of the adults. But what is the real nature of these differences and what is their origin?

Language is not a static resource. We mold it to suit our purposes – to emphasize, to elaborate, even to bring new things into being. Speakers – communities of speakers – in the course of mutual engagement in shared enterprise, create innovations in the areas they are engaged in. They develop new ways of doing things, and new ways of talking about what they are doing – ways that suit their purposes as a group. And the fate of these innovations will depend on the status of the innovators. If the innovators are viewed as doing important things, their innovations will be judged useful; if they are viewed as doing trivial or harmful or dirty things, their innovations will be judged trivial, or harmful, or dirty. Depending on the community and the endeavor, **lexical** innovations, for example, might be called "technical terminology," "jargon," or "slang." So what are adolescents and adults doing with language that is different?

Engaged in a fierce negotiation of the social landscape, social values, differences, tolerances, and meanings, adolescents are continually making new distinctions and evaluations of behavior. In the course of this endeavor they come up with new terms for evaluation and social types (*dweeb, homie*) as well as for emphasis (*totally*, or *hella*, as in *She's hella cool*). Middle-class adults, on the other hand, engaged in the negotiation of other space, come up with words like *software, Hispanic, throughput*. The main difference between these new coinages is in the situations in which they emerge – the landscape that the innovators are negotiating, and the social work that the innovations accomplish. The linguistic and social processes are the same. Lexical innovations mark new distinctions. When a community takes up a new word, it recognizes, ratifies and expands the importance of that new distinction. If the innovating community has sufficient power and influence, that innovation will spread well beyond it. Kids who use words such as *dweeb, homie*, and *hella* may well at some point come to refer to themselves or others as *Hispanic* – or at least check a box on a form that says *Hispanic*. The chances that the people who coined the term *Hispanic* will use the term *dweeb, homie*, or *hella* are fairly small.

I have seen any number of media pieces on adolescents' use of *like*, as in *I'm like, just standing there, you know, and she like comes up to me and like pushes me like that, you know?* and on **rising intonation** (which is heard as question intonation) in clearly affirmative sentences such as *my name is Penny Eckert(?)*. These innovations are touted as evidence of adolescent inarticulateness, sloppiness, vagueness, unwillingness to commit – you name it. By contrast, all kinds of innovations come from adult quarters and barely attract public attention. Particularly trendy these days is the spate of **nouns** used as **verbs** (technically called denominalized verbs), as in *that should impact the market, please access the mail file*, and *let's team*, and *I recently accessed my hotel's messaging service*. These snappy turns of phrase seem to suggest that we are dealing with people of action. I am willing to bet that if it were adolescents introducing these forms, we would see a considerable negative public reaction, with claims that adolescents were unwilling to go to the trouble of using the longer forms *have an impact on, gain access to, work as a team*. While I have seen many articles on the evils of *like*, I have yet to see one on the use of *okay* with a rising intonation, as in *We need to prepare a presentation, okay(?), and that will make it absolutely clear, okay(?), that we're the only people who can do this kind of work. Okay(?)*. Like *like* and rising intonation, *okay* is not just a random insertion; it serves to help organize the discourse – to highlight certain things, to guide the listener's interpretation of the finer points of the speaker's intent. But *okay* isn't used by teenagers; it's used by business people, as a way of asserting their authority, and it is hardly noticed.

Consider a couple of crutches for the inarticulate that have become popular among adults in recent years: *What we have here is a situation where the market is extremely unpredictable* and *What it is, is that the market is extremely unpredictable*. One might say that both of these devices allow the speaker to hold the **floor** without saying *uh*, while figuring out what to say or how to say it. (One might also say that both of these devices also **reify** what follows, elevating it in importance by setting it apart as a thing, a situation, something of note sitting on its little verbal pedestal.) One could dwell on the fact that these devices point to the inarticulateness of the average middle-aged person. Or one might say that they are evidence of speakers' fluency since the speaker does indeed maintain the floor without a pause. Which evaluation one chooses depends entirely on one's attitude toward the speakers.

Just a few years ago, people were laughing about kids using *go* (as in *she goes* or *I go*) as a quotative. What is interesting about *go* is that an entire interaction can be reported in which action and speech are treated equivalently because, of course, *he goes* doesn't just mean 'he says.' You can say, *he goes* and shrug or make a face. This makes for a very lively narration. More recently, attention has been drawn to the new quotative use of *be like* and *be all*, as in *she's like, "go away"; he's like* (shake head); *I'm all – "what?!"; She's all "yeah right."* One difference between *go* and *be like* or *be all* is the nuance in reporting. *He goes* reports one of a sequence of actions. *He's like* invites the listener to interpret the slant on the events being reported.

What *like*, rising intonation, *I'm like, I'm all*, and *she goes* have in common is their ability to dramatize a narration – and narration is a genre central to adolescent discourse. Narration is a difficult skill to learn, and the ability to tell competent narratives and have an audience actually attend to these narratives is an important sign of growing up and of social entitlement. Preadolescents engage intensely in narration, and as they move towards an adolescent peer controlled social order, narration becomes an important resource for the construction of this order. In a population that is continually negotiating identity and the social order, narrative is used to go over events in the negotiation of norms, values, and beliefs. Narrative is a means of holding people accountable and of putting actions on the table for consideration and evaluation. It is central to working out the peer social order.

Linguists are frequently confronted with popular beliefs about language that count certain speakers as "irresponsible," certain speech varieties as "ungrammatical," and certain speech practices as "illogical." These judgments are systematically passed on language spoken by the poor, by minorities, by women, and by children. From a linguist's point of view, none of these judgments have value. Rather, such beliefs are commonly based on selective observation and on biased judgment of what those observations mean. Adolescents are just going about their business, trying to make the best of a marginalized position in society – and using language to do so. While adults may be concerned about the linguistic products, they should be more concerned with the marginalization that provides the conditions for adolescent linguistic production.

Linguistic movers and shakers

So far I have been defending adolescents against common attacks on the way they speak. But in doing this I run the risk of reifying the notion of "adolescent language." Before I do so any further, I would like to emphasize that while one might be able to point to certain linguistic features that are currently being used primarily by adolescents (such as certain expressions like *hella* and the quotative *be all*), these are relatively fleeting and have already spread well beyond the age group in which they appear to have originated. At the same time, not all adolescents use them. Like middle-aged people, adolescents do not all speak alike.

With the focus on adolescence as a unified life stage comes an assumption that adolescents constitute a homogeneous category. Social scientists talk of "teen culture" or "youth culture," and people of all sorts generalize about the beliefs and behavior of "teenagers." But adolescents are as diverse as any other age group. First of all, they do not constitute a unified place in the path to adult status. While they all have in common their subjection to the national discourse of adolescence, they vary hugely in the extent to which they fit into this discourse and the ways in which they deal with this subjection. For example, the mythologized "typical" adolescent is fancy free, with no responsibilities such as contributing financially to their families or caring for children or elders. But, in fact, this model of adolescence does not apply to many people in the adolescent age group, for many of them have considerable family responsibilities. Nonetheless, it is the standard against which all are compared – and it marginalizes those who have such responsibilities. And while adolescents are all subject to the societal norm that they stay in school until they graduate, they differ in their ability and willingness to stay in school, and those who do stay in school differ widely in their orientation to the institution. Differences in orientation to adolescence and to the school institution that defines adolescence are fundamental to adolescent life, and language is a prime resource for signaling and maintaining these differences.

One of the important properties of language is its potential to convey social meaning somewhat independently of the sentences that are being uttered. As we use language to convey content, our choice of linguistic resources simultaneously signals who we are, what we're like, where we're from, what we qualify for, who we hang out with. The resources among which we choose may be words, pronunciations, grammatical constructions, **prosody**, idioms, etc. Different speakers combine such resources in distinctive ways, and if these combinations come to be associated with particular people or groups of people, one could say that they constitute styles. Style in language, as in dress, home decoration, and demeanor, is one of our most important assets. It represents who we are and how we align ourselves with respect to other styles. Our style can gain us entrée, elicit trust, attract people and resources. And just as easily, it can exclude us and frighten or alienate others.

When we speak, we draw on a multitude of resources – not just any resources, but those that are available through exposure to people and places. We all have a way of speaking that is centered in a **dialect**, depending on where we're from and who (or whom!) we hung out with when we were young. But we also may modify that dialect – for instance if we move away or if we dis-identify with the locality. In addition to our native dialect, we may draw on pronunciations associated with other regions, countries, ethnic groups, or specific localities, and sometimes even small groups develop their own special pronunciations. These linguistic resources are structured, and not random.

The term *vernacular* has many uses and is somewhat controversial in sociolinguistics. In this chapter it refers to language that is the most closely associated with locally based communities – and the product of life in those communities. It exists in opposition to the *standard* – the language variety embraced by and required for use in globalizing institutions (financial, business, governmental, and educational institutions). The success and credibility of these institutions depends, to some extent, on their ability to appear to transcend the local – to serve the interests of the more general population. As a consequence, the language they endorse is devoid of obvious local or ethnic features. Standard language is a powerful tool of membership, or at least of commitment to gaining membership, in the halls and homes of global power. Vernaculars, by contrast, emphasize local and regional difference and must be learned in the neighborhood, in locally based families and **social network**s; consequently, they are tied up with local flavor and membership. Those whose loyalties and aspirations are tied to this local milieu are most likely to embrace the vernacular, as part of a construction and an expression of local identity and solidarity. And those who orient more towards globalizing institutions are more likely to embrace the standard. The high school is the globalizing institution that dominates the life of most adolescents, and adolescents' adoption of more standard or more vernacular speech is related, among other things, to their orientation to that institution.

African American Vernacular English (AAVE) is a very important vernacular resource for many adolescents in the USA. For example, white kids in Northern California use AAVE features as a way of laying claim to coolness (Bucholtz 1999). Immigrant teenagers in urban areas often adopt AAVE as their dialect of English, not simply as a matter of exposure but also often as an act of identity. A study of the development of English among a group of adolescents in Northern California shows that as they moved into American adolescence, those who became school-oriented developed standard English, while the speech of those who moved into the street culture showed more AAVE features (Kuwahara 1998). The relation between the use of AAVE features and engagement in local street culture is reflected among native speakers of AAVE as well. Preadolescent African American boys in a friendship network in a New York housing project show a relation between the use of features of AAVE and the speaker's place in the peer network (Labov 1972). While members of the group as a whole prided themselves on their engagement in street life, some members were more engaged in school than others. The boys more engaged in school were somewhat peripheral in the group, and their peripheral status showed up in their language use. In particular, their speech showed far fewer occurrences of zero copula, as in *he bad* (an AAVE feature) and of more general non-standard features such as non-agreement between subject and verb (*he don't*) than did the speech of their peers more centrally engaged in the peer group.

White regional vernaculars play a similar role. My work in predominantly white high schools in the Detroit suburban area showed a repeated opposition between two class-based categories: the "jocks" and the "burnouts" (Eckert 1989). The jocks (who in an earlier era in the same school were called *soshes*, short for socialites) constitute a middle-class, school-oriented culture. Planning to continue to college after graduation, they base their social lives in the school and in its extracurricular sphere, intertwining their public institutional roles with their identities and their social networks. On the other hand, the burnouts (who in an earlier era were called *greasers*) are mostly bound for the local work force and reject the school as their social base. Preferring to function on their own terms in the urban area, they find the school's practices and activities infantilizing. Differences of this sort cannot be neutral in an environment where the jocks' way of life is the institutional norm, and where their activities give them institutional status and freedoms denied to others. The opposition between the jocks and the burnouts, therefore, can be an extremely bitter one, and is manifested not only in interpersonal and intergroup conflict, but in stylistic manifestations of every sort.

The linguistic styles of the jocks and burnouts reflect their orientations to the globalizing institution of the school, on the one hand, and to the local urban area on the other.

The linguistic variable that most clearly reflects the different stances of jocks and burnouts toward the school and everything it represents is negation. Negation is a powerful sociolinguistic variable throughout the English-speaking world. **Negative concord**, commonly referred to as double negation or multiple negation (as in *I didn't do nothing*), is strongly non-standard, and generally evaluated as reflecting lack of education. But this grammatical strategy is as much a device for expressing attitude toward educational institutions and the values associated with them, as a reflection of one's actual academic background. While there are speakers whose native dialect requires negative concord, and who have not mastered the simple negatives of standard English, far more speakers know both forms and alternate between them. Given their attitude toward school, it is not surprising that the burnouts use more negative concord than the jocks. Overall, the burnouts in my study use negative concord 42 percent of the time, while the jocks use it 13 percent of the time. This differential use is not a matter of grammatical knowledge: there are no burnouts who make exclusive use of negative concord.

But the difference between jocks and burnouts with respect to negation does not apply across the board. As shown in Table 18.1, jock girls are the most standard users of negation, while jock boys use negative concord one-fifth of the time. Both burnout girls and burnout boys, on the other hand, use negative concord almost half the time. This difference points to the important fact that gender is inseparable from other aspects of social identity. If we assume that the use of linguistic features is a way of constructing differences between groups, then the difference between jocks and burnouts is far greater among the girls than among the boys. And, indeed, the consequences for a jock girl of looking, acting, or talking like a burnout are far greater than for a jock boy doing the same thing. Jock girls are expected to maintain a squeaky-clean image, while burnout girls pride themselves in their disregard for institutional authority and their claim on adult prerogatives (such as controlled substances, sexual activity, and mobility). Because norms of masculinity dictate autonomy, jock boys must maintain a clean-cut image without appearing to be under adult or institutional domination. As a result, the difference between jock and burnout boys, in language as in dress and general behavior, is never as great as that between jock and burnout girls.

Negative concord has similar social significance around the USA. By contrast, features of pronunciation are more regionally specific. In the Detroit area, several **vowels** have distinctive local and regional pronunciations, and particularly characterize the dialect of white speakers. Of these, three are clearly new pronunciations, showing up only in the speech of the younger generation. They are:

> raising of the **nucleus** in /ay/, so that, for example, *buy* and *rice* sound like *boy* and *Royce*;
> backing of /ɛ/ so that, for example, *flesh* and *dell* sound like *flush* and *dull*;
> backing of /ʌ/ so that, for example, *but* and *fun* sound like *bought* and *fawn*.

The innovative variants of /ay/, /ɛ/, and /ʌ/ occur more in the speech not only of young Whites, but particularly those living closer to urban Detroit. This reflects the

Table 18.1: Percentage use of negative concord by jock and burnout girls and boys

Jock girls	Jock boys	Burnout girls	Burnout boys
2	19	40	45

fact that these are actually sound changes in progress, which tend to spread outward from urban centers. While the use of negative concord is associated with education and attitudes towards normative institutions, vowels such as these have a different social significance. As sound changes traveling outward from the city, they have the potential to carry urban significance – to be associated with urban life, and the street smarts and relative autonomy of urban kids. In keeping with this, within schools throughout the suburban area, it is the burnouts who lead their classmates in the use of these innovations. The pattern shown in Table 18.2, based on speakers in one high school, is repeated in schools across the urban area.

The category differences in Table 18.2 are statistically significant, but it is important to note that they are far less pronounced than the difference in use of negative concord shown in Table 18.1. This suggests that the differences in pronunciation are not quite as socially salient as the prominent and well-ensconced negative pattern.

The equivalent of jocks and the burnouts are **hegemonic** categories in white-dominated schools across the country. While the jocks and the burnouts (or their equivalents) are working to distinguish themselves from each other, other categories arise – among other things, in opposition to the hegemony of the jock-burnout split. In a Northern California school, a group of girls who embraced a *geek* identity distanced themselves from their peers' concerns with coolness and from what they viewed as demeaning norms of femininity (Bucholtz 1996). They prided themselves on their intelligence and freedom from peer-imposed constraints, and they based their common practice in intellectual pursuits. They did well in school but considered their intellectual achievement to be independent of the school, priding themselves in catching their teachers' errors. Their linguistic style was an important resource for the construction of their more general joint intellectual persona, and two aspects of their linguistic style are particularly salient. Living in Northern California, their peers – particularly their "cool" peers – make high stylistic use of current California sound changes – the **fronting** of **back vowels** /u/ as in *dude* (pronounced [dɪud] or [dyd], and /o/ as in *no* (pronounced [nɛw]). These girls use these changes, which seem to convey "cool California," far less than their peers, preferring to move away from that cool image through the use of more conservative pronunciations of both vowels. Another linguistic feature they exploit is the release of /t/ between vowels and at the ends of words. Generally in American English, /t/ is pronounced the same as /d/ when it occurs between two vowels as in *butter* or *at a*. At the ends of words before a pause, as in *you nut* or *what's that?*, the /t/ is generally not released at all. In British English, on the other hand, /t/ in both of these environments is generally released or **aspirated**: [bʌtʰ], [nʌtʰ]. This aspirated pronunciation of /t/ serves as an important stylistic resource for the geek girls' style. By aspirating many of their occurrences of /t/, they mark themselves as "articulate," in keeping with the American stereotype of the British and their speech. The geeks are quite consciously using conservative and prestige

Table 18.2: Percentage use of innovative vowel variants by jock and burnout girls and boys

Variable	Jock girls	Jock boys	Burnout girls	Burnout boys
ay	1	1	4	2
ɛ	23	27	31	33
ʌ	40	40	51	49

features of English to construct a distinctive style – not so much to claim social status within the adolescent cohort as to disassociate themselves from the adolescent status system altogether, and what they clearly see as trivial adolescent concerns.

In immigrant groups, adolescents play an important role in negotiating their community's transition to life in the new community. Immigrant children divide their lives between the home culture and the Anglo-American school culture. In both cases, they are primarily under the control of adults. But as they move toward adolescence and begin to develop a peer-based culture, the negotiation of home and school cultures is appropriated into the social norms and arrangements of the age group. Issues such as immigrant status, and ethnic and national orientation, become issues of identity and status among adolescents. A study of adolescent Latinas in California's Silicon Valley noted ways in which styles of English, on the one hand, and choices between English and Spanish, on the other, served as resources for constructing and disputing Latina identities (Mendoza-Denton 1996a). Immigration history and class, among other things, are important terms of difference in a community that is seen as monolithic from the outside. Of particular importance was the differentiation between opposed gangs, the Norteños and the Sureños. These gangs are not based on territory as is common with gangs, but on **ideologies** with respect to orientations towards Mexico and the USA. The Norteños emphasize their American, *Chicano*, identities, while the Sureños consider themselves *Mexicano*, emphasizing their ties to Mexico. Extensive **ethnographic** work with girls affiliating with either of these gangs showed that the two were set apart by subtle and not-so-subtle differences in the use of stylistic resources (Mendoza-Denton 1996a). Most striking – and not surprising – is the issue of language choice: the Sureñas making greater use of Spanish in their peer interactions than the Norteñas.

In addition, there were interesting linguistic dynamics in the development of styles of English. While linguists tend to focus on the use of the linguistic system strictly defined, Mendoza-Denton (1996b) draws explicit connections between linguistic and bodily style. She shows how a Chicana gang style is constructed through the combination of speech patterns and material resources such as makeup and dress. But she also connects speech to the body through an examination of voice quality, focusing on the girls' strategic use of "creaky" voice. This style is constructed in distinct opposition to the hegemonic Anglo culture and to the Anglo styles that dominate the high school, as well as to the styles of more assimilated Latinas.

References

Bucholtz, Mary (1996) "Geek the Girl: Language, Femininity, and Female Nerds," in N. Warner, J. Ahlers, L. Bilmes, M. Oliver, S. Wertheim and M. Chen (eds.), *Gender and Belief Systems*, Berkeley, CA: Berkeley Women and Language Group, pp. 119–131.

—— (1999) "You Da Man: Narrating the Racial Other in the Production of White Masculinity," *Journal of Sociolinguistics* 3(4): 443–460.

Eckert, Penelope.(1989) *Jocks and Burnouts: Social Categories and Identity in the High School*, New York: Teachers College Press, Columbia University.

Gramsci, A. (1971) *Selections from the Prison Notebooks*, London: Lawrence and Wishart.

Kuwahara, Yuri L. (1998) "Interactions of Identity: Inner-city Immigrant and Refugee Youths, Language Use, and Schooling," unpublished PhD dissertation, Stanford University, CA.

Labov, William (1972) "The Linguistic Consequences of Being a Lame," in William Labov, *Language in the Inner City*, Philadelphia, PA: University of Pennsylvania Press, pp. 255–292.

Mendoza-Denton, Norma (1996a) "Language Attitudes and Gang Affiliation among California Latina Girls," in N. Warner, J. Ahlers, L. Bilmes, M. Oliver, S. Wertheim and M. Chen (eds.), *Gender and Belief Systems*, Berkeley. CA: Berkeley Women and Language Group, pp. 478–486.

—— (1996b) "Muy Macha: Gender and Ideology in Gang Girls' Discourse about Makeup," *Ethnos* 61(1–2): 47–63.

PART EIGHT

Language and social class

Eva Eppler

INTRODUCTION

THE READINGS RELATING to the topic of language and social class are a good mix: they were written for different audiences/purposes, are accordingly pitched at different levels of difficulty, and address three different areas where language and social differentiation interact. The first one explores class-related linguistic socialization and its consequences for education. The second discusses the phasing out of regional dialects and how this process is related to changing social structures. The third one deals with the relationship between language use and reasoning, (perceived) intelligence and academic achievement.

Let's approach the texts in order of difficulty and start with the most accessible one. Michael Gos' short paper is an educational resource for teachers. Gos' paper is placed in an US context, but based on the British sociologist and practitioner's Basil Bernstein's distinction between working class students' **'restricted'** and middle class students' **'elaborated' codes**. The text focuses on two factors that greatly diminish the chances for success in college of working class students: communication protocols, and position within a family or a community organization. Communication protocols refer to the conventions of speech in the local communities of the two classes. Gos discusses what middle- and high-school teachers can do to better prepare working class students for the tasks ahead in the areas of memorization, critical thinking and speech patterns.

The concepts the paper is based on, 'restricted' and 'elaborative' codes, their characteristics and their association with social class are quite controversial. The controversy is not about the fact that social background shapes our linguistic experiences and results in social differences in communicative styles, but about the evaluative labelling of the two codes, the rigid distinctions implied, and the generalizations made about working and middle class students' language use.

The second text 'Mobility, meritocracy and dialect levelling: the fading (and phasing) out of Received Pronunciation' by Paul Kerswill is based on an oral conference presentation to an audience of practitioners and academics in Estonia interested in British issues in the New Millennium. It is an accessible and focused summary of what has been happening to traditional rural as well as modern mainstream **dialects** in the UK in the lead up to the twenty-first century, and how this is related to social developments.

In this reading Kerswill, a British sociolinguist, illustrates how speakers of traditional rural dialects have moved towards a type of English that is more like the urban speech of the local town or city in its pronunciation, lexicon and grammar. These modern or mainstream dialects are then subject to further **levelling**, that is, reduction in the linguistic differences between them, as they become more and more like standard English. Kerswill argues that these changes in the linguistic makeup of the UK were triggered by social changes: disintegrating traditional rural **social networks**, an expansion of the range of individual personal ties, and a change in social roles within the family, with both men and women going out to work and meeting people from a wider range of geographical and social backgrounds.

Kerswill first surveys the linguistic 'survivors' of **dialect levelling**. The second section of this reading looks in more detail at the socio-economic factors that caused regional **accents** and dialects to converge during the twentieth century. In the third section Kerswill first investigates Standard English as a class dialect, and then explores '**Estuary English**'. Estuary English is a 'new intermediate' variety of British English which is characterized by a mixture of non-regional and local south-eastern pronunciation. Kerswill uses Estuary English to illustrate the resistance that dialects (and their speakers!) show against becoming fully standardized and homogenized. In the last section he asks whether dialect levelling and standardization are signs of a move towards a classless society. He has to conclude on a slightly more pessimistic note, arguing that Estuary English is more likely to be 'a product of [a] trend towards greater upward mobility'.

The third text is an abridged version of a seminal academic publication entitled 'The logic of non-standard English' by William Labov (1969). In 'Academic Ignorance and Black Intelligence' Labov pioneered for **African American Vernacular English (AAVE)** what many other linguists have done (and are still doing) for other varieties: he convincingly argues that AAVE is a fully formed language with all the capacity necessary for logical thought. This was groundbreaking at a time when black children were thought to be verbally 'deprived': they were thought to receive little verbal stimulation, to hear very little well-formed language, and as a result were unable to speak complete sentences, form concepts, or convey logical thoughts.

Based on research carried out in Harlem between 1965 and 1968, Labov and colleagues set out to prove this '**deficit theory**' wrong. They did so by showing that the language (AAVE), family style and ways of living of lower-class inner-city children are significantly different from the standard American English and culture prevalent in the classroom. In the central section of this text Labov contrasts two speakers, one working-, one middle-class, dealing with roughly the same topic: matters of belief. He shows that the AAVE speaker is more than capable of dealing with abstract or hypothetical questions and that his opinions come through without qualification or reservation. Labov concludes that the middle-class speakers' arguments are rather vague and verbose; the AAVE speaker, on the other hand, can sum up a complex argument in a few words.

Like Gos, Labov and colleagues therefore conclude that it is not lack of intelligence or verbal or cultural deprivation that cause the low educational achievement of working-class students in inner city schools. He blames academics for failing to see that it is the difference between standard English and middle-class interactional styles on the one hand, and lower-class AAVE norms of language use on the other hand that explains many of the problems non-middle-class (and non-white) children face in the educational system. The readings for the social class chapter thus come full circle, despite the fact that there is a quarter of a century between the publication of the first and the last text.

Issues to consider

1. Think about what features might determine class; on the basis of this, assign yourself to either working or middle class. Does your personal experience of communication protocols and social structure coincide with what Gos (1995) describes? If not, or not entirely, outline the differences.
2. Do we know how Gos (1995) arrived at these conclusions? In other words, do we know which methodology he used, i.e. how many students he issued questionnaires to, interviewed etc? If not, what is this paper is based on? Do you think this is a valid research methodology?
3. Are dialect levelling and standardization the same thing? If not, what's the difference? Explain both terms to a family member or friend who is not studying language. This will help you define the two terms. What's the relation between dialect levelling and standardization? Ask the family members or friends who you explained dialect levelling and standardization to if they think that these two processes are signs of a move towards a classless society.
4. Labov and his colleagues collected examples of language produced by black working-class children which are AAVE and bear the hallmarks of 'restricted code' (Bernstein 1971) and 'public language' (Gos 1995). What are they? (See Examples 1 and 2.) Imagine you are a teacher. How would you deal with these verbal productions?
5. What are the main similarities and the big differences between Gos' and Labov's arguments?

Suggestions for further reading

For work on variation by class:

Nichols, P. (1983) 'Linguistic Options and Choices for Black Women in the Rural South', in Thorne, B., Kramerae, C. and Henley, N. (eds.), *Language, Gender, and Society*, Boston, MA: Heinle and Heinle, pp. 54–68.
Eckert, P. (2003) 'Social Variation in America', in Preston, D.R. (ed.), *Needed Research in American Dialects*, Publication of the American Dialect Society 88. Durham, NC: Duke University Press, pp. 99–122.

Foulkes, P. and Docherty, G. (eds.), (1999) *Urban Voices*, London: Arnold.

For texts that look at the way language is changing:

Britain, D. (2005) 'The dying dialects of England?' in Bertacca, A. (ed.), *Historical Linguistic Studies of Spoken English*. Pisa: Edizioni Plus, pp. 35–46, online, available at: http://homepages.tesco.net/~david.britain/13.pdf.
Kirkby, T. (2004) 'Linguists get chuddies in twist over dialects', *The Independent*, 1 April, online, available at: www.independent.co.uk/news/uk/this-britain/linguists-get-chuddies-in-twist-over-dialects-568408.html [accessed 16 May 2010].
Watt, D. (2002) '"I don't speak Geordie, I speak Northern": contact-induced levelling in two Tyneside vowels' *Journal of Sociolinguistics*, 6(1): 44-63.

To explore issues related to language, class and education:

Brice-Heath, S. (1996 [1983]) *Ways with Words: Language, Life, and Work in Communities and Classrooms*, Cambridge: Cambridge University Press.
Lawton, D. (1998) *Social Class, Language and Education*, London: Routledge.
May, S. and Hornberger, N.H. (eds.), (2007) *Encyclopaedia of Language and Education, Vol 1 Language Policy and Political Issues in Education*, second edition, New York: Springer.

For more theoretical work on the issue of class in sociolingusitics:

Rickford, J.R. (1986) 'The Need for New Approaches to Social Class Analysis in Sociolinguistics', *Journal of Communication*, 6(3): 215–221.
— (2001) 'Style and Stylizing from the Perspective of a Non-Autonomous Sociolinguistics', in Eckert, P. and Rickford, J.R. (eds.), *Style and Sociolinguistic Variation*, New York: Cambridge University Press, pp. 220–231.

Suggestions for further viewing

Educating Rita (1983) (for a UK context) Gilbert Lewis.
Erin Brockovich (2000) (for a US context) Steven Soderbergh.
People like us: Social Class in America (for a US context) Louis Alvarez and Andrew Kolker. See www.pbs.org/peoplelikeus/.

References

Bernstein, B.B. (1971). *Class, codes and control Vols. 1–3*, London: Routledge and Kegan Paul.
Labov, W. (1969) 'The logic of nonstandard English', *Georgetown Monographs on Language and Linguistics*, Vol. 22.

Chapter 19

Paul Kerswill

MOBILITY, MERITOCRACY AND DIALECT LEVELLING: THE FADING (AND PHASING) OUT OF RECEIVED PRONUNCIATION

1. Introduction: dialect levelling in Britain, 1900–2000

BRITISH ENGLISH IN the twentieth century has been characterised by **dialect levelling** and standardisation. It is probably useful to see this as composed of two stages, running in parallel. The first stage affects the traditional rural **dialects** of the country, once of course spoken by a majority of the population, but by the beginning of the twentieth century probably spoken by under 50 per cent. These dialects are very different from standard English in their pronunciation and in their grammar. What has happened is that, over one or more generations, families have abandoned these dialects in favour of a type of English that is more like the urban speech of the local town or city. These more urban ways of speaking have been labelled modern dialects or mainstream dialects by Peter Trudgill (1998). What most characterises them is that they are considerably more like standard English in phonology, grammar and vocabulary. The outcome of this first stage is that there are fewer differences between ways of speaking in different parts of the country – an example of dialect levelling. The second stage affects these urbanised varieties of English themselves. As anyone who travels round Britain quickly discovers, there are distinctive ways of speaking in each town and city. Sometimes these differences are quite large, and cause difficulties even for British people when they travel round. These dialects are subject to still further levelling, to such an extent that, in the south-east of England around London, it is now quite difficult to tell where a person comes from. The differences are very subtle, purely phonetic ones.

Let us examine some of these features.

1.1 Traditional dialects

Many of the features that made traditional dialects distinctive have been lost; only some are still found in British speech today. Below are some which can still be heard, though in most places they have replaced by standard English forms:

Grammar

1. Noun plurals: *shoon* 'shoes', *een* 'eyes', *kine* 'cows'
2. Pronouns
    *   in the North and Midlands: *tha* 'you' (singular), *hissen* 'himself', *I washed me* 'I washed myself'
    *   in the Southwest: *her* 'she' (south-west), *I do go shopping on Saturdays* 'I go shopping on Saturdays'
3. Verbs
    *   *gang* 'go' (Scotland), *fa* 'fall' (Scotland)
    *   Forms for 'I am': I is (Northwest), I are (Midlands), I be (Southwest), I am (North and East)

Vocabulary:

*   Scotland *luin* 'boy', *quine* 'girl', *greet* 'cry'
*   Yorkshire: *beck* 'stream', *bairn* 'child'

Phonology

*   Scotland: *nicht* 'night', *dochter* 'daughter', *hame* 'home'
*   North: *spian* 'spoon', *bian* 'bone', *reet* 'right'
*   North-east: *fower* for 'four', *sivven* for 'seven'
*   South-east Midlands: *fut* 'foot', *umman* 'woman'

Sources: Peter Trudgill (1998) *Dialects of England* and Wakelin (1978) *Discovering English Dialects*.

1.2 Modern dialects (1): Which features are the 'survivors' of dialect levelling?

Modern dialects preserve some of the features of traditional dialects. These are some of the 'survivors' which have not yet been levelled out:

Grammar

1. Present tense -*s* in whole verb paradigm, e.g., *I likes, you likes, she likes, we likes, they likes*, in South and Southwest of England

2.   Multiple negation: *We don't want none*
3.   Use of *ain't* for negative auxiliaries *isn't, aren't, hasn't, haven't*
4.   Past tenses of irregular verbs: *I done, I writ, I come, I see*
5.   Use of *never* as past tense negative marker: *I never went there yesterday*
6.   *them* as demonstrative adjective: *Look at them big spiders*
7.   Absence of plural marking on measures of distance and quantity: *two pound, ten mile.*
8.   Absence of adverb marking: *he came really quick*

Phonology

1.   Vowel of FOOT appears in *cup* in the Midlands and North of England
2.   Vowel of TRAP in words like *bath, dance, last, laugh* in the North and Wales, vowel of PALM, FATHER in the South.
3.   Monophthongs in words like GOAT and FACE in the North and Scotland, diphthongs in the South
4.   Post-vocalic *r* pronounced in words like CAR, NURSE, FATHER, NORTH in the Southwest and Scotland. It is absent in the Southeast and North.

1.3 Modern dialects (2): Changes happening right now

The following are recent changes, documented for example in Cheshire *et al.* (1989) and Williams and Kerswill (1999):

Grammar

Use of *was* in the positive, but *weren't* in the neg.:

I was	*I weren't*
you was	*you weren't*
she was	*she weren't*
we was	*we weren't*
they was	*they weren't*

Phonology

CONSONANTS

1.   Use of glottal stop [ʔ] for /t/ at the end and in the middle of words:

   (i)   before a consonant: *let[ʔ] me*
   (ii)   before a vowel: *get[ʔ] over*
   (iii) before a pause: *street[ʔ]*
   (iv)   in the middle of a word between vowels: *lett[ʔ]er*

This feature has been in London and Glasgow for at least 150 years (why it appeared in two cities so far apart is not known). Since then, the sound has appeared in most of the regional accents and dialects spoken in between. It is also encroaching on **RP**, so that in the first environment it is now normal, and is frequently heard in the second. (See John Wells's work on this (1994) and on his website.)

2.   Replacement of the two 'th' sounds by 'f' or 'v', so that *thin* is the same as *fin*, and *brother* rhymes with *lover*. This is a characteristic London feature, this time not traditionally found in Glasgow, which is spreading very rapidly. Outside the London area, the spread of this feature has taken place in the past 20–30 years only. For instance, in Norwich it is found in speakers born after about 1970, likewise for young adults in the Midlands towns of Birmingham and Derby, teenagers in Hull and young children in Newcastle and Glasgow. The order of spread seems to be as follows:

1.   London area
2.   Southeast: e.g. Reading, Milton Keynes
3.   Central England (Midlands, East Anglia, South Yorkshire): e.g. Birmingham, Derby, Norwich and Sheffield
4.   Northern England: Hull
5.   Northeast of England and Lowlands of Scotland: e.g. Newcastle, Glasgow

The feature is not yet reported for Cardiff, Liverpool and Edinburgh, or at least it is only sporadic there. (Source: Foulkes and Docherty 1999 (eds.), *Urban Voices*, various chapters.)

VOWELS

1.   The vowel of MOUTH. This vowel has a range of pronunciations in the South of England, including: [ɛʉ], [ɛɪ], [ɛː], [aːə], [æʊ], [aʊ]. The first two of these are typically rural pronunciations, the fifth a typical London variant, the last similar to Received Pronunciation. The third and fourth can be regarded as fast-speech variants, even though they are also characteristic of London speech.

Table 19.1: Percentage use of variants of /aʊ/ (MOUTH), Reading Working Class, interview style

	[ɛʉ]	[ɛɪ]	[ɛː]	[aːə]	[æʊ]	[aʊ]
Survey of English Dialects informants, 1950–60s (Orton *et al.* 1968)	✓					
Elderly age 70–80 (n=4)	53.5	38.1	3.3	0	4.1	0.7
Girls age 14 (n=8)	0	2.3	0	8.0	0	90.4
Boys age 14 (n=8)	3.8	3.2	0	5.7	0	87.1

Table 19.2: Percentage use of variants of /aʊ/ (MOUTH), Milton Keynes Working Class, interview style

	[ɛʊ̯]	[ɛɪ]	[ɛ:]	[a:ᵊ]	[æʊ]	[aʊ]
Survey of English Dialects informants, 1950–60s (Orton *et al.* 1968)	✓					
Elderly age 70–80 (n=4)	63.2	25.6	9.8	0	1.2	0
Women age 25–40 (n=48)	0	0	11.7	17.2	38.6	31.5
Girls age 14 (n=8)	0	0	0	5.9	4.7	88.8
Boys age 14 (n=8)	0	0	0	12.3	3.8	83.1

Tables 19.1 and 19.2 show that, in two south-eastern towns, Reading and Milton Keynes, there is a rapid shift from [ɛʊ̯] and [ɛɪ] towards a more RP-like [aʊ].

2. The vowels of GOOSE and GOAT are being **fronted**. GOOSE is moving from [ʉ:] to [ʉ:] or [y:], sounding like Estonian or German <ü> or even Norwegian <y>. (See Bauer 1985 and Kerswill 2000.) GOAT is likewise being fronted, so that it can be confused with *gate*. Thus, some people mistake 'coke' for 'cake'. These two changes are found in all southern speech, including RP. They are more advanced among non-RP speakers.

In sum, the outcome has been levelling: a **convergence** of accents and dialects towards each other. In some cases, this leads to southern features being adopted in the whole country. For other features, particularly vowels, this is not so: levelling, instead, is regional in character, usually centred on a big city like Glasgow or Newcastle or Leeds.

2. Economic change in the twentieth century as a cause of dialect levelling

Arguably, dialect levelling can be seen as due to three interrelated trends:

*   economic changes leading to a more efficient agriculture and hence the loss of rural employment – a process almost complete today. The following figures for the proportion of people living in rural areas shows this:

    1831   34 per cent lived in cities
    1931   80 per cent lived in cities
    1991   90 per cent lived in cities

    1990s 1.2 per cent working in agriculture

- though the increase of people living in towns and cities has been small since the 1930s, this period is characterised by the reduction of the number of people working in agriculture. Although 10 per cent today live in rural areas, only 1.2 per cent work on the land. Rural employment has become more diversified, and commuting is common, leading to a loss of traditional local networks and an expansion of the range of individual personal network ties.
- two world wars meant a change in social roles within the family: women went out to work, and hence had a wider range of social contacts, in addition to family and neighbours. Men, especially in World War 2, met people from a wider range of geographical and social backgrounds.
- the construction of suburbs in the first half of the century, and new towns in the second half (Kerswill and Williams 2000), led to considerable migration out of the big cities to formerly rural areas. This led to great changes in people's networks, and to widespread **dialect contact** (Trudgill 1986; Kerswill 2002) in the new neighbourhoods.

One can distill these three factors by saying:

(1) The movement of people led to greater dialect contact
(2) The movement of people led to radical changes in people's **social networks**, away from strictly local ones comprising family and neighbours to ones that encompass far more strangers and people in different walks of life.

The result is **dialect levelling** with standardisation.

3. The social class factor

3.1 Standard English as a class dialect based on written norms

So far, I have deliberately not mentioned a very obvious difference in British English speech: that related to the social class of the speaker. As in all European countries, speakers with a higher level of education and higher-paid jobs speak in a manner that is closer to the standard language than do other people. This happens in a social and political environment where there is a strong economic and social elite which has associations with political and economic power. Usually, the written word is held up as a type of benchmark, or 'standard', against which good and bad language is measured. Command of the written word has always been important for the maintenance of these elites, but it is even more important nowadays with the increase of written communication via e-mail and the Internet. In a very real sense, if you want to be socially and economically upwardly mobile, you need a high level of literacy and a good command of a form of the spoken language which is close to written, literate norms. Unusually, in England, the standard language is strongly associated with a powerful class accent, Received Pronunciation (or BBC, Queen's, Oxford, etc. English)

How does this relate to dialect levelling? I am going to suggest that the answer is more complex than might at first be thought. The most obvious result is the standardisation that I have already described. But as I have indicated, standardisation does not necessarily follow from dialect levelling: it is perfectly possible for dialects to converge without getting closer to the standard – and this happens in some situations.

The mechanism for standardisation lies in the kinds of social networks people have. People with more broadly based (more varied) networks will meet people with a higher social status, most typically at work. They will **accommodate** to them (Giles and Powesland 1997[1975]; Giles and Smith 1979) – a phenomenon known as **upward convergence**. The opposite, **downward convergence**, where a higher status person accommodates to a lower status person, is much rarer. This accommodation is thought to happen mainly among adults, not children or adolescents, because in Western societies children and adolescents have much more self-centred, narrower peer groups. This means that standardisation is something that adults do (while children and adolescents do other kinds of levelling).

3.2 The grassroots strike back: Estuary English and its equivalents

The mechanism just discussed is indeed straightforward. But there is a problem with the model. This is that standardisation is *not* an all-pervasive (universal) force. As we have already seen, various aspects of regional speech are being preserved, despite dialect levelling. There are still many non-standard features which are *not* disappearing, and there are some *new* non-standard features, especially pronunciations, like the fronting of GOOSE and GOAT. I will go on to talk about a particular example of the resistance that dialects show against becoming fully standardised and homogenised. This is the kind of southeastern speech that has become known as Estuary English.

In the past 10 years, the newspapers have given a good deal of converage to a 'new' accent of the Southeast, said to be centred on the Thames Estuary. This is how the originator of the term, David Rosewarne, defined it:

> Estuary English is a variety of modified regional speech. It is a mixture of non-regional and local south-eastern English pronunciation and intonation. If one imagines a continuum with RP and popular London speech at either end, Estuary English speakers are to be found grouped in the middle ground. They are 'between Cockney and the Queen', in the words of *The Sunday Times*.
>
> (Rosewarne 1994a: 3)

According to Rosewarne, people arrive at it from two directions, from below and from above. To deal first with the movement from below: people down the years have been 'correcting' their speech as they have been increasing their social status. What they get rid of is grammatically non-standard features, such as double negatives and the word 'ain't', and past tense forms like *writ* for 'wrote', *come* for 'came'. But, inevitably, they do something with their accent, too. In the Southeast, they avoid the most stigmatised phonetic features. The first to go is so-called h-dropping. It is not 'done' to say 'the 'amster is in the 'ouse'. Some of the **glottal stops** might be replaced with /t/, as in *water*. Some vowels may change. Thus, for words like MOUTH, a Londoner would replace [ɛː] (a strong marker of London dialect) with [æʊ] or with RP-like [aʊ]. But much would remain. In other regions, the same effect happens, with people ending up with a regional accent rather than a very local dialect.

Rosewarne claims that this form of speech, at least in the Southeast, is a new sort of standard, replacing RP. He says it is the favoured accent of young upwardly mobile people in all walks of life, including the professions. A claim that is sometimes made is that RP speakers will actually adopt it themselves, and he cites the British violinist Nigel Kennedy as a case in point. The effect is a sort of pincer movement, with both the higher and lower groups converging on this variety. Estuary English has been popularised by Coggle (1993).

The following are characteristic features of Estuary English, heard on a recent talk show:

- glottal stops for /t/, including some between vowels
- vocalised /l/ as in *fill*, giving pronunciations sounding like 'fiw'
- 'Cockney' (London) vowels (broad diphthongs, so that *mace* sounds like RP 'mice', *buy* sounds like RP 'boy', and *rice* has a vowel resembling that of RP 'choice')
- a general absence of h-dropping
- no use of non-standard grammar

I agree with most of what has been said about Estuary English. What I do not agree with is the idea that it is new. 'Intermediate' varieties have existed for a long time, as I indicated earlier. What is new, however, is the sheer spread of these kinds of accents. Non-RP versions of standard English can be heard on every radio and television station. The exception, for the time being, is newsreaders on the BBC. But even there, there are now Welsh and Scottish accented speakers – though not, as yet, Estuary speakers! To illustrate the strength of this new movement away from RP I will cite a story told by a friend of mine who explained that he had been disqualified from becoming an announcer on a local radio station because his voice was too 'cultured'. This is someone who speaks near-RP with a very few Merseyside (Liverpool) features. Doctors, scientists, lawyers, teachers, lecturers, industrialists and politicians who appear in the media can be heard using mild Estuary English or another mild regional accent, whereas 30 years ago that would have been the exception. The NATO spokesman during the 1999 Kosovan war, Jamie Shea, was entrusted with this highly responsible presentation job despite being a speaker of quite marked Estuary English with a number of London features in his pronunciation. And all this culminated in the appointment in 2000 of Greg Dyke, an Estuary speaker, as Director General of the BBC.

Let us see what kind of provisional conclusion can be drawn at this point in the argument. We are apparently confronted with a situation where there is greater tolerance of variety in British speech. This fits in with the freer moral atmosphere following the 1960s and 1970s, with the introduction of more relaxed legislation concerning abortion, contraception and homosexuality, as well as gender equality and race relations laws. There is general agreement that ther is greater tolerance of, it not always respect for, ethnic minorities today than 30 years ago. Greater access to education may have increased social mobility. Some commentators have said that all of this is a sign of a move towards a 'classless society', something which former Prime

Minister John Major said he was aiming for. By this analysis, society and language are following the same democratic path.

3.3 But is it all as rosy as it seems?

However, there is huge resistance to Estuary English among quite large sections of society, as revealed in the persistent complaints in the media. In the past 15 years the papers have been full of editorials, articles and readers' letters deploring the state of the language. Estuary English – together with, briefly in 1994, Milton Keynes English as we described it in our study (see Kerswill and Williams 2000) – was seen as the root of the evil.

Here is what the late playwright John Osborne wrote about the Milton Keynes accent on 7 August 1994 in the *Daily Mail:*

> It was announced last week that **Essex girl** has been supplanted by the children of Milton Keynes, who uniformly speak with a previously unidentified and hideously glottal accent … Nothing is more depressing than [Milton Keynes], this gleaming gumboil plonked in the middle of England. And now there is a home-grown accent to match.

More recently, we find this from a reader (in this case, a well-known singer) on 17 June 2000 in the *Daily Telegraph*:

> It is all very well for people to complain about the abuse hurled by fans at the England v Portugal match, but this is hardly surprising when one hears our spoken language under constant attack from the all-pervading virus of "London lad" speak – via the "meeja", including, alas, Radio 3. I am tired of hearing presenters – from weather girls to news readers – refer to "Chewsday" [Tuesday] … and to "Alec Shtewart" [Stewart] (who keeps wicket for England) and using "jew" as a word to replace many others, as in "Jew agree?" [Do you agree] or "Jew [due] to rain there was no play at Chrent [Trent] Bridge today" … The insidious degradation of spoken English saddens me and someone ought to stand up and say "enough".
>
> (P. Skellern)

The following week, seven letters were published agreeing with this correspondent, as against one (mildly) disagreeing. One of the former was the following:

> Further examples of mispronunciation involve the "double-o" sound in "noon", now commonly pronounced "neen", and the "yew" sound in "news", which has become "knees". You don't believe me? Just listen carefully.
>
> (K. Marsden)

All the features parodied in these and other letters and articles are characteristic of working-class speech in Britain. So these pronouncements can be regarded not as 'racist' (that would be unacceptable) but as 'classist' – even though the features arc mostly also used by so-called educated speakers as well – a fact which the correspondents don't seem to realise.

So what is happening? Where is this tolerance and democracy? If we look at public attitudes as revealed in opinion polls, we do not find the tolerant and open society one might have expected. In the summer of 2000, there was much debate among the media and politicians about asylum seekers, with claims that these individuals were illegal immigrants – and worse. At the same time, there were a number of vigilante campaigns against real and supposed child abusers. Racial abuse is apparently on the increase. So the linguistic views expressed are very much in line with these trends.

There is another way of looking at this. I will start with a paradox. In 1979, Mrs Thatcher came to power as the first woman prime minister. In her 11 years, she transformed certain aspects of British society. She is perhaps best known for destroying the power of the trade unions, which had had a huge influence up until that time on the economy through their encouragement of economically damaging and socially divisive strikes. The paradox is this. Not only did she undermine the representatives of the workers (the unions), but she also set herself against any kind of traditional, entrenched power base or vested interest. In particular, she set herself against the power of the 'old school tie', an expression which means that people who went to particular prestigious schools or universities, especially Eton College (a well-known 'public school') and Oxford and Cambridge universities, stood a much better chance than other people of getting a good job in banking, the law, the civil service and the diplomatic service, as well as in other professions. What she espoused was what Michael Young in his 1958 book called 'the rise of the meritocracy' – meritocracy being a term which he coined to refer to the outcome of the following formula:

$$IQ \text{ (intelligence quotient)} + effort = merit$$

In 1980s Britain, we saw the media creations of the 'yuppies' and **'Essex man'**, referring to well-to-do, self-made young people who were seen by the establishment as lacking in 'culture' and 'taste'. These people, typically, spoke Estuary English – they were upwardly mobile, and so had wider social contacts than their parents would have had. As a result, they accommodated to members of their new networks by removing some of the more marked features of their local accents and dialects. Mrs Thatcher had a number of non-RP speakers in her cabinet, notably Norman Tebbit, who spoke with a marked Essex (or Estuary English) accent.

On this analysis, Estuary English is simply a product of this trend towards greater upward mobility. It is not, therefore, a reflection of any greater democratic **ideology** in society, but a brutal result of new power bases (the newly-wealthy) replacing older ones. The old establishment is very resistant to change, and sticks by RP – even if, like at least one of the letter writers I've quoted, they are not RP speakers themselves.

But Estuary English – and the regionally accented speech of the other regions – does serve a useful function. It has drawn attention to the ridiculousness of having a single, monolithic accent, which, moreover, is very much a class accent. Few other countries share this belief in the 'rightness' of such a class accent. Many people do not think Mrs Thatcher did much good for Britain. Paradoxically, breaking down the old class barriers might have been one good thing she achieved, and the concomitant rise of Estuary English another.

Websites

If you are interested in Estuary English and recent changes in British English, look first at the *Estuary English website*, run by John Wells at University College London. It contains numerous articles, newspaper reports, commentaries, and even whole theses written on the subject:

www.phon.ucl.ac.uk/home/estuary/home.htm

Also have a look at the *Routes of English* website, based on the BBC Radio 4 series:

www.bbc.co.uk/radio4/routesofenglish

Annotated bibliography

Bailey, R.W. (1991) *Images of English. A cultural history of the language*. Ann Arbor, MI: University of Michigan Press. [Concerned with contemporary writings on English around the world.]

Bauer, L. (1985) Tracing phonetic change in the received pronunciation of British English, *Journal of Phonetics*, 13(1): 61–81.

——— (1994). *Watching English Change*, London: Longman. [Good data on British English in the twentieth century; interesting discussions.]

Cheshire, J. (ed.), (1991) *English Around the World: Sociolinguistic Perspectives*, Cambridge: Cambridge University Press. [Comprehensive collection of sociolinguistic articles grouped according to territory, with introductory articles on each territory.]

———, Edwards, V. and Whittle, P. (1989) Urban British dialect grammar: the question of dialect levelling, *English World Wide* 10(2): 185–225. Also in Milroy and Milory (eds.), 1993 (see below).

Coggle, P. (1993) *Do you speak Estuary?* London: Bloomsbury. [The best popular account]

Crystal, D. (1995) *The Cambridge Encyclopedia of the English Language*, Cambridge: Cambridge University Press. [A good source of information; lavishly furnished with examples and illustrations.]

Foulkes, P. and Docherty, G. (1999) (eds.), *Urban Voices*, London: Arnold. [Collection of articles on British pronunciation set in a sociolinguistic perspective.]

Freeborn, D., French, P. and Langford, D. (1986/93) *Varieties of English. An Introduction to the Study of Language*, Basingstoke: Macmillan. [Basic-level textbook on history, attitudes, registers, and standardisation. With exercises.]

Giles, H. and Powesland, P. (1997[1975]). Accommodation theory, in N. Coupland and A. Jaworski (eds.), *Sociolinguistics: A Reader*, Basingstoke: Macmillan, pp. 232–239. (Reprinted from H. Giles and P. Powesland, P. (1975) *Speech Style and Social Evaluation*, London: Academic Press, pp. 154–170.)

——— and Smith, P. M. (1979). Accommodation theory: optimal levels of convergence, in H. Giles and R. St Clair (eds.), *Language and Social Psychology*, Oxford: Blackwell, pp. 45–65.

Graddol, D., Swann, J. and Leith, D. (1996) (eds.), *English: History, Diversity and Change*, London: Routledge. [Textbook-style collection written for Open University students. Recommended.]

Gramley, S. and Pätzold, K.-M. (1992) *A Survey of Modern English*. London: Routledge. [Useful survey of grammar, phonology and sociolinguistics, with an international emphasis.]

Hughes, G.A. and Trudgill, P. (1997) *Accents of English*, third edition, London: Arnold. [Excellent straightforward survey with tape.]

Kachru, B.B. *The Alchemy of English*, Oxford: Pergamon. [World Englishes.]

—— (1992) *The Other Tongue. English Across Cultures*, second edition, Urbana, IL: University of Illinois Press. [Good collection of articles on English in ESL contexts.]

Kerswill, P.E. (1996) Milton Keynes and dialect levelling in south-eastern British English, in Graddol, D., Swann, J. and Leith, D. (eds.), *English: History, Diversity and Change*, London: Routledge, pp. 292–300.

—— (2000) *Accent levelling in the south-east of England: a comparative instrumental study of short and long vowels*, paper given at Sociolinguistics Symposium 2000, University of the West of England, Bristol, April.

—— (2002) Koineization and accommodation, in J.K. Chambers, P. Trudgill and N. Schilling-Estes (eds.), *A Handbook of Language Variation and Change*, Oxford: Blackwell, pp. 669–702. [Deals with the formation of new dialects, or 'koines'.]

—— and Williams, A. (2000). Creating a new town koine: children and language change in Milton Keynes, *Language in Society*, 29(1): 65–115. [Full details of the 'Milton Keynes' project; see also Williams and Kerswill 1999.]

Lass, R. (1987) *The Shape of English*, London: Dent. [A largely historical treatment, with phonology.]

Leith, D. (1983/1999) *A Social History of English*, London: Routledge. [A sociolinguistically-informed history.]

McCrum, R., Cran, W. and MacNeil, R. (1986) *The Story of English*, London: BBC Publications. [Good, illustrated interested lay person's survey, accompanying BBC TV series.]

Milroy, J. and Milroy, L. (1985) and later, *Authority in Language: Investigating Prescription and Standardisation*, London: RKP. [Very good treatment; sociolinguistic approach.]

—— and —— (eds.), (1993) *Real English: The Grammar of English in the British Isles*, London: Longman. [Articles on regional grammar; review of sources for different regions; review of educational issues.]

O'Donnell, W.R. and Todd, L. (1980) and later, *Variety in Contemporary English*, London: George Allen & Unwin. [Covers standardisation, registers, education.]

Orton, H., Dieth, E. and Wakelyn, M. (1968) *The Survey of English Dialects Vol. 4 (the Southern Counties)*, Leeds: E.J. Arnold.

Quirk, R. and Widdowson, H.G. (1985) *English in the World: Teaching and Learning the Language and Literatures*, Cambridge: Cambridge University Press.

Rosewarne, D. (1984) Estuary English, *The Times Educational Supplement*, 19 October.

—— (1994a) Estuary English: Tomorrow's RP? *English Today*, 10(1): 3–8.

—— (1994b) Pronouncing Estuary English. *English Today*, 10(4): 3–7.

Trudgill, P. (ed.), (1984) *Language in the British Isles*, Cambridge: Cambridge University Press.

—— (1986) *Dialects in Contact*, Oxford: Blackwell. [On face-to-face and longer-term contact between speakers of different varieties; Australian English as a koiné.]

—— (1998) *The Dialects of England*, second edition, Oxford: Blackwell. [Intended for the informed lay person; readable.]

—— and Chambers, J. (eds.), (1990) *Dialects of English*, London: Longman. [More technical collection of articles on grammatical variation.]

Wakelin, M. (1978/1994) *Discovering English Dialects*, Princes Risborough: Shire Publications. [A short (64 pp.), very cheap paperback meant for casual reading, but full of excellent information on older dialects.]

Wells, J.C. (1982) *Accents of English* (3 vols), Cambridge: Cambridge University Press. [Informative and readable.]

—— (1994) The Cockneyfication of RP? in G. Melchers and N.-L. Johannessen (eds.), *Nonstandard Varieties of Language: Papers from the Stockholm Symposium*, Stockholm: Almqvist and Wiksell, pp. 198–205. [Read John Wells's articles on this and on Estuary English on his website (see above).]

Williams, A. and Kerswill, P.E. (1999) Dialect levelling: change and continuity in Milton Keynes, Reading and Hull, in P. Foulkes and G. Docherty (eds.), *Urban Voices*, London: Arnold, pp. 141–162. [Assesses evidence for dialect levelling in England.]

Young, M. (1958) *The Rise of the Meritocracy*, Harmondsworth: Penguin.

Chapter 20

William Labov

ACADEMIC IGNORANCE AND BLACK INTELLIGENCE

THIS IS A slightly abridged version of "The logic of non-standard English," prepared for the *Atlantic Monthly* in June 1972. It argued the case that **AAVE** was a fully formed language with all the capacity necessary for logical thought, and that the conclusions of the "deficit model" that black children had no language were based on unscientific and biased methods. It is reprinted in the electronic version of *The Atlantic Unbound* at: www.ling.upenn.edu/~wlabov/papers.html.

The controversy over why children in the inner-city schools show such low educational achievement has been examined in several recent issues of The Atlantic. *In the September, 1971, Atlantic, R.J. Herrnstein summarized the position of psychologists and others who believe that heredity is substantially more important than environment in determining intelligence, as measured by IQ tests. In its issue of December, 1971,* The Atlantic *published a number of letters (the correspondents included sociologists, anthropologists, economists, educators, and a few psychologists) taking issue with Professor Herrnstein's article. Many of those who wrote maintained that environmental factors, rather than any genetic deficit, explain the poor performance of lower-class inner-city children.*

A third position held by linguists and many anthropologists locates the problem not in the children, but in the relations between them and the school system. This position holds that inner-city children do not necessarily have inferior mothers, language, or experience, but that the language, family style, and ways of living of inner-city children are significantly different from the standard culture of the classroom, and that this difference is not always properly understood by teachers and psychologists. Linguists believe that we must begin to adapt our school system to the language and learning styles of the majority in the inner-city schools. They argue that everyone has the right to learn the standard languages and culture in reading and writing (and speaking, if they are so inclined); but this is the end result, not the beginning of the educational process. They do not believe that the standard language is the only medium in which teaching and learning can take place, or that the first step in education is to convert all first-graders to replicas of white middle-class suburban children.

*This article grew out of my own attempt to state the linguistic position on these issues at a Georgetown Round Table in 1968. While psychologists are obviously divided, linguists find (somewhat to their own surprise) that they all agree. My own statement here is based on research carried out in South Central Harlem from 1965 to 1968 by a team of two white and two black investigators, supported by the Office of Education. Our aim was to describe the differences between the standard English of the classroom and the **vernacular** language used by members of the street culture. We carried out long-term participant-observation with a number of black adolescent peer groups: the Jets, the Cobras, the Thunderbirds, the Aces, the Oscar Brothers. Their **dialect** will be referred to below as the **Black English Vernacular (BEV)**. It is a remarkably consistent grammar, essentially the same as that found in other cities: Detroit, Chicago, Philadelphia, Washington, San Francisco, Los Angeles, New Orleans. It is important to note that this Black English Vernacular is only a small part of what might be called "Black English." Black Americans do not, of course, speak a single dialect, but a wide range of language forms that cover the continuum between this vernacular and the most formal literary English.—W.L.*

In the past decade, a great deal of federally sponsored research has been devoted to the educational problems of children in ghetto schools. To account for the poor performance of children in these schools, educational psychologists have tried to discover what kind of disadvantage or defect the children are suffering from. The viewpoint which has been widely accepted and used as the basis for large-scale intervention programs is that the children show a cultural deficit as a result of an impoverished environment in their early years. A great deal of attention has been given to language. In this area, the **deficit theory** appears as the notion of "verbal deprivation": black children from the ghetto area are said to receive little verbal stimulation, to hear very little well-formed language, and as a result are impoverished in their means of verbal expression. It is said that they cannot speak complete sentences, do not know the names of common objects, cannot form concepts or convey logical thoughts.

Unfortunately, these notions are based upon the work of educational psychologists who know very little about language and even less about black children. The concept of verbal deprivation has no basis in social reality; in fact, black children in the urban ghettos receive a great deal of verbal stimulation, hear more well-formed sentences than middle-class children, and participate fully in a highly verbal culture; they have the same basic vocabulary, possess the same capacity for conceptual learning, and use the same logic as anyone else who learns to speak and understand English. The myth of verbal deprivation is particularly dangerous because it diverts the attention from real defects of our educational system to imaginary defects of the child; and as we shall see, it leads its sponsors inevitably to the hypothesis of the genetic inferiority of black children, which the verbal-deprivation theory was designed to avoid.

The deficit theory attempts to account for a number of facts that are known to all of us: that black children in the central urban ghettos do badly on all school subjects, including arithmetic and reading. In reading, they average more than two years behind the national norm. Furthermore, this lag is cumulative, so that they do worse comparatively in the fifth grade than in the first grade. The information available suggests that this bad performance is correlated most closely with socioeconomic status. Segregated ethnic groups, however, seem to do worse than others: in particular, Indian, Mexican-American, and black children.

We are obviously dealing with the effects of the caste system of American society—essentially a "color-marking" system. Everyone recognizes this. The question is, By what mechanism does the color bar prevent children from learning to read? One answer is the notion of "cultural deprivation" put forward by Martin Deutsch and others: the black children are said to lack the favorable factors in their home environment which enable middle-class children to do well in school. These factors involve the development, through verbal interaction with adults, of various cognitive skills, including the ability to reason abstractly, to speak fluently, and to focus upon long-range goals. In their publications, the psychologists Deutsch, Irvin Katz, and Arthur Jensen also recognize broader social factors. However, the deficit theory does not focus upon the interaction of the black child with white society so much as on his failure to interact with his mother at home. In the literature we find very little direct observation of verbal interaction in the black home: most typically, the investigators ask the child if he has dinner with his parents, and if he engages in dinner-table conversation with them. He is also asked whether his family takes him on trips to museums and other cultural activities. This slender thread of evidence is used to explain and interpret the large body of tests carried out in the laboratory and in the school.

The most extreme view which proceeds from this orientation—and one that is now being widely accepted—is that lower-class black children have no language at all. Some educational psychologists first draw from the writings of the British social psychologist Basil Bernstein the idea that "much of lower-class language consists of a kind of incidental 'emotional accompaniment' to action here and now." Bernstein's views are filtered through a strong bias against all forms of working-class behavior, so that he sees middle-class language as superior in every respect—as "more abstract, and necessarily somewhat more flexible, detailed and subtle." One can proceed through a range of such views until one comes to the practical program of Carl Bereiter, Siegfried Engelmann, and their associates. Bereiter's program for an academically oriented preschool is based upon the premise that black children must have a language which they can learn, and their empirical findings that these children come to school without such a language. In his work with four-year-old black children from Urbana, Illinois, Bereiter reports that their communication was by gestures, "single words," and "a series of badly connected words or phrases," such as *They mine* and *Me got juice*. He reports that black children could not ask questions, that "without exaggerating ... these four-year-olds could make no statements of any kind." Furthermore, when these children were asked, "Where is the book?" they did not know enough to look at the table where the book was lying in order to answer. Thus Bereiter concludes that the children's speech forms are nothing more than a series of emotional cries. and he decides to treat them "as if the children had no language at all." He identifies their speech with his interpretation of Bernstein's restricted code: "The language of culturally deprived children ... is not merely an underdeveloped version of standard English, but is a basically non-logical mode of expressive behavior." The basic program of his preschool is to teach them a new language devised by Engelmann, which consists of a limited series of questions and answers such as *Where is the squirrel? / The squirrel is in the tree.* The children will not be punished if they use their vernacular speech on the playground, but they will not be allowed to use it in the schoolroom. If they should answer the question "Where is the squirrel?" with the illogical vernacular form "In the tree," they will be reprehended by various means and made to say, "The squirrel is in the tree."

Linguists and psycholinguists who have worked with black children are likely to dismiss this view of their language as utter nonsense. Yet there is no reason to reject Bereiter's observations as spurious: they were certainly not made up. On the contrary they give us a very clear view of the behavior of student and teacher which can be duplicated in any classroom. Our own research is done outside the schools, in situations where adults are not the dominant force, but on many occasions we have been asked to help analyze the results of research into verbal deprivation in such test situations.

Here, for example, is a complete interview with a black boy, one of hundreds carried out in a New York City school. The boy enters a room where there is a large, friendly white interviewer, who puts on the table in front of him a block or a fire engine, and says, "Tell me everything you can about this!" (The interviewer's further remarks are in parentheses.)
[12 seconds of silence]
(What would you say it looks like?)
[8 seconds of silence]
A spaceship.
(Hmmmmm.)
[13 seconds of silence]
Like a je-et.
[12 seconds of silence]
Like a plane.
[20 seconds of silence]
(What color is it?)
Orange. [2 seconds] An' whi-ite. [2 seconds]
An' green.
[6 seconds of silence]
(An' what could you use it for?)
[8 seconds of silence]
A je-et.
[6 seconds of silence]
(If you had two of them, what would you do with them?)
[6 seconds of silence]
Give one to some-body.
(Hmmm. Who do you think would like to have it?)
[10 seconds of silence]
Cla-rence.
(Mm. Where do you think we could get another one of these?)
At the store.
(Oh-ka-ay!)

We have here the same kind of defensive, monosyllabic behavior which is reported in Bereiter's work. What is the situation that produces it? The child is in an asymmetrical situation where anything he says can, literally, be held against him. He has learned a number of devices to avoid saying anything in this situation, and he works very hard to achieve this end.

If one takes this interview as a measure of the verbal capacity of the child, it must be as his capacity to defend himself in a hostile and threatening situation. But unfortunately, thousands of such interviews are used as evidence of the child's total verbal capacity, or more simply his verbality: it is argued that this lack of "verbality" explains his poor performance in school.

The verbal behavior which is shown by the child in the test situation quoted above is not the result of ineptness of the interviewer. It is rather the result of regular sociolinguistic factors operating upon adult and child in this asymmetrical situation. In our work in urban ghetto areas, we have often encountered such behavior. For over a year Clarence Robins had worked with the Thunderbirds, a group of boys ten to twelve years old who were the dominant preadolescent group in a low-income project in Harlem. We then decided to interview a few younger brothers of the Thunderbirds, eight to nine years old. But our old approach didn't work. Here is an extract from the interview between Clarence and eight-year-old Leon L.:

CR:	What if you saw somebody kickin' somebody else on the ground, or was using a stick, what would you do if you saw that?
LEON:	Mmmm.
CR:	If it was supposed to be a fair fight—
LEON:	I don't know.
CR:	You don't know? Would you do anything? … huh? I can't hear you.
LEON:	No.
CR:	Did you ever see somebody get beat up real bad?
LEON:	… Nope ???
CR:	Well—uh did you ever get into a fight with a guy?
LEON:	Nope.
CR:	That was bigger than you?
LEON:	Nope.
CR:	You never been in a fight?
LEON:	Nope.
CR:	Nobody ever pick on you?
LEON:	Nope.
CR:	Nobody ever hit you?
LEON:	Nope.
CR:	How come?
LEON:	Ah 'on' know.
CR:	Didn't you ever hit somebody?
LEON:	Nope.
CR:	[incredulous] You never hit nobody?
LEON:	Mhm.
CR:	Aww, ba-a-a-be, you ain't gonna tell me that.

This nonverbal behavior occurs in a relatively favorable context for adult-child interaction, since the adult is a black man raised in Harlem, who knows this particular neighborhood and these boys very well. He is a skilled interviewer who has obtained a very high level of verbal response with techniques developed for a different age level, and has an extraordinary advantage over most teachers or experimenters in these respects. But even his skills and personality are ineffective in breaking down the social constraints that prevail here.

When we reviewed the record of this interview with Leon, we decided to use it as a test of our own knowledge of the sociolinguistic factors which control speech. We made the following changes in the social situation; in the next interview with Leon, Clarence:

1. Brought along a supply of potato chips, changing the "interview" into something more in the nature of a party.
2. Brought along Leon's best friend, eight-year-old Gregory.
3. Reduced the height imbalance. When Clarence got down on the floor of Leon's room, he dropped from 6 feet, 2 inches to 3 feet, 6 inches.
4. Introduced taboo words and taboo topics, and proved to Leon's surprise that one can say anything into our microphone without any fear of retaliation. It did not hit or bite back. The result of these changes is a striking difference in the volume and style of speech.

[The tape is punctuated throughout by the sound of potato chips.]

	CR:	Is there anybody who says. "Your momma drink pee"?
{	LEON:	[rapidly and breathlessly] Yee-ah!
	GREG:	Yup.
	LEON:	And your father eat doo-doo for breakfas'!
	CR:	Ohhh! [laughs]
	LEON:	And they say your father—your father eat doo-doo for dinner!
	GREG:	When they sound on me, I say "C.B.M."
	CR:	What that mean?
{	LEON:	Congo booger-snatch! [laughs]
	GREG:	Congo booger-snatcher! [laughs]
	GREG:	And sometimes I'll curse with "B.B."
	CR:	What that?
	GREG:	Oh, that's a "M.B.B." Black boy. [Leon crunching on potato chips]
	GREG:	'Merican Black Boy.
	CR:	Oh.
	GREG:	Anyway, 'Mericans is same like white people, right?
	LEON:	And they talk about Allah.
	CR:	Oh, yeah?
	GREG:	Yeah.
	CR:	What they say about Allah?
	LEON:	Allah—Allah is God.
	GREG:	Allah—
	CR:	And what else?
	LEON:	I don't know the res'.

GREG: Allah i—Allah is God, Allah is the only God, Allah—
LEON: Allah is the son of God.
GREG: But can he make magic?
LEON: Nope.
GREG: I know who can make magic?
CR: Who can?
LEON: The God, the real one.
CR: Who can make magic?
GREG: The son of po'—(CR: Hm?) I'm sayin' the po'k chop God! He only a po'k chop God! [Leon chuckles]

The "nonverbal" Leon is now competing actively for the **floor**; Gregory and Leon talk to each other as much as they do to the interviewer. The monosyllabic speaker who had nothing to say about anything and could not remember what he did yesterday has disappeared. Instead, we have two boys who have so much to say that they keep interrupting each other, who seem to have no difficulty in using the English language to express themselves.

One can now transfer this demonstration of the sociolinguistic control of speech to other test situations, including IQ and reading tests in school. It should be immediately apparent that none of the standard tests will come anywhere near measuring Leon's verbal capacity. On these tests he will show up as very much the monosyllabic, inept, ignorant, bumbling child of our first interview. The teacher has far less ability than Clarence Robins to elicit speech from this child; Clarence knows the community, the things that Leon has been doing, and the things that Leon would like to talk about. But the power relationships in a one-to-one confrontation between adult and child are too asymmetrical. This does not mean that some black children will not talk a great deal when alone with an adult, or that an adult cannot get close to any child. It means that the social situation is the most powerful determinant of verbal behavior and that an adult must enter into the right social relation with a child if he wants to find out what a child can do. This is just what many teachers cannot do.

The view of the black speech community which we obtain from our work in the ghetto areas is precisely the opposite from that reported by Deutsch, Engelmann, and Bereiter. We see a child bathed in verbal stimulation from morning to night. We see many speech events which depend upon the competitive exhibitions of verbal skills: singing, sounding, toasts, rifting, louding—a whole range of activities in which the individual gains status through his use of language. We see the younger child trying to acquire these skills from older children—hanging around on the outskirts of the older peer groups, and imitating this behavior. We see, however, no connection between verbal skill at the speech events characteristic of the street culture and success in the schoolroom; which says something about classrooms rather than about a child's language.

There are undoubtedly many verbal skills which children from ghetto areas must learn in order to do well in school, and some of these are indeed characteristic of middle-class verbal behavior. Precision in spelling, practice in handling abstract symbols, the ability to state explicitly the meaning of words, and a richer knowledge of the Latinate vocabulary may all be useful acquisitions. But is it true that all of the middle-class verbal habits are functional and desirable in school? Before we impose middle-class verbal style upon children from other cultural groups, we should find out how much of it is useful for the main work of analyzing and generalizing, and how much is merely stylistic—or even dysfunctional. In high school and college, middle-class children spontaneously complicate their syntax to the point that instructors despair of getting them to make their language simpler and clearer.

Our work in the speech community makes it painfully obvious that in many ways working-class speakers are more effective narrators, reasoners, and debaters than many middle-class speakers, who temporize, qualify, and lose their argument in a mass of irrelevant detail. Many academic writers try to rid themselves of the part of middle-class style that is empty pretension, and keep the part necessary for precision. But the average middle-class speaker that we encounter makes no such effort; he is enmeshed in **verbiage**, the victim of sociolinguistic factors beyond his control.

I will not attempt to support this argument here with systematic quantitative evidence, although it is possible to develop measures which show how far middle-class speakers can wander from the point. I would like to contrast two speakers dealing with roughly the same topic: matters of belief. The first is Larry H., a fifteen-year-old core member of another group, the Jets. Larry is being interviewed here by John Lewis, our participant-observer among adolescents in South Central Harlem.

JL:	What happens to you after you die? Do you know?
LARRY H:	Yeah, I know. (What?) After they put you in the ground, your body turns into—ah—bones, an' shit.
JL:	What happens to your spirit?
LARRY:	Your spirit—soon as you die, your spirit leaves you. (And where does the spirit go?) Well, it all depends. (On what?) You know, like some people say if you re good an' shit, your spirit goin' t'heaven ... 'n' if you bad, your spirit goin' to hell. Well, bullshit! Your spirit goin' to hell anyway, good or bad.
JL:	Why?
LARRY:	Why? I'll tell you why. Cause, you see, doesn' nobody really know that it's a God, y'know, 'cause, I mean I have seen black gods, pink gods, white gods, all color gods, and don't nobody know it's really a God. An' when they be sayin' if you good, you goin' t'heaven, thas bullshit, 'cause you ain't goin' to no heaven, 'cause it ain't no heaven for you to go to.

Larry is a gifted speaker of the **Black English vernacular (BEV)** as opposed to standard English (SE). His grammar shows a high concentration of such characteristic BEV forms as negative inversion [don't nobody know], **negative concord** [you ain't goin' to no heaven], invariant be [when they be sayin], dummy it for SE there [it ain't no heaven], optional copula deletion [if you're good ... if you bad], and full forms of auxiliaries [I have seen]. The only SE influence in this passage is the one case of doesn't instead of the invariant don't of BEV. Larry also provides a paradigmatic example of the rhetorical style of BEV: he can sum up a complex argument in a few words, and the full force of his opinions comes through without qualification or reservation. He is eminently quotable, and his interviews give us a great many concise statements of the BEV point of view. One can almost say that Larry speaks the BEV culture.

It is the logical form of this passage which is of particular interest here. Larry presents a complex set of interdependent propositions which can be explicated by setting out the SE equivalents in linear order. The basic argument is to deny the twin propositions:

(A) If you are good, (B) then your spirit will go to heaven.
(not A) If you are bad. (C) then your spirit will go to hell.
Larry denies (B), and allows that if (A) or (not A) is true, (C) will follow. His argument may be outlined:

(1)   Everyone has a different idea of what God is like.
(2)   Therefore nobody really knows that God exists.
(3)   If there is a heaven.[??] it was made by God.
(4)   If God doesn't exist, he couldn't have made heaven.
(5)   Therefore heaven does not exist.
(6)   You can't go somewhere that doesn't exist.

(not B) Therefore you can't go to heaven.
(C) Therefore you are going to hell.

This hypothetical argument is not carried on at a high level of seriousness. It is a game played with ideas as counters, in which opponents use a wide variety of verbal devices to win. There is no personal commitment to any of these propositions, and no reluctance to strengthen one's argument by bending the rules of logic as in the (2, 4) sequence. But if the opponent invokes the rules of logic, they hold. In John Lewis' interviews, he often makes this move, and the force of his argument is always acknowledged and countered within the rules of logic.

JL: Well, if there's no heaven, how could there be a hell?
LARRY: I mean—ye-eah. Well, let me tell you, it ain't no hell, 'cause this is hell right here, y'know! (This is hell?) Yeah, this is hell right here!

Larry's answer is quick, ingenious, and decisive. The application of the (3–4–5) argument to hell is denied, since hell is here, and therefore conclusion (not B) stands. These are not ready-made or preconceived opinions, but new propositions devised to win the logical argument in the game being played. The reader will note the speed and precision of Larry's mental operations. He does not wander, or insert meaningless verbiage. It is often said that the nonstandard vernacular is not suited for dealing with abstract or hypothetical questions, but in fact, speakers of the BE vernacular take great delight in exercising their wit and logic on the most improbable and problematical matters. Despite the fact that Larry H. does not believe in God, and has just denied all knowledge of him, John Lewis advances the following hypothetical question:

JL: But, just say that there is a God, what color is he? White or black?

LARRY: Well, if it is a God ... I wouldn' know what color, I couldn' say—couldn' nobody say what—

JL: But now, jus' suppose there was a God—

LARRY: Unless'n they say ...

JL: No, I was jus' sayin' jus' suppose there is a God, would he be white or black?

LARRY: He'd be white, man.

JL: Why?

LARRY: Why? I'll tell you why. 'Cause the average whitey out here got everything, you dig? And the nigger ain't got shit, y'know? Y'unnerstan'? So—um—for—in order for that to happen, you know it ain't no black God that's doin' that bullshit.

No one can hear Larry's answer to this question without being convinced of being in the presence of a skilled speaker with great "verbal presence of mind," who can use the English language expertly for many purposes.

Let us now turn to the second speaker, an upper middle-class, college-educated black man being interviewed by Clarence Robins in our survey of adults in South Central Harlem.

CR: Do you know of anything that someone can do, to have someone who has passed on visit him in a dream?

CHAS M: Well, I even heard my parents say that there is such a thing as something in dreams, some things like that, and sometimes dreams do come true. I have personally never had a dream come true. I've never dreamt that somebody was dying and they actually died (Mhm), or that I was going to have ten dollars the next day and somehow I got ten dollars in my pocket. (Mhm.) I don't particularly believe in that, I don't think it's true. I do feel, though, that there is such a thing as—ah—witchcraft. I do feel that in certain cultures there is such a thing as witchcraft, or some sort of science of witchcraft; I don't think that it's just a matter of believing hard enough that there is such a thing as witchcraft. I do believe that there is such a thing that a person can put himself in a state of mind (Mhm), or that—er—something could be given them to intoxicate them in a certain—to a certain frame of mind—that—that could actually be considered witchcraft.

Charles M. is obviously a "good speaker" who strikes the listener as well-educated, intelligent and sincere. He is a likable and attractive person—the kind of person that middle-class listeners rate very high on a scale of "job suitability" and equally high as a potential friend. His language is more moderate and tempered than Larry's: he makes every effort to qualm his opinions, and seems anxious to avoid any misstatements or overstatements. From these qualities emerges the primary characteristic of this passage—its verbosity. Words multiply, some modifying and qualifying, others repeating or padding the main argument. The first half of this extract is a response to the initial question on dreams, basically:

(1)   Some people say that dreams sometimes come true.
(2)   I have never had a dream come true.
(3)   Therefore I don't believe (1).

This much of Charles M.'s response is well directed to the point of the question. He then volunteers a statement of his beliefs about witchcraft which shows the difficulty of middle-class speakers who (a) want to express a belief in something but (b) want to show themselves as judicious, rational, and free from superstitions. The basic proposition can be stated simply in five words:

But I believe in witchcraft.

However, the idea is enlarged to exactly one hundred words, and it is difficult to see what else is being said. The vacuity of this passage becomes more evident if we remove repetitions, fashionable words, and stylistic decorations:

But I believe in witchcraft.

I don't think witchcraft is just a belief.

A person can put himself or be put in a state of mind that is witchcraft.

Without the extra verbiage and the OK words like *science*, *culture* and *intoxicate*, Charles M. appears as something less than a first-rate thinker. The initial impression of him as a good speaker is simply our long-conditioned reaction to middle-class verbosity: we know that people who use these stylistic devices are educated people, and we are inclined to credit them with saying something intelligent.

Let us now examine Bereiter's own data on the verbal behavior of the black children he dealt with. The expressions *They mine* and *Me got juice* are cited as examples of a language which lacks the means for expressing logical relations—in this case characterized as "a series of badly connected words." In the case of *They mine*, it is apparent that Bereiter confuses the notions of logic and explicitness. We know that there are many languages of the world which do not have a present copula, and which conjoin subject and predicate complement without a verb. Russian, Hungarian, and Arabic may be foreign, but they are not by the same token illogical. In the case of black English we are not dealing with even this superficial grammatical difference, but rather with a low-level rule which carries contraction one step further to delete single consonants representing the verbs is, have, or will. We have yet to find any children who do not sometimes use the full forms of *is* or *will*, even though they may frequently delete it.

The deletion of the *is* or *are* in black English is not the result of erratic or illogical behavior: it follows the same regular rules as standard English contraction. Wherever standard English can contract, black children use either the contracted form or (more commonly) the deleted zero form. Thus *They mine* corresponds to standard English *They're mine*, not to the full form *They are mine*. On the other hand, no such deletion is possible in positions where standard English cannot contract: just as one cannot say *That's what they're* in standard English, *That's what they* is equally impossible in the vernacular we are considering. The appropriate use of the deletion rule, like the contraction rule, requires a deep and intimate knowledge of English grammar and phonology. Such knowledge is not available for conscious inspection by native speakers: the rules we have worked out for standard contraction have never appeared in any grammar, and are certainly not a part of the conscious knowledge of any standard

English speakers. Nevertheless, the adult or child who uses these rules must have formed at some level of psychological organization clear concepts of "tense marker," "verb phrase," "rule ordering," "sentence embedding," "pronoun," and many other grammatical categories which are essential parts of any logical system.

Bereiter's reaction to the sentence *Me got juice* is even more puzzling. If Bereiter believes that *Me got juice* is not a logical expression, it can only be that he interprets the use of the objective pronoun *me* as representing a difference in logical relationship to the verb; that the child is in fact saying that "the juice got him" rather than "he got the juice"! If on the other hand the child means "I got juice," then this sentence form shows only that he has not learned the formal rules for the use of the subjective form *I* and oblique form *me*.

Bereiter shows even more profound ignorance of the rules of discourse and of syntax when he rejects "In the tree" as an illogical or badly formed answer to "Where is the squirrel?" Such elliptical answers are of course used by everyone, and they show the appropriate deletion of subject and main verb, leaving the **locative** which is questioned by wh + there. The reply *In the tree* demonstrates that the listener has been attentive to and apprehended the syntax of the speaker. Whatever formal structure we wish to write for expressions such as *Yes* or *Home* or *In the tree*, it is obvious that they cannot be interpreted without knowing the structure of the question which preceded them, and that they presuppose an understanding of the syntax of the question. Thus if you ask me, "Where is the squirrel?" it is necessary for me to understand the sentence from an underlying form which would otherwise have produced *The squirrel is there*. If the child had answered *The tree*, or *Squirrel the tree*, or *The in tree*, we would then assume that he did not understand the syntax of the full form, *The squirrel is in the tree*. Given the data that Bereiter presents, we cannot conclude that the child has no grammar, but only that the investigator does not understand the rules of grammar. It does not necessarily do any harm to use the full form *The squirrel is in the tree*, if one wants to make fully explicit the rules of grammar which the child has internalized. Much of logical analysis consists of making explicit just that kind of internalized rule. But it is hard to believe that any good can come from a program which begins with so many misconceptions about the input data. Bereiter and Engelmann believe that in teaching the child to say *The squirrel is in the tree* or *This is a box* and *This is not a box*, they are teaching him an entirely new language, whereas in fact they are only teaching him to produce slightly different forms of the language he already has.

If there is a failure of logic involved here, it is surely in the approach of the verbal-deprivation theorists, rather than in the mental abilities of the children concerned. We can isolate six distinct steps in the reasoning which has led to programs such as those of Deutsch, Bereiter, and Engelmann:

1. The lower-class child's verbal response to a formal and threatening situation is used to demonstrate his lack of verbal capacity, or verbal deficit.
2. This verbal deficit is declared to be a major cause of the lower-class child's poor performance in school.
3. Since middle-class children do better in school, middle-class speech habits are said to be necessary for learning.

4. Class and ethnic differences in grammatical form are equated with differences in the capacity for logical analysis.
5. Teaching the child to mimic certain formal speech patterns used by middle-class teachers is seen as teaching him to think logically.
6. Children who learn these formal speech patterns are then said to be thinking logically, and it is predicated that they will do much better in reading and arithmetic in the years to follow.

This article has proved that numbers 1. and 2. at least are wrong. However, it is not too naive to ask, 'What is wrong with being wrong?' We have already conceded that black children need help in analyzing language into its surface components, and in being more explicit. But there are, in fact, serious and damaging consequences of the verbal-deprivation theory. These may be considered under two headings: (a) the theoretical bias and (b) the consequences of failure.

It is widely recognized that the teacher's attitude toward the child is an important factor in the latter's success or failure. The work of Robert Rosenthal on "self-fulfilling prophecies" shows that the progress of children in the early grades can be dramatically affected by a single random labeling of certain children as "intellectual bloomers." When the everyday language of black children is stigmatized as "not a language at all" and "not possessing the means for logical thought," the effect of such a labeling is repeated many times during each day of the school year. Every time that a child uses a form of BEV without the copula or with negative concord, he will be labeling himself for the teacher's benefit as "illogical," as a "nonconceptual thinker." This notion gives teachers a ready-made, theoretical basis for the prejudice they may already feel against the lower-class black child and his language. When they hear him say *I don't want none* or *They mine*, they will be hearing, through the bias provided by the verbal-deprivation theory, not an English dialect different from theirs, but the primitive mentality of the savage mind.

But what if the teacher succeeds in training the child to use the new language consistently? The verbal deprivation theory holds that this will lead to a whole chain of successes in school, and that the child will be drawn away from the vernacular culture into the middle-class world. Undoubtedly this will happen with a few isolated individuals, just as it happens in every school system today for a few children. But we are concerned not with the few but the many, and for the majority of black children the distance between them and the school is bound to widen under this approach.

The essential fallacy of the verbal-deprivation theory lies in tracing the educational failure of the child to his personal deficiencies. At present, these deficiencies are said to be caused by his home environment. It is traditional to explain a child's failure in school by his inadequacy; but when failure reaches such massive proportions, it seems necessary to look at the social and cultural obstacles to learning and the inability of the school to adjust to the social situation.

The second area in which the verbal-deprivation theory is doing serious harm to our educational system is in the consequences of this failure and the reaction to it. As Operation Head Start fails, the interpretations which we receive will be from the same educational psychologists who designed this program. The fault will be found, not in the data, the theory, or the methods used, but rather in the children who have failed to respond to the opportunities offered them. When black children fail to show the significant advance which the deprivation theory predicts, it will be further proof of the profound gulf which separates their mental processes from those of civilized, middle-class mankind.

A sense of the failure of Operation Head Start is already commonplace. Some prominent figures in the program have reacted to this situation by saying that intervention did not take place early enough. Bettye M. Caldwell notes that:

> the research literature of the last decade dealing with social-class differences has made abundantly clear that all parents are not qualified to provide even the basic essentials of physical and psychological care to their children.

The **deficit theory** now begins to focus on the "longstanding patterns of parental deficit" which fill the literature. "There is, perhaps unfortunately," writes Caldwell, "no literacy test for motherhood." Failing such eugenic measures, she has proposed "educationally oriented day care for culturally deprived children between six months and three years of age." The children are returned home each evening to "maintain primary emotional relationships with their own families," but during the day they are removed "hopefully to prevent the deceleration in rate of development which seems to occur in many deprived children around the age of two to three years."

There are others who feel that even the best of the intervention programs, such as those of Bereiter and Englemann, will not help the black child no matter when they are applied—that we are faced once again with the "inevitable hypothesis" of the genetic inferiority of the black people. Arthur Jensen, for example, in his Harvard Educational Review paper (1969), argues that the verbal-deprivation theorists with whom he has been associated—Deutsch, Whiteman, Katz, Bereiter—have been given every opportunity to prove their case and have failed. This opinion forms part of the argument leading to his overall conclusion that the "preponderance of the evidence is ... less consistent with a strictly environmental hypothesis than with the genetic hypothesis."

Jensen argues that the middle-class white population is differentiated from the working-class white and black population in the ability for "cognitive or conceptual learning," which Jensen calls Level II intelligence as against mere "associative learning," or Level I intelligence.

Thus Jensen found that one group of middle-class children were helped by their concept-forming ability to recall twenty familiar objects that could be classified into four categories: animals, furniture, clothing, or foods. Lower-class black children did just as well as middle-class children with a miscellaneous set, but showed no improvement with objects that could be so organized.

In the earliest stages of language learning, children acquire "selectional restrictions" in their use of words. For example, they learn that some verbs take ANIMATE subjects, but others only INANIMATE ones: thus we say *The machine breaks* but not *John breaks*; *The paper tears* but not *George tears*. A speaker of English must master such subtle categories as the things which break, like boards, glasses, and ropes; things which tear, like shirts, paper, and skin; things which snap, like buttons, potato chips, and plastic, and other categories which smash, crumple, or go bust.

In studies of Samoan children, Keith Kernan has shown that similar rules are learned reliably long before the grammatical particles that mark tense, number, and so on. The experimentation on free recall that Jensen reports ignores such abilities, and defines intelligence as a particular way of answering a particular kind of question within a narrow cultural framework. Recent work of anthropologists in other cultures is beginning to make some headway in discovering how our tests bias the results so as to make normally intelligent people look stupid. Michael Cole and his associates gave the same kind of free recall tests to Kpelle speakers in Liberia. Those who had not been to school—children or adults—could only remember eight or ten out of the twenty and showed no "clustering" according to categories, no matter how long the trials went on. Yet one simple change in the test method produced a surprising change. The interviewer took each of the objects to be remembered and held it over a chair: one chair for each category, or just one chair for all categories. Suddenly the Kpelle subjects showed a dramatic improvement, remembered seventeen to eighteen objects, and matched American subjects in both recall and the amount of clustering by categories. We do not understand this effect, for we are only beginning to discover the subtle biases built in our test methods which prevent people from using the abilities that they display in their language and in everyday life.

Linguists are in an excellent position to demonstrate the fallacies of the verbal-deprivation theory. All linguists agree that nonstandard dialects are highly structured systems; they do not see these dialects as accumulations of errors caused by the failure of their speakers to master standard English. When linguists hear black children saying *He crazy* or *Her my friend* they do not hear a "primitive language." Nor do they believe that the speech of working-class people is merely a form of emotional expression, incapable of relating logical thought. Linguists therefore condemn with a single voice Bereiter's view that the vernacular can be disregarded.

There is no reason to believe that any nonstandard vernacular is in itself an obstacle to learning. The chief problem is ignorance of language on the part of all concerned. Our job as linguists is to remedy this ignorance: Bereiter and Englemann want to reinforce it and justify it. Teachers are now being told to ignore the language of black children as unworthy of attention and useless for learning. They are being taught to hear every natural utterance of the child as evidence of his mental inferiority. As linguists we are unanimous in condemning this view as bad observation, bad theory, and bad practice.

That educational psychology should be strongly influenced by a theory so false to the facts of language is unfortunate; but that children should be the victims of this ignorance is intolerable. If linguists can contribute some of their valuable knowledge and energy toward exposing the fallacies of the verbal-deprivation theory, we will have done a great deal to justify the support that society has given to basic research in our field.

Chapter 21

Michael W. Gos

OVERCOMING SOCIAL CLASS MARKERS: PREPARING WORKING CLASS STUDENTS FOR COLLEGE

> The educational system is not predicated upon equal education for all, but upon competition with professional/managerial class students starting from the fifty and working class students starting from the zero yard line in the one hundred yard dash. And then the working class students are told the reason they didn't win is because they were slow. —I. Peckham

I**T IS NO** secret that working class students who choose to pursue a university education begin their college careers in a deep hole relative to students with managerial/professional class origins. This problem has existed for decades, and college educators have attributed it, at least partially, to a lack of experience, both life and educational, on the part of working class students. Traditionally this problem has been addressed through remediation and other retention programs. It was believed that if we spent a little time and effort on these students, we could bring them to a point where they could compete with their peers. But, of course, the problem has persisted.

Several researchers have suggested that a more important factor in this phenomenon may be social class markers—patterns of behavior and communication—in working class communities that are both marginalized and selected against at the college level (Bernstein 1971; Peckham 1995; Gos 1993). To succeed, students must overcome these markers and instead adopt those of the managerial/professional classes. Contending with college work can be difficult for anyone, but to have to keep up with course work and overcome family background can be overwhelming. That may explain why so many students fail in spite of remediation. The time to overcome social class markers is when students are in middle school and high school, when the academic pressures are lower and there is not a sense of their futures being at stake if they fail.

Two of the factors that separate working class students from their managerial/professional class peers are communication protocols and how the individual fits in the family and community organization. Both are a function of a student's background and both greatly affect the chances for success in college and the work world beyond.

Communication protocols

Working class people often live in extended families and have aunts, uncles, cousins, even grandparents living nearby. These family groups tend to be extremely location-stable, often staying in the same neighborhoods for generations. They know their family members and neighbors well. As a result of this familiarity, they understand **paralinguistic** meanings that are conveyed by tone, gesture, perhaps a look in the eye, that outsiders would miss (Peckham 1995). According to Bernstein (1971), the conversations that take place are often merely placeholders, with the real meaning of an exchange being conveyed through other channels. Bernstein called this "public language" because the utterances themselves are public property—everyone in the group tends to use the same basic utterances. In a public language, parts of sentences do not have to be connected by subordinate structures because the listener knows those connections. The short, grammatically simple, often unfinished sentences are understood because the listener knows what the rest of the sentence would be.

In managerial/professional classes, however, communication is through what Bernstein calls a "formal language." Because these families travel more, move more frequently, and often live hundreds or even thousands of miles away from other family members, their communication must transcend the community they are in and be applicable to a wider range of communication situations. In a formal language, meaning is contained in the structure of the language itself, not in the gaps, as in a public language. Formal language tends to be rich in personal and individual qualifications as opposed to the public language's community orientation. Volume, tone, and nonverbal cues take second place to the content of the sentences. And of course, formal language is the language of the university.

The implications of public language are many. Sentences tend to be simple and, in many cases, unfinished. The working class student often is unaware that a sentence is incomplete as uttered because the thought itself has been communicated in toto through the paralinguistic means discussed above. He or she is unaware that the thought has not been communicated to persons outside the community.

The public language user is also unable to communicate his or her individual feelings and experiences within the limitations of the language. Because language reflects a group's world view, the communal nature of the working class extended family produces a language without means of expressing individuation. Instead, speakers must attach their feelings to the social counters that are present within the language. When asked to identify how they feel about something, they will often speak in detached, third-person terms or talk about events rather than feelings. Mechanisms for individuation of thought are absent from their communication repertoires.

Position within a family or community organization

Another difference between the working class and the managerial/professional class is the way in which position in the family or community is determined, and like communication protocols, this difference also works against the working class student's chances for success.

The managerial/professional class home is person-oriented, that is, roles are determined not by position or birth order, but rather by who the individuals are. These children are born into an environment where they are seen and responded to as individuals with their own rights. They have a specific social status. Roles are changeable, mainly through the process of negotiation. Children of the managerial/professional classes essentially get to create their own roles within the family and community.

On the other hand, working class social structure is position-oriented. Individuals are born into clearly defined roles determined by their position (father, mother, first son, second son, first daughter, and so forth). These roles are defined independently of the persons holding them, and lines of authority are implicit in the roles. These lines are clearly established and are not subject to change through negotiation (Bernstein 1971). They tend to be consistent from family to family and community to community.

Probably the greatest effect that position-orientation has on the successes of working class children is in this area of authority. In working class families, authority and legitimacy of a statement come from the form of social relationships rather than from reasoned principles ("Do it because I said so"). When a statement is challenged, it is the relationship that is being questioned, not the logic of the statement. The authoritarian environment that working class students experience discourages them from questioning, while the more open, relativistic environment of the managerial/professional classes encourages students from that background to question. It is not hard to see how this would affect critical thinking and, ultimately, the arts of persuasive and expository writing.

But the problems faced by working class students as a result of position-orientation go even deeper than this. Clearly, these students are at a disadvantage because they have not been taught how to question or to formulate support for contentions. But what may prove to be an even bigger obstacle is not what they were never taught to do, but rather what they were taught never to do. That is, the act of questioning or arguing a position is often considered unacceptable behavior for children in working class families. Because authority and legitimacy lie in the source of a statement, not in its metaphysical truth, to question a statement is an attack on the authority figure (parent, teacher, textbook author) and a contention is true because of the person who states it. To further argue it would be rude to the audience by wasting their time, and to argue against it would, of course, be a personal attack on the speaker. Either action constitutes an unacceptable breach of etiquette for children in working class families.

So when working class students are asked to write a persuasive paper, they have only one position they can take, that taken by the teacher. Using arguments in support of the teacher's stance would be rude, an overkill of sorts that wastes the teacher's time, and taking a contrary position is not an option available to them. If asked to take a stand on an issue without the knowledge of the teacher's position, working class students will search for what they believe the teacher wants to hear or try to find another authority figure whose position on the issue can be co-opted. That accomplished, a statement of position may be made but supporting arguments will be lacking.

What can teachers do?

The place to start helping working class students to succeed in college is in the middle and high schools. Postponing preparation till college has proved to be ineffective. Clearly, the students who fail in college suffer all of the fallout associated with that failure. But even those students who manage to succeed and go on to get a degree suffer serious consequences. Most of the researchers currently working in the field suggest a strong correlate with college success for working students—a separation from their family and community (Rose 1989; Peckham 1995; Gos 1993). By waiting until college to address the issue of class codes, and then presenting students with a "sink or swim" situation, we have created an environment where a student's severing of the ties with his or her background becomes either a prerequisite to, or a result of, success in school. These students find that an immersion into the social community they wish to enter is an effective way to make the border crossing, much as living in a foreign country is an effective way to learn the language spoken there. Apparently, they see the connections with the old neighborhood and, more seriously, with their families, as hindrances to their goals. It has even been suggested that the higher the aspirations of the student, the more complete the separations (Peckham 1995).

Clearly, this kind of separation from family and culture should be avoided, and yet, for generations, it has gone hand in hand with success. I believe this is largely because of the intense pressure to make the border crossing in four years or, more realistically, in even less time. If, instead, we can spread the process of overcoming social class markers out over a longer period of time, students may be able to face these difficulties with much less pressure because their success or failure in school will not be so intimately tied to their progress in this endeavor. I believe a good place to begin this process is in the middle schools, although even a year or two of help late in the high school career will ease the pressure on working class students with college aspirations.

There are several things that middle and high school teachers can do, both in the classroom and in advising, to better prepare working class students for the tasks ahead. These actions surround three main pedagogical issues: memorization, critical thinking, and speech patterns.

Memorization versus critical thinking

Probably the most important factor contributing to success is the student's skill with meaning making. Meaning is constructed and built upon. It is not accomplished by "collecting" the meanings made by others. Working class students' natural tendency will be to try to understand, and then memorize, the meaning made by others, particularly those in authority. Instead, these students need practice in making their own meaning, whether reading "against the text" or reading for information or pleasure.

Sometimes working class students need more than practice, however. Because of negative experiences with any type of questioning in the past, they need encouragement and assurance that this is indeed an acceptable activity and that their meaning has value. Teachers can expect resistance to persuasive essay assignments and other tasks involving critical thinking and meaning making. When asked to perform such tasks, these students will often try to support ideas by authority rather than rationale. Teachers need to place a greater emphasis on supporting ideas rationally and discourage heavy use of authority and credibility appeals as justification for the truth or validity of a contention.

Memorization is often the enemy of working class students engaged in learning meaning making. And yet, it is a common pedagogy in working class schools. This is ironic in that not only is it an activity that working class students feel comfortable doing, but it is also one in which they often excel. Although there may be some rare use for memorized data sets, memorization often diverts attention from more critical, higher-level skills such as synthesis and analogy. That is not to say that memorization should be done away with completely. When it is necessary to have instant access to some piece of information in order to do some higher-level activity, memorization may be a sound approach, but it should not dominate the pedagogy.

Instead, teachers should teach the conceptual nature of activities, helping students learn to construct meaning from classroom stimuli. An example of this might be to assign an essay on Thomas Hardy's philosophy in *Tess of the D'Urbervilles*, rather than just measuring the knowledge of plot lines and character names through an "identify" exercise. When students are forced to move from a story line, to a meaning, and finally to a philosophy, they are engaging in the kind of activity that will help them overcome social class markers and better prepare for college.

Speech patterns

Regardless of how we feel about the fairness of judging persons by their speech patterns, the fact is, it happens. Working class college students find their verbal patterns, both speech and writing, the biggest obstacle they must overcome if they are to successfully cross the border into the managerial/professional classes. This marker, in fact, will shadow them far beyond college; the work world will judge them in much the same way. Yet, if there is one thing we have learned from the Native American experience in the late nineteenth and early twentieth centuries, it is that students are entitled to their own language. What are teachers to do?

Work in discourse communities has determined that communications patterns in communities are set from within, and persons wishing to join in a community's conversation must adapt to the community's patterns (Bartholomae 1985; Berkenkotter *et al.* 1988). Such is the case with working class students. In order to effectively communicate with the managerial/professional classes, they will have to learn the speech codes of those classes. This is not to say that students must reject their own language (although that has certainly been one of the casualties in the jettisoning of family and community by many successful members of the working class) but rather that they must become adaptable—"bilingual," if you will. While communicating in the managerial/professional class environment, they will be expected to use a formal language, reserving the public language for communities where it is appropriate.

The teacher is often the working class student's first contact with the managerial/professional classes (while many secondary school teachers come from working class back grounds, being successful border crossers, they now function as managerial/professional class communicators). For many students, teachers will be the only members of those classes they encounter until they reach college. It is not sufficient for teachers to merely set an example by speaking the language of the managerial/professional classes. Bernstein (1971) suggests that the differences in language can only be detected while listening downwards; that is, managerial/professional class speakers can detect differences between their language and that of the working classes, but working class members have a much more difficult time recognizing a difference. Teachers must impart the new, formal language to their students in ways that allow them to experiment with, and successfully communicate in, these new discourse communities. By urging standard English in all verbal and written utterances within the classroom (which, in college, is indeed a managerial/professional discourse community) and gently correcting errors, teachers will help working class students acquire this new "language."

One exercise that is particularly helpful in demonstrating to students the "bilingual" nature of communicating in multiple discourse communities is the tailoring of a particular document to each of the two audiences. For instance, the student may write a paper about a personal experience with a close friend as the target audience. Later, as a separate assignment, he or she is asked to write the same paper but now for a school administration audience—the principal or a school board member, for example. When the students go through the process of "translating" a paper to make it appropriate for the new audience, they gain a better picture of the problems of communicating in this new discourse community.

Teachers can further assist in the acquisition of managerial/professional class literacies by giving students ample practice in the individualization of feeling and experience in writing assignments and class discussions. This can be accomplished by encouraging the students to go beyond simple narratives that allow a detachment from feelings and, instead, to confront the effect that events had on them. Working class students will resist this initially, but with practice, it will become easier.

Another area where teachers can help is in the study of vocabulary words. Working class students benefit more by exploring the nuances of meaning and usage of new words than by memorizing a dictionary definition of a word and using it in a sentence. One of the biggest difficulties students have in college is that they have an imperfect handle on many of the words in their vocabularies. This sometimes leads to embarrassing events such as the student's making a public statement in which a word is used incorrectly. Correction by the professor, or worse, ridicule from fellow students, will inhibit the student's willingness to experiment with language. Such students quickly learn to shrink their working vocabularies to include only words they have comfortable control over. This reduction does not help their long-term success.

It should be noted that training students to become "bidialectical" does not imply a judgment of one "language" as better than the other but rather a recognition that different discourse communities communicate in different ways and that to become a member of any community entails learning its language. This issue is dealt with in detail in the Conference on College Composition and Communication (CCCC) statement, "Students' Rights to Their Own Language," a document teachers will find useful in understanding this issue.

The earlier in a student's life this move toward a bidialectical ability begins, the easier the transition to different discourse communities becomes. In a recent discussion of this issue on Techwr-1, an electronic bulletin board for technical writers, one participant stated:

I was drilled in correct grammar throughout my childhood. Maybe some don't realize it, but there is an element of classism to our grammar patterns. My parents were working class people working up to the middle class, and my mother particularly wanted us to speak properly so we would fit in.

Another added:

My parents were right off the farm, just barely above poor white trash, and in moving upward to middle class my mother saw "proper" language as a way to fit in and as a way to move up; proper language was a symbol of respectability. Hence, every time I said "ain't," my mother corrected me.

Clearly, from their occupations, we can tell that these people became successful border crossers. While they had the advantage of a family that encouraged this transition, many students don't, and the teacher may be their only hope.

Recommendations

Some working class students can go to college and, with a little remediation and a lot of work, be successful. It has been happening for decades. But the percentages are against them, and those who do succeed come away from the battle suffering huge losses, most notably a separation from their families and communities—in effect, from their heritage. It is my belief that this carnage can be alleviated. If we can begin preparing students to overcome class markers at an earlier age, when the pressures are fewer, we can add a third option, a border crossing that is less traumatic and carries with it no lifelong scars. Perhaps we can even improve the percentage of those who make it. Teachers in secondary schools are in a position to make the difference. Whenever possible, the teacher should:

- teach the conceptual nature of activities rather than allowing the simple memorization of facts;
- teach meaning making rather than allowing students to understand or memorize someone else's meaning;
- give greater emphasis to supporting ideas rationally rather than by authority;
- explore the nuances of meaning and usage of new vocabulary words rather than allowing simple memorization of dictionary definitions and use of terms in a single sentence; and
- encourage standard English in all classroom utterances, both verbal and written, by analyzing various dialectal contexts and by gently correct[ing] errors.

We all hope our students will begin college on an equal footing with their peers. But in the past this has not been the case. Although there is very little we can do to level the playing field in the homes and communities of our students, I believe there is much that can be done in the secondary schools. As a college professor from a working class background, I hope to see the day when working class students can come to the university and direct all their efforts to their studies. But to do that, they must first overcome the social class markers that inhibit their success at the college level. For that, their greatest ally may be the secondary school teacher.

References

Bartholomae, D. (1985) Inventing the university, in M. Rose (ed.), *When a Writer can't Write*, New York: Guilford, pp. 134–165.

Berkenkotter, C., T.N. Huckin, and J. Ackemlan (1988) Conventions, conversations, and the student writer: Case study of a student in a rhetoric PhD program, *Research in the Teaching of English*, 22(1): 9–44.

Bernstein, B.B. (1971) *Class, Codes and Control, Vols. 1–3*, London: Routledge and Kegan Paul.

Gos, M. (1993) *The Blue Collar Professor: A Voice in the Wilderness*, paper presented at the Penn State Conference on Rhetoric and Composition, State College, PA (July).

Peckham, I. (1995) Complicity in class codes: The exclusionary function of education, in C.L.B. Dews and C.L. Law (eds.), *This Fine Place So Far From Home: Voices of Working Class Academics*, Philadelphia, PA: Temple University Press.

Rose, M. (1989) *Lives on the Boundary: The Struggles and Achievements of America's Underprepared*, New York: Free Press.

PART NINE

Language and identity

Suzanne LaBelle

INTRODUCTION

L **ANGUAGE MAY BOTH** reflect and create identity. When used to reflect identity, it serves as a cipher for the history of both an individual and a group to which that individual belongs, with certain associated attitudes about the power and prestige group members have. When used to create identity, stylistic variation shows allegiance to local groups marked by changes in linguistic variable(s). The three articles in this section offer very different perspectives on how language and identity interrelate and how we use those ciphers to create a consistent view of the world. Eckert examines the creation and reflection of large scale social categories like age and gender through language. She reconceptualizes the work done in sociolinguistics on how style operates as an expression of identity in order to focus on local and changeable norms. Olsson shows how idiolect and individual language patterns can have a practical and legal application, to rule individuals in or out of consideration as criminal suspects, based on the peculiarities of their language not liable to change for stylistic purposes. Gesser looks at the way hearing/deaf identities are negotiated in an environment where deaf is the majority culture. Eckert and Gesser explore the relationship between identity and language to help explain how the social world is created, while Olsson's work shows how the close ties between language and identity can be exploited for legal purposes. Each of the three works explain how we define difference, and once defined, how we use language to locate ourselves and others in the social world.

Gesser, a Brazilian native Portuguese speaker presents an **ethnographic** portrait of her time in Gallaudet Unviersity in Washington DC in the US. Gallaudet is the world's first university specifically catering to the deaf and hard of hearing. Established in 1864, its main language of communication is American Sign Language (ASL). Gesser chronicles her time in this environment seeking to explain ethnographically how difference in language can create different identities. Ethnography is a tool social scientists use looking to gain insights into the structure of a culture by chronicling everyday life from insider and outsider perspectives. Gesser is a participant observer at the university and is able to explore difference in identity both through her status as a non-native user of ASL and as a non-native speaker of English. She explains what it is like to be a language learner in a deaf environment, how the **hegemony** of 'deaf as deficient', something she claims is taken for granted in hearing culture, is not present in the culture of the university. Power here means being able to use the dominant language (ASL). As a second language speaker Gesser notes her amazement that using 'codes', her second and third languages, allows her to be understood. Her less powerful position as learner allows her to access and ask about social rules of language use that others might not be able to. In her efforts to explore deaf identity she also seeks to explain the difficulties of hard of hearing speakers. Their identity falls somewhere in-between the deaf and hearing world, and the use of both ASL and American English in the ASL dominant university reinforces this identity split. These hard of hearing individuals are portrayed as not fully accepted in either deaf or hearing culture. Their **hybrid** identity is reflected in their use of both languages. Gesser also looks at how those hearing students at Gallaudet will, as an act of accommodation to the Gallaudet norms, reject oral communication amongst themselves and use ASL. This is done, she claims, to avoid being seen as not sensitive to local power, and as an attempt to reverse the external 'deaf as deficient' mindset.

Eckert attempts to break down language and identity into their constituent parts, and theorize as to how these parts might be created and reinforced. She describes developments in the sociolinguistics of style and notes that more than just traditional categories like gender, age and ethnicity come into play when creating, evaluating and using different varieties of language. She looks at how local contexts can help create identity, and how certain linguistic variables can indicate more than one social identity dependent upon local context. For example, a highly sibilant 'hissing' 't' sound may indicate 'gayness' in one context, or 'nerdiness' in another. The local social environment and the speaker/listener dynamic will determine the meaning of a language variant. After reviewing work done on conception of style in the sociolinguistic tradition, she introduces the term '**bricolage**' (Hebdige 1984), that is, the use of existing symbols to create new identities. This practice is key to developing style. Variation in small pieces of language can signal social identity. Further, use of one or more feature known to speakers and listeners as affiliated with a certain group may allow for a borrowed or performed identity. Eckert also discusses how '**communities of practice**' or groups whose membership is determined by common, repeated social ritual, is where the creation of style occurs. This recognition that identity is locally constrained and highly changeable allows for a more fluid and complex theoretical model of the relationship between language and identity.

Moving on from identity creation to identity recognition, Olsson shows us how the tools of linguistic analysis can be used to pinpoint regularities and patterns in individuals' talk. These regular patterns create a kind of marker or identifier which can then be used to confirm or reject legal claims. It should be noted that there is no linguistic equivalent to the unique fingerprint (see Coulthard 2004; French 1994). Forensic linguistics, the study of these patterns for legal purposes, offers a practical application for the correlation between individual and language. Olsson relates how specific idiosyncracies of spoken language, local accent or dialect, use of pause and pitch modulation, can be quantified and then used to assist in identification. The discipline relies upon regular patterns of linguistic forms which vary according to the individual and do not change as a matter of stylistic or register selection. This may be accomplished by examining talk or written documents, by comparing historically known work to work of questionable authenticity or by exploring interaction between witnesses and legal professionals. By carefully cataloguing these individual-specific uses of language, forensic linguists can say something about the authenticity of texts or the identity of a recorded individual. Olsson discusses cases where repetition of specific phonetic features allows linguists to relate a recorded threat to a particular person. When linguistic evidence shows these systematic differences, strong claims about guilt and innocence can be made.

Identity and language relate in a complex, local and stylistically variable ways. By exploring work on style, language and the law, and the creation of local language norms, the power dynamics within any society come to light. Language can be changed to take on or deepen a particular persona, it can show an individual's history and allegiances, or it can give away guilt, proclaim innocence, depending upon changes in patterns of delivery. Identity is not fixed, but is regularized through language in specific contexts.

Issues to consider

1. What are the processes by which individuals work within and sometimes against their cultures' norms to create identities?
2. How do perception and production of identity interact through discourse?
3. Can a feature of identity be described as partially agentive? How so?
4. How is the use of differing styles and registers BOTH a way to create different identities in different contexts as well as a way to demonstrate knowledge about others in your culture?

Further reading

On forensic linguistics:

Olsson, John (2004) *Forensic Linguistics: An Introduction to Language, Crime and the Law*, London/New York: Continuum.
Schane, Sanford (2006) *Language and the Law*, London/New York: Continuum.
Shuy, Roger (2005) *Creating Language Crimes: How Law Enforcement Uses (and Abuses) Language*, New York: Oxford University Press.

On style in sociolinguistics:

Bucholtz, M. (2009) 'From Stance to Style: Gender, Interaction, and Indexicality in Mexican Immigrant Youth Slang', in Alexandra Jaffe (ed.), *Stance: Sociolinguistic Perspectives*, New York: Oxford University Press, pp. 146–170.
Eckert, P. and Rickford, J. (eds.), (2001) *Style and Sociolinguistic Variation*, Cambridge: Cambridge University Press.

On sign language:

Journal of Sign Language Linguistics (John Benjamins).
Sandler, Lillo-Martin (2006) *Sign Language and Linguistic Universals*, Cambridge: Cambridge University Press.
Sutton-Spence, R. and Woll, B. (1999) *The Linguistics of British Sign Language: An Introduction*, Cambridge: Cambridge University Press.

Suggestions for further viewing

Children of a Lesser God (1986) Randa Haines.
The Language You Cry In (1998) Ángel Serrano, Alvaro Toepke.
Mad Max: Beyond Thunderdome (1985) George Miller.

References

Coulthard, M. (2004) 'Author identification, idiolect and linguistic uniqueness', *Applied Linguistics*, 25(4): 431–447.
French, P. (1994) 'An overview of forensic phonetics with particular reference to speaker identification', *Forensic Linguistics*, 1(2): 169-181.
Hebdige, Dick (1984) *Subculture: The Meaning of Style*, New York: Methuen.

Chapter 22

Penelope Eckert

THE MEANING OF STYLE

I N HIS GROUNDBREAKING study of Martha's Vineyard, William Labov (Labov 1963) showed that phonological variables can take on very textured local meanings. The use of a raised **nucleus** in /ay/, commonly referred to as "Canadian Raising" is recognized all along the Atlantic coast as characteristic of various island dialects (Wolfram and Schilling-Estes 1996). In recent generations, the nucleus of this diphthong has been lowering to [a], presumably under the influence of the lowered variant that predominates in the mainland US and that characterizes mainstream US English. Labov's study found that the height of this nucleus was functioning as a symbolic resource in the struggle over the fate of the island. In the process, the height of the nucleus in /ay/ had taken on quite specific local meaning. It is on the nature of such meaning, and the mechanisms by which it is constructed, that I wish to focus in the following pages.

When Labov arrived on Martha's Vineyard, a growing tourist and summer home trade was bringing about major changes in the island's life and economy, and the island's inhabitants were split over the desirability of this mainland incursion. On the one hand, people engaged in the local fishing economy, dominated by old island families of English stock, saw this as a serious threat to local control of the island's life and economy. Some others saw the summer trade as an opportunity for themselves and for the island's viability more generally. The issue of mainland control vs. the traditional island culture, then, was a central ideological struggle in the local community. This was not a struggle between the mainland and the island so much as a struggle among islanders with respect to their relation to the mainland. Labov showed that the pronunciation of /ay/ had been appropriated as a symbolic resource in this struggle, as lowering of the nucleus came to be associated not simply with the mainland but with the local implications of a mainland orientation. Those engaged in the local fishing community, and youngsters who planned to remain on the island for their adulthoods, were resisting – and reversing – this lowering and showed a high rate of nucleus raising. The height of the nucleus, then, originally marking a geographic difference, became symbolic of a very local ideological struggle. Lowered /ay/ meant not simply 'mainland', but an ideological package created by the local struggle over mainland incursion.

It is probable that the height of the nucleus of /ay/ was never neutral. The mainland and the island have been in contact, and distinct, for as long as Europeans have been in both places. And as long as the pronunciation of /ay/ has been different in the two places, it has no doubt carried meaning associated with people's perception of the cultural differences between island and mainland. And this is where the study of the meaning of variation must begin. Whenever a linguistic difference becomes distinctive, the terms of this distinction are based in the social relations that surround it. Put differently, language difference can be called into service in the construction of social distinctions. People living far enough from the eastern seaboard to only know that islanders have a peculiar pronunciation of /ay/ may simply see this as a regionalism. But anyone within the area will have a "take" on the differences between mainlanders and islanders. And for them, the social meaning of the pronunciation of /ay/ will be based in that take. If they think the islanders are quaint, they will hear the raised nucleus as quaint; if they think they're dour, chances are they will hear the raised nucleus as dour. It is important to note that this characterization places the viewer as well as the viewed. Seeing islanders as quaint makes the mainlander feel sophisticated; seeing them as dour makes the mainlander feel good-hearted. The vowel itself is heard as quaint or dour, and as a natural outcome of the islanders' quaintness or dourness. This is the process that Judith Irvine and Sue Gal refer to as **iconization** (Irvine and Gal 2000). It is in the day-to-day give and take of social practice that communities come to construct a shared take on themselves, on others, and on the differences between them. As long as an aggregate of people have no particular reason to set themselves off from others, there will be little attention to what they have in common, and in contradistinction from others. When circumstances and events create an interest in difference, though, that difference can be constructed out of a variety of material, including small linguistic differences. And as the circumstances and events become sufficiently foregrounded, the social meaning of a variable may become quite specific.

It is also quite probable that /ay/ was not the only linguistic resource that people called upon in the Martha's Vineyard fray. Labov also examines its partner diphthong /aw/, which shows a somewhat different, but clearly related, distribution. And there were no doubt other resources – ways of speaking of those who were pushing the resistance probably ranged from characteristic **lexical** items to **discourse markers** and speech activities. In other words, the significance of /ay/ raising was no doubt embedded in a more general style, including clothing, movement, territory and leisure activities, that said something like "English stock fisherfolk." And it is probable that people on the island, standing in a variety of positions with respect to these political issues, showed some variability in the ways in which they selected, combined, and situationally deployed these stylistic resources.

In other words, the meaning of variation lies in its role in the construction of styles, and what I am proposing here is a study of the role of variation in stylistic practice. This involves not simply placing variables in styles, but in understanding this placement as an integral part of the construction of social meaning. This has several implications for our view of variation. First, variables do not come into a style with a specific, fixed, meaning, but take on such meaning in the process of construction of the style. This leads to the second point, that style (like language) is not a *thing* but a *practice*. It is the activity in which people create social meaning, as style is the visible manifestation of social meaning. And inasmuch as social meaning is not static, neither are styles.[1] Stylistic practice involves a process of **bricolage**, by which people combine a range of existing resources to construct new meanings or new twists on old meanings (Hebdige 1984). Small stylistic moves, such as the addition of a Mickey Mouse watch to a business ensemble, can tweak an already-existing style and the persona that it presents – in this case perhaps inserting a zest of playfulness. The tweaking, however, is not just about the tweaker, but adjusts the social world around the tweaker. Perhaps the businesswoman wearing a Mickey Mouse watch to a meeting wishes to convey a certain amount of liveliness and independence – not just for the fun of it, but more likely in order to distinguish herself from those that she sees as stodgy and uninteresting. And the nature of this stodginess is specific to the community in which she wears business clothing – it is probably not aimed at her boorish grandfather, but at her colleagues' office or business practices. And with this stylistic act, she puts the distinction on the table for all to see.[2]

The selection of variables for making stylistic moves is based, then, in the speaker's interpretation of the meaning potential of the available resources. The mainland-island separation, and the dialect differences that go with that separation, make /ay/ and /aw/ prime linguistic resources for building styles that embed that separation in some way. The general mainland-island significance of nucleus height in /ay/ is vivified locally by the foregrounding of current social issues. At another time, in other words, the issues associated with island-mainland difference may have been quite different, and speakers may have deployed /ay/ in very different ways. One has only to look at the way that features of African American Vernacular English were deployed in the minstrel tradition and comedy such as Amos 'n Andy, evoking a benign, shuffling, inept and foolish **stereotype** (Rickford and Rickford 2000), and contrast this with the more recent white adolescent use of **AAVE** features to lay claim to coolness (Bucholtz 1999). In these two eras, African American linguistic features have served as very different stylistic resources. In other words, the use of a stylistic resource affects not only the receiving style, but the resource itself, feeding back into discourses of race, ethnicity, class, etc. One might consider, for example, that the use of Chicano features in the Southwest that Jane Hill (Hill 1993) discusses has the effect of constructing Chicano features – and their speakers – as a comic population. Stylistic resources, whether features of racialized dialects or of geographically defined dialects, come with a meaning potential that becomes more precise in the local context.

The study of social meaning in variation, then, needs to trace two kinds of patterns – what /ay/ raising offers as potential meanings by virtue of its larger distribution (e.g. across the eastern seaboard – and in the opposition between mainland and island), and how it comes to be deployed locally and combined with other resources, to constitute a "fisherfolk" style.

Things in the world become stylistic resources by virtue of their place in local discourse – in the collaborative work of sense-making. While individuals make stylistic moves, such as wearing a Mickey Mouse watch, they do so in cooperation with, or with reference to, the people around them. Since a stylistic move is to be put out into a community for the purpose of being interpreted, speakers select resources on the basis of their potential comprehensibility in that community. This does not mean that people select only resources that will be comprehensible, since certain styles may call for some mystification. James Ferguson, in his study of the deployment of style in the Zambian Copperbelt (Ferguson 1999), notes that lack of interpretability is key to a cosmopolitan style. But the uninterpretability itself is invoked because it is interpretable on a meta level – the cosmopolitan is precisely someone who is supposed to have access to knowledge and resources that are locally inaccessible. And the Copperbelt cosmopolitan no doubt reaches out for resources that are mystifying but not random or off-the-wall.

I have argued elsewhere (Eckert 2000; Eckert and McConnell-Ginet 2003) that the community of practice (Lave and Wenger 1991; Wenger 2000) is a prime locus of stylistic construction. Every speaker participates in a variety of **communities of practice**, or collections of people who engage together in a particular enterprise – a garage band, a family, a gang, a car pool, an office. The community looks out jointly on the social landscape, interpreting the landscape, and constructing their place and stance within that landscape. And individuals' place in the community is closely related to their participation in that process of construction. An important part of this meaning-making is the social characterization and evaluation of people and groups out in that landscape, and of their stylistic practices. It is in this process of meaning-making that speakers assign meaning to stylistic resources, and assess them as potential resources for their own stylistic moves.

Stylistic practice, then, involves adapting linguistic variables available out in the larger world to the construction of social meaning on a local level. The association of Mickey Mouse watches with children and playfulness does not in and of itself predict that a businesswoman will wear it to work. But in doing so, that businesswoman transforms the watch into an expression of independence within the business context. I am advocating, therefore, a study of variation that traces the path of a variable from its general state of availability to its specific deployment. Ultimately, this means that one might begin with a style, tracing the contributions of individual resources to that style. This is a reversal of the traditional approach to variation, which focuses on variables in virtue of their role in the dialect system or in linguistic change in progress.

1. Style in sociolinguistic variation

The picture I am offering of style and of the social meaning of variation is a fairly radical departure from established practice in the field of variation (and it is certainly not intended as a challenge to that practice, but as an extension of it). The early and groundbreaking studies of variation, seeking patterns of variation across large populations (Labov 1966; Wolfram 1969; Trudgill 1974), focused on correlations of linguistic variables with the broad demographic categories of class, age and gender. From this tradition there emerged a view of social meaning as directly associated with – even determined by – these categories. Thus, it has been common to view variables as marking membership in, or affiliation with, class and gender categories (and to view age differences as representing apparent time). But these broad demographic patterns are as much the result as the source of social meaning in variation, and understanding them requires that we explore the relation between local meaning and these larger distributions.

The predominant approach to style in variation has focused on a continuum of casualness and formality. Introduced by William Labov in his study of New York City (Labov 1966), this view of style allowed Labov to locate intra-speaker variation seamlessly in the broader patterns of variation across large communities. It quite explicitly located stylistic variation in the speaker's class position. The class stratification of linguistic variables assigned prestige to the speech at the upper end and stigma to the speech at the lower end. Prestige and stigma, then, have come to be the primary social meanings associated with variables, and formality brings a focus on prestige and an attempt to avoid stigma. With social meaning located in demographic categories, stylistic agency emerged in variation studies as a means of tempering one's appearance of category membership. It is important to consider that Labov's emphasis, though, particularly in subsequent writing (Labov 2000), has been not on social meaning but on attention paid to speech, so that the importance of casualness and formality lies in their effect on speakers' self-monitoring – hence on their ability to avoid stigma.

This view of style has not gone unchallenged. Most notably, Allan Bell (Bell 1984) challenged attention paid to speech as underlying stylistic variation, arguing that it is a mediating variable and that we need to ask what in the situations is causing speakers to pay more or less attention.[3] His answer to the question is that speakers shift styles as accommodation to their audience – primarily their addressee. He argues, further, that shifts in style as a function of topic are due to an association of topics with particular audiences. In Bell's recent expansion of his theory (Bell 2001), he argues further that a speaker's spontaneous adoption of a style (i.e. not in response to topic or present audience) is done with an audience in mind. This is tantamount to saying that the speaker's identity is embedded in social relations, which is clearly true. But it also suggests that the speaker is focusing on a specific imagined audience, and limits the speaker's agency to adaptation to pre-existing styles and social categories. This is a serious limitation that does not allow for creativity and change.

Nik Coupland (Coupland 1980, 1985, 2000) provided an early exploration of the use of variation to construct personae. His study of a disc jockey on Cardiff radio (Coupland 2000) shows a speaker using a variety of dialect features, calling on a variety of social meanings, as he moves around a complex social space. His strategic use of a range of dialect features yields a fluid persona rather than an adaptation to static types. Variation, in this case, is a resource for calling on a variety of places in social space, reminiscent of the acts of identity described by Le Page and Tabouret-Keller (LePage and Tabouret-Keller 1985). Where Labov's treatment of style focuses on the vertical axis of social class, the work of Bell and Coupland brings in the horizontal. Coupland, furthermore, argues that stylistic practice involves not simply the use of native variables, but brings in resources beyond one's own native dialect. The disc jockey's use of Cardiff features reaches out into the social landscape, and assigns meanings to these features based on commonly-held views of their socio-geographical significance.

Before I move on to discuss this process of meaning-assignment further, I would like to come back to the relation between the axis of formality that dominates Labov's view of style, and the persona-construction view that I am exploring here. John Fischer, in the first quantitative study of variation (Fischer 1958), examined some schoolchildren's use of the suffix -*ing*, and found several interesting correlations. He found that boys reduced -*ing* more than girls, that more roustabout ('typical') boys reduced -*ing* more overall than boys who were teachers' pets. Finally, he found that all boys reduced -*ing* less in interviews than in conversation. One can argue that -*ing* is a stigmatized variant and that boys avoid stigma less than girls, and roustabout boys even less than teachers' pets, and that everyone is avoiding stigma when speaking with adults. However, it is hard to view reduced -*ing* on its own as stigmatized. While certain styles making extreme use of reduction may be stigmatized in the judgment of some hearers, this variant is not in itself stigmatized and is, in fact, generally quite well-received when an upper middle class speaker is acting casual and friendly. Such a speaker would be less likely to use **negative concord** or (in the case of a New Yorker) an extremely raised /aeh/ or a stop variant for /th/ to this purpose. The general meaning of -*ing* reduction around the English-speaking world, though, is 'informal' and the use of this variant will only be stigmatized where informality is viewed as inappropriate. An informal style may be seen as insolent, even threatening under certain circumstances. The frequent reduction of -*ing* probably contributed to a devil-may-care style among Fisher's roustabout boys. In interviews with adults, kids are no doubt being more formal, but one might consider that in their formality, they (or at least the roustabout boys) are also pulling back on the devil-may-care self-presentation.

Then what is the meaning of formality? Judith Irvine (Irvine 1979) has pointed out that the use of the notion of formality in the study of language has touched on several dimensions. For instance, formality can be related to seriousness, or unfamiliarity, or social distance, or deference. While multiples of these commonly co-occur, we can no longer afford to conflate them if we are to focus on meaning in variation. Seriousness itself can include gravity, earnestness, concern with important matters. And indeed, speaking formally can confer gravity or importance on situations and topics. A speaker may manage style in an effort to sound more formal in particular ways – to present oneself as a serious person, to show that one takes the subject matter seriously, to show respect or deference to another, to call upon a positional, public identity, to create distance. While these all merge to some extent in the kinds of interactions found in sociolinguistic interviews, in day-to-day life they may not.

2. Stylistic practice and the meanings of variables

Common practice views variables as directly **indexing** social categories, hence it is not uncommon to refer to sound changes that women lead in as "women's changes", and for divergence between male and female speech to be attributed to men's avoidance of sounding like women. It is particularly common for this kind of attribution to emerge in discussions of gender. In a similar spirit, the Japanese press has accused Japanese teenage girls who use assertive forms normally associated with male speech of trying to speak like men. In fact, the "like women" or "like men" refers not to women and men so much as to characteristics associated with women and men – characteristics that are commonly judged undesirable in the other gender. In fact, Japanese girls using assertive forms are not trying to be boys, but to be assertive. This assertiveness, in turn, is part of a very female teenage trendy style (Okamoto 1995). In other words, linguistic choices index such things as attitudes, stances, and activities that in turn are associated with social categories. Variables index these categories *indirectly* (Silverstein 1976; Ochs 1991). It is this indirect nature of the relation between variables and categories that allows variation to be a resource not simply for the indexing of place in the social matrix but for the construction of new places and of nuanced social meanings.

My own work in Detroit suburban high schools (Eckert 1989, 2000) was designed to get at the local meaning of class for adolescents. After all, the class categories upon which sociolinguists had theorized the social dynamics for the spread of change were adult categories, and their components – educational attainment, occupation, income – are still in the future for most adolescents. In an effort to understand how class is experienced in adolescence, I embarked on an ethnography in a high school and found that class is mediated in the high school by categories that re-cast class in the immediate school context. These categories lean heavily on style. In fact, style – in dress, in demeanor, in activity choice as well as in language – is central to the construction of social categories and meaning. In predominantly white schools around the Detroit area (and with variations across the US) there is a polarization between two opposed, class-based social categories. On the one hand, there are *jocks*, kids who base their social lives in the school institution, participating in the extracurricular and college-prep sphere, and constituting a middle class culture. In opposition to the jocks are the *burnouts*, a working class culture who reject the school as a locus of social life and activity, maintaining neighborhood ties and orienting to the urban area where they seek both stimulation and their working future.

It took no time to see that there was a major social opposition among the students – from the moment I walked into the school the opposition was clearly visible. What I later came to know were jocks were hanging around the student activities areas at lunchtime, wearing pastel colors, preppy styles, candy-colored makeup and feathered hair (the girls, anyway), and school jackets. What I came to recognize as burnouts were hanging out in the school smoking area, wearing dark colors, rock concert tees, dark eye makeup and long straight hair (the girls), jeans jackets or Detroit and auto factory jackets, and wallet chains (the boys). Variation does a tremendous amount of symbolic work, but language does not work on its own and no linguistic variant works on its own. First of all, language is part of a broader **semiotic** system that includes such things as clothing, territory, musical taste, activities, and stances. The burnouts' urban orientation emerges in the use of symbols of street smarts such as wallet chains, symbols of urban affiliation such as Detroit jackets and auto factory jackets. Their claim to engagement in the realities of life outside of school shows up in symbols of toughness (e.g. leather jackets, wristbands or boots with studs), and in dark-colored clothing. There is a seamless relation between these visual symbols and the burnouts' use of urban variants of the late stages of the Northern Cities shift. The backing of /e/, and /uh/, and the raising of the nucleus of /ay/ (Eckert 2000) are all changes that are apparently progressing outward to the suburbs from the urban area, and the burnouts are the primary carriers of these changes. As shown in Table 22.1, burnouts show a consistent lead over jocks in the use of advanced variants of these changes. Burnouts' rejection of the standardizing school institution emerges in evading school authority in a variety of ways, the flaunting of controlled substances, the refusal to use lockers and the cafeteria – and the use of negative concord. The jocks, meanwhile, offer a "clean

Table 22.1: Varbrul factor weights for use of urban sound changes and negative concord, by gender and social category

	Girls	Boys	Burnouts	Jocks	Input	Sig.
/uh/	n.s.	n.s.	0.571	0.437	0.494	0.000
/e/	n.s.	n.s.	0.540	0.467	0.262	0.016
/ay/	0.586	0.434	0.707	0.257	0.009	0.045
neg. concord	0.412	0.567	0.708	0.306	0.238	0.000

cut" image including symbols of institutional affiliation such as decorating their lockers, wearing school jackets, and using standard grammar. Their institutional orientation includes an anti-urban orientation, which shows up in not only an avoidance of urban phonological variables, but in some cases a reversal of the urban changes that the burnouts lead in (the lowering of /e/ and the **fronting** of /uh/).

Of course jock and burnout styles can be seen as fairly stable combinations of variables, and one could accord these variables the meanings of "jock" and "burnout." However, the jocks and the burnouts account for at most half of the student population of the school. The rest of the student population is quite **heterogeneous**, but nonetheless dominated by the **hegemonic** jock-burnout opposition. Thus, those who are not jocks or burnouts refer to themselves as "in-betweens" and describe themselves in relation to their distance from jocks and/or burnouts, or the characteristics they share with one or the other category. And for this entire cohort, the use of variables is related to individuals' navigation of the broader semiotic space. Most notably, if we look at the larger student body, we find that the use of urban vowel shifts is associated with urban orientation more broadly. Thus, as shown in Table 22.2, the kids in the school who spend leisure time "cruising" Detroit, whether jock, burnout or in-between, show a significantly higher use of urban variables than those who do not.

Other subtle personal differences show up in the distinct usage of different friendship groups, or network clusters, within and across social categories. Not all burnouts are alike, for example. Among the burnout girls, there are two main friendship clusters – the larger group who consider themselves "regular" or "normal" burnouts. These girls' identification as burnouts is based primarily in their working class orientation and their anti-school stance. While they are regularly at odds with authority for such things as skipping school, illegal substance use and a general rejection of adult intervention in their personal lives, they do not get into serious trouble. In contrast, a somewhat smaller cluster of girls pride themselves in being "the biggest burnouts" – I have heard "regular" burnouts refer to them as "burned-out burnouts." These girls are more wild, and pride themselves on coming to school stoned on a regular basis, being in serious academic trouble, staying out all night and getting in trouble with the police. There are also different kinds of girls involved in school activities – the "squeaky-clean" jocks, and a group of girls who participate enthusiastically in school activities, but who also like to "party" and some of whom have experimented with soft drugs. These girls are sometimes referred to as "partying jocks." Finally, there is a cluster of girls who participate in many school activities, but who eschew what they view as the jocks'

Table 22.2: Relation between use of urban variables and participation in cruising among white Detroit suburban adolescents

	Cruisers	Non-Cruisers	Input	Sig
(uh) backing	0.563	0.458	0.422	0.000
(e) backing	0.544	0.464	0.331	0.029
(ay) raising	0.765	0.381	0.011	0.000
negative concord	0.777	0.294	0.106	0.000

Source: Eckert 2000.

popularity orientation. They consider themselves more down to earth, and many of themselves consider themselves more serious. Figure 22.1 shows the use of negative concord across these five network clusters from the wild girls, or the burned-out burnouts at the **vernacular** extreme, through the more serious girls at the most standard extreme. As this figure shows, the percentage of use of negative concord is a delicate indication of one's engagement in the standard institutional culture.

Qing Zhang has taken the view of variables as stylistic resources a major step further, showing that variation can be a key resource for the forging of new categories and the identities with which categories are co-constructed. Zhang (2001) examined the speech of two kinds of managers in business in Beijing – managers in traditional state-owned business, and managers in the new foreign-owned businesses. The latter are part of a new and growing young elite, often referred to as "Chinese yuppies." The yuppies' engagement in the international market, including their engagement with non-mainland Chinese, pulls them into a cosmopolitan milieu and requires the production of a cosmopolitan persona. They are pioneering a materialistic and cosmopolitan life style in Beijing, and in doing so setting themselves quite apart from their peers in state-owned businesses. In addition to the active construction of "life style" through the consumption of home furnishings, clothing, toys and leisure activities – or one might say, to go with these – the yuppies are developing a new and distinctive speech style. Perhaps the most salient resource in this linguistic construction is the use of the full tone, which is a feature of non-mainland Mandarin. This variable, completely foreign to Beijing and never appearing in the speech of the managers in state-owned businesses, brings a very clear cosmopolitan quality to their speech. Zhang emphasizes that the speakers are not imitating Hong Kong speech, but calling on a Hong Kong feature to bring Beijing into the transnational sphere. This is accomplished, furthermore, with the selective use of more local features.

Zhang went on to delve into the construction of meaning in local Beijing variables: rhotacization, lenition and the interdental pronunciation of /z/, all of which are quite saliently associated with Beijing Mandarin. She traced the meanings of these variables to salient personae in Beijing culture – personae that appear commonly in modern literature: the "alley saunterer" and the "smooth operator" – quite distinct male urban personae. She shows that the yuppics selectively adopt (or reject) these variables as a function of the nature of the personae they are developing. Women avoid both the smooth operator and the alley saunterer variables, as neither of these character types is useful to a business woman. The men, on the other hand, reject the alley saunterer

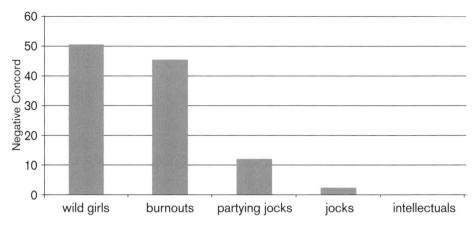

Figure 22.1: Relation between negative concord and girls' network cluster.

variable as reflecting a character who is too feckless for a transnational businessman, but adopt a moderate amount of the smooth operator variable. The yuppies, thus, recombine locally available resources to construct a new, cosmopolitan – yet still Beijing – persona. On the other hand, the managers in state-owned businesses, still linked to local networks, continue to use a high level of Beijing features, and never use full tone.

3. New variables

Growing out of dialectology on the one hand, and historical linguistics on the other, the study of variation has focused on variables in virtue of their status as regional markers or as interesting sound changes in progress. A couple of "stable" variables – *ing* and /th/ and /dh/ have also been studied – almost as touchstones of style and class. Otherwise, the net has not been cast very wide. A particularly interesting stable variable is the release of word-final stops. We're all aware of our use of t-release – and even aspiration – when we're being emphatic: "I did not[h]!", or when we're being exaggeratedly precise – particularly when we're annoyed at someone's failure to follow: "/a/ is not[h] a consonant[h]." We're also aware of our use of it when we're angry: "Cut[h] that[h] out[h]." It's worth noting that one would probably rarely release all the occurrences in this latter utterance, but the release of the /t/ in *that*, and then the release in *cut* signals a continuous increase in the level of anger or annoyance. /t/ also gets released in academic styles. So where does /t/ release get its meaning? British speakers of English regularly release their /t/s, and Americans adopt this feature when imitating British English. The age-old stereotype of the British, and British English, as superior, intelligent and educated, is no doubt at work here. A distinction made at the international level, then, seems to be providing American speakers with a resource for signaling superiority of a variety of sorts, but it seems to be primarily limited to intelligence, education, articulateness. Mary Bucholtz (Bucholtz 1996) has noted the use of this variable by a group of high school girls fashioning themselves as geeks. These girls saw themselves as intelligent – not as goody-goody good students, but as smarter than their teachers. Their use of /t/ release was a prominent resource in their development of a distinctive "intellectual" verbal style. /t/ release is also often heard as Jewish, and particularly as Orthodox. Sarah Benor (Benor 2002) examined this variable in a study of kids in an Orthodox community, and found that it indexed masculinity, inasmuch as masculinity is tied with Talmudic study. Further, she found that – among both boys and girls – those who had been to Yeshiva released /t/ more than those who had not. In addition, she has shown nice anecdotal evidence of the use of this variable in interaction, as boys release /t/ when they're making a point in Talmudic discussion.

At the same time, /t/ release has also been identified as a feature of gay speech. In a study of a radio debate between a gay-identified lawyer and a straight-identified lawyer, Kathryn Campbell-Kibler, Sarah Roberts and Robert Podesva found that the gay lawyer indeed released more /t/ than his opponent. Reluctant to subscribe to a monolithic view of "gay" speech, Podesva has continued this work in a study of gay professionals as they adjust their style moving from more to less saliently gay situations. Comparing the language of a medical student, in the clinic with patients and at a barbecue with his friends, Podesva found a subtle pattern in the use of /t/ release. The medical student, Heath, adopts a highly competent and educated persona in the clinic, but a playful "bitchy diva" persona among his friends at the barbecue. As it turns out, he uses significantly more /t/ release in the clinic than at the barbecue, in keeping with the meaning of preciseness, intelligence and education that one would certainly want to evoke when functioning as a physician. At the barbecue, however, the bursts of the /t/ releases are rarer but significantly longer. This offers a wholly new view of the nature of variables. Podesva's interpretation of this is that the long burst is a particular way of exaggerating /t/ release, and that what is being conveyed is a kind of fussy hyper-articulateness, to the point of prissiness. In other words, the exaggerated release is intended not to convey intelligence, but prissiness – in keeping with the "bitchy diva" persona that Heath enjoys performing with his friends.

It should not be ignored that until these people studied /t/ release, the only time linguists had paid attention to word-final stops is in the study of cluster reduction in AAVE. Are these independent linguistic facts? Probably not entirely. While cluster reduction in AAVE may be historically unrelated to unreleased /t/ in Standard American English, the presence or absence of word-final /t/ is highly salient in the social evaluation of the speech of African Americans. Andrea Kortenhoven (pc) reports that her group of African American friends in high school had a special stylistic feature, the use of *antyways* for *anyway*. Seen as school-teachery talk, this insertion of consonants was no doubt in recognition of the distinctiveness between standard English and AAVE. Sensitivity to /t/ release, then, seems to permeate US language ideology and offer material for the construction of local stylistic features. Building on the large-scale opposition between British and American English, combined with the historic construction of Americans as rough upstarts in opposition to the refined and educated British, /t/ release provides a global resource that can, in turn, be put to local use. The precise meaning of /t/ release in actual use depends on the particular style – Orthodox Jew (learned), California geek girl (smart), bitchy diva (prissy) – that it's incorporated into.

4. Conclusion

Sociolinguistic variation is a central means by which the social is embedded in language. To understand how variation works, we have to concern ourselves with the nature of the social meaning it carries, and the mechanisms by which variation comes to be endowed with meaning. Most particularly, we need to examine the use of variation up close, to understand how (and to what extent) it is used to express very local and personal meanings. To do this, we have to focus on the role of variation in constructing personae – to see how people deploy linguistic resources to create styles. This paper has argued for an approach to variation that beings with style and works down to individual variables, and one that begins with the potential social meanings of variables and works down to the unfolding of those meanings in styles.

Notes

1   Some styles (e.g. corporate male style) depend on an appearance of stability. One could say that they resist change, but I am inclined to say that they actively maintain stasis. Every time a corporate man buys a tie he aligns himself with respect to a range of ideologies, and the selection of a conservative one is as much a stylistic move as the selection of one with naked women or palm trees.

2   Of course, the move may backfire, as those around her can interpret the watch as they see fit, and this is where power enters into one's ability to make meaningful moves – hence to make meaning.

3   I believe that this is inherent in Labov's account, and that he intends attention paid to speech to be the cognitive consequence of situations, which in turn runs the process of variation. In other words, a casual situation, or fear, or distraction, leads a speaker to lose control of speech, and what emerges with this loss of control is the vernacular.

References

Bell, A. (1984) "Language Style as Audience Design," *Language in Society*, 13: 145–204.

——— (2001) "Back in Style: Reworking Audience Design," in P. Eckert and J.R. Rickford (eds.), *Style and Sociolinguistic Variation*, Cambridge: Cambridge University Press, pp. 139–169.

Benor, S. (2002) *Sounding Learned: The Gendered Use of /t/ in Orthodox Jewish English*, Penn working papers in linguistics: Selected papers from NWAV 2000.

Bucholtz, M. (1996) "Geek the Girl: Language, Femininity and Female Nerds," in N. Warner, J. Ahlers, L. Bilmes, M. Oliver, S. Wertheim and M. Chen (eds.), *Gender and Belief Systems*, Berkeley, CA: Berkeley Women and Language Group, pp. 119–131.

——— (1999) "You Da Man: Narrating the Racial Other in the Production of White Masculinity," *Journal of Sociolinguistics*, 3(4): 443–460.

Coupland, N. (1980) "Style-Shifting in a Cardiff Work Setting," *Language in Society*, 9(1): 1–12.

——— (1985) "'Hark, Hark, the Lark': Social Motivations for Phonological Style-Shifting," *Language and Communication*, 5(3): 153–171.

——— (2000) "Language, situation and the relational self: Theorizing dialect-style in sociolinguistics," in P. Eckert and J.R. Rickford (eds.), *Style and Sociolinguistic Variation*, Cambridge: Cambridge University Press, pp. 185–210.

Eckert, P. (1989) *Jocks and Burnouts: Social Categories and Identity in the High School*, New York: Teachers College Press.

—— (2000) *Linguistic Variation as Social Practice*, Oxford, Blackwell.

—— and S. McConnell-Ginet (2003) *Language and Gender*, Cambridge: Cambridge University Press.

Ferguson, J. (1999) *Expectations of Modernity: Myths and Meanings of Urban Life on the Zambian Copperbelt*, Berkeley, CA: University of California Press.

Fischer, J.L. (1958) "Social influences on the choice of a linguistic variant," *Word*, 14: 47–56.

Hebdige, D. (1984) *Subculture: The Meaning of Style*, New York: Methuen.

Hill, J.H. (1993) "Hasta la vista, baby: Anglo Spanish in the American Southwest," *Critique of Anthropology*, 13(2): 145–176.

Irvine, J.T. (1979) "Formality and Informality in Communicative Events," *American Anthropologist*, 81(4): 773–790.

—— and S. Gal (2000) "Language ideology and linguistic differentiation," in P.V. Kroskrity (ed.), *Regimes of Language: Ideologies, Polities, and Identities*, Santa Fe, NM: School of American Research Press, pp. 35–83.

Labov, W. (1963) "The Social Motivation of a Sound Change," *Word*, 18: 1–42.

—— (1966) *The Social Stratification of English in New York City*, Washington, DC: Center for Applied Linguistics.

—— (2000) "The Anatomy of Style Shifting," in P. Eckert and J.R. Rickford (eds.), *Style and Sociolinguistic Variation*, Cambridge: Cambridge University Press.

Lave, J. and E. Wenger (1991) *Situated Learning: Legitimate Peripheral Participation*, Cambridge: Cambridge University Press.

LePage, R.B. and A. Tabouret-Keller (1985) *Acts of Identity*, Cambridge: Cambridge University Press.

Ochs, E. (1991) "Indexing gender," in A. Duranti and C. Goodwin (eds.), *Rethinking Context: Language as an Interactive Phenomenon*, Cambridge: Cambridge University Press.

Okamoto, S. (1995) "'Tasteless' Japanese: Less 'Feminine' Speech Among Young Japanese Women," in K. Hall and M. Bucholtz (eds.), *Gender Articulated: Language and the Socially Constructed Self*, New York/London: Routledge, pp. 297–325.

Rickford, J.R. and R.J. Rickford (2000) *Spoken Soul: The Story of Black English*, New York: John Wiley and Sons.

Silverstein, M. (1976) "Shifters, Linguistic Categories, and Cultural Description," in K. Basso and H. A. Selby (eds.), *Meaning in Anthropology*, Albuquerque, NM: University of New Mexico Press, pp. 11–56.

Trudgill, P. (1974) *The Social Differentiation of English in Norwich*. Cambridge: Cambridge University Press.

Wenger, E. (2000) *Communities of Practice*, New York: Cambridge University Press.

Wolfram, W. (1969) *A Sociolinguistic Description of Detroit Negro Speech*, Washington DC: Center for Applied Linguistics.

—— and N. Schilling-Estes (1996) "On the Social Basis of Phonetic Resistance: The Shifting Status of Outer Banks /ay/," in J. Arnold, R. Blake, B. Davidson, S. Schwenter, and J. Solomon (eds.), *Sociolinguistic variation: Data, theory and analysis*, Stanford CA: CSLI Press.

Zhang, Q. (2001) *Changing Economics, Changing Markets: A Sociolinguistic Study of Chinese Yuppies*, unpublished PhD dissertation, Stanford, CA: Stanford University.

Chapter 23

John Olsson

THE MAN WITH THE BASEBALL BAT

I MAGINE YOU ARE about 17 years old and someone threatens you with a baseball bat. If this were not bad enough, imagine also that you are blind. One morning your mobile phone rings. You answer it and this is what you hear: 'I have a baseball bat for your kneecaps,' the voice at the other end says.

The background to the case was that two youths at a blind school in the south of England got into an argument with each other about a girl. Angry words were exchanged between the boys and there was a lot of bad feeling between them. The school did its best to sort the problem out but nothing was resolved and eventually one of the boys left the school. The boy who remained at the school was the one who received the threatening call. He believed that the voice belonged to the father of the other boy. The police were called and interviewed the suspect.

The boy who made the complaint had had the presence of mind to record the conversation as it took place. He had previously received an anonymous call and was almost ready for it. Being able to do this when you are blind takes not only ingenuity but a cool head as well, especially if you are being threatened at the same time.

The telephone call had also been made on a mobile phone, with the caller's number being suppressed. This is something you can do on a phone in the United Kingdom quite easily. However, in some countries it is not possible. The fact that the recording was from a mobile phone onto a mobile phone meant that the sound quality of the call was poorer than it would probably have been had the call been placed from a landline. My instructions from the police force[1] where the offence took place were straightforward: was the anonymous caller the same person as the known speaker?

For the reader who is interested in how this kind of inquiry is handled, you can break a voice identification down into a number of separate headings:

- First, are the two samples apparently of the same dialect/accent?
- Second, are the voices of the same type?
- Third, if we look at pronunciation of certain speech sounds (called 'phonemes') are they similar across the known and questioned voices?

As regards the first point, the voices both shared the same dialect, actually from the North West of Wales. One feature of this dialect is the way many speakers pronounce the sound 'k'. It is not unlike the way some Scottish speakers pronounce the last sound in the word 'loch'. It is partly produced towards the back of the mouth in an area known as the velum, hence the term 'velar sound'. This sound appeared in the word 'knee**c**aps', '**c**ollege', and also in the word '**g**ot'. The 'g' sound in 'got' is similar to 'k', except that when you say 'g' you actually vibrate your vocal cords, but when you say 'k' you do not. Try it and see. As you can hear, aside from the presence or absence of the vocal cords, it is the same sound. In the interview the suspect, referring to his son, said 'he doesn't know whether he's **c**oming or **g**oing'. The velar sound appeared in both these words in the 'k' and the 'g'. However, although we find the velar 'k' and 'g' in this speaker's dialect, in the case of this speaker it was particularly strong. In my view it was much stronger than is usually the case. I felt this was distinctive.

Another interesting feature of this speaker was the way he pronounced words like 'speak'. At one point in the phone call he taunts the blind boy by saying 'Speak to me'. When he says 'speak' he actually says 's**b**eak'. On listening to the word 'kneecaps' I noticed the same phenomenon, 'kneeca**b**s'. In the course of his police interview the suspect said, again referring to the time period of which his son and the other boy had been at loggerheads with each other, 'over a period of years'. Here, the word 'period' sounded more like '**b**eriod'.

The next question to consider was whether the voices were of the same type. Phoneticians use a number of descriptors for voice types. At one end of the spectrum you have a voice like Marilyn Monroe – especially when at its most persuasive. Listening to a voice like this you have the overwhelming impression of being 'soft-soaped' or seduced by the speaker. What you are listening to, for the most part, is simply breath. The vocal cords are wide open and the breath is continuous. It's like a constant rush of air. Hence phoneticians talk about a 'breathy' voice. At the opposite end of the spectrum you have a voice which sounds not unlike a door creaking. You may remember Dr Kissinger, the globetrotting Secretary of State for the United States of America back in the 1970s. His voice would literally creak as he talked. Try it yourself. How you do it, is to lower your voice as much as possible and say 'aah'. Listen to the creak in the voice. Not surprisingly, such a voice is known as a 'creaky' voice. Here the vocal cords are almost completely closed off at one end. The actor Humphrey Bogart tended to have a **creaky voice**, and you will often hear media pundits with such a voice. It is also known as the 'expert's' voice. Do not imagine, however, that only men have a voice like this: women can also have creaky voices. In the same way, you will also find men with breathy voices. A good example was the actor Derek Nimmo. In case these names are unfamiliar to you, if you are near a computer, do a search on Youtube. You will find many references to each of the people I have named here and you will be able to listen to the voices for yourself.

Right in the middle of *breathy* and *creaky* you have the normal, modal voice. This is what our suspect had: a completely middle of the road way of producing his voice – with, however, one exception. The voice was very tense, perhaps even stressed. This did not appear to be just because he was in a stressful situation, either on the phone or in the police interview room. It seemed to be a quality that was always there.

In the police interview he repeatedly denied having made the threatening phone call. However, based on the number of similarities across the known and questioned voices, I felt there was a high probability that it was him, and said so in my report. He continued to deny responsibility for a while, but then – as sometimes happens – changed his mind when he got to court, and decided to plead. The court found him guilty of sending a malicious communication, which is a serious offence and he was fined heavily. The magistrate said that had it not been for his age and health, the consequences for him might have been more serious.

At about the same time I began another voice identification from North Wales. A couple had been burgled at about 2 AM near Wrexham. Raiders had stolen credit cards, mobile phones and the couple's car. High on a cocktail of drinks and drugs the perpetrators had driven the car recklessly through the town, throwing out personal possessions they had found in the vehicle, including the male victim's works uniform. They then trashed the couple's car and left it on a housing estate. A little later the burglars received a phone call. The voice at the other end appeared to be the female victim, but what the burglars did not know was that they were actually speaking to a police officer. She very cleverly constructed the conversation to get the maximum amount of conversation out of the two young men. This is very helpful in voice identification cases, where you need as wide a range of speech sounds, indications of vocal expression and voice dynamic as possible.

Based on knowledge of the local criminal fraternity police officers thought they recognized the voices and the following morning several homes were raided in the Wrexham vicinity, including that of Andrew Caveney, aged 23 and Daniel Roberts, aged 21. Along with the conversation with the burglars in the car, I also received the interview tapes, one with each of the suspects.

The sound quality on interview tapes differs greatly from that found in phone calls, especially mobile phone calls. Interviews are conducted in what are known as PACE rooms. PACE stands for the Police and Criminal Evidence Act. It was introduced in 1985 to regulate, amongst other things, the way suspects and witnesses are interviewed by police in criminal cases. Prior to this, PACE interviews were not taped, but were written down in note form and then compiled into statements. This caused many suspects to claim that they had been 'verballed' by officers. Verballing is the process whereby a statement is altered to 'fit' someone up. The tape-recording of interviews has put a stop to most verballing claims since, if the quality of the sound on the tape is clear enough, usually there is no dispute as to what was said.

In contrast to the quality found on most interview tapes, mobile phones usually present the voice analyst with problems of clarity, signal interference and environmental noise. In the present instance the suspects were talking while driving. A moving vehicle is not the best place to try to identify a voice, especially if the car is being driven with the windows open.

Both of the voices appeared to be from the Wrexham area. The elder male's voice was particularly distinctive when pronouncing words like 'back' and 'smack'. At one point he tells the caller that she is lucky he did not come upstairs to her bedroom and wake her up. He says he often does this and enjoys giving his female victims a good 'smack' or 'slap'. I found this speaker's voice very distinctive: he had a loud, harsh voice with a nasal quality, which was evident both in the tape and the police interview.

The second voice was also very distinctive. The speaker appeared to have a stammer and often garbled his sentences in particular ways. Only about 3 per cent of the population have any kind of stammer, and it is not always accompanied by grammatical problems, which was the case here. Evidently, this was a very nervous speaker who, once he began to stammer, would then mangle up his grammar by putting in words which did not belong, and even inventing words on occasion.

Had the crime not been so serious the PACE interviews with the two perpetrators would have been amusing. Their efforts to deny their crime bordered on the inventively pathological. They fabricated the most marvellous excuses as to their whereabouts. However, their voices betrayed them completely. They finally admitted to their crimes when presented with the voice evidence and were sentenced to three years' imprisonment.

Note

1   To protect the victim in this instance I am not revealing any identifiable details of this case.

Chapter 24

Audrei Gesser

LEARNING ABOUT HEARING PEOPLE IN THE LAND OF THE DEAF: AN ETHNOGRAPHIC ACCOUNT

T HIS ARTICLE IS a personal account, grounded in some concepts of postcolonial/ cultural studies (Bhabha 1990, 1994; Hall 1992), interactional sociolinguistics (Gumperz 1986; Jacob and Ochs 1995), and in theoretical and methodological **ethnographic** perspectives (Agar 1980, 1994; Erickson and Shultz 1981; Hammersley and Atkinson 1983; Anzul *et al.* 1991), describing my journey in the land of the Deaf[1]— Gallaudet University. Even though I came to this place to learn about Deaf people's lives, in relation to their culture(s), language(s) and identity(s), what became more interesting to me during my stay at Gallaudet was hearing people's behavior, which in turn, revealed a lot about Deaf people's lives as well. In this sense, I consider that in some situations both hearing and Deaf individuals might overlap in their cultural, linguistic, and identity experiences.

Therefore, I want to start by stressing the importance of a variable that is important in ethnographic studies—*time*. I believe that *time* might work as a useful "tool," helping us to see things through a different light: changes only occur through the passage of time, and the changes I am referring to have mainly to do with my own personal/ academic growth and understanding during this process.

Linked to this view, I follow the notion that the "happenings," i.e. "[any] form, interpretation, stance, action, activity, identity, institution, skill, ideology, emotion, or other *culturally meaningful reality* [italics added]" within any social context (globally or locally) are "co-constructed" through social interaction among the participants (Jacob and Ochs 1995: 177), and they are "un-linear" (Bhabha 1990, 1994)—even though the historical narrative has to be told linearly due to written language limitations, the social happenings might overlap. In this sense, the discussion in this ethnographic account (whether speaking about individuals, identities, languages and/or cultures) is composed of layers and levels (and is not characterized by homogeneity) and by *continua* (as opposed to dichotomies). These assumptions become relevant because they help us to escape from an essentialist view,[2] and therefore, act against the tendency to construct stereotypes.

Entering the field

I arrived at Gallaudet University as a visiting researcher through the Gallaudet Center for Global Education (CGE),[3] and I was supported by the Brazilian government agency CAPES Foundation (Coordination of Higher Education and Graduate Training). I decided to pursue my research at Gallaudet under an anthropological perspective, because I was interested in broadening my view of Deaf people's lives; Gallaudet University appeared to be the ideal place to pursue this interest. To have a better sense of the institution and the people who comprise it, I decided to live in one of the campus residence halls and take my meals at the cafeteria. I also participated in many of the student academic activities: I took a course in ASL for beginners as a regular student and audited some other classes. Even though my formal status was that of a researcher, I believe that I was identified by my peers as an international hearing graduate student. During my stay at the university, I followed the daily routine of the other students, and my data are derived from that activity.

Data collection

This investigation relied on ethnographic research methods. According to Hammersley and Atkinson (1983), the primary goal of ethnography is the "detailed description of the concrete experience of within a particular culture and of social rules or patterns that constitute it" (p. 8). To understand *what is going on* in some of the social interactions, I investigated and analyzed the local meaning perspectives of the people involved in the context where interaction occurred (Gumperz 1986; Wardhaugh 1992).

The data for this study, then, were generated from field notes taken during the fall semester of 2004 at Gallaudet University. I kept a journal and, from time to time, I developed expansions of my notes trying to make the "unfamiliar" more "familiar" so that my interpretation could come to an approximation of the "inside" view (Erickson 1986; Agar 1980). Although the data were not recorded or videotaped, there are some points in my discussion in which I paraphrase the participants' comments using quotation marks in order to give them *voice* in the text. In this sense, the data are constructions of the researcher in at least two ways: in relation to the paraphrasing process and in relation to the selection and interpretation of the data themselves.[4]

Since Gallaudet comprises a huge anthropological context, it is not possible to cover all the physical spaces and issues in the ways in which they deserve. Therefore, this discussion is restricted to only some of the interactional moments in which I took part. Sometimes, the amount and quality of data I have generated vary from place to place and from person to person. In other words, the language, identity, and culture issues discussed here arose from some of my interactions with some students, teachers, and staff (whether Deaf, Hard of Hearing or hearing), and they occurred sometimes in the dorms, sometimes in classes, or at the cafeteria.

"You have to use ASL here!": Understanding language, identity and cultural issues

> Language has fundamentally three roles in bonding a group of speakers to one another and to their culture. It is *a symbol of social identity, a medium of social interaction, and a store of cultural knowledge.*
>
> (Lane *et al.* 1996: 67[italics added])

One of the things that first attracted my attention when I arrived at the university was the patience that many Deaf people had with me. My biased view was that they would strongly discriminate against me because of my lack of skill with ASL and because I am hearing. Since I was not able to communicate in sign language, most of them read my lips and mouthed in English and/or used written communication. With some hearing people I used mostly English (oral mode) to communicate—a language that is also foreign to me, but much less foreign than ASL. Yet, in both situations, I sometimes had a weird feeling that Agar (1994) metaphorically refers to in regard to his use of the German language: "I often feel, and still feel, that inside of German, I am driving a powerful car on ice without chains. I move, but God only knows where" (p. 97). As time passed by, and my knowledge of these two languages improved, I was always asking myself how is it possible that I am communicating in these two "foreign and weird" codes and these people actually understand what I'm saying? For sure—I always thought to myself—I am making sense, and therefore, doing something with these two languages. I never lost this feeling.

Since I was not proficient in ASL, I developed a strategy of speechreading in English (again, a very difficult skill for me if compared, for instance, to spoken American English speakers) because I noticed that most people at Gallaudet (even Deaf people) frequently mouth words and whisper in English. I relied strongly on this strategy until I was more proficient in ASL and, thus, more comfortable using signs. I also noticed that even ASL-proficient hearing people rely a lot on speechreading during their interactions with ASL users.

It is very common to see hearing people who are interacting with other hearing people using simultaneous communication (SimCom). Only in very rare situations is the English language not used at all. The use of ASL in public space at Gallaudet by hearing people is more a political-ideological issue, since they see themselves circulating in a context that a priori is a Deaf space. Then, the use of *hands*—whether conveying ASL, Signed Exact English (SEE), home signs, foreign sign languages, SimCom, wherever you are, whomever you are talking to—is, somehow, the shared linguistic channel for communication. Due to the fact that many languages co-habit this place, it can be observed that language use is circumstantial and it can occur at every point along a continuum: each language's placement will be influenced by the purpose, the content, and the speakers. Therefore, it can be said that these languages operate in a fluid and unstable medium, in the way that they are formed and transformed continuously during the interactions of the people who are using them. In sum, I agree with Fishman (1999) when he says that "languages are rarely hermetically sealed off from one another, so that they may influence each other somewhat, both orally and in writing, even though on the whole their social functions tend to differ" (p. 156).

Within this sociocultural-linguistic ocean, I experienced moments that made me reflect even more about language, culture, and identity issues. During this time I felt more Brazilian than ever. My Brazilian identity, especially with respect to my accent when speaking English, was always projected and co-sustained by me and by my peers in the course of interaction: *"It is so interesting you have nice insights and still have an accent!"* In addition to stressing the difference conveyed by my accent, this comment, not surprisingly, also represents a belief and (mis)concept about language: a biased view that people who have an accent might be lacking knowledge and or/intelligence.

One of the richest insights that led me to an understanding of hearing people's cultural assumptions, therefore, emerged from the following episode. A hearing person (very proficient in ASL) approached me in the cafeteria. At the very moment we started talking to each other she said: *"You HAVE TO use ASL, otherwise Deaf people are going to look at you and say 'who is that Brazilian hearing girl who is here at Gallaudet and does not sign?' ".* At the beginning, I was shocked about her comment and I took it personally, because she knew that I could not communicate in ASL at that time. But, what does this comment really tell us? On the one hand, it might show this person's concern with political correctness and a feeling of identification with Deaf people in their struggle for recognition and the survival of ASL (despite the efforts of hearing society to eradicate it). However, I started to reflect carefully upon it, and I asked myself to what extent this comment could also mirror **hegemonic** thinking based on a monolingual view of language use, which in turn, resembles the discourse of **linguistic imperialism**. Language is a powerful means to convey ideological baggage. It can be a means of solidarity, resistance, control, manipulation, oppression, as well as a representation of identity within a cultural and a social group (Phillipson 1992).

Looking back on that comment, it seemed to me that some hearing people still behave as the oppressors when it comes to Deaf issues, and how hearing people (especially those people who are fluent/proficient in ASL) oppress other hearing people (less or not proficient in ASL at all).[5] To check my observations in this regard, I also listened to other hearing people's comments (especially those having contact with ASL for the first time) about their experiences with ASL and about its use in interactions with Deaf and hearing people. Most of these people told me that they felt oppressed but the oppression did not come from Deaf people, instead, it came from hearing people:

> You know … I am really frustrated and sad with hearing people. They keep saying to me that I have to learn ASL and when I try to communicate they correct me all the time and say that my signs are wrong. When I am with Deaf people it is different. They help me a lot, because they want to communicate. Sometimes, I think that some hearing people just want to show their skills in sign, and they ignore other people who are starting to learn…. Sometimes, they do not care if you understand them or not. … I thought hearing people would help me here, but the help and comprehension is coming from the Deaf.
>
> (American hearing person/beginner in ASL)

I then spoke with a Hard of Hearing student who told me that he feels angry with some Deaf people because he thinks that they are behaving in the same way hearing people did in the past when they insist he use ASL on campus. "Why?" he says. "If I am in Japan do I have to use Japanese? What about my right of privacy? I can speak both ASL and English, what's the problem if I privilege one over another?"[6] Even though he has a point, and I do understand his perspective, it is important to keep in mind that there are issues between Hard of Hearing and Deaf people. The Hard of Hearing people's situation, from some Deaf—and even hearing—people's point of view, is a situation of "betweenness"—a sense of belonging to neither culture. Bhabha (1994) refers to this feeling as "unhomeliness"—some people are caught between two cultures, and have the feeling of belonging to neither, which, in turn, leads these people to a sense of cultural displacement. The dilemma then is clear—these individuals feel like they have to pick one of the "sides of the coin." If this is so, this behavior reflects both a very purist view of identity and culture, and a very negative view of bilingual/bicultural individuals who can live effectively with two languages and cultures. Still, these essentialist attitudes toward language use show, to a certain extent, the need for cohesion in the form of a core identity/culture. This cohesion, in turn, is strongly represented by the language you make use of—a valued and recognized cultural trait within the Deaf minority linguistic group (Lane *et al.* 1996; Ladd 2003).

As the time passed, I was "affected" by the underlying cultural assumption regarding ASL use, and this perception somehow shaped my reality, which in turn, reinforced my perception (Lane *et al.* 1996: 198). There were some moments when I started to feel obliged to use signs with hearing people. But how could I use ASL if I was not fluent? In order to reduce my anxiety in relation to ASL use, I started to simply wave and move my hands frenetically and randomly while speaking in an attempt to make my hands visible, as if I were "materializing a language" and conveying some sort of meaning through these actions. This was certainly an illusion, but I noticed that for some situations it worked as a way to show my attempt to use signs, and therefore, to diminish my "outsider" status (even though I felt silly doing it; still it was a strategy that I found to lower my anxiety as well as to be seen positively by my hearing peers).

I also observed some hearing people (with almost the same level of ASL proficiency as mine) making an effort to use signs—indeed the conversation could be understood because English was being spoken (signs were used only for a few words, put sporadically in the air, as if trying to fill some gaps—this was indeed, a use of fragmented signs). On the one hand, it was easier for me to understand these people's speech better (in English of course!), because by trying to express themselves in signs, these beginner signers also slowed down their speed in the English language. But I wondered how many Deaf people had suffered and missed information when interacting with hearing people using SimCom because the structure of sign language will always be compromised in favor of the use of an oral language.

I could see that SimCom was being used for a variety of reasons. It might work as a step toward the use of one language only (in this case, ASL). In addition, it might also be a strategy used by some hearing people who are just starting to learn sign language—and here I emphasize how *oral speech* (as opposed to sign) is inherent in hearing people's culture (Gesser 1999) and, therefore, hard to abandon completely. Yet, at other times, it might be a reflection of one's ideology. We would have to look closer to see if it was an attempt to reject and ignore Deaf people's sign language.

Following these comments derived from my data, it is possible to perceive that this imposition of ASL will vary from context to context and from speaker to speaker. But what they tell me so far, specifically in regard to hearing people, has to do with the motivations, beliefs, and/or rationales that might be involved. Some hearing and Hard of Hearing people feel oppressed by their hearing and Deaf peers. Hearing people may have numerous reasons for being militant about ASL use. Some hearing people come to Gallaudet to be immersed in Deaf culture and language. They may have invested a considerable amount in order to have this opportunity to live and study at Gallaudet, and for some this linguistic contact will be unavailable elsewhere, so signing 24 hours a day may be a very important goal. In other cases, hearing people may want to be accepted and recognized in the Deaf community.

"ASL is the golden key!": **Hearing people in the search for Deaf people's recognition and social acceptance**

It was a hot, sunny day. I entered the cafeteria as usual to have my breakfast. The place was not full. Some people were grouped together at one of the tables watching television. While I was walking to find a table a Hard of Hearing friend of mine waved his hands and invited me to sit with him. We started to chat about topics related to Deaf people, and I asked him about his impressions of hearing people at Gallaudet University. We had a great time discussing this issue, and he finally said to me: "You know, if it was a long time ago, I think that Deaf people would never accept the presence of hearing students here in the same way that they do today, but if you want to live well at Gallaudet University, and if you want to be valued and accepted by deaf individuals, then, *ASL is the golden key*!"

The vignette above is indicative of the overall feeling that rules hearing behavior at Gallaudet. I have observed that most hearing people who arrive here feel as if they were minorities in terms of number and prestige (something they have never experienced before outside this place, at least, in regard to hearing status). In this sense, the social dynamic is reversed: positions, social roles, statuses. This new experience leads these people to adopt a specific behavior pattern where acceptance from Deaf people is what matters most. In this setting, it is possible to perceive a feeling, a desire on the part of hearing people "to be Deaf," which in turn, is the same as "being accepted." Being at Gallaudet University in order to have contact with sign language and Deaf people (despite all true and good intentions) are not, I would say, the only reasons that bring hearing people here. It is more than that. It is, at one level, a search for acceptance, which makes this place work very well as a place for a *therapy session*—it is in this sense a huge *therapist's couch*. It is a place for the legitimization of hearing people's need for recognition and validity in the eyes of Deaf people. So, when I see these people associating only with Deaf people or when I see hearing people grouping themselves only with hearing people they consider "Deaf" in some way, using sign language to communicate among themselves even in situations where no Deaf person is present, and rejecting the use oral language (which is an illusion, since most of these people *mouth* when they are signing, and most hearing people rely on this linguistic device to understand each other), all these, reflect the ideology that to be hearing, at a certain level, is seen here as if it were a *sin*.

And what does this side of the coin show us? It shows us a reflection of a complicated double-movement—the attempt of hearing people to reconstitute themselves as a group that despite the "hearing label," does not want to be associated with the well-known oppression created by ("the evil") hearing people of the past. Therefore, the behavior of these hearing people and their use of language are fluid, unstable, and are revealed in fluctuations between two poles (sometimes being too Deaf at one end of the continuum, and at other times, too Hearing). Hearing people's rejection of the use of oral language in face to face interaction represents both a reaction against the past with respect to the treatment of Deaf people and also the hope for a different perception of hearing people in the future. At the same time, it may be that proficiency or fluency in sign language is not a guarantee of good intentions. History suggests (Fanon 19[6]7; Bhabha 1990, 1994) that language can be a powerful instrument of domination, and the history of Deaf people shows that this observation extends to the oppression of Deaf people by hearing society.

It makes sense for these hearing people to go through this process. Before arriving at Gallaudet University, some hearing people may not have detached from their "Deaf people's caretakers identity." Hearing people may have a sense of being Deaf people's *ambassadors* to hearing society. And if this is the case, I would say that hearing people are "superfluous" at Gallaudet. Put simply, Deaf people do not need hearing people's help, at least, not in *the way* or from the point of view hearing people might think they do—a biased, paternalistic, and/or hegemonic one.

Considering this dynamic, it might be true that there is a *disequilibrium* in the status quo, or, as some would prefer to say, there is a threat to hearing people's established social order (Lane 1992). There is a need for a dislocation from one way of seeing, feeling, and behaving to another. Hearing people's roles and status pass through a redefinition at Gallaudet. Then, it is possible to observe an inversion of behaviors, values and, especially, the construction of other social identities: from "caretakers/gatekeepers" to "dependent," from "majority" to "minority," from "norm" to "exception"—in sum, hearing people become "deviant" in this context.

I say this because at many points during my observations, I asked myself the questions "what is my problem?" and "what is my role here?" I felt so displaced myself that I started to see all hearing people in the same way. In fact, these questions were really tied to my prejudiced view of hearing people since I was attributing exclusively bad motives to hearing people's behavior. These questions arose from my initial judgments of hearing people, but they were also part of my own process of getting their points of view. Regarding this process, I understand Erickson (1992) when he stresses the importance in ethnographic research of making the "unfamiliar" "familiar" and the "familiar" "unfamiliar". He argues that it is only through this movement that one can make sense of "what is inside the black box" (p. 202) of a different culture.

"English has to be perfect, but ASL can be anything": Gallaudet University as the border between diverse worlds

Gallaudet University is a huge social space where many different people with diverse backgrounds, experiences, and views are grouped together. It is the borderland between different worlds. It is a place where the majority hearing group meets the minority Deaf group in the homeland of the latter. It is where diverse groups are in contact and for this reason, it is a place where ideologies, cultures, and identities collide: Deaf, hearing, Hard of Hearing, black, white, Asian, Blind, Catholic, Jewish, Muslim, Baptist, American, foreign, lesbian, gay, heterosexual, just to cite a few, are in contact. So, we have a **microcosm** where groups distinguished by gender, nationality, age, ethnic, religious, and sexual orientation are co-habiting in a very peculiar way. Even though their main tie and/or core group identification is that of the audiological condition (and here begins the misconception about the way people make sense of each other, because the label establishes an overgeneralization, suggesting a dichotomy between the "good" and the "evil"), it is the contact itself that accentuates this **heterogeneity**. Therefore, clashes are inevitable. As a consequence it is possible to see a complex and contradictory interface among these groups.

At one of the lectures I attended at the very beginning of my stay at Gallaudet, I remember one Deaf teacher saying: "English has to be perfect, but ASL can be anything." On the one hand, this statement shows Deaf people's frustration in regard to hearing people's expectation when it comes to Deaf people's English language use. But on the other hand, it also implies a view that most people might have toward ASL—that it is a language with a low social status. It was from this early moment that I started to make sense of this place and understand the meaningful role that Gallaudet plays in the lives of all the people who inhabit its community. Therefore, I see Gallaudet connecting all those different worlds, and all the people who, somehow, are engaged in crossing this path to reach each other—they have to pass through a sort of "therapy session." It is the first step for any sort of transition both at the individual as well as at the societal level. This institution is viewed from the outside as *the land of the Deaf,* which creates the false and illusory expectation that ASL is the only language to be used here. It creates the expectation that all people who are linked to Gallaudet have banished their biased views about Deaf people and their language/culture. It also creates the idea that no discrimination, oppression, or any sort of prejudice will be found. That was what I thought before arriving and spending six months here. It was also the view that many people who are part of this place shared with me:

> You know … before arriving here, I thought I would not find problems. I thought that everybody here would be sensitive to each other in this context. …I thought I'd be signing all the time, using only American Sign Language and that I wouldn't be using English at all. I am a little bit frustrated because I wanted to improve my sign skills.
>
> (hearing person who is proficient in ASL)

Therefore, all social contexts, the cafeteria, classes, meetings, offices, the dorms, all these contexts are potentially used by individuals to express political and ideological views, but also to adjust to diverse cultural frames. In this sense, Gallaudet University is not only a space for Deaf people's political/educational articulation, and for Deaf people's empowerment, it is also a huge therapy couch for hearing people. ASL plays an important role in the constitution of Deaf society and culture, and hearing people's language use and attitudes about its use are important indicators of social identity. ASL use here is a powerful vehicle for the construction and maintenance of selfhood during social interaction among members of different groups.

Concluding remarks

This essay is intended as an account of my experiences of face-to-face interaction at Gallaudet University, including attitudes and observed communication behaviors in relation to language, culture, and identity of Deaf, hearing, and Hard of Hearing people. It attempted to present a broad ethnographic account of the behavior of some hearing and Deaf people as they construct meaningful realities, including my own. In this sense, Gallaudet University was inspiring—my experience there was extraordinarily rich, both as a place to study human behavior in all its diversity and as a place to experience personal growth.

Acknowledgment

This research was supported by a Brazilian government scholarship granted by CAPES foundation (Coordination of Higher Education and Graduate Training), during the period of August 2004 to January 2005.

Notes

1   It is common practice in the specialized Deaf literature to use the capitalized term *Deaf* to refer to a particular group of deaf people who share a language, values and beliefs, and the term *deaf*, with a lower case, to refer to the audiological condition of not hearing. Some might argue that this distinction, even though relevant, is difficult to make because it is not possible to know "at what precise point do deaf become Deaf" (Baynton 1996: 12). Still, I believe that the distinction has to be made, because it mirrors "a movement in the identity of Deaf people that derives from their 'ethnic revival'" (Baker 1999: 122).
2   "Essentialism [is] the existence of fixed characteristics, given attributes, and ahistorical functions that limit the possibility of change and thus of social organization" (Grosz 1994: 84).
3   I would like to express my deepest gratitude to Dr. Robert E. Johnson who shared his knowledge with me during the development of this project.
4   It is important to stress that even transcription excerpts are, to a certain extent, constructions of the researcher (Atkinson 1993) [this reference is missing from the original - eds].
5   I believe that it might be true that there is still oppression from hearing people toward Deaf people in some interactions within the Gallaudet University context, but this was not investigated in this study.
6   Keeping to this issue of language oppression/discrimination, I have heard from a Deaf international student that she felt oppressed and discriminated against by some Deaf Americans, users of ASL. Many issues and variables might be involved here. Yet, it would be interesting to investigate the relations among Deaf people who are signers of different sign languages to see if ASL has a prestigious status over other sign languages.

References

Agar, M. (1980) *The Professional Stranger*, New York: Academic Press.
——— (1994) *Understanding the Culture of Conversation*, New York: Perennial.
Anzul, M., Margot Ely, Teri Friedman, Diane Garner and Ann Mccormack Steinmetz (1991) *Doing Qualitative Research: Circles within Circles*, London: Falmer.

Baker, C. (1999) Sign Language and the Deaf Community, in J.A. Fishman (ed.), *Handbook of Language and Ethnic Identity*, Oxford, UK: Oxford University Press, pp. 122–39.

Baynton, D.C. (1996) *Forbidden Signs: American Culture and the Campaign against Sign Language*, Chicago: University of Chicago Press.

Bhabha, H.K. (1990) *Nation and Narration*, New York: Routledge.

—— (1994) *The Location of Culture*, New York: Routledge.

Erickson, F. (1986) Qualitative Methods in Research on Teaching, in M. C. Wittrock (ed.), *Handbook of Research on Teaching*, New York: Macmillan, pp. 77–200.

—— (1992) Ethnographic Microanalysis of Interaction, in M. D. LeCompte, W. L. Millroy, and J. Preissle (eds.), *The Handbook of Qualitative Research in Education*, New York: Academic, pp. 201–25.

—— and J. Shultz (1981) When Is a Context? Some Issues and Methods in the Analysis of Social Competence, in J.L. Green and C. Wallat (eds.), *Ethnography and Language in Educational Settings*, Norwood, NJ: Ablex, pp. 147–160.

[Fanon, Franz (1967) *Black Skin, White Masks*, transl. Charles Lam Markmann (1967 translation of the 1952 book), New York, Grove Press.]

Fishman, J.A. (1999) Sociolinguistics, in J.A. Fishman (ed.), *Handbook of Language and Ethnic Identity*, Oxford: Oxford University Press, pp. 152–163.

Gesser, A. (1999) *Teaching and Learning Brazilian Sign Language (LIBRAS) as a Foreign Language: A Microethnographic Description*, master's thesis, Universidade Federal de Santa Catarina, Florianopolis, Brazil.

Grosz, E. (1994) Sexual Difference and the Problem of Essentialism, in N. Schor and E. Weed (eds.), *The Essential Difference*, Bloomington, IN: Indiana University Press.

Gumperz, J. (1986) Interactional Sociolinguistics in the Study of Schooling, in J. Cook Gumperz (ed.), *The Social Construction of Literacy*, Cambridge: Cambridge University Press, pp. 229–252.

Hall, S. (1992) The Question of Cultural Identity, in S. Hall, D. Held and T. McGrew (eds.), *Modernity and Its Futures*, Cambridge: Polity Press, pp. 273–326.

Hammersley, M. and P. Atkinson (1983) *Ethnography: Principles in Practice*, London: Routledge.

Jacob, S. and E. Ochs (1995) Co-Construction: An Introduction, *Research on Language and Social Interaction*, 28(3): 171–183.

Ladd, P. (2003) *Understanding Deaf Culture: In the Search of Deafhood*. Clevedon, UK: Multilingual Matters.

Lane, H. (1992) *The Mask of Benevolence: Disabling the Deaf Community*, San Diego, CA: DawnSign.

——, R. Hoffmeister and B. Bahan (1996) *A Journey into the Deaf-World*, San Diego, CA: DawnSign.

Lanehart, S.L. (1999) African American Vernacular English, in J. A. Fishman (ed.), *Handbook of Language and Ethnic Identity*, Oxford: Oxford University Press, pp. 221–225.

Phillipson, R. (1992) *Linguistic Imperialism*, Oxford: Oxford University Press.

Wardhaugh, R. (1992) *An Introduction to Sociolinguistics*, Oxford: Blackwell.

PART TEN

Standard Englishes

Suzanne LaBelle

INTRODUCTION

THESE PIECES LOOK at the consequences of the process of **globalization** from the point of view of language, specifically what happens to English in a global environment where new standards emerge and old standards are typically, though not exclusively, viewed as a positive marker of unity or group boundaries. All three pieces explore the globalization/**localization** of varieties of English, post-standardization, and the power correlates that can be seen as an outcome of globalizing and localizing processes. The Kachru interview provides a theoretical framework for thinking about different varieties of English, whilst highlighting theoretical changes in the field, and suggesting avenues for further research. The Evans study explores traditional language planning reasoning behind making 'English' an institutionalized official standard, and then goes on to explore what happens when global economic concerns intervene. In appealing to patriotism and sense of group identity through language, the very notion of drawing an 'official' boundary may create a problematic environment when a powerful 'other' is present. In Evans' case, this powerful other is a Japanese manufacturer looking to do business in the US state of Ohio. This presence arguably led to Ohioans unsuccessful attempt to enshrine English as the official state language. Her piece indirectly highlights the need to explore language for use both as a marker of identity and as a system of communication. Jenkins' piece looks the identity/communication divide more closely. She examines attitudes towards English used by non-native speakers. She does this by questioning non-native speaker views on the production of their second language, highlighting the power relations between native and non-native English users. All three pieces question the idea that English is simply a monolithic entity. They show that even though there are standard Englishes, that have been used as a tool of colonialism, power, and control, English is nevertheless locally used, in a way that is non-standard or non-native, or just non-official. Speakers bend language to their needs creatively and continuously, in response to global and local concerns to create and reinforce power structures.

In the Kachru interview, the term 'World English' is explained as an umbrella term for English used in an international context, and its history as a theoretical device for analyzing language varieties is introduced. Kachru notes that once specific varieties were recognized, the concept of 'Englishes' arose as a new noun and construct, where local and international varieties of English were recognized as competitors. Major research themes and prominent researchers in the sub-field are then discussed including issues of concern for macro-sociolinguistics, that is, the wide-ranging examination of the relationship between language and nation. Kachru takes us through issues of **linguistic imperialism**, **genetic versus functional nativeness** in English and the development of English as an International Language whilst explaining the history and development of World English. The use of English by so-called Outer Circle speakers, those nations where English is used alongside another language, as a tool for expressing a hybrid or multiplex local identity, is considered. For example, there is an institutional challenge to speakers of English in Africa and Asia where local varieties are not as powerful as Inner Circle Englishes, though development of associations between language planners and linguists suggests positive movement for the future. Kachru concludes the interview with a call to translators and other language professionals to work carefully around minority language and culture. He argues that English, though mutable, does have a deleterious effect on local language culture, and that sensitivity in both examining new Englishes and preserving traditional minority languages is needed.

Evans takes on the difficult task of teasing out what is behind the will to legislate an official language. She discusses how the traditional arguments of 'unity' and 'shared deep rooted values' can lead to enshrining a standardized language in law, and also how these concepts may be eclipsed in public and official imaginations by the need to secure economic power. Her profile of the failed attempt to make English the official language of the State of Ohio in the USA, brings these issues to light. In 2005 the 'Ohio English Unity Act' looked to establish English as the only language to be used in official proceedings within the state. This bill was not in response to a real threat to English in the state of Ohio, English had unofficially been the language of government without issue prior to the 2005 bill. Even though there seemed to be some support for the bill, a discourse arose in the news media in the state as to the desirability of such a bill in the face of potential overseas investment. Evans frames this discussion in the complex relationship between English as a medium of social advancement in the US and larger cultural **stereotypes** a group, in this case, Americans, have about how to achieve success.

On one level practicality won out in Ohio, the risk of causing offence to power trumped 'unity'. The desire to encourage overseas investment, and thus potentially local jobs, was stronger than associations of English with American identity. However, wrapped up in that outcome is the belief Americans have about themselves that striving for economic success is a part of the American ethos. Claims about the usefulness of English as an identity marker, though usually a part of that ethos, may be removed from the paradigm if economic success is in danger. Here a group has chosen to de-emphasize the institutionalization of a language variety to keep intact their worldview on what constitutes success. As Evans concludes, 'The **hegemonic** frameworks that drive English-language legislation are underpinned by "deep values" that are, themselves, a mélange of **ideologies** and experiences' (p. 343).

Jenkins looks at attitudes towards **English as a lingua franca** (**ELF**), or common shared language across cultures. She begins by making the case for removing the artificial boundaries around the different varieties that can be captured in the term 'World English'. She advocates an inclusive approach with native and non-native varieties as equals, standard and non-standard varieties as equals. She claims that in practical terms, English speakers from norm developing, native speaker nations participate in ELF discourse without 'set[ing] the linguistic agenda' (p. 347) as all participants make changes to their variety in interaction. 'ELF is thus a question, not of orientation to the norms of a particular group of English speakers, but of mutual negotiation involving efforts and adjustments from all parties' (p. 347).

Nevertheless, Jenkins notes that a current debate in the study of the standardizing practices amongst non-native Englishes includes the problem of whether to ascribe the status of 'error' to a linguistic form used in a way that significantly differs from that of a native speaker. She says this depends on the communicative effectiveness of the form. This approach is different from some English teaching professionals who view ELF as a substandard variety eliciting substantial negative evaluation. Her past work (2007) has shown that non-native speakers rank inner circle native speaker varieties like US and UK English as more correct and pleasant than other varieties, even if they are speakers of outer circle varieties. Jenkins suggests that course materials geared towards US/UK English as ideal is a source of these attitudes. She then surveys her students on ERASMUS programmes studying in the UK from around Europe and is able to suggest that after a period of adjustment ELF users can develop positive attitudes about their language variety, or at least neutral ones.

Through exploring language variety, nation, and attitudes towards perceived linguistic competence these authors carefully demonstrate that while language standardization may allow for ease of widespread transmission of a language variety, it also brings up complex issues of communication and identity, power and purpose, ownership and deference. Symbolic power and **soft power** are relevant. Note the re-analysis of the acronym for World Englishes, 'WE', as an inclusive first person plural pronoun. You should also pay attention to Kachru's comments about the commissioning of Crystal (2003) and Graddol's work (2006). This alludes to the soft power that inner circle nations seek to exert by exporting their standards to the rest of the world. The papers should make you think about how access to standard language creates and perpetuates power inequalities as well provides group identity.

Issues to consider

1. Why if linguists view all varieties of language as equal in their ability to express meaning do non-linguists spend such effort on prescriptivism, determining what counts as so-called 'good' or 'bad' varieties?
2. What issues arise when using a global language like English as a means of communication for second language speakers versus as a marker of identity for first language speakers?
3. What discourses are relevant in arguments for official or standard languages? Who benefits from these discourses? Who does not benefit?

4. What does the establishment of a standard language mean for communities of speakers who do not have access to that standard?

Further reading

On World Englishes:

Crystal, David (2003), *English as a Global Language*, second edition, Cambridge: Cambridge University Press.

Graddol, D. (2006) *English Next*, British Council, online, available at: www.britishcouncil. org/learning-research-englishnext.htm.

— (2010) *English Next India*, British Council online, available at: www.britishcouncil.org/ learning-english-next-india-2010-book.htm.

Pennycook, Alastair (2006) *Global Englishes and Transcultural Flows*, Abingdon: Routledge.

On language policy and planning:

Kachru, B.B. (ed.), (1992) *The Other Tongue: English Across Cultures*, second edition, Urbana, IL: University of Illinois Press.

Phillipson, R. (2003) *English-Only Europe?* London: Routledge.

Ricento, T. (1998) 'National language policy in the United States', in R. Ricento and B. Burnaby (eds.), *Language and Politics in the United States and Canada: Myths and Realities*, Mahwah, NJ: Earlbaum, pp. 85–112.

Schildkraut, D. (2005) *Press One for English: Language Policy, Public Opinion and American Identity*, Princeton, NJ: Princeton University Press.

Tsui, Amy B.M. and James W. Tollefson (2007) *Language Policy, Culture, and Identity in Asian Contexts*, Mahwah, NJ: Lawrence Erlbaum Associates.

Suggestions for further viewing

Monsoon Wedding (2001) Mira Nair.
Mango Souffle (2003) Mahesh Dattani.
Chicken Rice War (2000) Chee Kong Cheah.
Spellbound (2002) Jeffrey Blitz.

References

Crystal, David (2003), *English as a Global Language*, second edition, Cambridge: Cambridge University Press.

Graddol, D. (2006) *English Next*, British Council, online, available at: www.britishcouncil. org/learning-research-englishnext.htm.

Jenkins, J. (2007) *English as a Lingua Franca: Attitude and Identity*, Oxford: Oxford University Press.

Chapter 25

Jacqueline Lam Kam-Mei interviewing Braj B. Kachru

ASIA'S ENGLISHES AND WORLD ENGLISHES

[The following dialogue first appeared in *The Hong Kong Linguist*, the journal of the Hong Kong Branch of the Institute of Linguists (November 1999), after Braj Kachru's visit in 1998 as a guest of the University of Hong Kong. It is reprinted here with the permission of both journal and interviewee. Items in square brackets are *English Today* editorial additions.]

JLK   *When did you first begin to use the term "world Englishes"? Had anyone else used the term at that time or were you the first?*

BBK   The use of the term actually goes back to the 1970s. I had been using the term "world Englishes" in my seminars at Illinois before it was proposed to Pergamon Press, Oxford, as a title for a reincarnated journal when they invited Larry Smith [at the East–West Center, Honolulu, Hawaii] and me to "re-launch" the [British ELT-related journal] *World Language English*. In 1985, *World Englishes: The Journal of English as an International and Intranational Language* was launched. The term "world English," without pluralization, was used in some contexts earlier. The reincarnated journal, as Tom McArthur says, "has been a vehicle for the discussion, both general and specific, of varieties of English worldwide, and has in the process firmly underlined the neologism *Englishes* in linguistic and educational circles. The journal's editorial stance is that all 'world Englishes' (native and non-native) belong equally to all who use them and merit serious and consistent study both individually and collectively" (1998: 61).

One might say that *WE* captures several demographic and contextual characteristics of the current cross-cultural profile of the English language. The following come to mind: the functional range and the depth of penetration of the language in various levels of society; the resultant localized innovations and creativity in the language; the multi-cultural and literary identities of the language and its multiple canonicity; and, indeed, the agony and ecstasy about the global presence of the language.

In the use of this term, the emphasis, then, is on the "WE-ness" that is associated with the medium and its multiple messages (mantras). This conceptualization of

English, based on the pragmatics of its functions across cultures and languages, naturally rejects the perpetuated dichotomy between "us" and "them" – between "native" and "non-native." As we know, it is this dichotomy that the "ELT Empire" – to use Australian lexicographer Susan Butler's term – has cultivated and nurtured. It is again this dichotomy that underlies the on-going culture wars about the language. In this context I am thinking of, for example, the statements of Richard Bailey, Felipe Fernández-Armesto, and Samuel P. Huntington discussed in my recent paper, presented as the 1998 Sir Edward Youde Memorial Fund Lecture in Hong Kong. We must emphasize that this "WE-ness" is embodied in various strands of Englishes across cultures and languages; its reach and range of uses is unparalleled.

The English language is used in Asia and Africa as a medium to articulate various types of cultural emblems and also as a sociopolitical linguistic weapon. I have often mentioned in my writings the insightful and refreshing way Nigeria's Wole Soyinka, India's Raja Rao, the Philippines' F. Sionil José, and Singapore's Edwin Thumboo use the English language to represent their distinct native cultural identities – in other words, use the medium as an emblem: Soyinka believes that his people "carved new concepts into the flesh of white supremacy" by the "conversion of the enslaving medium into an insurgent weapon" (Soyinka 1993: 88).

India's Vivekananda (1863–1902) used the same linguistic weapon – both in his multilingual country and the West – for conveying the message of Vedanta and for setting up the Ramakrishna Mission for spiritual and social awakening. Vivekananda's pragmatic mind crossed the stifling linguistic boundaries and argued that "the British Empire has given us a machine and I will put the ancient truths of Vedanta in it, broadcast them to the world and make them run like fire." The Indian monk used the medium with elegance and success across the Western world. It is all these worlds the medium represents – the Asian world, the African world, and indeed, the Western world. This is, therefore, not a minor achievement, and I believe that we should celebrate it, and participate in using the medium for articulating our visions.

We at last have a medium that to a large extent realizes the dream of a "universal language." What we need, then, is to reevaluate our traditional conceptualizations – theoretical, methodological, and pedagogical – about the current functions of English in a variety of global contexts. That, of course, is happening, but with resistance because all types of interests are involved. And we should not underestimate the economic interests that determine the debate about whose standard, whose model, and whose pedagogical materials are to be used world-wide.

JLK	*You are well known for having taken a different position with regard to English around the world from Professor Randolph Quirk's, especially in the 1980s. How did that happen? Are you now closer or further apart in your views at the end of the century?*
BBK	This is a somewhat complex question to answer. Let me first clear up one misunderstanding. What I said in 1991 in "Liberation Linguistics and the Quirk Concern" (*ET*25, Jan 1991) refers not only to Professor Quirk's view. Actually, an identical view is held by the international English Language Teaching Empire, and a very recent articulation of this view – perhaps in more extreme form – comes from John Honey (1997). And Professor Quirk's position changed rather suddenly in the late 1980s.

His earlier position is summarized in the introduction that Professor Quirk and I jointly wrote for an edited volume (Smith 1981). When I pointed this out in 1991, Professor Quirk's response was, "I am pleased that Professor Kachru has detected some shift in my thinking over the years, since it is among a scholar's foremost duties to reach new conclusions as new evidence presents itself. ..." (see Tickoo 1991: 227). My response to Professor Quirk's very valid reply regarding his "shift in thinking, or changing of positions on intellectual issues" is given in the same volume (pp. 228–231). I might also mention here that the Tickoo volume also includes four papers relevant to this question (in Section III, pp. 153–226), two by Professor Quirk with an added "Note" and two by me with a "Response" to the "Note." There is no need for me to summarize the arguments of the two positions here.

JLK	*As a journal editor I must also ask you about your journal "World Englishes." Has it developed as you expected, or has it taken on a life of its own that sometimes surprises you?*
BBK	Well, the way the journal *World Englishes* has evolved has not exactly surprised us. Larry Smith and I had realized that there was actually a space for a professional journal to represent the sociolinguistic, cultural, political, and economic realities about the global presence of the English language – I mean all the dimensions of it, the linguistic and literary issues and also the agonies and ecstasies. The senior and aspiring researchers and educators in English studies received the journal with contagious excitement, especially in Africa, Asia, and other regions where English is an additional language. These were voices whose creativity in the language and identity with it in varied cultural contexts had hardly any international scholarly resource for expression or discussion. We believe that *WE* provided that scholarly resource.

I must share with you the experience Larry Smith and I had when we took the manuscript of the first issue of *WE* to Pergamon Press at Oxford (the journal is now published by Blackwell, Oxford). Vaughan James, who at that time represented the Pergamon Press on the Board of *WE* said, "Yes, you have an excellent first issue. But are you sure that you will have contributions of the same quality for the next issues?" Well, in retrospect, I must say that Vaughan James' fears have proved to be unfounded. *WE* has a unique character and represents multiple voices – and we have sustained that multidisciplinary representation and international presence – African, Asian, European, North American, and so on, during the past fifteen years.

I don't think that I can say it better than Tom McArthur did (1993: 334), referring to the logo-acronym of the journal. He observed that the logo "serves to indicate that there is a club of equals here." In McArthur's interpretation of the logo, he rightly emphasizes that the emphasis is on "the democratization of attitudes to English everywhere on the globe." I think the concept "world Englishes" certainly represents that fact about the current status and functions of global English.

JLK	*Can you tell us something about the IAWE (International Association of World Englishes)?*

BBK   I don't know where to begin. Actually, what is now IAWE was originally an unnamed group of like-minded people who met to share their thinking-in-progress at various times and places. IAWE has a rather loose organizational structure, and I'm not sure that any serious effort has been made to develop a constitution or a set of by-laws. But, in spite of that – or perhaps because of that – it is working well, and the members share both excitement about what they are doing and, I might add, a commitment.

The ideas that brought the group together may be traced back to two international conferences organized independently of each other in 1978 – just over two decades ago. These two conferences were organized about three months apart, one at the East-West Center and the other at the University of Illinois at Urbana-Champaign, the latter in conjunction with the 1978 Summer Institute of the Linguistic Society of America. It turned out that the two conferences had considerable shared concerns and conceptual cohesion. Professor Randolph Quirk played an important role in the Hawaii conference. In fact, he and I wrote a joint statement and a summary of the conference which has appeared in the volume edited by Larry Smith (Smith 1981). This volume includes selected presentations from the Hawaii meeting.

The Urbana conference was larger and included participants from Africa and several Asian countries, in addition to Europe and the USA. At the Urbana conference, as I have written elsewhere, "the English-using community in various continents was for the first time viewed in its totality. A number of cross-cultural perspectives were brought to bear upon our understanding of English in a global context, of language variation, of language acquisition, and of the bilingual's – or a multilingual's – use of English." (Kachru 1992 [1982]: xiii–xiv).

In later years, special colloquia were organized as part of several professional organizations, e.g. International TESOL, IATEFL (in Belgium), in which the late Peter Strevens played a vital role, and the Georgetown Round Table of Languages and Linguistics (GURT 86 and later). It was, however, in 1988 that a more focused group was coordinated that was rather informally called the International Committee for the Study of World Englishes (ICWE). In 1992 the committee met at the University of Illinois at Urbana, as a co-sponsor of a conference on "World Englishes Today." At that conference an informal proposal was discussed and the IAWE was launched. In the past years, the IAWE annual conventions have been held in, for example, Nagoya, Japan (1994), Honolulu, USA (1996), and Singapore (1997), and the next one is scheduled to be held at Tsukuba, Ibaragi, Japan (1999). The past Presidents have been Larry Smith and Braj B. Kachru, the current President is Anne Pakir, and Ayo Bamgbose is President-elect. The journal *World Englishes* is in a loose way associated with IAWE.

JLK   *David Graddol and the British Council recently published a book with the title* The Future of English. *What do you think the future might be?*

BBK   Yes, you are right that the Graddol book is yet another attempt at "forecasting the popularity of the English language in the 21st century." That the project was initiated by the British Council helps to contextualize the genesis of the book. But having said that, what concerns me about the study is that it is very selective of what it includes. As researchers we all are selective in some sense, but Graddol's selectivity distorts the profile of world Englishes. In that sense, the study is misleading.

Let me be specific about my point. In Graddol's study, I looked in vain for references to what the English-using and non-English-using Africans and Asians have to say about the current or future uses of English in their countries; I looked, for example, for the distinction the Africans (e.g. Chinua Achebe, Wole Soyinka) and Asians (e.g. Raja Rao, R.K. Narayan, Vikram Seth, Salman Rushdie), and African-Americans (e.g. Henry Gates, Jr.) make between the use of English as a medium to present identities of their cultures, their experiences and their native contexts, as opposed to English as the medium of Western culture. In other words, the study does considerable crystal-gazing and reading of tea leaves on highly selective positions of some users of English – primarily Western. In my view, the future of English – in a global sense – is now in the hands of the other two Circles – the Outer and Expanding Circles. The Inner Circle has had its linguistic innings. The signs are not those of a monolithic English, but of Englishes with multiple identities. That vision and those indicators are muted in the Graddol volume.

JLK *Tom McArthur recently published* The English Languages. *How does his position relate to your views on World Englishes?*

BBK First, let me say that, in the UK, McArthur is almost unparalleled in his vision, vitality and understanding of and empathy with the world users of Englishes. I think his cross-cultural experiences are fascinating. How many scholars do we know who can talk with amazing competence and experience about Scottish writers, the Scottish nationalist movement, Baha'ism, Yoga, the *Bhagavad Gita*, English **lexicography**, the evolution of writing, and so on? We see McArthur's subtle grasp of issues and complexities of English around the world in his planning of the monumental resource book *The Oxford Companion to the English Language* (1992). *The English Languages* (1998) is certainly vintage McArthur. I have used this book with considerable success in my seminars. It is both comprehensive and provocative and integrates elegantly all voices relevant to our understanding of the subtle questions about English around the world.

JLK *David Crystal has also recently published* English as a Global Language. *In it, toward the end, he focuses on a possible World Standard Spoken English (WSSE). Is such a thing possible?*

BBK As you know, David Crystal's *Cambridge Encyclopedia of the English Language* (1995) is now one of the two major reference sources for the English language, the other being McArthur (1992). Crystal's *English as a Global Language* (1997), however, belongs to a different genre and is aimed at a specific readership. The suggestion for this book, as Crystal tells us, came from the "Chairman of US English, the largest organization which has been campaigning for English to be made the official language of the USA" (p. ix). This volume was written "for private circulation"

(p. ix) among the members of that organization. There is also an edition printed by US English and circulated in the USA. One might say that out of the three books mentioned, Graddol has the British Council perspective, and Crystal perhaps has a specific intended readership in mind – the US English membership. However, Crystal does raise some interesting questions, particularly in Chapter 5. In my classes, the book certainly generates some discussion – both pro and con.

And now, about a World Standard Spoken English (WSSE): I have some difficulty in understanding what Crystal means by the tricky word "standard" here. Who will set the standard? How? He certainly is aware of the complexities of the issues related to this question. In 1985, Crystal made an insightful observation at the 50th Anniversary Celebration of the British Council in London about Professor Quirk's position. On this issue, he said, "What concerns me, however, is the way in which all discussion of standards ceases very quickly to be a linguistic discussion, and becomes instead an issue of social identity, and I miss this perspective in his [Quirk's] paper" (1985: 9–10). I now – almost fifteen years later – have the same problem with Crystal's position. I miss the issues of identity – and distinct canonicity – of Englishes in his *English as a Global Language*.

> **JLK**   *You have recently given some presentations in Manila and Bangkok on English as an Asian language. This concept would naturally interest our readers in Hong Kong. Is English really an Asian language?*
>
> **BBK**   A short answer to the question is: Yes, English is an Asian language if we make a distinction between the GENETIC NATIVENESS of a language and its FUNCTIONAL NATIVENESS. In terms of functional nativeness, there are several shared characteristics in Asian Englishes. This raises relevant epistemological questions, which I discussed, as you know, in Manila and Bangkok. In fact, a more detailed version was also presented in Hong Kong in November 1998. There are certain criteria that one has to use to determine the functional nativeness of Asian Englishes: for example, historical, functional, formal, sociocultural, creative, educational, interactional, and attitudinal.

The understanding of the Asianization of English, then, entails study of Englishes in Asia with reference to the paradigms of contact literatures, contact linguistics and sociolinguistics. I believe that there is enough evidence to support – within this trimodel approach – the argument that the Asianization of English shows a variety of shared features. Now, I will not go into all the details here. A preliminary version of a paper with details of the trimodel approach has already appeared in Bautista (1997) and another version is forthcoming. And now to answer your question: Yes, English is an Asian language in the sense that I have discussed in Manila and later.

JLK   *How do you see English relating to other languages in Asia and elsewhere? Will there still be room for them all in the next century?*

BBK   It depends on what you mean by the word "relating." In Asia's numerically overwhelming profile, English now has a significant presence. This profile of English has developed and grown during the post-Colonial period. And this has occurred essentially due to the initiatives of the Asians – their resources, their institutions, and their administrative and educational networks: they are setting the agendas for the language. In just two Asian countries, China and India, there are 200 million and 333 million users of the English language, respectively, with of course various degrees of competence.

These figures, then, add up to 533 million! This number surpasses the populations of the USA, the UK and Canada combined. This indeed is a staggering figure, and, naturally, its implications are immense: **ideological**, cultural, linguistic, ethical, and in terms of creativity in English by the Asians, and in other Asian languages (e.g. Bengali, Chinese, Hindi, Japanese, Malay). This might sound like a triumphalistic statement, but then that is a fact of a major current linguistic reality of Asia. There is understandably agony, guilt, atonement, and so on about this, as there is also ecstasy. But, you know, in dynamic societies there is always room for yet another language, and for adding yet another code to one's linguistic repertoire. In this process, we have seen both societally – and individually – larger and functionally more potent fish eating smaller fish. That, of course, opens up a Pandora's box of a different kind: The questions of linguistic human rights and the protection of minority languages, and so on.

I am very concerned about that too, since my "mother tongue" is spoken by less than 0.8 percent of India's population and, in terms of its users, is restricted mainly to the valley of Kashmir. I know how it feels to see the attrition of one's mother tongue in one's own family, community and even the state. I have seen that happen. I know what it means to see minority literatures go unrecognized and almost undiscovered. That is happening now to Kashmiri literary creativity. That is yet another reality. But overall, the presence of the English language – a major language of wider communication – has provided the Asians a potent linguistic tool. The Asians – and I might add the Africans – are making use of this tool very effectively in a variety of functions, for success, for mobility and for articulating their identities across various types of boundaries.

JLK   *Will there be less or more work for translators in future?*

BBK   I will refrain from crystal-gazing on this topic. But I would like to say that, as the languages of wider communication spread within a nation (for example, Hindi in India) or across nations (for example, Arabic, English, Spanish, and Chinese), there will be more need for sensitive, creative, and competent translators. There is a greater need to bring to the larger readerships the traditions, the cultures, the wisdom, the experimentation in creativity, and other innovations that occur in what are called the minority languages.

It is sad that this wisdom, cultural treasure and creativity is not always – and not fully – shared with the users of other languages. What we need is access to the world's minority – or "minor" – languages through the mediums of the languages of wider communication. English, of course, has the widest cross-cultural and cross-linguistic currency from this point of view. I have just completed a monograph on a Kashmiri poet and social activist, Dina Nath Nadim (1916–1988), and have raised several of these points in it.

In discussions on translation there is also a cluster of other issues. I am particularly thinking of the ethical issues and those related to ethnocentrism. We are often told that FitzGerald's translation of the *rubais* of the Persian poet Omar Khayam is a superb example of the translator's craft. Perhaps so. But we are generally not told about FitzGerald's ethnocentrism and the liberties he took in his translation. It is worth knowing that in a letter that FitzGerald wrote to a friend, he mentioned the 'liberties' he took in translating Omar Khayam. Note what he said: "It is an amusement for me to take what Liberties I like with these Persians who (as I think) are not Poets enough to frighten me from such excursions, and who really want a little Art to shape them" cited in Lefevere (1990: 19).

Well, it is refreshing that in various recent books on translation a string of such questions is being discussed within new theoretical and methodological perspectives with reference to the craft of translation. That is an excellent beginning.

References

Bautista, M. (ed.), (1997) *English is an Asian Language: The Philippine Context*, Sydney: Macquarie.

Crystal, David (1985) "Comment," in R. Quirk and H.G. Widdowson (eds.), *English in the World*, Cambridge: Cambridge University Press.

Honey, John (1997) *Language is Power: The Story of Standard English and its Enemies*, London/ Boston, MA: Faber & Faber.

Kachru, Braj B. (ed.), (1992 [1982]) *The Other Tongue: English Across Cultures*, Urbana, IL: University of Illinois Press.

—— (1997) "World Englishes 2000: Resources for Research and Teaching," in L. Smith and M.L. Forman (eds.), *World Englishes 2000*, Honolulu, HI: University of Hawaii Press.

Lefevere, A. (1990) "Translation: Its Genealogy in the West," in S. Bassnett and A. Lefevere (eds.), *Translation, History and Culture*, London/New York: Pinter Publishers.

McArthur, Tom (ed.), (1992) *The Oxford Companion to the English Language*, Oxford: Oxford: University Press.

—— (1993) "The English Language or the English Languages?" in W.F. Bolton and D. Crystal (eds.), *The English Language* [Vol. 10 of the *Penguin History of Literature*], London: Penguin Books, pp. 323–341. (Originating as the *Sphere History of Literature*, 1987.)

—— (1998) *The English Languages*, Cambridge: Cambridge University Press.

Smith, Larry E. (ed.), (1981) *English for Cross-Cultural Communication*, London: Macmillan.

Soyinka, Wole (1993 [1978]) *Language as Boundary: In Art, Dialogue and Outrage*, New York: Pantheon Books.

Tickoo, Madhan L. (ed.), (1991) *Language and Standards: Issues, Attitudes, Case Studies*, Singapore: SEAMEO Regional Language Centre.

Chapter 26

Betsy E. Evans

ENGLISH AS OFFICIAL STATE LANGUAGE IN OHIO: ECONOMY TRUMPS IDEOLOGY

I N THIS CHAPTER, I examine a case of proposed language legislation in the US state of Ohio in which market concerns appear to override the **ideological** beliefs typically found in the English-only debate. Exploring the roots of the motivations for the English-Only movement in the United States has been taken up by many scholars. This considerable amount of research devoted to discovering these common pillars of the arguments for establishing legislation to designate English as the official language of various municipalities in the United States has established that the movement is fuelled by several ideologies including power, nationalism, demographic and cultural change (e.g. Schildkraut 2005; Schmid 2001; Tatalovich 1995). These notions are often described as unwavering steadfast beliefs, and only rarely do the discussions consider the possibility that they might take a back seat in a language legislation debate among the general public (e.g. Baron 1990; Citrin *et al.* 1990; Escamilla *et al.* 2003). Here, the framework of Ricento's (1998) 'deep values' is used to explore the failure of language legislation in the state of Ohio.

In 2005, a bill was introduced in the Ohio House of Representatives to make English the official language of the state. The stated purpose of House Bill #553 (HB553) [Ohio House Bill 553] was to 'require the use of the English language by state and local government entities in official actions and proceedings'. Government actions, proceedings and records in Ohio were already conducted in English. In fact, even The Ohio Commission on Hispanic/Latino Affairs, a state government agency, also conducts all of its official business in English. This legislation, therefore, simply assures the status quo with regard to the use of English and government business. Ohio, a Midwestern state that is comprised of 84.9 per cent persons reporting 'white' as their race in 2006 (United States Census Bureau), is not terribly diverse in terms of ethnicity. In addition, according to the US Census Bureau, in 2000 61 per cent of Ohioans reported that they speak a language other than English at home. By comparison to the national average (17.9 per cent) and states like California (39.5 per cent) and New York (28 per cent), it seems that English is not 'under threat' in Ohio. These factors have certainly raised the issue of the utility of such a bill. Nevertheless, even when *imaginary*, threats to the social order can propel members of the dominant group into action (Ricento 1998: 100). The arguments for proposing the Ohio bill rely heavily on the notion of 'unity': State Representative Courtney Combs, the bill's sponsor, refers to it as the 'Ohio English Unity Act'. Unity, and similar notions, are often invoked in language legislation campaigns in the United States.

In the Ohio case, however, the fear of the potential economic repercussions caused by the bill seemingly overrode the 'unity' and concurrent ideologies in spite of the ostensibly steadfast and unmovable nature of English-only ideologies. That is, after formal discussion in the House of Representatives, the bill was tabled[1] by a 65–28 vote. Newspapers reported that Ohio House Representatives were worried that the bill might negatively influence a pending Honda motor company decision about choosing Ohio or Indiana for the location of a new automobile plant. It appears that, in this case of English language legislation, the strong ideologies that support such legislation among Americans are not as powerful when pitted against money and jobs. This case-study explores, via interviews and relevant texts, the role of 'deep values' in language legislation and posits a weakness of the ideologies supporting such legislation in the face of practical issues. It concludes by suggesting that the complexity and the limitations of the ideologies behind the English-only position are often oversimplified.

Deep values

Unity is one of the more salient themes in the HB 553 debate as it is invoked by the bill's sponsor in naming the bill the 'Ohio English Unity Act'. Ricento (1998) provides a very useful and productive evaluation of unity and other factors that influence language policy in the United States and breaks down the complexity of the motivations that drive this kind of legislation. Via an analysis of the US Bilingual Education Act of 1968, he examines language policy in the United States and concludes that there are 'underlying, usually unstated or hegemonic frameworks' created by 'deep values' (1998: 89). For Ricento, 'deep values represent an accretion of national experiences, influenced by certain intellectual traditions' (ibid.). 'Deep values' are flexible, however. Each society has its own set of 'deep values' and they can change over time. In addition, it is not the case that all members hold all the same values. That is, 'deep values' are dominant but not universal. For Americans, one of these widely held 'deep values' is that 'unity and cultural integrity of the United States cannot abide cultural, including linguistic, pluralism' (1998: 90). Ricento describes other major dominant values that comprise American 'deep values'. They relate to shared historical experiences, belief in freedom from government intrusion and the belief that ethnolinguistic minority groups should not receive special protection to ensure the maintenance of their group. Examples of how the language of HB 553 and support for it, especially from the bill's sponsor, provide many examples of Ricento's 'deep values' will be discussed below.

Other research on English-only legislation also provides examples of the key role of deep values. For example, in their exploration of public attitudes to English-only legislation across the United States, Frendreis and Tatalovich (1997) conducted a **multivariate analysis** on data from a nationwide sample of the 1992 American National Election Study (NES). Respondents were asked 'Do you favour a law making English the official language of the United States, meaning business would be conducted in English only, or do you oppose such a law?' Frendreis and Tatalovich found that support for official English legislation was broad: 64.5 per cent indicated that they did support such a law (1997: 359). In addition, contrary to previous claims, they found that cultural/attitudinal variables are more important than demographic factors (e.g. partisanship, social class) in predicting support of English-only legislation (1997: 365). That is, they did not find that the commonly suggested hypotheses of racism, ethnic rivalry, class politics or partisanship were good predictors of responses to official English legislation. Their findings indicated that attitudes about an official national language in the United States 'are mostly tied to attributes regarding national identity and individuals' normative views about common identity and cultural diversity' (1997: 366). These attributes share many characteristics with Ricento's 'deep values' of unity and shared national experience.

Citrin *et al.* (1990) also explored survey data on English-only legislation in order to understand the mass appeal of such legislation. They conducted multivariate analyses on a variety of socio-political factors to find correlates among them (e.g. voting records, political party affiliation, social indices). They were specifically interested in 'the role played by feelings of national identity' (1990: 536). To that end, they constructed a 'Language Policy Index' (1990: 554) from responses to a questionnaire that aimed to indirectly measure a respondent's position on 'official English'. Their analyses of public opinion and language issues led them to the conclusion that the widespread support for English-only legislation is based largely on feelings of nationalism. They suggest that the popularity of official English legislation is the 'pervasive public desire to reaffirm an attachment to a traditional image of Americanism' (1990: 536). Here, again, we see the importance of "deep values" in the support for official English-language legislation.

Palozzi (2006) explored the role of multiculturalism and 'deep values' in official English legislation in Colorado. His data were comprised of surveys of Colorado voters before a 2002 election, which included official English legislation and surveys of university students in 2003. He found that both groups agreed that multilingualism is a good thing but also that a common language is important to national unity. 'This apparent discrepancy may illustrate the tension between espousing English as an important marker of American national identity and symbol of political unity, and acknowledging personal freedom' (2006: 34). That is, Americans are of two minds on the issue of official English; they feel that speaking English is part of what defines American citizenship but an individual's right to speak the language they choose also defines what it is to be an American. This duality is also present in the 1994 General Social Surveys (GSS), which reported that while 60 per cent of respondents favoured making English the official language of the United States and that government business should be conducted only in English, 61 per cent of those same respondents supported bilingual voting ballots. Palozzi (2006) shows us an example of duality in beliefs around language legislation. I suggest below, in conjunction with examples from the Ohio case, that this duality helps to weaken the strength of 'deep values' and enables it to be overruled by practicality.

The research discussed above has attempted to show a unifying theme in public opinion research on language legislation. That is, the strongest underpinnings for support of official English legislation are Americans' notions of what defines being American rather than issues such as overt racism, hostility, and social class conflict (see also Schildkraut 2005). Having examined the patterns in the ideologies supporting language legislation, we move on to the discourse about Ohio House Bill 553.

The sponsor of HB 553

It is important to note that the discussion surrounding the Ohio language legislation is not different from that of other US states' attempts at making English their official language and these themes have been widely discussed elsewhere (e.g. Baron 1990; Escamilla *et al.* 2003; Schildkraut 2005; Tatalovich 1995). The point of interest here is the reason for the failure of the bill. The bill's sponsor, Representative Courtney Combs (a Republican representing Hamilton County) states that '[The bill's] purpose was to promote a unifying stance by the state and allow everyone to celebrate cultural differences through a common language'. In interviews with the author and the press, Combs invokes aspects of 'deep values' such as unity and 'assimilation' to gain support for his bill. For example, in a newspaper article Rep. Combs refutes the idea that the bill is an 'English-only' bill by calling that nomenclature a 'scare tactic'. He said that he preferred the term 'unity' instead (Kidder 2006). In Rep. Combs' request to his House colleagues for co-sponsorship of HB 355, he exhibits Ricento's dominant American values:

> English is the common bond that holds us together as a nation … We are not dispelling those who do not speak English from our society; rather we are adding a bond between Ohioans … By creating a common bond among all people, we are preserving the strong and rich histories that each culture brings to our great state.
>
> (Ohio House of Representatives Internal Memorandum, personal communication)

Combs maintains consistently in interviews that he believes the bill is a means for uniting people.[2] When it was suggested to Combs by a colleague that the bill is 'divisive', he insisted that it was not divisive but 'uniting'. In an interview with the author, he cites a case in Cincinnati (the largest city in his district) where residents of a neighbourhood were not getting along because of the 'language barrier', suggesting that everyone could get along if they all spoke English. […] Other ideologies were also present in the discussions in the HB553 debate.

Two other typical themes dominate Rep. Combs' discussion about why this bill should be passed: 'assimilation', and the 'American dream' (i.e. self-sufficiency). Assimilation to American culture, or the 'deep value' of rejecting pluralism, is something, for Combs, that immigrants should want to do and also requires speaking English. He indicated that he was inspired to propose the bill because he felt that it should be emphasized that if a person becomes an American citizen, he or she should learn English. As an example, he told a story of a friend who has a Mexican 'housekeeper' who does not speak English and does not want to learn English. He said that that [a] friend's German parents had immigrated to the United States and learned English, and he wondered why it is not 'emphasized' that people who come to the United States should learn English. He felt that being American means speaking English. Combs was quoted in *The Columbus Dispatch*: 'It makes us, in my opinion, all Americans if we speak the same language' (Siegel 2006b).

Another dominant value, achieving the American dream (i.e. anyone can achieve economic prosperity), is present in Combs' discussions about HB553. He believes that not learning English stands in the way of immigrants' economic success because learning English 'can make them very self-sufficient'. For Combs the belief in self-sufficiency and the achievement of the American dream are largely tied to economics. For example, he stated in an interview with the author that an immigrant's income increases by 23 per cent if they learn English and indicated that the answer for breaking 'the bonds of poverty' and having a 'better life' for immigrants is to learn to speak English. [...] In addition, according to Combs, learning to speak English is a way for immigrants to have power. He maintained that people who speak English exert control over immigrants who do not speak English because they cannot speak for themselves. They are controlled and suppressed for the benefit of those who can speak English. According to Combs, if encouraged properly, immigrants will learn English, assimilate, be self-sufficient and be able to control their own destiny. In sum, there are familiar dominant values in the discussions about HB553, and these values are taken up in the next section with regard to their weakness in the face of perceived economic pressure.

The HB 553 debate in the public

In this section, the public debate on HB553 is explored with special attention given to how that debate among the Representatives and in the media exemplifies the importance of market forces with regard to this bill. On 23 May 2005, the House voted in favour of 'tabling' the bill (sending the bill back to committee for revision or more research) with 65 votes for and 28 against. In these discussions about the bill, the negative economic ramifications of HB553 are frequently mentioned. The main economic arguments centered on assumptions that the construction of a Honda factory would provide jobs and income for Ohioans and, additionally, that a Honda factory would employ many Ohioans long-term. For example, a newspaper article by Jim Siegel of *The Columbus Dispatch* reporting on the 'English-only proposal' pointed directly at the opportunity to land a deal for a Honda plant in Ohio as the reason for the failure of the bill with this headline: 'House tables language bill: Lawmakers feared ruining Honda deal'. He indicated that some House representatives expressed fear that English-language legislation would ruin chances at securing a deal with Honda motor company to build a $400 million plant in Ohio (Siegel 2006a). He wrote: 'Worried about how it might affect the state's efforts to lure a Japanese-owned automobile plant to Ohio, the Ohio House defeated a proposal to make English the official state language.'

He highlighted the economic ramifications of the bill further by stating that the plant would employ about 1500 people and that '… state officials don't want to give Honda any reason to choose Indiana over Ohio for its new plant.' Representative Jon Husted, the Speaker of the House, quoted by Siegel in the same article, confirmed his own concerns about the economic ramifications of the bill 'If it … prohibits success of things like recruiting Honda to Ohio, we want to make sure we're not creating barriers for those types of situations.' Another newspaper article about the bill echoed the context of 'barriers' expressed by the Speaker of the House and pointed directly to economics as the key reason for the failure of the bill:

> The efforts of some Ohio lawmakers to have English declared the state's official language were defeated by their toughest opponent: common sense. House members' recent vote to kill an English-only measure isn't a matter of backing down; it's a case of embracing opportunity. The top spot on many lawmakers' agendas right now isn't what language people speak, but jobs for Ohioans … Ohio is competing with Indiana for the [Honda] plant, and many House members wisely figured that a law that might make life difficult for Honda's Japanese executive and their families wouldn't help Ohio's chances. This is a perfect illustration of the global nature of business and why erecting barriers to the rest of the world is a bad idea.
>
> ('Carrot, not stick' 2006)

An editorial from the *Akron Beacon Journal* applauded the economic 'logic' of the tabling of the bill while emphasizing the highly symbolic nature of the measure:

> An Ohio yearning to please Honda, hoping the Japanese automaker will build a $400 million plant within the state's borders, would do well to resist making English its official language, signalling something less than open arms and bright smiles. Thankfully, a majority of the Ohio House embraced the logic last week, squashing a measure that would have unnecessarily stated the obvious: speak English here if you wish to succeed.
>
> ('Language lesson' 2006: 3)

Representative Combs, however, felt that the Honda factory should not have played a role in the fate of the bill. In an interview with the author, he indicated that he personally spoke with representatives of the Honda Corporation about how they felt about the bill: 'Basically their comment was "we're neutral on the bill".' However, other House members were not convinced about Honda's neutrality. House Representative, David R. Evans (R-77th District), who was present when the vote was taken to table the bill, indicated that the issue of the potential Honda plant was part of the discussion of the vote and the Speaker, Jon Husted, did not seem to support the bill (personal communication). In fact, according to Combs, Speaker Husted recommended that they delay voting on the bill until the Honda decision was made so as not to jeopardize Ohio's chances at landing the deal for a plant.

Although not as widely discussed, there were other kinds of economic objections. For example, the Director of the northern Ohio Sandusky County Department of Job and Family Services, in another newspaper article about HB553, discussed the important role that migrant workers played in that community: '[migrant workers are] a very important part of our economy here. It does not make sense to make it more difficult for them' (Sanctis 2005:1A). This strategy of emphasizing the economic importance of migrants also signals that the economic utility argument is strong among the competing ideologies of language legislation.

There were, to be sure, other objections to the bill that were not related to the economy, the Honda plant or migrants' influence on the economy. Racism, for example was not absent from the discussion. *The Columbus Dispatch* reported on comments on the bill by the president of the Ohio Hispanic Coalition who called it 'a bill about intolerance' (Courtney 2005). These kinds of objections were not, however, attributed to any legislators who had the power to vote against the bill. While some of the legislators voting against the bill may have held objections of this nature, they were not reported as having them.

Conclusion

In conclusion, the failure of Ohio HB 553 is an example of the inadvertent (and what linguists would regard as positive) effect market forces may have on language policy and shows how the support for English-only legislation can be overruled by domestic economic concerns. However, the 'about turn' in relation to Honda is not as contradictory as it first appears. Ohio HB 553 has the typical English-only ideologies at its core. These ideologies are strong but the point here is that the 'commitment' to the ideology in this case depends in part on a strong economy. That is, 'the way in which an issue is framed is a crucial determinant of which attitudes influence preference formation' (Citrin *et al.* 1990: 536). Further, Citrin *et al.* (1990: 556) acknowledged that the surveys they analyzed were conducted during prosperous economic times and that the results may have been different if conducted during a period of economic uncertainty. In addition, another factor contributes to the weakness of the ideologies in this case. Because Americans believe that it is important for Americans to speak English while at the same time they believe people have the right to speak whatever language they want, there is a certain amount of duality at the centre of the ideologies. English-only legislation is underpinned by a cultural consensus about national identity that can be challenged by its own complexity. Therefore, such legislation is subject to being overruled by more salient transitory practical issues such as the local economy.

Schildkraut (2005) also provides compelling evidence of the complexity of the American belief system that provides a platform for language legislation and warns against 'monolithic scale measures' (2005: 199) of American identity. Citrin *et al.* (1990) point out, 'for most members of the majority language group in the United States the *tangible* [emphasis in original] personal costs and benefits of bilingual government services or "official English" are neither clear nor substantial' (1990: 535). Perhaps when the personal costs and benefits become tangible such as that highlighted by the possibility of the Honda factory, 'deep values' are backgrounded. The **hegemonic** frameworks that drive English-language legislation are underpinned by 'deep values' that are, themselves, a mélange of ideologies and experiences. As such, when some of the 'deep values' conflict with one another or important external factors, they cannot serve as a solid underpinning, allowing for the ideological support or 'framework' for a particular issue to tumble.

The Ohio case is certainly not the only case of practicality overriding traditional American values. Palozzi (2006: 34) also found in the Colorado case that for some voters it was 'disdain for overly punitive and potentially costly litigation that turned otherwise pro-amendment people against it'. While 'symbolic values rather than material concerns are the predominant influence on mass preferences' (Citrin *et al.* 1990: 536), we must be mindful of the complexity of these symbolic values or 'deep values' and be aware of how that very complexity may render them weaker than they appear.

The debate is not yet over. Ohio House Bill 553 underwent revisions after its introduction; after it was tabled by the House of Representatives by a vote of 64 to 28 in May of 2006, it remained with the committee without being brought to the House floor for another vote. Representative Combs' office reported that illegal immigration issues had taken priority over HB 553. Honda ultimately chose the state of Indiana, Ohio's main competitor (and a state that does have an 'English-only' law), for the site of its new auto plant. Interestingly, in May 2008, the Ohio House passed a different bill (HB477) with a 54–42 vote that requires the use of the English-language by state and local government entities in official actions and proceedings, subject to certain exceptions. It awaits passage by the Senate, although Ohio Governor Ted Strickland indicated that he will veto the bill if it reaches him.

Notes

1   When a bill is "tabled", it is returned to the committee responsible for it for amendment or further consideration/research because the legislators feel it is not ready for a final vote.
2   While there are many points of interest in dissecting Comb's beliefs, it is not the purpose here to examine the fallacies of his arguments.

References

Baron, D. (1990) *The English-Only Question: An Official Language for Americans?* New Haven, CT: Yale University Press.

'Carrot, not stick; Encourage English in Ohio through education, not ban on foreign languages'. (6 June 2006) *Columbus Dispatch*, p. 12A. Retrieved from LexisNexis database.

Citrin, J., B. Reingold, E. Walters and D. Green (1990) 'The "Official English" Movement and the Symbolic Politics of Language in the United States', *The Western Political Quarterly*, 43(3): 535–559.

Courtney, J. (2005) 'Opponents speak out against English Only bill', *Columbus Dispatch*, 31 October, Retrieved from LexisNexis database.

Escamilla, K., S. Shannon, S. Carlos and J. García (2003) 'Breaking the Code; Colorado's Defeat of the Anti-Bilingual Education Initiative (Amendment 31)', *Bilingual Research Journal*, 27(3): 357–382.

Frendreis, J. and R. Tatalovich (1997) 'Who supports English only language laws? Evidence from the 1992 National Election Study', *Social Science Quarterly*, 78(2): 354–368.

General Social Surveys (1971–2000) *Cumulative Codebook*, conducted for the National Data Program for the Social Sciences at National Opinion Research Center, University of Chicago, online, available at: www.onenation.org/fiscalan.html [accessed 17 March 2005].

Huebner, T. and Davis, K. (eds.), (1999) *Sociopolitical Perspectives on Language Policy and Planning in the U.S.A.*, Amsterdam/Philadelphia: John Benjamins Publishing Company.

Kidder, K. (2006) 'Audience leery of English mandate', *Columbus Dispatch*, 28 July, pp. 1–2 E.

'Language lesson: The Ohio House grasps the many flaws in English-only', (1 June 2006) *Akron Beacon Journal*, p. 3. Retrieved from LexisNexis database.

Ohio House Bill 553, online, available at: www.legislature.state.oh.us/bills.cfm?ID=126_HB_553 [accessed 5 May 2005].

Palozzi, V. (2006) 'Assessing voter attitude toward language policy issues in the Unites States', *Language Policy*, 5(1): 15–39.

Ricento, T. (1998) 'National language policy in the United States', in R. Ricento and B. Burnaby (eds.), *Language and Politics in the United States and Canada: Myths and Realities*, Mahwah, NJ: Earlbaum, pp. 85–112.

Sanctis, M. (2005) 'Language Barrier', *The News-Messenger* (Fremont, Ohio), 2 August, page 1A. Retrieved from LexisNexis database.

Schildkraut, D. (2005) *Press One for English: Language Policy, Public Opinion and American Identity*, Princeton, NJ: Princeton University Press.

Schmid, C. (2001) *The Politics of Language: Conflict, Identity, and Cultural Pluralism in Comparative Perspective*, New York: Oxford University Press.

Siegel, J. (2006a) 'House tables language bill', *Columbus Dispatch*, 27 May, p. A1.

—— (2006b) 'Raising their voices across the US; let's speak English in Ohio, legislators says; Bill would make it the state's official language', *Columbus Dispatch*, 11 April, p. 01A.

Tatalovich, R. (1993) 'Who sponsors official English legislation? A comparative analysis of California's illegal immigration initiative', *Southeastern Political Review*, 21: 721–735.

—— (1995) *Nativism Reborn? The Official English Language Movement and the American States*, Lexington, KY: The University Press of Kentucky.

United States Census Bureau *State and County Quick Facts*, online, available at: http://quickfacts.census.gov/qfd/states/39000.html [accessed 9 September 2008].

Chapter 27

Jennifer Jenkins

ENGLISH AS A LINGUA FRANCA: INTERPRETATIONS AND ATTITUDES

World Englishes and English as a lingua franca

AS IS WELL known to readers of this journal, the study of WE has been in progress for several decades, and apart from the fact that the plural, 'Englishes', still occasionally causes raised eyebrows among non-linguists, there seems to be a general acceptance of what the field entails. My own use of the term 'world Englishes' is thus one that is likely to be non-controversial for most scholars of WE in that it refers to *all* local English varieties regardless of which of Kachru's three circles (Kachru 1985) they come from. All, according to this interpretation, are bona fide varieties of English regardless of whether or not they are considered to be 'standard', 'educated', and the like, or who their speakers are. In other words, my interpretation does not draw distinctions in terms of linguistic legitimacy between, say, Canadian, Indian, or Japanese English in the way that governments, prescriptive grammarians, and the general public tend to do.

The only possible area of controversy that I can see here, then, is that some WE scholars may not consider Expanding Circle Englishes as legitimate varieties on a par with Outer and Inner Circle varieties. Yano, for example, argues: 'In Japan, English is not used by the majority, nor is it used often enough for it to be established as Japanese English' (2008: 139). For reasons concerning their historical origins and current patterns of use, Expanding Circle Englishes are still perceived, even by some WE experts, as norm-dependent: that is, as 'interlanguage', or 'learner English', of greater or lesser proficiency depending on their proximity to a particular Inner Circle variety.[2]

Moving on to 'English as a lingua franca',[3] in using this term I am referring to a specific communication context: English being used as a lingua franca, the common language of choice, among speakers who come from different linguacultural backgrounds.[4]

In practice this often means English being used among non-native English speakers from the Expanding Circle, simply because these speakers exist in larger numbers than English speakers in either of the other two contexts (see e.g. Crystal 2003; Graddol 2006). However, this is not intended to imply that Outer or Inner Circle speakers are excluded from a definition of ELF. The vast majority of ELF researchers take a broad rather than narrow view, and include all English users within their definition of ELF. The crucial point, however, is that when Inner Circle speakers participate in ELF communication, they do not set the linguistic agenda. Instead, no matter which circle of use we come from, from an ELF perspective we all need to make adjustments to our local English variety for the benefit of our **interlocutors** when we take part in lingua franca English communication. ELF is thus a question, not of orientation to the norms of a particular group of English speakers, but of mutual negotiation involving efforts and adjustments from all parties.

At its simplest, ELF involves both common ground and local variation. On the one hand, there is shared linguistic common ground among ELF speakers just as there is shared common ground among the many varieties of the English that are collectively referred to as 'English as a native language' (ENL). ELF's common ground inevitably contains linguistic forms that it shares with ENL, but it also contains forms that differ from ENL and that have arisen through contact between ELF speakers, and through the influence of ELF speakers' first languages on their English. On the other hand, ELF, like ENL, involves a good deal of local variation as well as substantial potential for accommodation – the scope for its users to adjust their speech in order to make it more intelligible and appropriate for their specific interlocutor(s). This can involve, for example, **code-switching**, repetition, echoing of items that would be considered errors in ENL, the avoidance of local idiomatic language, and paraphrasing (see Cogo and Dewey 2006; Kirkpatrick 2008).

The common ground in ELF is being identified in the speech of proficient speakers of English. While the majority of speakers providing data for analysis come from the Expanding Circle, ELF databases usually also include Outer Circle speakers, and most also include Inner Circle speakers. However, in the case of the Inner Circle, numbers are restricted to ensure that they do not distort the data with a surplus of ENL forms or (unwittingly) act as norm-providers, making the other speakers feel under pressure to speak like them. VOICE (the Vienna-Oxford International Corpus of English), for example, allows up to 10 per cent of native speakers to be present in any interaction.

ELF researchers are as interested in the kinds of linguistic processes involved in ELF creativity as they are in the resulting surface-level features, and these processes, such as regularisation, have already been found to operate in ways similar to those that occur in any other language contact situation (see also Lowenberg 2002). Examples of features resulting from these processes are likely to include the countable use of nouns that in ENL are considered uncountable (e.g. *informations, advices*), and zero marking of third person singular *-s* in present tense verbs (e.g. *she think, he believe*; see e.g. Breiteneder 2005). At present there is insufficient evidence for researchers to be able to predict the extent of the common ELF ground. And it is also likely that researchers working on ELF in different parts of the world, e.g. the VOICE and ELFA (English as a Lingua Franca in Academic Settings) teams in Europe (e.g. Seidlhofer *et al.* 2006; Mauranen 2006), and Deterding and Kirkpatrick (2006) in Southeast Asia will identify different branches of ELF, just as there are different branches of ENL such as North American English, Australian English, British English and so on, and different sub-varieties within these. But at present it is still too early to say.

Two further provisos need stating in relation to ELF research. First, ELF distinguishes between *difference* (i.e. from ENL) and *deficiency* (i.e. interlanguage or 'learner language'), and does not assume that an item that differs from ENL is by definition an error. It may instead be a legitimate ELF variant. This does not mean, however, that all ELF speakers are proficient: they can also be learners of ELF or not fully competent *non*-learners, making errors just like learners of any second language (see Jenkins 2006). At present it is still to some extent an empirical question as to which items are ELF variants and which ELF errors, and depends on factors such as systematicity, frequency, and communicative effectiveness. Sufficient patterns have nevertheless emerged for ELF researchers to be in a position to make a number of hypotheses about ELF, including the two features described in the previous paragraph.

The second proviso is that even if and when ELF features have been definitively identified and perhaps eventually codified, ELF researchers do not claim that these features should necessarily be taught to English learners. In other words, they do not believe either that pedagogic decisions about language teaching should follow on automatically from language descriptions or that the linguists compiling the **corpora** should make those decisions. In this, ELF corpus researchers take a rather different approach from compilers of most corpora of British and American English (often, oddly, referred to as 'real' English), who tend to transfer their findings immediately to English language teaching publications for circulation all round the Expanding Circle, without seeing any need for the mediation of pedagogic and sociolinguistic considerations.

Two positions on ELF

ELF is seen as non-controversial and is taken for granted by many professionals working internationally (businesspeople, technicians and suchlike), although their positive orientation is rarely verbalised, let alone published. By contrast, it is the negative responses to ELF, coming primarily from within the field of English studies, which are most often published. Those who criticise ELF tend to orient to one of two (curiously opposing) perspectives on English. First, a number of scholars working within the field of WE argue that ELF is monolithic and monocentric, a 'monomodel' in which 'intercultural communication and cultural identity are to be made a necessary casualty' (Rubdy and Saraceni 2006: 11). This seems to me to be a strange interpretation of ELF, as it is Inner Circle models such as 'standard' British and American English and their respective 'standard' accents, **RP (Received Pronunciation)** and GA (General American), that are monomodels and which regularly make casualties of Expanding Circle speakers' identities. And this was certainly borne out in the words of the Expanding Circle speakers who participated in interviews with me for my recent research project (Jenkins 2007, and see below).

In fact it seems to me that ELF's pluricentric approach is precisely why those who favour a monolithic approach to the English of its second language speakers – i.e. those who take the second and opposite perspective to the WE critics of ELF – object to ELF so much. According to this second perspective, ELF lacks any standards and by default exhibits errors wherever it departs from certain Inner Circle Englishes (usually British and American). According to this position, ELF and EFL (English as a foreign language) are one and the same. No distinction is made between English learnt for intercultural communication (ELF) – where native English speakers may be, but often are not, present in the interaction – and English learnt specifically for communication with English native speakers (EFL).[7]

If people wish to learn English as a 'foreign' language in order to blend in with a particular group of its native speakers in an Inner Circle environment or because of a personal aspiration to acquire 'native-like' English, then that is their choice, and of no concern to ELF researchers provided that the choice is an informed one. However, this is a completely different linguacultural context from the one that ELF researchers are investigating. The problem is that because the monolithic position on ELF conflates it with EFL, those who subscribe to this position believe that any differences from native speaker English in the speech of *ELF* speakers have exactly the same status as differences from native speaker English in *EFL* speakers: that is, they are by definition deficiencies rather than legitimate ELF variants. It is worth reminding ourselves at this point that the people who have this **ideological** frame of mind used to say the same sorts of things about Outer Circle Englishes such as Indian English, Lankan English, and Singapore English – that they were interlanguages rather than legitimate varieties of English with their own norms of use. Now they have simply transferred their attention and derogatory comments to ELF.

Underlying attitudes and their potential effects

Turning to attitudes, the language that people use when they put forward the second perspective outlined at the outset – that ELF means errors and 'anything goes', and that it is simply interlanguage – is often very revealing. For one thing, the language tends to be emotive. These are three typical examples (emphases added in each case):

- Sobkowiak (2005: 141) describes an ELF approach to pronunciation as one that will 'bring the ideal [that is, Received Pronunciation] down into the *gutter* with no checkpoint along the way'.
- Prodromou, in several similarly worded articles, describes ELF as 'a *broken* weapon' and its speakers as '*stuttering* onto the world stage' (e.g. 2006: 412).
- Roy Harris, referring, in a letter to the *Times Higher Education Supplement* (14 September 2007, p. 14), to the fact that Korean Airlines had reportedly chosen to use French speakers of English, rather than British or American English speakers, because Koreans found the English of the French more intelligible, makes this comment: 'I couldn't care less what kind of English Korean Airlines *inflict* on their passengers.'

The derogatory nature of the kinds of language used in comments such as these demonstrates the strength of antipathy towards ELF forms among supporters of ENL. And although it is not possible to make direct causal links between such attitudes and ELF speakers' identities, the staunchly native English speaker ideology that underpins these attitudes, and also pervades much of the English language teaching material available in Expanding Circle countries, seems to be exerting an influence on Expanding Circle English teachers and their learners. This was suggested, for example, by a questionnaire study of Expanding Circle English speakers' attitudes towards English accents that I conducted (see Jenkins 2007: Ch. 6). The results showed that an attachment to 'standard' Inner Circle native speaker models remains firmly in place among many non-native English speakers, despite the fact that they no longer learn English to communicate primarily with its native speakers.

The respondents even showed little sign of acknowledging the fact that Outer Circle Englishes are now, in the main, firmly established varieties with their own norms. Thus, they rated Indian English as poorly as Chinese and Japanese English for both acceptability and pleasantness, and only slightly higher for correctness. Meanwhile, they consistently oriented most positively to 'standard' British and American English accents, not only in relation to the 'correctness' and 'pleasantness' variables, but also for 'acceptability for international communication'. This is surprising, given the increasing evidence that British and American accents are not the most easily intelligible in lingua franca contexts because of their copious use of features of connected speech such as elision, assimilation, and weak forms.

Similarly, the questionnaire respondents evaluated non-native English accents according to their proximity to these two Inner Circle accents. This meant that they were reasonably well disposed towards a Swedish English accent, which they referred to as 'native-like', 'natural, like native speakers', etc. On the other hand, they made extremely pejorative comments about the accents they perceived as furthest from native English accents, particularly China English, Japanese English, and Russian English accents. For example, the Japanese English accent was described as 'weird' and 'menacing', the China English as 'quarrel-like' and 'appalling', and the Russian English as 'heavy', 'sharp', and 'aggressive'. The respondents even volunteered these kinds of comments about the accent of their own first-language group, making them, in Lippi-Green's (1997: 242) words, 'complicit in the process' of their own subordination.

I was surprised by the extent of the negativity towards non-native English accents demonstrated in many of the responses to my questionnaire study. However, things were less clear-cut and polarised, and more explanatory, in the interview study (mentioned above) that I conducted in parallel. In this study, most of the participants, themselves young teachers of English, expressed a fair degree of ambivalence and even conflicted feelings about their English. On the one hand, they felt some kind of obligation to acquire 'near-native' English accents, by which they meant near-(North) American or British English, in order to be seen – and to see themselves – as successful English speakers and teachers. So at one level they were unable to separate the notion of good English from the notion of an Inner Circle native speaker 'ideal'. This is not surprising in view of the point made above about the ideological underpinnings of much of the material that is available to them: course books, teaching manuals, applied linguistics writings, and so on, whose negative effects on their confidence are doubtless enhanced by comments of the sort made by the likes of Sobkowiak.

On the other hand, the participants also expressed the desire to project their own local identity in their English, and some of them even felt themselves to be part of a community of lingua franca English speakers, and to share a common identity with other ELF speakers. This supports Seidlhofer's point: 'Alongside local speech communities sharing a dialect, we are witnessing the increased emergence of global discourse communities, or communities of practice sharing their particular registers, with English being the most widely used code' (2007: 315).

According to my interview participants, the freedom to express their own local and ELF identities in their English would give them greater confidence as both English speakers and English teachers. It seems clear, then, to paraphrase Rubdy and Saraceni (2006: 11), that these interview participants felt their identities were casualties of the pressures on them to learn American or British English, and that the opposite would be true if ELF became acceptable and those pressures were removed. The following five extracts are typical of the ambivalent and 'conflicted' comments they made (see Jenkins 2007 for full details):

> Taiwanese English speaker: 'I really feel bad about this you know, I feel like I have to lose my identity. I'm a Taiwanese person and I should feel comfortable about this, and I just feel that when I'm speaking English, I will want to be like a native speaker, and it's really hard, you know.'

> Japanese English speaker: 'Yes, that's lots of contradiction in the view. So in theory I can understand varieties of English and non-native accent, it's good, it's accepted as far as intelligibility exists. But at a personal level still I'm aiming at native-like speaking.'

> Italian English speaker: 'The materials they have, it's mainly videos and tapes, it's all native speakers' accents, so that's the only model they have. Maybe if more materials around was with different accents and non-native speaker accents, then it's like recognizing, it's like codifying, it's like accepting it worldwide.'

> China English speaker: 'First of all I am Chinese. I don't have to speak like American or British, it's like identity, because I want to keep my identity, yeah. ... I feel that it's quite conflicted for me because I feel happy when they say okay you have a native accent, but erm if they cannot recognize from my pronunciation and they think that okay, you are definitely American, I don't feel comfortable because I am indeed a Chinese.'

> Polish English speaker: 'I've still got a little bit of linguistic schizophrenia ... I know that I don't need to speak like a British person, but because I've been taught for so many years that I should do it, when I hear, let's say, someone speaking British English like a nice RP pronunciation, I like it.'

The fact that most of my interview participants seem to have reached a point at which they no longer consider it, at least in theory, a foregone conclusion that it is essential to imitate ENL speakers in order to communicate effectively in ELF contexts of use is cause for optimism for ELF researchers. In this, there seems to be something of a divide between these younger Expanding Circle English users and those from older generations such as Sobkowiak (see above), with the younger ones being more likely to have experienced ELF communication at first hand, and (perhaps partly for this reason) being more receptive to ELF in theory and to (English) language change in general. Further evidence of younger English speakers' more favourable orientations to ELF can be found in data collected by Peckham *et al.* (2008) among Erasmus students in Hungary and the Czech Republic. For example, a German participant in their study says:

> I liked very much with the English here to speak English with non-native speakers. It's the funny new words or new pronunciations that emerge and then you just keep those because you like them so much and not important anymore to say in the right way, and even more fun to create this new language.

This German student still considers her differences from ENL to be errors (not 'right'), but she is clearly aware of the creative potential of the kind of English she produces with other non-native speakers. The next student, a French speaker, takes the same deficit approach to the kind of English he speaks as compared with ENL (which he calls 'real English'), but is also well aware of its communicative value:

> Erasmus English is totally different than the real English, but it's like we have different accents, we use these words and it's not correct at all, it's like quite awful sometimes [*laughs*] but it's good, we can understand each other.

A third student, also French, again considers her English to be faulty by comparison with ENL ('I don't speak perfectly English') but is aware of the major advantage of being bilingual and the major disadvantage ('it's not my problem') of being monolingual:

> I was really embarrassed in the beginning. I was like 'oh, I'm really sorry for my level' because I was ashamed I think. And now I don't care about the native speaker because most of them don't speak any other language, so it's not my problem, I don't speak perfectly English but I speak some other language.

Finally, an Italian student points out how effective ELF communication is, and the fact that it tends to be English native speakers who are the source of problems:

> I see that if I'm in the middle of people that are not English and they're speaking English and so there is no problem understanding them, probably my obstacle was that to understand like really English people talking.

Regardless of their perspective on their English and whether they still perceive their differences from ENL as errors, all these younger English speakers seem at least to appreciate their advantage as bilingual speakers of English in ELF communication contexts, and to view the claim that effective communication in English involves deferring to ENL norms as a fiction – something that WE research has, of course, long demonstrated.

Finally, as the purpose of the original workshop at the 2007 IAWE Conference in Regensburg (of which my current paper formed a part) was to explore similarities and differences in orientation to English of WE and ELF scholars, I will end with a short comment on this topic. Over the past few years, ELF research has often been seen as having a very different agenda from WE research. However, it seems to me (and always has done) that world Englishes and English as a lingua franca have a lot more that draws them together than sets them apart. And, to quote myself, 'we need to find ways of bringing WE and ELF scholars together in recognition of their shared interests, whatever their circle or research focus' (Jenkins 2006: 175). The colloquium organised by Margie Berns and Anne Pakir at the IAWE conference in Regensburg in 2007, the first of its kind bringing together WE and ELF scholars, was thus a very important first step in this direction, and I look forward to much future collaboration of this kind.

Notes

1   The Erasmus Programme is a European Union education and training programme that enables students to study and work abroad, as well as supporting collaboration between higher education institutions across Europe.

2   Arguments such as Yano's ignore the fact that there are established English varieties in some Outer Circle countries where 'English is not used by the majority', but is the preserve of a largely elite educated minority.

3   ELF is sometimes known as EIL (English as an international language). However, to avoid confusion with other uses of the word 'international' (e.g. 'International English' is sometimes equated with North American English), most researchers prefer 'ELF'. This is also generally preferred to the term 'lingua franca English', as the latter implies the existence of one single lingua franca variety of English, which is most certainly not the case.

4   Note that by 'communication context' I am not referring to any specific geographical context. ELF communication, in this interpretation, is not tied to any particular geographical area, but is defined by who the participants are and how they orient to English.

5   Note that I normally use the term 'native English speaker' to refer to both Inner and Outer Circle speakers. But because those who subscribe to the second position outlined above reserve 'native speaker' for the Inner Circle, I am using it in this sense in this part of my discussion.

References

Breiteneder, Angelika (2005) The naturalness of English as a European lingua franca: the case of third person -s, *Vienna English Working Papers 14*, pp. 3–26.

Cogo, Alessia and Dewey, Martin (2006) Efficiency in ELF communication: from pragmatic motives to lexicogrammatical innovation, *Nordic Journal of English Studies*, 5(2): 59–94.

Crystal, David (2003) *English as a Global Language*. Cambridge: Cambridge University Press.

Deterding, David and Kirkpatrick, Andy (2006) Emerging South-East Asian Englishes and intelligibility, *World Englishes*, 25(3–4): 391–409.

ELFA website: www.uta.fi/laitokset/kielet/engf/research/elfa.

Graddol, David (2006) *English Next: Why Global English May Mean the End of English as a Foreign Language*, London: British Council.

Jenkins, Jennifer (2006) Current perspectives on teaching world englishes and English as a lingua franca, *TESOL Quarterly*, 40(1): 157–181.

——— (2007) *English as a Lingua Franca: Attitude and Identity*, Oxford: Oxford University Press.

Kachru, Braj B. (1985) Standards, codification and sociolinguistic realism: the English language in the Outer Circle, in Randolph Quirk and Henry G. Widdowson (eds.), *English in the*

World: Teaching and Learning the Language and Literatures, Cambridge: Cambridge University Press, pp. 11–30.

Kirkpatrick, Andy (2008) English as the official working language of the Association of Southeast Asian Nations (ASEAN): features and strategies, *English Today*, 24(2): 27–34.

Lippi-Green, Rosina (1997) *English with an Accent*, London: Routledge.

Lowenberg, Peter (2002) Assessing English proficiency in the Expanding Circle, *World Englishes*, 21(3): 431–435.

Mauranen, Anna (2006) Spoken discourse, academics and global English: a corpus perspective, in Rebecca Hughes (ed.), *Spoken English, TESOL and Applied Linguistics*, Houndmills: Palgrave Macmillan, pp. 143–158.

Peckham, Don, Kalocsai, Karolina, Kov´acs, Emöke and Sherman, Tamah (2008) English and multilingualism, or English only in a multilingual Europe? In *Languages in a Network of Excellence in Europe*, unpublished project report, Work Package 7.

Prodromou, Luke (2006) A reader responds to J. Jenkins's 'Current perspectives on Teaching World Englishes and English as a Lingua Franca', *TESOL Quarterly*, 41: 409–413.

Rubdy, Rani and Saraceni, Mario (eds.), (2006) *English in the World: Global Rules, Global Roles*, London: Continuum.

Seidlhofer, Barbara (2007) English as a lingua franca and communities of practice, in Sabine Volk-Birke and Julia Lippert (eds.), *Halle 2006 Proceedings*, Trier: Wissenschaftlicher Verlag, pp. 307–318.

Seidlhofer, Barbara, Breiteneder, Angelika and Pitzl, Marie-Luise (2006) English as a lingua franca in Europe: challenges for applied linguistics, *Annual Review of Applied Linguistics*, 26: 3–34.

Sobkowiak, Włodzimierz (2005) Why not LFC? In Katarzyna Dziubalska-Kołaczyk and Joanna Przedlecka (eds.), *English Pronunciation Models: A Changing Scene*, Frankfurt am Main: Lang, pp. 131–49.

VOICE website: www.univie.ac.at/voice

Yano, Yasukata (2008) Comment 5 in the Forum on Colingualism, *World Englishes*, 27(1): 139–40.

Glossary

AAVE   African American Vernacular English; used interchangeably with BEV

accent   features of variation in speakers' pronunciation that can signal their regional or social background.

accommodation theory   adjusting the way one speaks to be more like a real or imagined interlocutor. Thus a speaker who accommodates changes the way they speak to be more like the person they are speaking to in order to facilitate closeness and solidarity. It is also possible that a speaker changes their language away from their interlocutor in order to signal distance. There need not be co-presence for accommodation to take place; in the media, television and radio presenters adjust their speech to accommodate their audience (e.g. national or local).

adjective   a class of words which is generally used to describe or modify a noun. The adjectives in the following examples are in small capitals: 'The LUCKY cat ran away'. 'The PERSIAN cat ate my trout.' 'That cat is BIG.'

adverb   a class of words which is generally used to describe or modify a verb, but can also modify other parts of speech which aren't nouns. They can also signify when, where, how, or to what extent something happened. The adverbs in the following examples are in small capitals: 'The girl QUICKLY solved the problem'. 'The dog wagged its tail FURIOUSLY'. 'He came to class LATE because he was tired'.

androcentric/androcentrism   as 'andro' means 'man', androcentric means to be male centred.

apartheid   a system of racial segregation in South Africa between 1948 and 1994. The segregation was effected through law.

aspirated stop   a stop is a consonant where the airstream is stopped by one of the articulators (lips, tongue, palette), such as 'p', 'b', 't', 'd', 'k' and 'g'. Aspiration refers to breath after this stop is released. An unaspirated voiceless stop (p/t/k) can sound very much like the voiced consonant at the same place of articulation (b/d/g).

authentic/authenticity   in sociolinguistics, discussion of authenticity appears to have taken the place of the vernacular. While previously it was thought that individuals had a 'natural' way of speaking (the vernacular) now sociolinguistics argue that speakers are always constructing an identity. As this leaves the concept of the natural vernacular in a precarious position, scholars now talk about accepted constructions of identity as 'authentic'.

backchannel feedback   the feedback that listeners give to speakers, by verbal expressions such as *mmm, uhuh, yeah*, and by nodding, frowning or other facial and body gestures. See also **minimal responses**.

back vowels   see **vowel**

BEV   Black English Vernacular; used interchangeably with AAVE.

binomial   two names or categories.

bricolage   in French this literally means 'tinkering'. Bricolage refers to the process of making something new out of existing materials and resources; it is most often used in sociolinguistics to refer to the construction of new identities by combining pre-existing variables into a new style.

cant   the specialized language of a particular group, hence, like 'jargon' or 'argot'. Usually used pejoratively.

CDA Critical Discourse Analysis   an approach to discourse analysis that explores the connection between language and power. It is explicitly political and analyzes language using a variety of tools in order to say something about how language is used to do things, including promoting a particular ideology.

closed question   as opposed to an **open question**, a closed question is one that syntactically requires a 'yes' or 'no' response. A closed question is often constructed by using a declarative with an interrogative tag at the end: 'It's cold in here, isn't it?'

code-switching   when lexical items and grammatical features from two languages occur in one utterance, turn or conversation.

collocation   refers to the co-occurrence of words. Some words are in frequent collocation such as *happy* and *event* as in 'happy event'. Collocation can also affect the meaning of a word in a particular context. For example *white* in collocation with *wine* denotes a different colour from *white* in collocation with *snow*.

commodification   turning something into a thing that can be sold.

communicative competence   in contrast to **competence and performance**, communicative competence is what a speaker needs to do to construct appropriate utterances in a speech community. Communicative competence is also called 'sociolinguistic competence' or 'pragmatic competence'.

communities of practice   a group of people who come together for a common aim or activity. Communities of practice often develop their own ways of using language. The model is influenced by a move in sociolinguistics to look locally at language use, as opposed to large scale variationist investigations.

competence and performance   competence is opposed to performance, in a distinction made by Chomsky. Competence is refers to the grammar, or the rules of the language which need to be followed for grammaticality. Performance is what people actually do in their speech.

connotation   the personal associations conjured up by a word, although they are not strictly part of its definition. For example, a *spinster* is an adult female human who has never been married, but for many people this word also carries connotations of 'old', 'unattractive' and 'not sexually active'.

convergence   a process in which speakers change their speech to make it more similar to that of their hearer, or to that of other people in their social group. When applied to the convergence of whole dialects or accents it is also termed levelling. Upward convergence describes speakers moving from a less to more prestigous variety; conversely, downward convergence is a move from a more to less prestigous variety.

conversational dominance   when a speaker takes more turns or more time than is equitable in a conversation. Such dominance may be exercised through **interruptions**, self-allocation of turns or simply not giving up a turn (that is, not stopping speaking).

corpus/copora (pl)   corpus means 'body' and in linguistics a corpus is a collection of spoken or written texts which are then used as data in order to say something about patterns in the text. Corpora may be general, in order to cover as much language variety as possible, or more specific, in order to investigate a particular area.

covert prestige   covert means 'hidden' or 'non-obvious'. Sometimes speakers use a seemingly less prestigious or non-standard language variety to identify with a group that uses that variety. Thus, the language variety of that group can have a covert prestige. See also **overt prestige**.

creaky voice   a way of modifying the voice by constricting the lower part of the vocal tract so that it sounds creaky. This is meaningful in some languages' sound systems; in English it is used to affect a style.

deficit theory   a theory that claims differences in speech can be described in terms of one variety being less correct or powerful than another. There are deficit theories for differences between men and women's speech as well as for differences between the speech of social classes.

derivational morphology   making a new word from an old one. This may change the part of speech of the word; for example, the verb 'defect' can be changed into a noun 'defection' through addition of the '-ion' suffix, or shift a base to a different sub-class within the same broader word class, e.g. pig ➔ piglet, or changing the meaning of the base, e.g. lock ➔ unlock.

dialect contact   when the speakers of two dialects interact for a long period of time. This may result in **dialect levelling**.

dialect levelling   the reduction of differences between ways of speaking in different parts of the country, as a result the number of variants in the output is dramatically reduced from the number in the input.

dialect   a variety of a language that can signal the speaker's regional or social background. Unlike accents which differ only in pronunciation, dialects differ in their grammatical structure – *Do you have …?* (US) versus *Have you got …?* (UK) – and in their vocabulary: *sidewalk* (US) versus *pavement* (UK).

dialectic   while this has specific meanings in philosophy and logic, it is used more generally to refer to the presence of two factors which interact with each other. It is also sometimes used simply to mean 'mutually related' or dialogue. It is not related to dialect.

dichotomous   the splitting into two parts and two parts only.

diphthong   a complex speech sound that begins with one vowel and glides into another vowel, e.g. the middle sound in 'mine'.

directives   asking someone to do something; this will usually be in the **imperative** form. If a directive is in a more mitigated form, it is likely to be described as a request.

discourse   this term has a number of meanings. The particular meaning that is intended will either be defined or be clear from the context. One meaning is simply what people say, thus as a synonym for talk. It is more likely to be a way of describing the structuring features and principles of stretches of language. These features can also be understood as an ideology; the discourse is the realization of this ideology in language. Thus, it can be used to refer to the way belief systems and values are talked about, as in 'the discourse of capitalism'. The prevailing way that a culture talks about or represents something is called the dominant discourse, that is, the 'commonsense' or 'normal' representation.

discourse marker   a word with a function more than a meaning, which is to structure speech. 'So', 'well', 'now', 'really' and the like are all examples of discourse markers. They do have a function in displaying affect and also in structuring arguments.

divergence   a process in which speakers choose to move away from the linguistic norms of their hearer or social group. This can involve using a style or language variety not normally used by the group or even speaking an entirely different language.

downward convergence   see **convergence**.

dyadic   involving two actors; generally applied to conversation in which two people are interacting.

elaborated code   see **restrictive and elaborated code**.

ELF English as a Lingua Franca   refers to the use of English by native and non-native speakers of different varieties to communicate. As English is a World or Global language, ELF signals the importance of examining how users of different varieties actually interact and communicate. In part, this is to move discussion away from questions about which variety is 'correct' or 'standard'.

emoticons   the use of ASCII characters to communicate affect in written language, especially when mediated by technology such as email or texting. The use of emoticons is important in supplying information about affect, stance and irony in the absence of face to face interaction, and thus the absence of intonation and **paralinguistic** information.

entailment   a logical and often semantic relationship between propositions. Entailments are logically necessary, as opposed to implicature which are conventional.

Essex girl/man   stereotypical figures well known in England. Essex is a county in the south-east of England. 'Essex girl' is a pejorative term for women, indicating lack of intelligence, aspirant behaviour, poor taste and sexual proclivity. 'Essex man' suggests 'average' though not necessarily in a positive way, as the suggestion of low intelligence and aspiration remain.

Estuary English   the label for a variety spoken in the south-east of England, found roughly around the Thames river estuary.

ethnographic   a research methodology which seeks to describe a particular society or event through such methods as participant observation and interviews, usually over a long period of time.

etymology   the history of a word, that is, from which language a word seems to have developed. It is not always possible to establish the etymology of a word.

face   see **positive/negative face**.

floor   in relation to conversation, this is used in two senses. The first, and more usual, sense refers to the 'space' available in the conversation. When a speaker is talking s/he is said to 'hold the floor'. The second sense refers to the general landscape of the floor. A shared floor, for example, is said to exist when it is permissible for more than one speaker to speak at one time. This is the marked floor; the default floor is that only one person speaks at a time.

folk linguistics   can refer to the beliefs that non-linguists have about language, and in this sense is often pejorative. The term also refers to the study, by linguists, of these beliefs.

fresh talk   from the work of Goffman, 'fresh talk' is speech that sounds natural even though it is scripted/planned. It is designed to seem natural.

fronting   see **vowel**.

fushaa   a prestige form of Tunisian Arabic which fuses classical and Modern Arabic.

generic   generally, an expression which is used to refer to a class of things. For example, a distinction is drawn between the generic use of *man* in *Man has walked the earth for millions of years* where this term refers to humans in general and *I now pronounce you man and wife* where this term refers only to male humans.

genetic versus functional nativeness   the myth of genetic transmission of a language refers to cases where a group has their language because of inheritance from a 'founding' community. Thus, former colonies like Australia, New Zealand and Canada inherited their English from Britain. In contrast functional nativeness is determined by the range of social circumstances a language can be used in.

Gestalt psychologists   a kind of psychology that emphasises patterns and focuses on the way the human mind takes account of them in perception and thought processing.

globalization   a process variously defined in relation to economics, governance and culture. Globalization approaches questions and issues acknowledging the interconnectedness between different parts of the world. In contrast to internationalism, globalization does not privilege the nation state as actor. The clearest examples of globalization are to do with economics. Institutions like the IMF, WTO and World Bank are arguably the most global agents.

glottal stop   a consonant made by a tight closure of the vocal chords followed by an audible release of air. It can be heard in several British accents where this consonant replaces the /t/ in a word such as *butter* pronounced *buh-uh*. The phonetic symbol for a glottal stop is /ʔ/.

hedges   linguistic devices such as *sort of* and *I think* which 'dilute' an assertion. Compare *he's dishonest* and *he's sort of dishonest; she lost it* and *I think she lost it.*

hegemonic (adj) /hegemony (n)   the common meaning of the concept originates in the work of Antonio Gramsci. While initially it was related to dominance and leadership in economic matters and means of production, it was later extended to include all forms of dominance and leadership, especially in relation to dominant (or hegemonic) ideologies (Gramsci 2000[1]).

heterogeneity   difference, or variety; as opposed to homogeneity (uniformity).

honorific   in general refers to the use of language to express respect or politeness. More specifically it can refer to certain address forms which express respect such as *Sir/Madam, Your Highness, Reverend* and the 'formal' version of *you* in languages which make that distinction.

HRT   High Rising Terminal; also known as 'uptalk' or 'rising intonation'. While this intonation is typical of questions, it is also a marker of identity and style in some speech communities.

hybrid/hybridity   two or more features/things together treated as one. In relation to language, a hybrid genre, for example, will be one that takes features from more than one established genre. Thus, 'infomercials' are hybrid forms which incorporate features of advertising (commercials) with features of informational programming (like news or documentaries).

iconization   a process described by Irvine and Gal[2] whereby stereotypes about a group become attached to features of their language. Thus, women are stereotypically thought to speak a lot; hence, verbosity is 'iconized' as a feminine characteristic.

ideational   a function of language proposed by Halliday as part of systemic functional grammar. The ideational function of language refers to the way language organizes experience; both objects and events.

ideology   a set or pattern of beliefs.

imperative   in grammatical terms, a verb form, which is expresses a command 'Come!' or 'Speak!' are both imperative forms.

implicature   a meaning which can be extracted but is implicit rather than explicit. Implicatures are conventional rather than strictly logical (see **entailment**).

indexical/indexing   an index points to something. In grammar, an index may also be called a deictic. What a deictic ('this', 'I', 'now') refers to can only be established by the context of the utterance. It is now more commonly used to discuss the significance of a linguistic feature. Thus, the pronunciation of a particular phoneme can index membership of a social group if that feature is associated with that group.

infixing   is a morphological process where a **morpheme** is inserted inside a word, rather than as a prefix or suffix. Infixing is very important in some languages, English has few examples of infixing as in 'abso-bloody-lutely'. (This may also be called tmesis.) This is not the kind of thing that occurs in languages where infixing is common. Rather, in those languages infixing is part of, for example, verb conjugation.

interlocutor   another way of describing an addressee or partner in talk.

interruption   variously defined as **simultaneous speech** and an utterance that stops the interrupted person speaking.

intertextuality   generally used to refer to the referencing of or allusion to one text by another. This may be done by obvious quotation, parody or borrowing any textual feature.

intransitive   see **transitive**.

kitsch   objects (or their characteristics) which are highly sentimental or even vulgar. While 'kitsch' has in the past been used to cast aspersion on others' taste, in postmodern times it is celebrated for exactly the reasons it was derided. The celebration of kitsch is usually one of ironic detachment.

language maven   a non-linguist who takes a strong interest in and strong position on how language should be used.

latching   to describe the way a speaker in a conversation starts speaking just as the last turn finishes. Thus, there is no gap between the two speakers (between the two turns).

late modern   the period in which we live now; the term draws attention to the social construction of identity that people are compelled to engage in because of the breakdown of traditional/stable identity categories.

lexical   relating to lexemes, that is, words.

lexicography   the work involved in as well as the construction of dictionaries.

linguistic determinism   the strong version of the Sapir-Whorf hypothesis that holds that limits of language are the limits of thought.

linguistic diversity   the fact that languages encode the world differently. This is also connected to the Sapir-Whorf hypothesis. Linguistic determinism and relativism do not make sense without linguistic diversity.

linguistic imperialism   the imposition of one culture's language upon another culture.

linguistic relativism   the weaker version of the Sapir-Whorf hypothesis that holds that the categories encoded in language influence the habits of our thought.

localization   used in contrast to globalization as well as being recognized as part of it. In terms of products, like films, video games and computer programmes, localization refers to adaptation of the product to suit local language and culture. The same process can be seen when global languages (like English) or language genres are adapted in a similar way by local populations to suit their cultural context.

locative   relating to location; in particular, a verb form which relates to location.

marked   generally speaking, 'marked' means noticeably unusual. More specifically, marked terms refer to anything which deviates from the norm and this deviation is signalled by additional information. **Unmarked** linguistic forms are neutral in so far as they represent the 'norm', and carry no additional information. For example, the unmarked form *nurse* is often assumed to refer to a woman. To refer to a nurse who is a man, the additional term *male* is often added: *male nurse* (the marked form). The notion of markedness can be applied to any set of terms where there is a 'default' that only has limited application.

metalingual/metalinguistic   literally, above the linguistic, thus, language used to talk about language.

microcosm   a small area which has the complexity and structure of larger areas.

minimal responses   in conversations, the contributions that speakers make to show that they agree or that they are listening; for example, 'mm hm', 'yeah' and so on. See also **backchannel feedback**.

mitigate/mitigation   making an utterance less forceful, usually with epistemic modals, such as 'may', 'might' or with verb forms that indicate a lack of complete certainty, such as 'I think' (as opposed to 'I know').

modal (verb)   the modal auxiliary verbs of English are *will, shall, would, should, can, could, must, may, might*. Modal auxiliaries have several meaning functions. One important meaning function is epistemic. That is, speakers use modals to express their attitude towards the 'certainty' of what they are saying. Note the meaning difference between *That is a bird* and *That could be a bird*.

moral panic   a moral panic arises in response to a perceived threat to society. Usually this threat is exaggerated (and thus incorrect) and often fuelled by media representation.

morpheme/ morphology   the study of the smallest meaningful part of language, the morpheme. Morphemes can be 'bound' or 'free'. Bound morphemes cannot stand by themselves, while free can. In 'smallest', 'small' is a free morpheme and '-est' is a bound morpheme.

multivariate analysis   a kind of statistical analysis which examines more than one variable.

negation   sentences can be negated in English by using *not*: *I knew* versus *I did not (didn't) know*. They can also be negated by the use of other negative words like *nothing, never, nowhere: I knew nothing*. The grammar of standard American and British English does not allow a sentence like *I didn't know nothing* because it contains *multiple negation*, the use of *not* plus the negative word *nothing*. However, the grammatical rules of other **dialects** of English, as well as other languages such as Italian and Spanish, require the use of multiple negation.

negative concord   otherwise known as multiple negation. See **negation**.

negative face   see **positive face**.

neoliberalism   a political and economic ideology which asserts capitalist values such as free trade.

non est disputandum   there is no disputing.

noun   class of words which, generally speaking, name people or things, but more importantly share certain grammatical characteristics. For example, in English nouns (in small capitals) can be preceded by *the: the MUSIC*. They can be marked for plural: *CAT/CATS*. They can be modified by **adjectives**: *the big BRIDGE*.

nucleus   the central part of a syllable or the first part of a **diphthong**.

open question   as opposed to a **closed question**, an open question invites a fuller response than 'yes' or 'no'. Typically, open questions begin with a 'wh-' interrogative such as 'what', 'who', 'where' and 'why'.

overt prestige   a type of prestige attached to forms of language use that are publicly acknowledged as 'correct' and as bestowing high social status on their users. See also **covert prestige**.

paradigmatic   as opposed to **syntagmatic**. The paradigmatic axis of language describes the way words are chosen from among all possible choices and, as a consequence, can be said to be meaningful. For example, to call a woman a 'girl' rather than a 'lady' depicts her as young. This is part of the structuralist view of language. Is also used more generally as the adjectival form of paradigm, where paradigm means a patterned structure. Thus, it is possible to talk about a verb paradigm to describe the way a verb is conjugated according to person etc. Paradigm may also be used as a synonym for **ideology**, though this use background value judgements about the values contained in the paradigm.

paralinguistic   that which is beyond language but is nevertheless communicative, such as intonation, pitch and volume. It may also be used to refer to facial expression and body language.

performative   this term has two uses and which is meant should be clear from the context. In the first sense, a performative is a speech act which does something. This comes from Austin and Searle's speech act theory. Performatives differ from other propositions in that they are neither true nor false. Thus, 'I promise' is a performative as the speaker does something by saying this, namely promises. It makes no sense to say that 'I promise' is true or false (though it can be sincere or insincere). The second sense of performative relates to identity and social constructionism. Thus, we can talk about gender as being performed and in that sense, performative (rather than given).

positive/negative face   positive face is the desire to be positively valued; negative face is the desire to be unimpeded in one's actions. Face is a concept that helps to analyze and understand some features of communicative competence, especially politeness.

presupposition   a background assumption embedded within a sentence or phrase. The assumption is taken for granted to be true regardless of whether the whole sentence is true. For example *We will introduce a fairer funding formula* presupposes that the current funding formula is not fair. This presupposition will remain even if the proposition is negated.

prosody   in phonology, prosody refers to intonation and stress. It may also be used in relation to **semantics**, semantic prosody, though the 'semantic' is often elided when it is used in this way. Semantic prosody relates to the **connotations** of a word which are a direct result of the other words it is most used with. This involves the investigation of what the most common collocates of a word are (see **collocation**).

received pronunciation or **RP**   the **accent** which is generally used by newsreaders on national television in the UK. Sometimes called a 'BBC accent' or an 'educated British accent'. An RP accent is not marked for a particular region of Britain, but is marked for relatively 'high' social class. It is thought that only about 3 per cent of the British population normally use RP.

referential   one of Jakobson's six functions of language. The referential function of language is what we might normally think of as information, or the denotative function of language, but also includes the ideas, objects and conventions which speakers share knowledge of.

reflexive/reflexivity   in grammatical terms, a reflexive verb is a verb where the subject does something to her/himself. Thus, 'I wash myself' is reflexive. Some languages have special forms for these verbs. More generally, 'being reflexive' or 'reflexivity' refers to thinking about actions or ideologies. Such reflexivity is said to be typical of late modernity and as such as related to social constructionist theories of identity. That is, as we perform and construct our identities, we need to think about the language we use and the actions we engage in, so that we can project the identity we want to.

reify   to treat something (usually a theoretical category) as though it is a thing. Reification often also involves treating that thing as stable and homogenous.

restricted and elaborated code   from the work of Basil Bernstein, the restricted code is said to be used by working class individuals, while the elaborated code is used by middle class speakers. The restricted code is said to be characterized by lack of explicit detail as it is generally used by speakers from cohesive, tight-knit speech communities with a great deal of shared knowledge. As this shared knowledge can be taken for granted in conversation, it does not need to be made explicit. Such a code only works in the appropriate context. Conversely, the elaborated code is very explicit and as such, can be said to be context free.

rising intonation see **HRT**.

semantics the study of the meaning of words.

semiosis that which is semiotic.

semiotic signs and their study, whether linguistic or otherwise.

sexist language language that treats one sex as less equal than another. Sexist language generally refers to language which treats women as inferior to men.

simultaneous speech when participants in a conversation speak at the same time. It is helpful to distinguish between disruptive simultaneous speech (interruptions) and supportive or collaborative simultaneous speech. In relation to the latter, some conversational floors allow simultaneous speech without this being seen as interruptive or inappropriate. This collaborative floor is remarked upon as the default rule for conversation in Anglo culture is said to be that one speaker speaks at a time.

social capital see **symbolic capital**.

social network a way of describing the way people are connected to each other in a community. Social networks can be closed (where everyone knows each other) or open. Closed networks are said to be dense. Networks can also be uniplex or multiplex depending on whether individuals have more than one relationship with each other. For example, if A is only a work associate of B their relationship is uniplex. If they are also related, or spend time together socially, they will be connected in more than one way and thus their relationship can be said to be multiplex.

soft power while hard power usually refers to military strength, soft power refers to the cultural capital and influence that (usually) nations may exercise on the international scene. This may include capitalizing on the cultural capital of a language variety by exporting the variety in the form of cultural associations, language teaching materials and language teachers.

sophist in Ancient Greece, a man of learning, with particular skill in argument and composition. It is often used as a disparaging term, suggesting someone who will happily make the weaker argument the stronger, especially for payment.

speech acts an utterance which does something as well as saying something. Thus, 'I'm sorry' says something but also performs an apology. See **performative**.

stereotype This has at least two meanings. The first is that which is understood by 'stereotype' in its usual sense, that is, a set of ideas (often negative) about a group of people. Stereotypes are culturally specific and comprise a set of attitudes which are widely known and generally accepted as true at some level (see also **iconization**). The second meaning is more specific and refers to one of Labov's three kinds of linguistic variables. A variable is a stereotype when the association of a group with a variable is so well known and has attracted such negative or archaic associations that the form is actively avoided by in-group speakers.

symbolic capital from the work of Bourdieu, symbolic, cultural or social capital refers to assets that individuals accumulate based on their presentation, speech, relationships, education and so on. Like real capital (money) symbolic capital can be used to procure things.

syntagmatic as opposed to **paradigmatic**. The syntagmatic axis of language describes the way words are ordered in relation to each other.

transitive/intransitive   kind of verb used in a clause. A transitive verb requires a direct object in order to make sense, whereas an intransitive verb does not. For example, in *Lucy loves Fred*, 'Fred' is the direct object of the verb 'love'. 'Love' is a transitive verb and would be incomplete without its direct object, as you can see from *Lucy loves* … On the other hand, in *Fred snores*, 'snores' is an intransitive verb; there is no direct object and the verb is complete on its own. Not to be confused with **transitivity (model)**.

transitivity (model)   model, used in the analysis of utterances, to show how the speaker's experience is encoded. It is part of systemic functional grammar. In the model, utterances potentially comprise three components. (1) *Process*, which is typically expressed by a verb. (2) *Participants* in the process. The participant who is the 'doer' of the process represented by the verb is known as the *actor*. The *goal* is the entity or person affected by the process. (3) *Circumstances* associated with the process. In utterances such as *she cried loudly* or *he jumped from the cliff*, the underlined components provide extra information about the process, and can be omitted.

turn-taking   the way speakers change from time to time in a conversation. Particular settings may have turn taking rules, for example, that you can only speak if asked a question.

unmarked   see **marked**.

upward convergence   see **convergence**.

verb   grammatical class of words, which commonly refer to 'acting' or 'doing', although many verbs such as *to seem* or *to know* do not quite fit into this meaning category. More importantly, verbs take characteristic forms or endings such as those marking tense and voice, and they perform a specific function in a sentence. The verbs in the following sentences are in small capitals: *He LAUGHED a lot. She WAS ELECTED president. I AM WALKING quickly. They MIGHT WANT some. I HAVE SEEN her. Bob SEEMS nice. SIT there.* See also **modal verb**.

verbiage   though this can mean verbose, that is, talking too much, in linguistics it is more likely to be used as a technical term for what is said when describing propositions in the framework of systemic functional grammar. See **transitivity (model)**.

vernacular   this term has at least two meanings. The first refers to the most natural form of an individual's language and which they do not consciously alter (see **authenticity**). The second meaning contrasts the vernacular variety with a prestige variety. Thus, the vernacular is lower on a hierarchy of language with the standard at the top as prestigious (see **overt prestige** and **covert prestige**).

vowel   speech sound made with no obstruction to the air flow from the lungs. The bold letters in the following examples represent some of the vowel sounds in English *s**a**t, t**o**p, h**ea**lth, s**i**lly*. There is a vocabulary to describe vowels and which describes them as front/back, high/low, open/closed. The first two refer roughly to the position of the tongue in the mouth; the last refers to whether the lips are open/rounded or not.

World English(es) (WE)   also known as global English(es). The plural is conventional as it indicates that there is no single variety that could be called World English or global English. The term refers to the spread of English as well as the many varieties that exist, whether first languages or not.

Xhosa   a Bantu language spoken in southern parts of Africa. The language has three clicks as consonants.

Zipf's law   an empirical theory that describes the frequency of word occurrence in a language.

Notes

1.   See Gramsci, A. (2000).
2.   See Gal, Susan and Irvine, Judith (2000) Language ideology and linguistic differentiation, in Paul V. Kroskrity (ed.), *Regimes of Language: Ideologies, Polities, and Identities*, Santa Fe, NM: School of American Research Press, pp. 35–83 and Gal, S. and Irvine, J.T. (1995) 'The boundaries of languages and disciplines: how ideologies construct difference', *Social Research*, 62(4): 967–1001.

Index

Note: bold page number indicates relevance of whole chapter